ASIA as METHOD

Kuan-Hsing Chen

ASIA as METHOD

Toward Deimperialization

Duke University Press
Durham and London
2010

© 2010 Duke University Press

All rights reserved

Printed in the United States of America on acid-free paper ∞

Designed by Heather Hensley

Typeset in Arno Pro by Tseng Information Systems, Inc.

Library of Congress Cataloging-in-Publication Data appear
on the last printed page of this book.

CONTENTS

vii   PREFACE

1   INTRODUCTION
Globalization and Deimperialization

17   CHAPTER 1
The Imperialist Eye: The Discourse of the Southward Advance and the Subimperial Imaginary

65   CHAPTER 2
Decolonization: A Geocolonial Historical Materialism

115   CHAPTER 3
De–Cold War: The Im/possibility of "Great Reconciliation"

161   CHAPTER 4
Deimperialization: Club 51 and the Imperialist Assumption of Democracy

211   CHAPTER 5
Asia as Method: Overcoming the Present Conditions of Knowledge Production

257   EPILOGUE
The Imperial Order of Things, or Notes on Han Chinese Racism

269   NOTES

287   SPECIAL TERMS

291   BIBLIOGRAPHY

305   INDEX

Centering its analysis on historical forces in modern East Asia, this book calls for critical intellectuals in the former and current colonies of the third world to once again deepen and widen decolonization movements, especially in the domains of culture, the psyche, and knowledge production. It further calls for critical intellectuals in countries that were or are imperialist to undertake a deimperialization movement by reexamining their own imperialist histories and the harmful impacts those histories have had on the world. Dialectical interaction between these two processes is a precondition for reconciliation between the colonizer and the colonized, and only after such a reconciliation has been accomplished will it be possible for both groups to move together toward global democracy.

Much of this book was written from 2004 to 2006, while I was a visiting senior research fellow at the Asia Research Institute (ARI) at the National University of Singapore. This time also turned out to be an important opportunity for me to physically feel Southeast Asia and sense what it meant to live in a small country. While at ARI, I met the young Singaporean director Tan Pin Pin, who was there on a visiting basis to finish postproduction work on her film *Singapore Ga Ga*. According to the promotional materials, the film is "a 55-minute paean to the quirkiness of the Singaporean aural landscape. It reveals Singapore's past and present with a delight and humour that makes it a necessary film for all Singaporeans. We hear buskers, street vendors, school cheerleaders sing hymns to themselves and to their communities. From these vocabularies (including Arabic, Latin, and Hainanese), a sense of what it might mean to be a modern Singaporean emerges." The director uses sounds familiar to Singaporeans as a means of articulation. Interviews with several "average" Singaporeans document the details of their daily lives, including their fantasies, such as the old man who plays the harmonica and dances to his own rhythms in the subway, and who claims to be a Singapore national treasure recognized by the National Arts Council. Pin Pin's Singapore is composed of these energetic nobodies. The film includes no government officials lecturing the audience, nor any dissident intellectuals critiquing the state.

The closing scene of the film is set in a crowded auditorium during the celebration of Singapore's national day. With the music growing louder, a young man is seen slowly climbing up a tower to place on its top the national flag, symbol of the nation's glory. Suddenly the scene switches to a singer performing outside a subway entrance. With an air of hopelessness he sings:

> Wasted days and wasted nights,
> I have left you behind
> For you don't belong to me —
> Your heart belongs to someone else.

> Why should I keep loving you
> When I know that you're not true?
> And why should I call your name
> When you're to blame for making me blue?

Singapore Ga Ga is not a conventional documentary, but rather a film that resonates on the level of sentiment, drawing its viewers in through widely shared experiences and memories. The film's expert use of nostalgia and emotion accounts for the enthusiastic response it received in Singapore. The D harmonica played by the old man is part of the national music curriculum, and its soulful tones are immediately familiar to anyone who has attended school in Singapore. Subway announcements are also a daily encounter for Singapore's citizens, and their sound automatically registers deep in the nerve center of every commuter. The audience does not have to seriously ponder what *Singapore Ga Ga* wants to say. Memory, stored in desire and the body, becomes the medium of dialogue. The film is propaganda, serving both to cultivate national sentiment and to show the humane side of Singapore, but this type of propaganda could not possibly have been produced by a government public-relations office or tourist board.

What the film seems to have captured most insightfully is that the most powerful way to reflexively address the issue of nationalism is to operate on the same affective plane where nationalist energy arises: one has to sincerely identify with the nation, genuinely belong to it, and truly love it in order to establish a legitimate position from which to speak. Only in this way can Pin Pin's closing critique be as sympathetically received as she intended.

The first chapter of this book violates this logic. Its frontal critique of Taiwanese nationalism could easily be rejected on the ground that it assumes no identification with Taiwan. When a very early version of the chapter was published in the mid-1990s, it ignited a bit of a controversy. At that time, a highly respected scholar commented that my treatment of the subject was not sympathetic enough to be accepted. When you are young and self-righteous, it is not easy to appreciate or accept such criticism. It wasn't until I started moving around to different parts of Asia that I realized how sturdy were the walls that nationalism has thrown up between countries and people in the region. In the third world, nationalism has been a force forged in response to colonial conquest, and in order to eventually move beyond it, we must first dig into local histories and distinguish the different effects that nationalism has manifested in different locations. At this point in history, a total negation of nationalism is nothing but escapism.

I do not believe that nationalism in a small country constitutes a big problem. Singaporeans can identify with the nobodies seen through Pin Pin's camera; viewers and subjects become linked together, triggering a sense of belonging that empowers both groups. Drawing attention to the rich details of everyday life returns at least a minimal dignity to those who have no hope for change through local electoral politics, but who nevertheless have to go on living as the docile subjects of an authoritarian regime, as they are often described by outsiders. Recognizing the complexity of such subjectivity is the first step toward letting go of our own nationalist complex.

In a different vein, South Korean nationalism has also been transformed into a powerful critical force that has moved that nation forward. Nationalist pride in South Korea's democratic achievements, expressed in the form of a strong civil-society movement, is connected with the deep-seated desire to build a more democratic, progressive, and modern country.

My own attitude toward nationalism has thus changed over the years from pure negation to a conditional acceptance. As presented in the following chapters, nationalism is a common element of three even more fundamental problems: colonialism, the structure of the world during the cold war, and the imperialist imaginary. Corresponding to this entangled problematic are the often combined movements for decolonization, deimperialization, and what I call "de–cold war," confronting the legacies and continuing tensions of the cold war. The mediating site for these forces and movements is the imaginary Asia. It would be wrong to consider these interwoven problems as theoretical abstractions. On the contrary, they exist in our bodies and minds, and the related desires and psychic pain that must be overcome are palpable parts of our everyday lives. In short, they are matters of subjectivity, and it is on the plane of subjectivity that we must reopen the past for reflection in order to make moments of liberation possible in the future.

Methodological Notes

This project is deeply indebted to the critical traditions and works of Lu Xun, Chen Ying-zhen, Frantz Fanon, Stuart Hall, Partha Chatterjee, and Mizoguchi Yūzō, among others who came out of the colonized world to honestly confront the limits of their times. In different ways, they all understood that the task of decolonizing culture and mind, desire and body, and the production of knowledge has to proceed from the inner logic of the colonized social formation. Moreover, the struggle cannot be waged only in terms of the statist rearrangement of international relations. Subjectivity, they have argued, is also a key site of decolonization work. Only through the process of self-analysis can new strategies be formulated to overcome the limits imposed and shaped by the history of imperialism.

The arguments presented in this book could not have been arrived at without a moving trajectory. The thoughts and discourses presented here were developed over the past sixteen years or so in rather scattered contexts and in dialogue with various critical circles in Asia, where I have been engaged intellectually, physically, and psychically. In particular, involvement in the Information Center for Labor Education, *Taiwan: A Radical Quarterly in Social Studies*, and *Inter-Asia Cultural Studies: Movements* has contributed to my intellectual formation. Many of the ideas presented in the following chapters were first articulated in response to political and theoretical issues that emerged in specific historical situations; most of them were delivered in public forums and meant for a general audience. During this process, a pattern emerged: each of my attempts to understand and intervene in a specific context required pushing beyond the limits of my own knowledge; therefore, each attempt generated my next stage of reading, research, and thought. The theses of decolonization, de-imperialization, and de–cold war now serve as an umbrella problematic, which links together work that grew out of different historical moments and required analyses at different levels of abstraction.

At the same time, this book continues the spirit of critical cultural studies, which involves working and intervening in local spaces without losing one's commitment to be in dialogue with general theoretical arguments. Rereading Lu Xun's popular criticism has made me realize how much my own mode of writing is, in a way, a continuation of his method. Some of Lu Xun's most seductive writings are the ones responding to concrete events. He puts himself inside the event itself and, with no trace of self-indulgence, attempts to intervene. Lu Xun seldom begins or ends a discussion with theoretical abstractions, though the political and intellectual implications of his writing often go far beyond the event to which he responds. To reclaim this mode of intellectual practice through the space opened up by cultural studies is to ground ourselves in the cultures of our own — that is, to address the issues arising out of our own puzzling environments. As readers will notice, most of the chapters of this book do not begin with an analytical concept or a set of theoretical propositions. Social and political contradictions manifested in concrete events are always at the center of my analysis; dialogue with different strands of academic discourse is in the background, not the foreground. My primary concern is with the social world, and I engage with academic discourse only when this kind of explanatory machinery is necessary to understand real conditions. As a result, the object of dialogue often emerges after the analysis. I see this mode of operation as continuing one strand of Lu Xun's critical tradition. There is no desire to formulate theoretical concepts which are applicable to all events and in all contexts. The point is to generate historically grounded explanations so that specific interventions can be waged more effectively.

Events taking place in different moments of history in Taiwan are at the center of analysis throughout this book. For our purposes, the advantage of such a focus is that Taiwan has never been a closed space. On the contrary, it has been decisively shaped by the political and economic dynamics of East Asian history. Its history with mainland China before the twentieth century, its colonization by Japan in the first half of that century, and its subordination to U.S. hegemony after the Second World War are, in some ways, a perfect compression of the region's modern history. To place Taiwan at the center is a strategic choice, one that draws out the transnational dynamics of the region, allowing us to go beyond the limits of national and nationalist historiography. On a deeper level, in thinking of Asia as method, I am testing the usefulness of shifting points of reference. Analyzing Taiwan by systematically referring to different parts of East Asia will allow us to see if a different understanding of Taiwan — as well as of the region — is possible.

The Chapters

The first chapter analyzes the discourse of southward advance that emerged in Taiwan in the 1990s and lays out the current problematic state of cultural decolonization in Asia. The next three chapters theorize linkages between three intersecting historical processes: decolonization, deimperialization, and de–cold war. These three concepts are intimately linked, but for the sake of clarity, each chapter focuses on one of them. Chapter 2 traces the trajectories of decolonization since the Second World War. Chapter 3 tackles the complex relation between colonialism and the cold war. Chapter 4 focuses on the question of deimperialization. The accounts in these chapters build on each other in order to uncover the overlapping relationships between the three processes. Chapter 5 places the arguments of the book in dialogue with several academic disciplines and discusses their implications and possibilities for knowledge production.

The analysis of the discursive formation of the southward advance in chapter 1 unmasks sub-imperialist tendencies in Taiwan, specifically the triumphalist sense of pride Taiwanese felt when their country was finally able to export its capital, in the form of investments in Southeast Asia. Critically engaging with essays published in a leading literary supplement, the chapter discovers a reproduction of colonial knowledge in mainstream cultural circles. These writings make use of scholarship on the Japanese colonial period, a time during which an earlier southward advance was launched. That project of the 1930s used Taiwan as a strategic point from which to invade several Southeast Asian countries, suddenly pushing Taiwan to the center of the region in the process. This mapping of Taiwan as the center of Asia was rediscovered by Taiwanese intellectuals and used to support the state's southward advance in the 1990s, but surprisingly the appropriation of this history came without any critical understanding of its obviously imperialist origins. The chapter then traces the historical logic in play, in order to explain how this postcolonial state of mind came into being through the formation of Taiwanese nationalism after the Second World War. What we discover is that decolonization in Taiwan has not yet really taken place. This conclusion is the point of departure for the central argument of the book, which emerges step by step in the following chapters.

Chapter 2 traces the practices of decolonization in other, specifically third-world contexts to begin to explain why a decolonization movement has not effectively unfolded in Taiwan. Focusing on the level of subjectivity, the chapter identifies the historical effects of decolonization, expressed in forms of nationalism, nativism, and civilizationalism. Alongside these practices and through the mediation of earlier psychoanalytic work on colonial identification by Fanon, Memmi, and Nandy, the chapter formulates an alternative historical trajectory of cultural studies in the third world, one which has not yet been fully articulated. Having identified the limited extent of decolonization in Taiwan, the chapter proposes a strategy of critical syncretism to move beyond the limits of colonial identification on the one hand, and the postcolonial politics of resentment on the other hand. Finally, in dialogue with earlier attempts to revise historical materialism, the chapter formulates an analytical framework: a geocolonial historical materialism. Drawing on the work of radical geographers and making links with the third-world trajectories of cultural studies, the chapter distinguishes and then reintegrates geographical spaces in a move to develop a more adequate understanding of the formerly colonized world in the new context of neoliberal globalization. The chapter, in short, is a theoretical formulation that attempts to elucidate the current state of decolonization in East Asia.

The third-world approach to decolonization initiated by theorists such as Fanon has tremendous explanatory power, yet it cannot fully account for the incomplete project of decolonization in East Asia. The cold war's succession of the Second World War as both a structural divide and a blocking device needs to be theorized. Chapter 3 attempts to do this by connecting the problems of colonialism and the cold war. Through an analysis of contemporary ethnic conflicts in Taiwan, the chapter argues that the confluence of these two historical and structural forces has over-determined the characteristics of modernity in Asia. In most national and social spaces, the dominant contradictions and conflicts are the result of deep-seated structural issues. The entanglement of colonialism and the cold war in Taiwan has produced and shaped local structures of senti-ment, which, in turn, have become the emotional (more than the ma-terial) basis for political mobilization, the dominant forms of which are ethnic politics and ethnic nationalism. The resulting clashes occur within the nation, within and among the regions of the nation, and even, sadly, within the family. The formation of this structure of sentiment has ren-dered reconciliation on all levels difficult, if not impossible. To overcome cold-war antagonism and move toward regional peace and reconciliation, we can no longer buy into mainstream political practices, which have been ahistorical and purely self-interested. Instead, confronting histori-cally constituted structures of sentiments on the psychoanalytic terrain of the social and the cultural opens up new possibilities of reconciliation within the nation and throughout the region.

The previous chapters' focus on decolonization and its relation with the cold war brings us to our third area of emphasis: deimperialization. Chapter 4 argues that if the process of decolonization and de–cold war within the former colonies is to be executed critically and effectively, the imperialization question has to be brought back to center stage. This is necessary to enable a reflexivity that can undercut the desire to identify with the empire and support imperialist projects. This chapter is an at-tempt to theorize the failure of these processes through an analysis of Club 51, a group which promotes the idea that Taiwan should become the fifty-first state of the United States. The desire to join the United States is found not only in Taiwan but also in the Philippines, Okinawa, South Korea, and other locations. The chapter suggests that the phenomenon is a result of the long-term historical effects of imperial identification, which—especially in the current context of globalization—generate overwhelming insecurity and uncertainty. After tracing the changing images of the United States in global politics before and after September 11, 2001, the chapter argues that in the instance of Club 51, we find a continuing commitment to identify with the empire, a clear result of three earlier moments of imperialization: those of the Chinese empire, the Japanese military occupation, and U.S. imperialism in the period after the Second World War. To transform the existing knowledge structure in such a way that the projects of decolonization, deimperialization, and de–cold war can be better advanced, the final chapter puts forward "Asia as method" as a critical proposition. Presented as a series of dialogues with frameworks and arguments emerging at the intersection of postcolonial critiques, globalization studies, and Asian studies in Asia, this chapter proposes that Asia as method creates new possibilities for intellectual work. The implication of Asia as method is that using Asia as an imaginary anchoring point can allow societies in Asia to become one another's reference points, so that the understanding of the self can be transformed, and subjectivity rebuilt. Pushing the project one step further, it becomes possible to imagine that historical experiences and practices in Asia can be developed as an alternative horizon, perspective, or method for posing a different set of questions about world history.

Acknowledgments

The ideas presented in this book first began to unfold in 1994, and their publication sixteen years later is very much like finally paying a debt to family members, friends, and myself. Bringing together and reworking ideas that have emerged over such a long period has been difficult, and it has been humbling to confront my own immature impulses and naiveté. At the same time, these writings bear the traces of battles fought in the concrete social milieu, and I hope any remaining rough edges help to distinguish the book from typical ivory-tower ramblings.

Much of the basic skeleton of the book first appeared in Mandarin in the journal *Taiwan: A Radical Quarterly in Social Studies*, or *Taishe*. Since 1989, *Taishe*, which also refers to the intellectual community that has grown up around the journal, has provided me a hospitable space to inhabit. A group blissfully free of disciplinary consciousness, *Taishe* members are forced to speak from positions outside their own professional fields. I don't know of any other intellectual group in the Chinese-speaking world with such a disposition. With the arrival of the Internet, the community moved beyond its regular monthly meetings and began to organize public forums, conferences, and political rallies. *Taishe* is a group whose members disagree and quarrel with each other, yet go on working together. None of us is satisfied with what we have done, and we all hope that more can be achieved. I thank all the members of the group for their support and tolerance. Special thanks to Chu Wan-wen, Zheng Hongsheng, Chao Kang, Feng Jian-san, Josephine Ho, Karl Ning, Chen I Chung, Frank Wang, Hsia Hsiao-chuan, Hsu Jinnyu, Fred Chiu, Sechin Chien, Hsia Chujeo, Chu Wei-cheng, Wei Ti, Chen Hsin-hsin, and Lee Shangjen. Thanks also to Lin Tsai-chueh and Shen Sung-chiao, close friends of *Taishe*.

A common practice of intellectual work is to use personal anxieties as a type of energy to drive research forward. This book avoids that circuitous process and confronts personal anxieties directly. I believe this is the only approach that allows deeply rooted problems, such as the emotional structure of sentiment in ethnic politics in Taiwan and the Japanese and American complexes embedded in Taiwanese subjectivity, to be adequately addressed. Taiwan is my anxious home.

Admittedly, the analyses and calls for collective action presented here can be seen as consequences of my personal apprehensions, but these personal apprehensions are also the result of real conflicts in the social space. Its resources include worrisome daily-life experiences, such as tension triggered among friends over which candidate to vote for in an election. The intensity of the emotional investment makes it clear that even in the so-called era of globalization, analysis cannot ignore the local conditions of sentiment. Therefore, rather than equivocating about or suppressing the emotional conditions of the subject, I have found that critical cultural studies works best when it brings sentiment to the forefront, making it a source of thought and analysis. I personally expect cultural studies to engage more with the social subject, including on the level of the psyche, so that a more liberating form of knowledge may be generated.

In addition to *Taishe*, the Information Center for Labor Education has been a site where I have joined social movements in Taiwan. I have not been able to be fully involved as some of my friends, but their ongoing fights have provided me with the inspiration and energy to move ahead. Special thanks to Hsia Linching, Zheng Chun-chi, Wuo Young-Ie, and Lee Yi-qun, among others, for their long-term support.

From its inception, the *Inter-Asia Cultural Studies: Movements* journal project has given me the privilege of speaking out, as well as the opportunity to move throughout Asia to work with intellectuals in various critical circles. This experience has proven to me that online interaction is no substitute for physical encounter. No matter where I went — the offices of nongovernmental organizations in Sri Lanka or Hong Kong, the sidewalk food stalls of Manila or Kuala Lumpur, the hawker centers of Singapore, the *noraebang* (karaoke bars) of Seoul, the Paris Commune in Taipei (a bar and leftist meeting spot), or home after infinite rounds of drinks in Tokyo, Beijing, or Bangalore — I felt strongly the physical tension, anxiety, and restlessness that exists between friends living in different locales. At the same time, the shared friendships and concerns among those living in third-world Asia have somehow created new possibilities of solidarity and provided a shared sense of urgency. Unpacking the affective effects of the cold war, colonialism, and imperialization are attempts to break down the complex barriers between us. But it is more than this: getting to know each other better through our transient encounters is also an occasion for each of us to understand ourselves anew at home. The driving energy behind this book comes from this dialectical tension between anxiety felt in Taiwan and the uneasiness of my encounters throughout Asia.

There are more friends involved in the Inter-Asia project than can be named here. I can list only some of them who have supported this book project: Kim Soyoung, Cho Hee Yeon, Kim Seongnae, Kim Hyun Mee, Baik Youngseo, Yoo Sunyoung, Kang Naehui, Kang Myungkoo, Paik Wookinn, Sakiyama Masaki, Tomiyama Ichiro, Ikegami Yoshihiko, Shunya Yoshimi, Ota Yoshinobu, Kang Sanjung, Ueno Toshiya, Mouri Yoshitaka, Marukawa Tetsushi, Kojima Kiyoshi, Minoru Iwasaki, Koichi Iwabuchi, Diana Wong, Shamsul A. B., Francis Loh, Hilmar Farid, Melani Budianta, Quah Sy Ren, Ngoi Guat Peng, Kwok Kian-woon, W. L. Wee, Tejaswini Niranjana, Ashish Rajadhyaksha, Madhava Prasad, S. V. Srinivas, Nishant Shah, Firdous Azim, Ien Ang, Jeannie Martin, Stephen Muecke, Brian Massumi, Fran Martin, Audrey Yue, Chang Hsiaohung, Joyce Liu, Allen Chun, Amie Perry, Wang Chih-ming, Eva Tsai, Rob Wilson, Colleen Lye, Petrus Liu, Jing Wang, Leo Ching, Ralph Litzinger, Michael Hardt, Arif Dirlik, Masao Miyoshi, Gail Hershatter, Chris Connery, Paul Willemen, Dave Morley, Larry Grossberg, Briankle Chang, Daniel Mato, Tani Barlow, Naoki Sakai, and Chris Berry.

I wish to thank my Chinese friends in Hong Kong and mainland China who have also been supportive: P. K. Hui, Law Wing Sang, Stephen Chan, Eric Ma, Lau Kinchi, Oiwan Lam, Yan Hairong, Zhang Jingyuan, Shen Yuan, Dai Jinhua, Sun Ge, Wang Xiaoming, Wang Hui, Huang Ping, and He Zhaotian, among many others.

Stuart Hall, Hanno Hardt, Chen Ying-zhen, Mutō Ichiyō, Cho Hae-joang, Meaghan Morris, Mizoguchi Yūzō, Partha Chatterjee, Qian Liqun, Jomo K. S., Paik Nakchung, and the late Edward T. Ch'ien are intellectual models and personal friends. I thank them for their inspiration and support.

In the fall of 2001, I was invited to teach for a term in the Sociology Department at Yonsei University, where some sections of this book were first taught. Graduate students there patiently read and discussed early versions of the manuscript. I thank them for letting me test out some ideas on them, and also Haejoang and Hyun Mee for their hospitality.

In March 2005, I delivered a series of five talks, based on the chapters of this book, at the Center for the Study of Culture and Society in Bangalore. The discussions led to a radical reframing of the entire project. I thank Teju, Ashish, and S. V. for their continuing conversations and friendship.

At Tsing Hua University, where I taught from 1989 to 2008, Vice President Chen Wen-Hwa supported my two-year leave of absence, which I used to complete this project. My old friends, comrades, and drinking partners Chen Tsun-shing, Yu Chih-chung, and Lu Cheng-hui must be acknowledged in particular. I am especially grateful to Liu Jen-peng, who took over some of my responsibilities during my leave and who has been a rare friend.

I thank Chua Beng Huat for his friendship and support. For the past decade, during our coeditorship of the *Inter-Asia* journal, I have learned a tremendous amount from him. He reached out to rescue me when I was sinking into a bad work environment. ARI and its staff have created an unusual institutional milieu that enabled me to successfully complete the Chinese version of the book and the first draft of the English version. I thank Professor Tony Reid for his warm support. I thank Laavanya Kathiravelu for helping to edit the draft manuscript. Two years in ARI is like living outside history—I cannot imagine having a privilege like that again. Living in Singapore will always be an important memory. I particularly thank those who helped to make my daily life there more humane.

An earlier version of chapter 1 appeared as "The Imperialist Eye" in *Positions: East Asia Cultures Critique* 8, no. 1 (2000): 9–76; a portion of chapter 2 appeared as "The Decolonization Effects" in the *Journal of Communication Inquiry* 21, no. 2 (1997): 79–97; an earlier version of chapter 3 appeared as "Why Is 'Great Reconciliation' Im/possible?" in *Inter-Asia Cultural Studies: Movements* 3, nos. 2 and 3 (2002): 77–100 and 235–52; a portion of chapter 4 appeared as "America in East Asia" in the *New Left Review* 12 (2001): 73–87; and a portion of chapter 5 appeared as "Civil Society and Min-jian" in *Cultural Studies* 17, no. 6 (2003): 876–96. I wish to thank the editors and publishers of these journals.

At Duke University Press, I thank Ken Wissoker for his guidance and patience, Courtney Berger, Timothy Elfenbein, and Leigh Barnwell for their support, and three anonymous reviewers for their sympathetic and careful readings.

I thank Liu Chun-yu (Emma) and Lin Chia-hsuan, managing editors of *Inter-Asia Cultural Studies*, for their detailed editorial work.

I am deeply grateful to my friend and editor David Katz, who worked meticulously to transform my Chinese expressions into readable English, and helped with the indexing. This intellectual debt cannot be fully repaid except with bottles of cold sake. David, we'll just have to drink more together.

Bai Lang, my running mate, is a peaceful force. Whatever worries I have are always stripped away by his playful jumping whenever I come home.

Ding Naifei has lived with this project for too long. Most of this book has come out of conversations with her during our morning walks. In the end, it's no longer possible to tell if this is her work or mine. I once again thank Naifei for her unconditional support, criticism, and love.

I dedicate this book to friends affiliated with *Taiwan: A Radical Quarterly in Social Studies*, the Information Center for Labor Education, and *Inter-Asia Cultural Studies: Movements*.

GLOBALIZATION AND DEIMPERIALIZATION

> Men make their own history, but they do not make it as they please; they
> do not make it under self-selected circumstances, but under circumstances
> existing already, given and transmitted from the past. The tradition of all
> dead generations weighs like a nightmare on the brains of the living. And
> just as they seem to be occupied with revolutionizing themselves and things,
> creating something that did not exist before, precisely in such epochs of
> revolutionary crisis they anxiously conjure up the spirits of the past to their
> service, borrowing from them names, battle slogans, and costumes in order
> to present this new scene in world history in time-honored disguise and bor-
> rowed language . . . In like manner, the beginner who has learned a new lan-
> guage always translates it back into his mother tongue, but he assimilates
> the spirit of the new language and expresses himself freely in it only when he
> moves in it without recalling the old and when he forgets his native tongue.
> KARL MARX, *THE EIGHTEENTH BRUMAIRE OF LOUIS BONAPARTE*

This project formulates an analytical framework—a geocolonial historical materialism—in order to develop a more adequate understanding of
contemporary cultural forms, practices, and institutions in the formerly
colonized world. As a whole, the book is in dialogue with three main currents of cultural studies: postcolonial studies, globalization studies, and
the emerging field of Asian studies in Asia.

The Field

Postcolonial cultural studies is at an impasse. The central problem lies
in its obsessive critique of the West, which bounds the field by the object of its own criticism. The result of this impasse is to put in doubt the

proposition that the world has reached the postcolonial era: if modern colonialism has been initiated and shaped by the West, then the postcolonial enterprise is still operating within the limits of colonial history and has not yet gone beyond a parasitic form of critique (Chen 1996). This book seeks to overcome the limits of the postcolonial critique by shifting the terrain of analysis to the question of deimperialization in the context of Asia. This turn toward Asia is suggested by the argument that only by multiplying the objects of identification and constructing alternative frames of reference can we undo the politics of resentment, which are too often expressed in the limited form of identity politics. Only by moving beyond such fixations can new forms of intellectual alliance be built and new solidarities forged in the new context of globalization.

If postcolonial studies is obsessed with the critique of the West and its transgressions, the discourses surrounding globalization tend to have shorter memories, thereby obscuring the relationships between globalization and the imperial and colonial past from which it emerged. This book puts the history of colonialism and imperialism back into globalization studies. In my view, without the trajectories of imperialism and colonialism, one cannot properly map the formation and conditions of globalization. Most importantly, the critical desire for a progressive form of globalization can be endorsed only if it puts the intent to deimperialize before all else. Globalization without deimperialization is simply a disguised reproduction of imperialist conquest. If this era of globalization is built on the assumption that to reconstruct a livable earth we can no longer allow any form of imperialism to prevail, then the movement toward deimperialization, starting with rethinking the wrongs and pains of past imperialist interventions, is the minimum requirement of the present.

The third area which the book addresses and intends to shape is the general field of Asian studies. In the past, this field was seen as having been largely constituted by studies done outside the geographical site of Asia, mainly in the United States and Europe. The emerging phenomenon of Asian studies in Asia seems to suggest that the reintegration of Asia requires a different sort of knowledge production. This is necessary to generate self-understanding in relation to neighboring spaces as well as the region as a whole, while at the same time removing the imperative to understand ourselves through the imperialist eye. Interestingly, with the rise of Asia, we have suddenly found that we have been doing Asian studies in our own way, without using that name. The absence of the name, in fact, indicates our own lack of consciousness about Asia. If Asian studies is broadly defined as the field whose object of analysis is located in Asia, we will find that most of the research carried out in different parts of the region is in fact Asian studies. If one accepts this observation, it is clear that the largest number of practitioners of Asian studies are indeed in Asia, rather than outside the region—although, having learned from mainstream academics in the West to look down on the particularism of area studies, we have not admitted that we are a part of it. The challenge, however, cannot be simply to reclaim the territory of Asian studies from U.S. or European experiences, but to define Asian studies in Asia and its potential achievements. This book's objective is to offer some thoughts on how we might meet this challenge.

The epistemological implication of Asian studies in Asia is clear. If "we" have been doing Asian studies, Europeans, North Americans, Latin Americans, and Africans have also been doing studies in relation to their own living spaces. That is, Martin Heidegger was actually doing European studies, as were Michel Foucault, Pierre Bourdieu, and Jürgen Habermas. European experiences were their system of reference. Once we recognize how extremely limited the current conditions of knowledge are, we learn to be humble about our knowledge claims. The universalist assertions of theory are premature, for theory too must be deimperialized.

An Argument

This book makes the theoretical and political argument that decolonization and deimperialization could not have unfolded until the emergence of an era of globalization. By decolonization, I do not simply mean modes of anticolonialism that are expressed mainly through the building of a sovereign nation-state. Instead, decolonization is the attempt of the previously colonized to reflectively work out a historical relation with the former colonizer, culturally, politically, and economically. This can be a painful process involving the practice of self-critique, self-negation, and self-rediscovery, but the desire to form a less coerced and more reflexive and dignified subjectivity necessitates it.

If decolonization is mainly active work carried out on the terrain of the colonized, then deimperialization, which is no less painful and reflexive, is work that must be performed by the colonizer first, and then on the colonizer's relation with its former colonies. The task is for the colonizing or imperializing population to examine the conduct, motives, desires, and consequences of the imperialist history that has formed its own subjectivity. These two movements — decolonization and deimperialization — intersect and interact, though very unevenly. To put it simply, deimperialization is a more encompassing category and a powerful tool with which we can critically examine the larger historical impact of imperialism. There can be no compromise in these exercises, if the world is to move ahead peacefully.

My use of the word "globalization" does not imply the neoliberal assertion that imperialism is a historical ruin, or that now different parts of the world have become interdependent, interlinked, and mutually beneficiary. Instead, by globalization I refer to capital-driven forces which seek to penetrate and colonize all spaces on the earth with unchecked freedom, and that in so doing have eroded national frontiers and integrated previously unconnected zones. In this ongoing process of globalization, unequal power relations become intensified, and imperialism expresses itself in a new form.

Placing the modern history of East Asia at the center of our analysis, the book argues that the decolonization and deimperialization movements in the period immediately after the Second World War were interrupted by the formation of a cold-war structure. Only after the cold war eased, creating the condition of possibility for globalization, did decolonization return with the full force of something long repressed. But unlike the immediate postwar period, this moment of decolonization requires us to confront and explore the legacies and ongoing tensions of the cold war — an imperative I designate as "de–cold war." In fact, these three movements — decolonization, deimperialization, and de–cold war — have to proceed in concert, precisely because colonization, imperialization, and the cold war have become one and the same historical process. Unless these three movements can proceed together — that is, unless the deimperialization movement is globalized in both the former colonies and the current and former imperial centers — events like those of September 11, 2001, are bound to happen again and again.

A Narrative

Let me slow down and unpack this abstract proposition. It has now become clear that one crucial aspect of globalization is actually regional integration. The African Union, the Latin American Integration Association, the European Union, and the Association of Southeast Asian Nations are expressions of this regionalism. This process was accelerated in the aftermath of September 11, as groups in various parts of the world came together to oppose U.S. imperial desire. In East Asia, however, regional history has prevented a coherent framework from emerging; as a result, regional integration here has proceeded relatively slowly.

Starting in the middle of the nineteenth century, the "Chinese empire"[1] at the center of East Asia began to collapse, and the Sinocentric system of trade and tribute—which had been a relatively coherent world order—started to erode.[2] The periphery (Japan) sought to replace the center (China), significantly altering power relations in the region. But the decline of the feudal tribute system did not end deep-seated historical tensions in the region. Although the political structure of East Asia has been reshaped along the lines of the modern nation-state, the dense history of the region has prevented it from complete or rapid disintegration. The current configuration of big and small nation-states in the region, for example, closely mirrors the historical arrangement of suzerain and vassal states that existed before the Second World War.[3] Simply put, the current international order in East Asia is a reconfiguration of the old Sinocentric structure combined with the so-called "modern" system of the nation-state.[4] This heterogeneous and internally contradictory historical experience complicates the existing narrative of colonialism.

The mainland Chinese territory, for instance, was never colonized, but it was split up, and parts of it were ceded or leased to Western imperialist forces. Note that I am making a distinction between colony and concession, which have different legal statuses; more importantly, the distinction implies different forms of governing and governed subjectivities. The first real colony in the modern history of Northeast Asia was arguably Hong Kong, which was ceded to England in 1842 after the shameful Opium War.[5] Japan annexed Okinawa in 1872 and occupied Taiwan in 1895, after the First Sino-Japanese War. At the end of the Russo-Japanese War in 1905, Korea became a Japanese protectorate; it was formally absorbed into the Japanese empire in 1910.[6] Although in 1911 the first republic in Asia was established in mainland China, Taiwan, still occupied by Japan, was not part of it. Then in 1932, the Japanese puppet state of Manchukuo was established in the northeast part of China.[7] The Japanese officially invaded China in 1937, which marked the beginning of an eight-year war that became part of the Second World War, ending in 1945 with the defeat of Japan and its Axis partners. In retrospect, the difficulty with Northeast Asian regional integration is partially caused by the discomfort the region's population felt under first the long-term dominance of the Chinese empire, and then the strain of prewar Japanese imperialism and colonialism.

Here I am making another analytical distinction between colonialism and imperialism. The Japanese state's operations in Taiwan and Korea were colonialism proper, but in China, which was never colonized or completely occupied in the way that Taiwan and Korea were, Japan's involvement is best understood as imperialism. Subjects in the colonies were directly governed by the foreign regime, and unlike foreign concessions such as Hong Kong, Macao, and parts of Shanghai (in an earlier period), the colonies of Taiwan and Korea were established without any indication that colonial rule would end. This implies a completely different condition of life. To put it in abstract terms, colonialism is a deepening of imperialism. Whereas colonialism is necessarily a form of imperialism, imperialism is not necessarily a form of colonialism. (To echo the discussion in the previous section, deimperialization is theoretically a much wider movement than decolonization.)

To mobilize the populace in the colonies for what was called the Great East Asian War, the Japanese colonial state launched an "imperialization of the subject" (*kominka*) movement in 1937 to transform the colonized people in Taiwan and Korea into its imperial subjects (Chou 1996). While imperialization was aimed at further assimilating the colonized subject, it was also a process which took place at the imperial center, as the center's own subjects became imperialized.[8] This is a critical point in my argument. In conventional usage, assimilation is thought to be the process by which the colonizer attempts to transform the colonized, to initiate the colonized subject into a more civilized way of life. In this view, assimilation is a one-way street: the colonized learns to become like the colonizer, never the reverse, as if the empire's own subject has nothing to do with the colony, and the colonial machine need not do anything to adjust to new situations resulting from the incorporation of the conquered territories. The fact that imperialization is a double process, one that takes place in the imperial center as well as in the colonies, has only recently begun to be realized. Much recent historical research, in particular the work of Catherine Hall (2002), has forcefully demonstrated that the identity of the empire is directly shaped by its relation with the colony. In light of this discussion, the Japanese kominka movement can now be read as one instance of a historical practice, one that allows us to foreground the problematic of this double process. If this theoretical move stands, it raises a more burning question: what would be the consequences if deimperialization did not happen? When the empire is eroded and the decolonization process gathers momentum, we expect deimperialization to occur in both the imperial country and the colony, but the experience in East Asia after the Second World War has shown us that this process can be interrupted. As we proceed, readers will see that the notion of deimperialization is central to this book. A detailed analysis of this problematic will be presented in chapter 4.

In 1945, when Japan was finally defeated, the deimperialization process had just begun, but Japan was then occupied for seven years by the Allies, who put General Douglas MacArthur in charge of the country, and its status shifted quickly from that of colonizer to colonized. This new condition prevented Japan from doing the reflexive work of deimperialization within its own territory and from grappling with its historical relations with its former colonies (Korea, Taiwan, and others) or its protectorate (Manchukuo).[9] The Korean War, which broke out in 1950, entailed not only a bloody fight among the Koreans themselves, but also the partitioning of Korea into two states.[10] By the end of the Korean War in 1956, a stable cold-war structure in East Asia was in place. The cold-war segregation of the region went on for two decades, until the Chinese mainland began to reopen to the world in the late 1970s. It was during these difficult cold-war times that Japan, Okinawa, South Korea, and Taiwan became U.S. protectorates. As I see it, one of the lasting legacies of this period is the installation of the anticommunism–pro-Americanism structure in the capitalist zone of East Asia, whose overwhelming consequences are still with us today.

First, this structure produced an image of the communists as evil, which supplied rhetorical justification for an alliance of antidemocratic forces. The othering of the imaginary communist is the precise historical reason why the suppression of grass-roots democratic movements by authoritarian military regimes and right-wing governments was strongly supported by U.S. neoimperialists. According to the ideological fantasy generated by this structure, being antigovernment was equivalent to being communist. The authoritarian state could therefore legitimately intimidate and arrest dissidents, and the critical tradition of leftist thought in the region was effectively discontinued.

Second, energies for deimperializing Japan and decolonizing Japan, Okinawa, Taiwan, and Korea (and arguably Hong Kong and Macao) were depoliticized, postponed, and channeled into economic development, where the conditions for thinking reflexively about the former relations between the colonizer and the colonized were prohibited. Such critical work, apparently, would have given the communist enemy an opportunity to break up the U.S.-led democratic alliance. Addressing the historical question of colonialism was therefore forbidden.

Third, the momentum required to rediscover and rebuild subjectivity in the former colonies after the Second World War and the Korean War was lost. Japan, Okinawa, Taiwan, and South Korea became U.S. protectorates, but since subjectivities in East Asia were so heavily colored by the favor of American influences the countries might more accurately be described as American subcolonies. The United States has become the inside of East Asia, and it is constitutive of a new East Asian subjectivity. In short, the cold war carried within itself moments of disruption and continuity, whereby U.S. neoimperialism both disrupted and continued Japanese colonialism.[11] The cold war mediated old colonialism and new imperialism.

The Vietnam War reinforced the anticommunism–pro-Americanism structure. The defeat of U.S. imperialism in Vietnam, however, did not sufficiently push the U.S. antiwar movement into a full-fledged deimperialization movement at home. (If it had, U.S. militarism would probably not have increased in the following decades.) The defeat in Vietnam helped consolidate cold-war anticommunism, which did not soften until China announced its open-door policy in the late 1970s. Anticommunism entered a new stage in the late 1980s, when the collapse of socialism and the triumph of capitalism was heralded around the globe. This was when the rhetoric of globalization began to take off, and by the early 1990s, "globalization" had become a buzzword in the academy.

By now, it has become clear that during the cold-war era, everyone lived in a divided world. In contrast, the world today is being molded by various attempts to replace the anticommunism–pro-Americanism structure with one of globalization. Masquerading behind the rhetoric of "the end of ideology" or the "third road," these attempts, which are being put forward primarily by neoliberals based in Europe and the United States, are of course heavily charged with ideology and intent on removing barriers that prevent capital from conquering all the planet's "free markets." Nevertheless, capital-driven, neoliberal globalization has created a new condition of possibility in Northeast Asia. For example, once mutually exclusive zones now permit exchanges of people and goods. Travel between mainland China and Taiwan has been allowed since the late 1980s, and limited visits between North and South Korea began in 2000. Regional reconciliation is beginning. More importantly, thanks to the lessening of cold-war tensions and the drive for globalization, democratic opposition movements in places like South Korea and Taiwan have found more sympathy for their legitimate grievances in the international community.

This postponed period of political democratization is indeed the beginning of a new process of decolonization. It is made up of movements that were first organized to fight against U.S.-backed authoritarian states, and later struggled to decolonize their countries by reopening the history of prewar colonialism. Supporting the emergence of opposition political movements has been the nativist movement. To use Ashis Nandy's (1983) words, this is a movement defined as a "loss and recovery of the self." Rediscovering traditions and rewriting national histories are the dominant forms of expression of this movement. I would argue that the Korean cultural revitalization movement and the Taiwanese nativization (*běntǔhuà*) movement, which began in the 1970s and 1980s and are continuing, have been the cultural and social basis of the political democratization movements;[12] and precisely because of nativization's ethnic-based politics, these democratic movements are running into trouble today. Chapter 2 deals with this issue in depth.

But in the new context of globalization, the complexity of decolonization goes far beyond the anticolonial, national independence movements of an earlier era. Current decolonization movements must confront the conditions left behind by the cold-war era. It has become impossible to criticize the United States in Taiwan because the decolonization movement, which had to address Taiwan's relation with Japan, was never able to fully emerge from the postwar period; the Chinese communists were successfully constructed as the evil other by the authoritarian Kuomintang regime; and the United States became the only conceivable model of political organization and the telos of progress. Consequently, it is the Chinese mainlanders (those still in China as well as those who moved to Taiwan in 1949) who have, since the mid-1980s, become the figures against whom the ethnic-nationalist brand of the Taiwanese nativist movement has organized itself. In contrast, the Americans and Japanese are seen as benefactors, responsible for Taiwan's prosperity.

Despite these political constraints, the colonial history of the Japanese occupation has become a booming field of study in Taiwan since the 1990s. Although there are tremendous problems with the way colonial history is being studied, divided as it is into separatist and integrationist lines of research, the project of decolonization in Taiwan is under way, however limited and incomplete it might seem. Like Taiwan, South Korea has started to work out its colonial relations with Japan (on such issues as the "comfort women," history textbooks, and popular television dramas jointly produced by Japanese and Koreans) and with the United States (on issues like the removal of military bases). The publication of the *Modern History of Three East Asian Countries* (2005), written and edited by scholars from Korea, China, and Japan, is a further indication of South Korea's important role in the regional reconciliation process.[13] Compared with their Taiwanese counterparts, South Korean democratic forces have a much stronger presence in civil society, but in what direction and how far the decolonization movement in Taiwan and South Korea can push remain unanswered questions.

The complexity evident in Taiwan's and Korea's history is manifested even more fully in Japan's dual status as both colonizer and colonized. As colonizer, Japan has to resolve its guilt for the damage it caused its neighbors by the imperialist Greater East Asia Co-Prosperity Sphere project. As colonized, Japan has to work out its contradictory attitudes of resentment and gratitude toward the United States. In a way, the entire intellectual history of Japan since the Second World War can be read as a critique of the self, specifically the complicity between the population and the prewar militarist state. Maruyama Masao's account of the Japanese fascist personality is devoted to precisely this topic (Maruyama 1963). But, once again conditioned by the cold war, the internal configuration of political forces in Japan—with the left and right wings successfully checking each other's ambitions—has prevented critical intellectual circles from dealing with Japan's former colonies and conquered lands. The Left projected its romantic longing onto China but became confused and disillusioned by the Cultural Revolution. The Right projected its colonial nostalgia onto Taiwan (seen as the real China as well as a shadow Japan) and South Korea.

The moment of "decolonialization" (this is how the activist thinker Mutō Ichiyō refers to what I have described as deimperialization), when Japanese critical intellectuals finally took up Japan's imperialist relations with its former colonies, only came into being in the 1990s. This moment first concerned itself with the issue of the comfort women, but in the late 1990s, it expanded into a series of heated debates on a variety of issues (Hanasaki 2000). Today, critical circles in Japan are also actively dealing with their country's relations with the United States through issues such as the Okinawa military base, responses to September 11, and participation in Asian peace movements. But the U.S. question, in my view, remains the most difficult challenge for mainland Japanese intellectuals to work through.[14]

We began our narrative with a discussion of the Chinese empire, and now we come back to it. After a century of imperialist invasion, the Chinese socialist revolution reunified most of China's sovereign territories.[15] However, due to the century-long accumulation of anti-imperialist sentiment, the modern Chinese national identity can be said to have been formed by its relation with the former imperialist countries of the West, a relation which has still not been resolved. Western imperialism has long been part of the Chinese psyche and, in my view, will only be adequately addressed when China has been fully modernized.

Within Chinese history, the 1945–49 civil war between the Chinese Communist Party (CCP) and the Nationalist Party (the Kuomintang, or KMT) was in fact a struggle between different versions of modernity, or—looked at from another perspective—between different strategies of decolonization and deimperialization. Taiwan's move toward capitalism on its road to modernity was cemented in 1949 when it became a KMT-ruled U.S. protectorate, whereas mainland China's pursuit of socialist modernity was heavily influenced by the Soviet Union. If we understand socialist revolution as a form of decolonization opposed to capitalist expansionism and conducted in the name of class politics, then an important episode in the story of Chinese decolonization was the moment of its third worldism. Chinese solidarity with the colonized third world, which began in the context of the 1955 Bandung Conference in Indonesia, was a crucial step in the opening up and reformulation of the self-centered worldview found throughout the history of the Chinese empire. For instance, from the 1950s to the late 1970s, an intellectual movement engaged in the translation of literatures from all over the third world was able to break out of the binary opposition between China and the West, successfully showing how such conventional limitations could be overcome. Although the third worldist decolonization era was short-lived, its long-term impact on the contemporary Chinese intellectual scene cannot be underestimated.[16]

China's reopening to the world in the late 1970s was an important condition for the formation of neoliberal globalization, especially in East Asia. Inside China, Deng Xiaoping's southern tour (*nánxún*) in 1992 officially marked the country's market turn, and the changes brought about by this shift have only escalated since then. Much like the immediate postwar era, when the countries of the East Asian capitalist block put their full energies into economic development, China is now in a turbulent mood, and economic development has become a national—if not nationalist—movement. The profit-seeking drive is indeed a form of redemption, payback for the history of lack that China experienced from the 1950s onward. If—as happened in Japan, Okinawa, Taiwan, and South Korea—the release of repressed energy for decolonization and deimperialization coincides with economic prosperity, this may be the moment for China to take up the historical question of imperialism again.

The improvement of the Chinese economy has not only put China back in the center of global power, it has facilitated imaginings—both positive and negative—of regional reintegration in Northeast Asia. Although it is true that a new regional structure is forming as the center of gravity in Asia shifts, it would be ridiculous and unacceptable to understand the situation as simply the return of the old Chinese empire in the form of an updated tributary system. Nevertheless, the view of China as a threat has been widespread and deeply felt in other parts of East Asia and is being reinforced by the Chinese leadership's own slogan of a "peaceful rise," which was an attempt to assuage anxiety in the region. These two sentiments—the hope for regional integration and the fear of China—seem to have resulted from the overlapping of two moments in history. It is still too early to know precisely what the new regional structure will look like, but I think that critical circles in the region first need to recognize that the relative sizes of these countries is significant, and then learn to work out equitable mechanisms of interaction, including the distribution of responsibilities, big or small.[17]

Indeed, if regional integration is to be pushed forward, it is precisely at this moment that a reflexive politics of decolonization and deimperialization needs to be formed. This, as I see it, is the major challenge and responsibility facing critical intellectuals in China and in other parts of Asia. For critical Chinese intellectuals (I count myself one), the political difficulty of this work is twofold: on the one hand, there is the real sentiment of suffering that is the legacy of Western and Japanese imperialist invasions, and the corresponding reactive dangers inherent in the presently emerging Chinese triumphalism; on the other hand, there is the deeper necessity to reflexively take up China's empire (if not imperialist) status in relation to the rest of Asia, which—though from an earlier historical moment—has generated lasting hegemonic pressure on the whole of East Asia. The point is not so much to debate, on the Chinese mainland and beyond, whether China is or will become the next imperial power, but to rework the historically grounded ideals formulated in the third worldist moment of internationalism, or perhaps even earlier, in the moment of Sun Yat-sen's Great Asianism.[18] These ideals would serve as a reflexive mechanism to challenge the scenario in which the Chinese empire is pitted against the American one, in what would surely be a disastrous reproduction of the imperial desire. The severe competition for global power would bring China back to the old binary logic of China and the West, and Sinocentrism would once again cause China to ignore the rest of the world.

Implications

This condensed and partial narrative of colonization and decolonization in the modern history of East Asia has been an attempt to locate exactly where in the process we currently find ourselves. Although as critical intellectuals we would like to imagine that the global decolonization project is over and done with—especially if one recalls that Fanon teased out the problems of decolonization decades ago in his seminal texts *Black Skin, White Masks* (1967 [1952]) and *The Wretched of the Earth* (1968 [1961])—contemporary East Asian experiences contradict that naive hope. We are actually at an initial and critical stage of decolonization and deimperialization, which was made possible only by the arrival of the so-called post-cold-war era of globalization. It is initial because these reflexive movements have not yet progressed very far. It is critical because the directions these movements might take are not yet fixed, and the movements could quickly fall into the traps Fanon pointed to.[19] Unless the decolonizers make the effort to sort out the myriad complexities of the situation, we could see a return to imperialism, as manifested by the support for U.S. military expansionism that various East Asian states extended in the wake of September 11.

If this is the picture in East Asia, where decolonization and deimperialization have just begun, what is the situation in the rest of the world? Have the former colonies in other parts of Asia, Africa, and Latin America really decolonized? Have current and former empires in Western Europe and North America really deimperialized? I am not a global historian and cannot answer these questions with precision, but my hunch is that in this regard East Asian experiences are not at all exceptional. In 1957 Albert Memmi made a clear demand: "The disclosures having been made, the cruelty of the truth having been admitted, the relationship of Europe with her former colonies must be reconsidered. Having abandoned the colonial framework, it is important for all of us to discover a new way of living with that relationship" (Memmi 1991 [1957], 146). Half a century later, it seems that neither side of the colonial divide has sufficiently responded to Memmi's call to work out a way to live with the historical legacy of colonialism. In Southeast and South Asia, decolonization in the form of national independence has been achieved, but the countries' relations with their former colonizers have not yet been properly addressed. And the imperial powers involved—England, France, Portugal, Spain, the Netherlands, and the United States—have not deimperialized themselves enough to be able to acknowledge the harm they did to these regions. I believe that critical studies of experiences in Asia might be able to offer a new view of global history, and to pose a different set of questions. This is the true potential of Asia as method.

September 11 and its aftermath clearly show the range of sentiments — from admiration to resentment — that exists around the world in relation to the American empire. The reactionary popular support that George W. Bush's military invasion of Iraq initially enjoyed within the United States makes clear that the country has never gone through a deimperialization movement. And even though the coordinated global movements against the U.S. imperialist invasion of Iraq in 2003 were among the first of their kind, their nascency is also an indication that the global decolonization and deimperialization movements have just begun. The U.S. hegemony in the capitalist bloc after the Second World War has, since the end of the cold war, extended to the entire globe. Not only have third-world spaces in Asia, Latin America, and Africa been colonized politically, economically, and culturally by the U.S. military empire, but so have Europe and the former European empires. It is then the meeting of the colonizer (the United States) and the colonized (the rest of the world) that has made September 11 a truly global event. If this observation has any validity, then the call for a global decolonization and deimperialization movement is urgent.

At this juncture, Asian regional integration is strategically central. But this integration cannot be understood simply in regional terms; it has to be placed in the context of global politics since September 11. It is a regionalism, but also an internationalism and a globalism. If all of Asia can be integrated as other regions have started to do through organizations such as the African Union, the European Union, and the Association of South East Asian Nations, that integration would increase the likelihood that the global balance of power vis-à-vis the U.S. military empire could shift. At this historical moment, the global formation of regional blocs seems necessary to prevent the United States from continuing to abuse its position as the single superpower. Without such critical recognition and practices, regionalization is about nothing more than making a seat for oneself at the table of free-trade negotiations. If maintaining regional balances is a significant step toward a peaceful transformation of the world, the integration of Asia is a global demand.

Iraq is in Asia, in the center of West Asia. Imagine for a moment that an Asian Union existed to resist intervention from outside: would it have been quite so easy for Bush, with his imperialist desire, to arrogantly invade Iraq? But to counter neoliberal globalization, a global decolonization and deimperialization movement must first be carried out. If the colonized and colonizer do not address the history of imperialism and colonialism together, it is impossible to build solidarity among the so-called global multitudes.[20] If the world is not to go on as a theater of imperial conquests and rivalries, then deimperialization is a necessary intellectual and political commitment.

CHAPTER 1

THE IMPERIALIST EYE
The Discourse of the Southward Advance and
the Subimperial Imaginary

I look hard for
The origin of my blood.
Some say I'm from the Malay archipelago,
On the southwest border of China . . .
But my parents said:
We are all children of the sun,
The eggs of the snake,
The race nurtured by the earth . . .
No clear answer after all.
But retracing assures me,
That I now understand (we are) the real master of the beautiful island,
And page after page of broken history.
MONANEN MALIALIAVES, "BURNING"

In early 1994, the government of Taiwan announced a policy called "moving southward" (*nánxiàng*). The policy encouraged Taiwanese companies to invest in Southeast Asia, and it was applauded by business executives, scholars, and politicians as an important counterbalance to the existing overinvestment in mainland China. The opposition party—the Democratic Progressive Party, or DPP—endorsed the policy, which received a flood of enthusiastic responses in the media. The few dissenting voices noted the unsatisfactory investment conditions in Southeast Asian countries: political instability, backward infrastructures, inefficient government administration, skyrocketing real-estate prices, and rising salaries.[1] The arguments of both sides, however, were framed by the same narrative, which effectively silenced critical reflection on the underlying structure of the southward advance. Not a single voice was raised to challenge the fact that advancing toward the South (or the West or the North, for that matter) was a projection of the same expansionist ambitions that we recognize from the seventeenth and eighteenth centuries. A Taiwanese imperial desire was being formed.[2]

To be more precise, an inchoate ideological desire for a Taiwanese subempire was emerging out of this project initiated by the state. Under the neocolonial structure, Taiwan's economy, international politics, and culture have been subordinated to those of the United States and Japan. As a result, Taiwan's targets for expansion were not in the more solidly established capitalist zones, already also dominated by the United States and Japan, but in less politically and economically advantaged areas, where Taiwan's economic interests could be exploited with less competition. I use the word "subempire" to refer to a lower-level empire that is dependent on an empire at a higher level in the imperialist hierarchy. Neocolonial imperialism here refers to a form of structural domination in which a country with more global power uses political and economic interventions in other countries to influence policy and exercise control over markets. Unlike the earlier colonial imperialism, which depended on invasion, occupation, and usurpation of sovereignty to further economic interests, neocolonial imperialism uses military force as a support mechanism and employs it only as a last resort. The history of the third world has proven that many colonies have won independence only to become subcolonies, falling prey to their former colonizers once again because of their economic, cultural, and political dependency on the new imperial (formerly colonial) power. The stratified hierarchical construction of neocolonial imperialism is the present phase of global capitalism.

Taiwanese subimperial practices began in the 1980s with westward (toward mainland China) and southward (toward Southeast Asia) flows of capital, but these were mostly uncoordinated investments made by small- and medium-size businesses seeking access to cheap labor. Not until the creation of state-led expansionist projects—such as Taiwan's "fourth" Export Processing Zone in the Philippines,[3] the Taiwan Industrial Area in Vietnam, and the Taiwan Development Project in Indonesia—did Taiwan finally express its true subimperialist nature. The establishment of these physical zones is reminiscent of the classical imperialist practice (itself closely associated with traditional territorial colonialism) of building bases in overseas territories from which to organize exploitative activities.

As businesses in Taiwan closed factories there and moved their operations to mainland China and Southeast Asia in the late 1980s, cases of unsafe working conditions and worker abuse began to multiply. In Thailand, workers died in a fire at a Taiwanese-owned toy factory. In the Philippines, women workers went on strike to protest Taiwanese factory owners' militaristic management style and physical abuse. Women in mainland China were subjected to brutal physical mistreatment in the workplace as well as exploitative personal relationships with Taiwanese businessmen.[4] Meanwhile, the flow of capital continued apace. In 1988, Taiwan's investment in Thailand amounted to 10 percent of foreign investment in that country and was second only to Japan's. In 1989, Taiwan's share of foreign investment in Malaysia was 24.7 percent, again second only to Japan's. In 1990, Taiwan's investment in China's Fujian Province amounted to one-third of foreign investment. In the same year, Taiwan's investment in the neighboring Guangdong Province was second only to Japan's. In short, Taiwan's capital expansion was well under way in Southeast Asia and mainland China by the end of the 1980s (Tan 1993, 63, 65). In the context of our analysis, the implication of this is clear. Taiwanese capital was already in Southeast Asia long before 1994, when the government announced its policy of a southward advance. The policy was ideological maneuvering, the result of political anxiety brought about by stronger economic ties with China. Taiwan has sought to influence other countries' trade and diplomatic policies. The government negotiated with Thailand, Indonesia, and Vietnam to set a ceiling on the number of laborers from those countries allowed to work in Taiwan, and it pressed the government of Indonesia to suppress workers' protests in that country against Taiwanese capital. Interventions like these display the logic of dominance characteristic of neocolonialism.

Could the alliance of state and capital in Taiwan succeed in building a subempire? Should the state intervene to control the flow of capital? Where and in what situations is capital investment justified? These are not the questions I am concerned with. What is truly at issue here is imperialist desire. The imperialist expansionist mentality not only justifies exploitation of all kinds, but it also generates hardships and long-term resentment among other peoples which may become the seeds of future regional conflicts.

Taiwan itself experienced numerous waves of colonization, starting with the Dutch in the seventeenth century, and followed by the Han Chinese during the Ming and Qing Dynasties and the Japanese during the first part of the twentieth century. The process of decolonization began in Taiwan after its liberation from fifty years of Japanese occupation, but was interrupted by the KMT's colonization and U.S. military and economic subjugation after the Second World War, during which Taiwan was gradually subsumed into the U.S. neocolonial agenda. Throughout the 1960s and 1970s, Taiwan was integrated into the global capitalist system, primarily through the severe exploitation of its laborers, which produced the so-called Taiwan economic miracle and enriched today's bourgeois state. Unfortunately, capital recognizes no national boundaries. When business owners closed their factories in Taiwan and moved overseas in the 1980s and 1990s, they left behind their own families and the laborers who had made them rich.

The state-capital alliance is the engine for the formation of Taiwanese subimperialism.[5] The emergence of the southward-advance discourse in the 1990s demonstrated that capital accumulation in Taiwan had accelerated to the extent that within fifty years, the island had metamorphosed from a colony into a quasi-empire, no longer occupying a marginal position on the map of global capitalism. Constricted economically by a mega-empire, it joined the game of imperialist competition by investing downward in order to seize markets, resources, and labor in less developed countries. Taking into consideration the three-worlds theory put forward at the 1955 Bandung Conference, we may ask if this means that some third-world areas — such as the so-called Four Little Tigers (Hong Kong, Singapore, South Korea, and Taiwan) or other newly industrialized countries — have acquired the strength to expand abroad and have thereby redrawn the world map.[6] Or do we need to produce a layered analysis to chart the political meanings of the emerging internal differences within the third world?

The Problematic of Third-World Cultural Studies

In Taiwan, the third world never became a critical-analytic or political category. Politicians, intellectuals, and business people have always identified themselves with advanced, first-world countries and felt it shameful to be put into the category of the third world. The absence of a third-world consciousness has been a basic condition of intellectual life in Taiwan, including among left-leaning circles. This absence, I wish to argue, was a necessary condition for the formation of the southward-advance discourse.

In the field of cultural studies, the third world as an analytical category has also been ignored. Although, since the 1990s, this field has been going through a process of internationalization, the third world has not been taken up as a coordinating concept around which to organize dialogue. This has immense methodological and political consequences. First, if historical materialism is the assumed methodology of cultural studies, and industrial capitalism its assumed reference system of practices, then what sort of analytical machinery can be developed to engage with agricultural societies in third-world spaces, where peasants are still the dominant group in the population?[7] Second, without a category such as the third world, local analysis is shaped by concept of the nation-state, which explains the emergence of British, American, Canadian, Australian, and other "national" cultural studies. Third, questions of colonialism and imperialism have been pushed to the side in former imperial centers. For instance, British colonialism and U.S. imperialism have not been central to cultural studies as it is practiced in the United Kingdom and the United States. Instead, the work of posing these questions has fallen to critics who reside in places where historical colonialism remains an inescapable problem, and where neoimperialism continues to exercise its power. Finally, with the rejection of the third world as an outdated category, globalization has become an alibi that is used to erase history and politics. One overt example of this is John Tomlinson's *Cultural Imperialism* (1991). The concluding chapter, "From Imperialism to Globalization," exemplifies the strategy of replacing the pejorative "imperialism" with the neutral "globalization."[8] According to Tomlinson, imperialism implies a strong desire to impose one system on the whole world, whereas globalization is less overbearing and implies an international interdependence and conditions more favorable to addressing common human problems resulting from modernity, which is seen as the predestined fate of the human race. In his argument, globalization involves no unequal distribution of resources and power. The structural differences between oppressor and oppressed, first and third worlds, capital and labor, and state and social subject are all dissolved under the banner of globalization.

The rapid disintegration of the socialist second world, the internal colonization within the third world, and the transformation of the world's political power structure have made it necessary to challenge and revise the three-worlds theory (Pletsch 1981; Ahmad 1992, 287–318). But to deny the importance of colonialism and imperialism is to ignore the history of the third world, and this is theoretically and politically unacceptable.

The particular forms and practices of neocolonial imperialism began to take shape in the wake of the decolonization movements of the first half of the twentieth century and continued to evolve throughout the second half, changing most dramatically during the 1970s and 1980s. By September 11, 2001, it is fair to say that territorial conquest, military oppression, and the direct usurpation of political sovereignty had been largely displaced by the operating logic of hegemony. Transnational companies and superstate organizations have become the new agents of imperialism. Backed by strong capital, mighty military power, and the dominant position in the structure of international politics, contemporary neocolonial imperialism is producing a new form of political and economic dependency. Nevertheless, the critical conditions and constitutive effects of imperialism have not changed and may have intensified: (1) the corporate monopoly system persists in core metropolitan centers; (2) the continuous expansion of economic power in the center intensifies its ambition to control resources and markets elsewhere; (3) the international division of labor continues to enrich the advanced capitalist zones; (4) powerful industrialized countries continue to increase their exports and investments abroad; (5) the exploitation of labor deepens; (6) the gap between the rich and the poor grows around the world; and (7) the environment in colonized areas continues to deteriorate.[9] As Herbert Schiller (1991) has argued, the postimperialist era has not yet arrived.

Masao Miyoshi (1993) has argued that colonialism becomes even more dynamic when driven by global capitalism. According to Miyoshi, with the transition from colonialism to global capitalism, the nation-state gradually gives way to transnational companies as the primary agent of history. This observation may well be true for advanced capitalist countries, but for those living in third-world locations such as South Korea, Taiwan, mainland China, India, and Sri Lanka, the nation-state and nationalism are playing an increasingly important role.[10] While we must acknowledge the strength of global capitalism, we should also recognize that the role of the nation-state is not really in decline; instead, it is in transition. The formation of superstate organizations — such as the European Union, the NAFTA Free Trade Commission, and the Association of Southeast Asian Nations — results when states in these regions cut up territory, divide markets, and achieve the restructuring and redivision of labor required by international capitalism. Viewed in this light, it is incumbent on us to not only differentiate the powerful from the weak and the central from the peripheral, but also to avoid idealizing the states of the third world and making the nation-state our primary locus of identification.

Frantz Fanon, writing *The Wretched of the Earth* (1968 [1961]) just before Algeria gained its independence from France, was already taking issue with states' nationalist practices. In the process of anti-imperialism, he argues, decolonization must transform nationalist energy into a liberating consciousness of sociopolitical needs; otherwise, once the common enemy (the colonizer) disappears, the most resourceful among the national bourgeoisie will occupy the dominant positions in the apparatuses of nation building and state making and will collaborate with the former colonizer, thus turning the colony into a neocolony. Meanwhile, this national bourgeoisie will exercise internal colonization,[11] suppressing the subaltern populations and often fostering long-term ethnic clashes by inventing or emphasizing cultural differences in order to gain an advantage in the internal struggle for power. Fanon's theoretical analysis predicted the structural experience common throughout the third world: colonization is followed by decolonization, which is then followed by a stage of internal colonization and eventually incorporation into the system of neocolonial capitalism. The following chapter will argue that the formulation of a geocolonial historical materialism, an approach more pertinent to third-world spaces, may be useful in confronting problems at all levels in the global–local dialectic. This direction of research is not meant to create a third-world-centrism or to deny the importance of first-world cultural studies. Quite the contrary: the dialectic cannot complete its work without the involvement of both parties. As suggested in the introduction, the decolonization work performed by the colonized will not be complete without the colonizer's deimperialization, and vice versa. The articulation of dialogue and alternative so that counterhegemonic alliances can be forged — at least on the level of knowledge production — will depend on collective will, interaction, and effort.

Refusing to duplicate existing power structures requires that third-world cultural studies not limit itself to critiquing Western imperialism and capitalism. It will also have to overcome its overinvestment in nationalism, so as to bring out the complexity of power relations within third-world spaces; make transparent its own internal hierarchical divisions; and counter the emerging third-world subimperialism. The analysis in this chapter is a starting point in this line of research.

Said, Culture, and Imperialism

Returning to the concrete issue of the southward-advance discourse, I want to emphasize again that the imperial consciousness, ideology, and desire so frankly manifested in the discourse are my main concerns, while subjectivity is the primary focus of my analysis. History has proven that the formation of empire is never merely a matter of political, economic, and military control. Cultural discourse also plays an active role in providing the theoretical justification needed for empire building. When considering this cultural dimension, the first question that we need to ask is: what are the sources of its theoretical formulation?

The late Edward Said's analysis of the cultural production of imperialist ideology in *Culture and Imperialism* (1993) is instructive. Although his argument is based on the analysis of major works and figures in the Western literary canon, the problematic he opens up is intimately connected with the present and the future. The colonial structure quickly disintegrated with the end of the imperialist era after the Second World War, he argues, but the moment of high imperialism has cast a long shadow and remains culturally influential in the present (ibid., 7). Critical discourse on imperialism has disproportionately focused on its political and economic aspects, while the role of culture in the experiences of modern imperialism has not received adequate attention. For Said, imperialism and colonialism are not simply matters of capital accumulation and the seizure of territory and resources. Only with the backing of a powerful ideological formation can a state overcome internal differences while at the same time amassing enough energy and resources to conquer external territories (ibid., 9). During the process of imperial expansion, the imperial power projects its own understanding onto the colony in its attempt to define the colonized culture. Through its continuously changing relations with the colony, the imperialist country reaches self-definition and self-affirmation. Its imperialist subjectivity is constituted by its power relations with the colony.

Said's analysis convincingly demonstrates that—consciously or not—cultural discourse, together with cultural practices and politics, produces a system of domination that extends throughout the space of the cultural imaginary, shaping the parameters of thought and defining the categories of the dominant and the dominated. It justifies and affirms the imperialist right to expand, and it closes off possibilities for alternative modes of imagination. The insights presented in *Culture and Imperialism* can provide useful entry points for our analysis. In light of our theoretical concern, three interpretive directions emerge from reading Said: (1) the formation of imperialism is inevitably supported by cultural discourse and ideology; (2) the imperialist subject's identity can only be affirmed in relation to the colonized; and (3) the imperialist cultural imaginary conditions the vision and horizon of the colonized. To be sure, Said's historical analysis of the relation between Western imperialism and its cultural canon cannot be directly mapped onto the new phenomenon of subimperialism in the third world. Shifting the site of analysis from the imperialist to the subimperialist requires that we place the nation-state and nationalism at the center of our analysis.

The Imperialist Eye: Reading a Special Issue on the Southward Advance

The first three months of 1994 saw the dissemination of images, narratives, arguments, and opinions which became woven together into a remarkably coherent southward-advance discourse. This wave of media attention generated a social mood which conditioned a particular encounter with an imaginary Southeast Asia. Among these texts, the daily literary supplement of the *China Times* newspaper—called Human Space (Rénjiān)—stands out as not only the most influential, but also the most orchestrated. With its long history as the preeminent platform for cultural circles in Taipei, Human Space occupies a strategically important position. From 2 March to 4 March 1994, the *China Times* put out a full-page special issue of Human Space on Taiwan's southward turn, called "A Black Tide from the South." The following analysis is based on this collection of essays, but it will not be confined solely to the texts. The impact of the special issue lies in its immediate involvement and intervention in the social space and its interpellating of a "southward advancing subject." Through this analysis, I intend to open up the multilayered ideological structures in the special issue. I do not presume that this discourse easily and successfully recruited into the project subjects in the social space, but its potential to do so should be recognized.

The questions to be raised are: What exactly are the cultural, political, and ideological implications of the southward-advance discourse? How does it operate? What are the discursive content, form, and direction of the argument put forward? What ideological structures does it assume and connect with? As a cultural imaginary, what are its sources and its resources? A deeper theoretical concern is the question of whether there are ideological linkages between imperialism, colonialism, nationalism, and statism to be brought to the surface in our analysis of the discourse.[12]

The timing of the Human Space special issue, which appeared just after President Lee Teng-hui's visit to Southeast Asia during the lunar new year holiday, has clear political connections. Lee was born in Taiwan and educated in Japan and the United States; after he returned to Taiwan, he rose quickly through the ranks of the KMT. The special issue contained five essays by well-known writers, scholars, and editors: Yang Changzhen, Liu Kexiang, Wu Micha, Yang Bo, and Yang Zhao. Many critical intellectuals were surprised that these self-proclaimed "native leftists," who were usually considered to be in the opposition during the KMT era, had suddenly turned around to support the KMT political establishment and had laboriously searched for historical, cultural, and theoretical justifications for the state-led southward-advance policy. How does one account for this sudden shift?

The five essays included in the special issue were published in the following order: Yang Changzhen's "Gazing at the Low Latitudes: Taiwan and the 'Southeast Asian Movement'" and Liu Kexiang's "A Disappeared Line" both appeared on 2 March; Wu Micha's "Revisiting Taiwan's Location" and Yang Bo's "Mysterious Chinese" were printed on the following day; and Yang Zhao's "From China's Periphery to the Center of *Nanyang*: A Neglected Episode of History" appeared in three installments, from 2 March through 4 March. I shall begin with the short editorial introduction to the special issue.

The editor's note about the special issue, placed prominently in the center of the page in the 2 March issue, was written in the context of Taiwan President Lee Teng-hui's trip to Southeast Asia and the Southeast Asia project of the president of the Academia Sinica, Lee Yuan-tseh. The note lays out the background and motives of the special issue and guides readers toward a particular view of Taiwan's relationship with *Nanyang* (Southeast Asia). Here is the text of the editor's note:

> President Lee's trip to Southeast Asia during the lunar New Year has provoked many responses; most of the news reports and analyses, however, focus on political, economic, and trade issues. Taking into consideration Taiwan's cultural and historical connections with *Nanyang* countries, we launch this special issue, in part, to echo — or make a preliminary start toward realizing — the plan of President Lee [of the Academia Sinica] to make Taiwan the center of Southeast Asian historical studies within ten years.
>
> A black tide advancing north annually from the South Sea; an unnoticed biogeological line; a *Nanyang* Chinese man in the eyes of a French female writer; and a "(military) base for southward advance" in the Thirties . . . We hope this series of humanist reflections from the margin will show Taiwan from a new angle, and reflect its past and future relations with Southeast Asia and the surrounding areas.
>
> — The Editor

This editorial guide mixes a rational mode of discourse with poetic language, and each both subverts and supplements the other. Designed as a dialogue between humanist reflections from the margin and political and economic concerns from the center, the editor constructs a new angle, a "new" past, in order to push Taiwan toward the future — that is, toward the South.

The editor specifies from the very beginning the strategic position of the special issue by echoing the double-Lee structure: politics and the economy versus culture, current policies versus historical connections. The mode of thinking here is not binary but the Chinese yin-yang logic of bipolar complementarity. The two Lees need each other to round out a whole, although Lee Yuan-tseh repeatedly denied there were any political implications in his grand scholarly plan to make Taiwan a center of Southeast Asian historical studies.[13] The editor's note makes at least a rhetorical attempt at balance, but considered as an ideological construction, it is clear that the ambition of the special issue was to support the current political and economic policy by giving it cultural and historical justifications.

From the perspective of area studies, Lee Yuan-tseh's southward-advance plan very likely predated Lee Teng-hui's, and the former's denial of political connections may well be credible. But whatever his claims, it is impossible to disassociate Lee Yuan-tseh's vision for Taiwan as a center for Southeast Asian historical studies from his particular geopolitical location. Lee is a scientist (he won the Nobel Prize in Chemistry in 1986), and although he later became involved in Taiwan politics, he does not have a background in history or area studies. A long-term resident and one-time citizen of the United States, Lee taught at several leading American universities, including the University of California, Berkeley, a stronghold of Asian studies, where he was based for over twenty years. His championing of an area-studies center should be seen in the context of his own education and career, which were essentially American. The Second World War brought with it a realization in the United States that global economic and cultural development—what we now understand as neocolonialism—would require a massive amount of location-specific knowledge of the kind generated by serious scholarly research. Area-studies programs at American universities were created or aggressively expanded in the years after the war. Over a half-century later, the United States has established itself as the leading force in area studies. Today the world's leading research institutes specializing in East Asia, Southeast Asia, and South Asia are all at American universities such as Harvard, the University of Chicago, and Berkeley, which created their Asian-studies institutes after the war (Barlow 1993). In order to catch up with such places within ten years, Lee Yuan-tseh would first have needed to quickly produce a team of linguists capable of working productively in a large number of Southeast Asian languages. Or he could have taken a shortcut and imported large numbers of American scholars and their archives. Unsurprisingly, the plan to become the center of Southeast Asian research turned out to be a daydream. Lee's Southeast Asia project was nevertheless a pioneering event in Taiwan's academic history: it was the first large-scale attempt to steer the direction of the academy through the control of research funding in the humanities and social sciences.[14]

One point needs to be clarified. The state policy (southward advance), the academic direction (looking toward Southeast Asia), and the object of cultural production (the special issue) were interconnected neither through a linear alignment of motives, nor through simple administrative coordination. Rather, their connections lie in a homologous relationship in the structure of discursive space: the complex ideological relationship between knowledge and power can be revealed only by tracing the connections running through the fabric of discursive content, argument, and form.

In the second paragraph of the note quoted above, the editor lists the broad assemblage of topics to be found in the special issue, such as the black tide, the biogeological line, the colonial woman writer's narrative imaginary, and the "(military) base for southward advance" of the 1930s. These natural, literary, and historical discursive forms and directions are intended to recover a very particular collection of historical memories. By retrieving these marginalized or forgotten stories, Taiwan can be repositioned along a new political horizon, so as to discover its "genuine" connections with the black tide from the South and "the surrounding areas" both in the past and for the future.[15] The southward-advance special issue has its impetus in the need to recover the forgotten past so as to complete the present, in order to secure a stable future. Likewise, the South has always throbbed with the blood of Taiwan's own history.

This is a puzzling point in the editor's note. The editor mentions the "southward advance" of the 1930s, but that reference is followed by ellipsis points, as if the editor is hesitating, seemingly aware that there might be a connection between the special issue and the southward advance of Japanese imperial conquest in the 1930s.[16] But he does not complete the thought. Equally curious is the illustration that accompanied the phrase "a black tide from the South," which appeared in bold Chinese characters at the very top of the newspaper for two successive days. In the drawing, trees lean together along the horizon, arching over an ocean view. It is not clear whether the drawing was meant to give a stereotypical Nanyang flavor or to indicate Taiwan's southern coastline embracing the southern black tide. What is clear is that a bird with spread wings (perhaps a symbol of freedom or of Taiwan) is flying toward and landing on the characters *nánfāng* (the South). What then is the semiotic work that the "black tide" is supposed to perform?

Naturalizing Power and Knowledge

In his essay, "Gazing at Low Latitudes: Taiwan and the 'Southeast Asia Movement,'" Yang Changzhen leads off the special issue by returning Taiwan to the "black tide cultural sphere [to which] it has always belonged." Yang's argument is based on "natural geography." Due to differences in ocean temperature, the rotation of the earth, and geological divides, an ocean current known as the black tide has formed around the Indochinese peninsula. East Asia's "rice civilization" developed beside this tide's warm and nutritious flow and in time came to form the "black tide cultural sphere." The author cites archeological and anthropological evidence to argue that a group of Taiwan's aboriginal tribes called the Pingpu "belong to the Malay race." This argument is then used to support the proposition that Taiwan has always been a member of the black-tide cultural sphere and was incorporated into "the Chinese system" only after the Han Chinese invasions of Taiwan during the Ming Dynasty.

The discursive effect is to naturalize Taiwan's rightful place as an original part of the Southeast Asian black-tide cultural sphere and attribute its later Chinese affiliation to human factors. Underlying this argument is a set of oppositions: nature versus human, original versus alien, and Southeast Asia versus China. The logic of equivalence links the concepts of "Taiwan," "original," "natural belonging," "Southeast Asia," and the "black tide," an attempt to win the reading subject's consent to binding Taiwan and the black-tide cultural sphere tightly together. The sign value of the black tide, then, is to be found in its restoration of Taiwan to its natural membership in the black-tide cultural sphere, as opposed to the Chinese sphere, which is understood as a more recent historical aberration. This argument has a critical element. The opposition between "aboriginal Pingpu tribes" and the Han Chinese suggests hostility on the part of the former toward the latter, and further implies the aboriginal population's full entitlement to Taiwan. However, the marginal Pingpu subject is mentioned only once in the essay, as support for Taiwan's natural identification with Southeast Asia. Throughout the rest of the narrative, Taiwan is homogenized, a place completely deprived of social differences. Yang's starting point could have led him to argue for the restoration of Taiwan's territory and sovereignty to "nature," or to the "real" Taiwanese—that is, the aboriginal tribes. But he deploys the aboriginal figure only for the purpose of connecting the Han Chinese Taiwan with Southeast Asia. There is no reflection on the Han Chinese colonization of Taiwan's aboriginal population.

Yang moves forward from natural geography to human history. At its zenith, the Chinese empire expanded its political and economic power through the entire black-tide cultural sphere. Taiwan's incorporation into "history" was initiated by Chinese pirates, who established a sea route from Japan through Chinese waters to Southeast Asia for their own trading purposes. From that point on, Taiwan entered "Chinese history, Southeast Asian history, as well as world history." Yang's next move touches on an important theme: imperialism and the formation of Southeast Asian nationalism. He argues that Southeast Asian nationalism has been fashioned through two waves of what he calls the "Southeast Asian Order Reconstruction Movement" (Dōngnányǎ zhìxù chóngjiàn yùndòng). The first wave was the expansion of Japanese capitalism in the years leading up to the Second World War, and the second was the rise of socialism in "Red China." The failure of these two movements, which were engineered by the region's most powerful nations, led to a series of regional collaborations, which culminated in the founding of the Association of Southeast Asian Nations (ASEAN) in 1967. Yang explains that ASEAN was created "to cultivate a parallel sub-regional system of cooperation as the basic strategy for the autonomy and freedom of the [member] nation-states."

There are obvious problems with the argument. To begin with, Yang's view that the Greater East Asia Co-Prosperity Sphere put forward by Japan was once "welcomed by Southeast Asian nationalists and intellectuals as its salvation" is not really correct. Renato Constantino, the nationalist historian of the Philippines, has demonstrated that, except for a handful of opportunists, the majority of Filipinos paid little regard to Japanese propaganda, which they considered ridiculous (Constantino 1990, 14–15). In Malaya, although some of the Malay and Indian colonialists were influenced by Japanese anti-British rhetoric, the Chinese community had begun an anti-Japanese movement long before Japan's 1941 invasion (Sundaram 1989, 217). In Singapore, strong anti-Japanese sentiment was evident by 1931, escalated from 1937 on, and reached a climax during the Japanese occupation during the Second World War (Lee 1992, 12–15). Yang is inflating the importance of selected historical episodes and passing them off as representative.

Second, Yang credits the Japanese imperialists with destroying the existent colonial structure "that was oppressing Southeast Asian nationalism" and laying the foundation for later regional integration. Again, history does not support this claim. Instead of supporting local nationalist forces, Japanese colonizers suppressed nationalism with numerous policies, many based on racial discrimination. At the same time, the original colonial power structure was not destroyed. Almost twenty years after the end of the Second World War, for example, British imperialists were heavily involved in the formation of the Malaysian Federation. Their purpose was to place all of England's Southeast Asian colonies under a single umbrella, which, they imagined, could become its own sphere of influence (Sundaram 1989, 219). In Singapore, the British colonizers' cruel suppression of local nationalism, and especially of the leftists, actually intensified after the Japanese occupation (Lee 1992, 127–30). All these historical situations contradict Yang's story. Nevertheless, he goes on to argue that "the Greater East Asia Co-Prosperity Sphere can be regarded as East Asian societies' great fight back against Western colonial invasion," and that the Japanese imperialist "reconstruction of an Eastern Asia order left an important legacy, namely, a mature modern nationalism." His constant affirmation of Japanese imperialism is nothing less than a discursive exoneration of the invaders.

Third, Yang believes that "after the establishment of Red China, the socialist movement triggered a wave of Sinophobia in the Southeast Asian countries . . . which led to the eventual rejection of socialism." He goes on to argue that the success of the Vietnamese revolution was "even more terrifying" and hence "catalyzed the birth of ASEAN." But anti-Chinese sentiment in Southeast Asia did not begin in 1949. As far back as the end of the sixteenth century, Chinese merchants' control of the food and the textile industries in the Philippines provoked discontent (Constantino 1992, 58–60). More recently, the Philippine Communist Party (PKP) won great public support in the 1930s and 1940s. By 1949, the year the Chinese Communist Party came to power, the PKP was strong enough militarily to claim that it would take control of the country within two years. Its failure was due not to "Southeast Asian people's favoring of nationalism over socialism," as Yang believes, but to the antisocialist interventions of the United States (Constantino 1991, 289). Critical studies coming out of the region, exemplified by Constantino's (1990, 1991, 1992) historical work, show that it was the imperialists' top-down control over the colonies that was the main mechanism suppressing socialist forces, and that had little to do with "the people's preference" for nationalism, socialism, or anything else. Yang's socialism-nationalism dichotomy is not sustainable. These two forces were often combined, rather than being mutually exclusive, in Southeast Asia. Until recently, elements of socialist-nationalist movements were still active in the Philippines, Malaysia, and Thailand. Yang's views reveal more about his anxieties over socialist movements than they do about the history of Southeast Asian nationalism.

"Gazing at Low Latitudes" concludes with a back-to-nature call: "Existing among the order of East Asian subaltern countries, with similar historical experiences and present conditions, Taiwan moves naturally towards Southeast Asia." Indeed, this imaginary location within the category of the third world has great potential to open a new worldview. However, Yang's selective and misleading account of East Asian history, his justification of Japanese imperialism, his retreat from any substantive engagement with the role of the United States in the region, and his attack on socialism all indicate less progressive motives. Coming from nature and returning to nature, Yang's Taiwan fits perfectly into the new map that was being drawn by the state.

Yang's strategy of naturalizing the southward advance resurfaces in Liu Kexiang's "A Disappeared Line." Liu attempts to connect Taiwan with Southeast Asia by retrieving the Wallace Line, a biogeological boundary identified in the nineteenth century. Liu's argument displays the intimate relationship between knowledge and power, between scholarship and empire. He begins by pointing out that Alfred Russel Wallace was a pioneer in the field of evolutionary theory, but nowhere does he mention how the theory was misapplied to provide theoretical support for Western imperialist expansion.[17] This is a significant omission, given that the Wallace Line, which was discovered at the time of the British colonial conquest of the Malaysian archipelago, was later used by Japanese scientists. Liu himself gives a vivid account:

The biological and anthropological knowledge implied by such bio-geological lines and the areas that surround them, including the South-east Asia archipelagos and peninsula, attracted the interest of Japanese biologists who were visiting Taiwan. They were eager to go there to conduct systematic scientific research, in order to understand the area's relationship with Taiwan, and even with Japan. For the Japanese government, Southeast Asia was the target of its southward advance, while for many scholars of biology and anthropology it was a place so tantalizing it seemed as if they were whales returning to their breeding waters.

Liu struggles to separate government from scholarship in order to leave room for the latter's aesthetic naiveté, but the desire for scientific knowledge is not simply a desire for knowledge or science for its own sake, but a desire to explore and establish the relation between colony and home country via the domain of science. This fatal attraction, this interpellation of the South, stimulated scholars to march in lock step with their nation's military imperialists, even at the risk of their lives. Practically speaking, without the empire's southward advance as the material basis for this type of research, this knowledge would not have been so quickly produced. Without the scientific evidence of an ancient "cultural affinity and cultural layer" between Japan, Taiwan, and Southeast Asia, the Japanese empire would lack a critical justification for its southward advance. One need not wait for the future to see whether knowledge produced under such circumstances could shoulder this heavy task. Our reading of Yang Changzhen has shown how his essay is carrying out precisely the kind of knowledge work that lays the foundation for future imperial expansion. Liu Kexiang's analysis draws out the complicity between cultural production and empire formation, so one has to wonder how he could be blind to the implications of his own knowledge production—which, in this case, is quite blatantly being used to support the state's southward-advance policy. And if he does sense the connection, why is he not willing to tease out that complicity?

The analysis thus far shows that the southward-advance discourse delivers ideological support for the formation of state policy and demonstrates how that formation operates according to the logic of naturalization. Antonio Gramsci's theory of ideology remains a powerful explanatory tool here. For Gramsci, the most "natural" is also the most ideological, and naturalization is one of the principles of ideological production. My analysis also describes how the imperial subject (Taiwan) moves close to the target of colonization (Southeast Asia), while anxiously distancing itself from the enemy (communist China) in order to discover its new (but also already existing) self-identity. It reveals that the old imperialist cultural imagination (in the form of the Greater East Asia Co-Prosperity Sphere and the Wallace Line) still conditions the imagination of the colonized. The new empire's imagination, as constructed by the southward-advance discourse, is a copy—a new, pirated edition—of the Japanese imperial thought of a half-century ago.

Taiwan-centrism: The Incarnation of Imperialism

Wu Micha's "Reconsidering Taiwan's Location" is a historian's chronological account. It starts in the fourteenth century with the formation of the trading system between East and Southeast Asia, continues to the seventeenth-century arrival of the Dutch East India Company, which pushed Taiwan onto "the stage of world history," moves to colonization by Japan in the late nineteenth century, and ends with the defeat of the Japanese in 1944. Wu's writing has the effect of a slide show: scenes are thrown up on the screen and shuffled through, one by one, accompanied by a voice-over so flat and emotionless that it seems unlikely ever to arouse the audience's sympathy. Nevertheless, precisely because the screen puts the reader squarely in the position of spectator, the invisible narrator can let his history unfold as he patiently walks us through the past. Wu provides the reader with a Taiwan-centered linear history, supplemented in the introduction and conclusion with the frame of "Taiwan's real location." Complementing Yang's and Liu's nature-based discourses, Wu gives the southward-advance discourse in the special issue the weight and depth of history.

The byline Wu Micha guarantees academic authority. A history professor at National Taiwan University who was educated at the University of Tokyo, Wu is a leading expert on the history of Taiwan (Wu 1991). How does someone speaking from Wu's academic position engage with state policy? Appearing in the opening and closing paragraphs of his essay is his protagonist, President Lee Teng-hui, who serves to establish the political context for Wu's account. Wu writes that "President Lee's trip down to Nanyang [enables] us to finally 'discover' the neighboring areas which have always been around us."[18] Wu's main argument is that:

> President Lee's route limns for us the long-existent, but unnoticed, geographical location of Taiwan. Traveling from Taiwan to the Philippines, Indonesia, and Thailand before returning to Taiwan, [he] encircled an oceanic world. Mainland-centered cartography leaves unclear Taiwan's real location and its historical unfolding in the region. Once Taiwan is placed at the center of the map, we see an entirely new scene: Taiwan stands right at the junction of East Asia (the East China Sea) and Southeast Asia (the South China Sea). To a considerable degree, this location has determined Taiwan's historical unfolding and foreshadows its potential.

Simply put, "Reconsidering Taiwan's Location" is intended to correct a wrongheaded Sinocentric positioning. Repositioning Taiwan at the center of the map enables us to find Taiwan's "real location," which is the center of both East Asia and Southeast Asia. Wu's view diverges here from Yang's "back to nature" argument. While Yang is content to push Taiwan toward Southeast Asia, Wu undertakes the more ambitious project of approaching Southeast Asia without giving up East Asia.

What exactly is the basis for Wu's Taiwan-centrism? His chronology captures several relevant historical instances. The first occurred when the Dutch East India Company set up trading posts throughout Japan, Taiwan, Southeast Asia, and the Indian subcontinent in the seventeenth century, though at this historical moment, Taiwan-centrism was not yet obvious. A clearer version appeared in the twentieth century during the Japanese occupation of Taiwan. The Japanese southward-advance project used Taiwan as a base from which it launched its colonization of Southeast Asia from southern China all the way to Australia. The geographical zones encompassed by the Dutch and Japanese colonial projects do not align perfectly, yet according to Wu, the second episode "naturally reminds us of the seventeenth century East India Company."

Wu's text is accompanied by a remarkable map, which was placed in the center of the page of the 3 March edition of the *China Times*. Originally included in a book published by the Japanese newspaper *Asahi Shimbun* in 1944, the map shows Taiwan with a series of concentric circles around it; as Wu emphatically notes, it is an image that "puts Taiwan at the center of the Greater East Asia Co-Prosperity Sphere!" More telling is the map's caption: "In the 30s and 40s, Japanese scholars often used Taiwan as the center to think through the whole of Greater East Asian relations!" Wu notes that Lee Teng-hui's Nanyang trip is simply a more recent instance of an earlier Taiwan-centrism: "The course Lee's aircraft flew seems to once again evoke the very map."

What exactly do these three historical episodes "inspire" us to do? Wu's unreflexive and uncritical discourse leads us to the realization that his proposal for a new Taiwan-centrism is clearly derived from the colonialist cultural imaginary. Putting Taiwan at the center of a map literally drawn by the colonizer is the reincarnation of a fifty-year-old imperial desire on the part of the colonized.

But was Taiwan ever really the center of the Japanese empire?

The Sexual Intercourse of Empire, Capital, and Race

Yang Bo's "Mysterious Chinese" is a first-person narrative interspersed with memories of childhood travel. The author's sentimental literary style contrasts sharply with the dryness of the other essays in the special issue, giving readers an unexpected breathing space. Yang's disarming style also allows him to amplify his subjective voice into a collective psychological projection. His very selectively constructed "popular memory" displaces the historical master narrative, and more powerfully articulates together the subject, capital, empire, gender, and sexuality as positions of identification. In this form of writing, the slogan "the personal is political" fully manifests its meaning; through a retelling of family history, the political basis of Yang's "cultural China" is revealed.

Assuming the role of an amateur anthropologist, the author enters Southeast Asia to carry out what he calls "postcolonial studies." Once he begins his Southeast Asia narrative, his desire fluctuates through the dialectic of "me" and the "mysterious Chinese," which is then transformed into the dialectic between the Chinese and the colonizer. Left out of the narrative is the subjectivity of the "other local races," who appear only when they are in conflict with the Chinese.

The author's "postcolonial" curiosity leads his readers back to his family history, first during the turmoil of the Vietnam War, and then to the earlier era of Japanese colonial occupation. This retrospective and affective account enables him to work through the guilt of his childhood Oedipus complex. He writes, "I disapproved of our relatives' *pǎo dānbāng* [small-capital trading] in Southeast Asia and my father's insurance and shipping business, but now I'm sure *pǎo dānbāng* was no more shameful than what the *táishāng* [Taiwanese business people] of today do."[19] The ambivalent sentiment, largely due to the traditional Chinese literati disdain for commerce, can be resolved by attributing these actions to a courageous struggle for life. Only through this self-justification can the author's reidentification with the father be achieved: "After all, having the courage to prioritize business over petty benefits is a basic requirement of life among overseas Chinese, including, naturally, the Taiwanese." The identification with overseas Chinese is reached through the sympathetic recognition of small-capital businessmen in the past and the vanguard of southward-advancing Taiwanese merchants in the present. This is a highly selective construction of popular memory, relying on class, race, and gender exclusion. In the narrator's desire for identification, his mother, his father's workers, and the "other" peoples dwelling alongside the overseas Chinese never emerge over the horizon of his historical memory.

Yang's real concerns are what kind of people the Nanyang Chinese are, and how they are viewed. The importance of these questions lies in their potential to constitute one's own subjectivity, which can be established only in constant interaction with the Other. As Yang puts it, "This is a basic task like [the Chinese expression] *zhījǐ zhībǐ* [know yourself and know your opponent]." Interestingly, his search is not based on written accounts by these "other peoples";[20] rather, his (Chinese) self-identity is sought in two colonial literary texts. The first text, Joseph Conrad's *Lord Jim* (1900), with its "negative image" of the Chinese is quickly dismissed. In the second text, Marguerite Duras's *The Lover* (1986), however, Yang finds the possibility of a Chinese identity—but a Chinese identity with a Taiwanese core.

Yang's discussion of Duras is the only mention of women in the entire special issue. Above the text of the article is a still image of the actor Tony Leung Ka-Fai set in a circular frame; below the picture is the caption: "The Chinese man in the film *The Lover*." Under the photo is the essay's title, "Mysterious Chinese," with the author's name below that. At the very bottom of the page is an oblong picture that shows two women, one standing, the other sitting; its caption reads: "Indochina, 1930. The sixteen-year-old Duras in her Vietnamese dress, taking a picture with her companion. The same year, on a Mekong River ferry, she encountered a Chinese man who later became the prototype for the protagonist in *The Lover*." In the picture, Duras is comfortably seated, whereas her female "companion" is standing behind and to the right of Duras's chair. Both women are looking into the camera—that is, directly at the reader. This picture is a display of hierarchy—the sitting colonizer (the master, or mistress) and the standing colonized (the maid)—definitely not the portrayal of two "companions" with equal status. More interestingly, in Yang's rewriting, the lover is no longer "the Chinese" (*Huárén*) but "the Chinese man" (*Zhōngguó nánrén*). Throughout the essay, Yang slides between these terms, carefully linking the invisible Taiwanese (man), the Nanyang Chinese (man), and the "Chinese man." On the surface, this slippage seems like evidence for a neo-Confucian affinity for "cultural China," but the order of the slippage actually marks the shifting identity of the author himself. In his reading of *The Lover*, we read one such mechanism of identification:

> This novel describes the encounter and love affair between a young girl, Duras, and a Chinese man along the banks of the Mekong River. Their economic and physical relationships represent a reversal of the relation between the white colonizing class and the colonized . . . Whatever else it is, this book is a milestone in the representation of the Chinese: the very rich Chinese lover, graceful and attractive, mysterious as ever (mischievous even). Once presented in the novel and on the big screen (after much editing), it becomes a recognition of the Chinese, a serious treatment.

It is definitely not Duras here who is constructing her female subjectivity by means of the nonwhite man; rather, it is the colonized, with recourse to his dominant position with regard to sex and capital, who recovers his male and racial identity through their intercourse. The colonized finally achieves redemption through becoming the object of the white woman's desire. This is indeed a reversal. Backed by capital, the colonized assumes the position held by the white male colonizer. Yang strongly identifies with this "cultural China" man, who is rich, graceful, and mysterious. But what kind of identification and recognition is this?

In *Black Skin, White Masks*, Fanon gives an account of desire in the relationship between the colonized man and the white woman:

I wish to be acknowledged not as *black* but as *white*.

Now—and this is a form of recognition that Hegel had not envisaged—who but a white women can do this for me? By loving me she proves that I'm worthy of white love. I am loved like a white man.

I am a white man.

Her love takes me onto the noble road that leads to total realization . . .

I marry white culture, white beauty, and whiteness.

When my restless hands caress those white breasts, they grasp white civilization and dignity, and make them mine. (Fanon 1967 [1952], 63)

Fanon's self-psychoanalytic account suggests that the writing subject's strong desire is to replace the white colonizer and become him, rather than to recognize his own existence as a black man. This is a reversal. Although Fanon's analysis may be helpful in understanding the structural tendencies and theoretical logic of Yang's writing position, the categories of "Chinese" and "black man" are not historically equivalent. In the neo-Confucianist theorization of cultural China, blacks (whether from Africa, the Caribbean, or elsewhere) are essentially invisible. In sharp contrast, in the Chinese world, French civilization represents the pinnacle of the mysterious and romantic Western culture. Viewed from the framework of cultural China, the "intercourse" between Tony Leung Ka-Fai and Duras on the page of the special issue is the miscegenation of the cream of the Occidental and Oriental civilizations. It signifies a recognition by the most highly civilized nation of the West, a proof of Chinese culture's permanent vitality. In Yang's cultural China, there exists a sexually charged anxiety over not being recognized. And Chinese (male) dignity must therefore be ransomed with the advantage of capital.

The identification with cultural China can be very oppressive to ethnic Chinese who do not live in mainland China. They are marginalized in their local environment, but at the same time they are often asked to be Chinese.[21] A strong ethnocentric tendency often operates in the concept of cultural China. In "Mysterious Chinese," the identity of the Chinese subject identity can only be constructed vis-à-vis a "Western, white colonizer," while the many racial and ethnic groups in Southeast Asia do not even enter the relational space of identification. Cultural China as a strategy to counter Western hegemony ends up being a reproduction of imperialist desire, locked in the binary opposition of China versus the West.

"Taiwanese Woman" versus "Mainland Man": Sexual Triumphalism

Yang Bo's reading of the Chinese and Western characters in *The Lover* reminds us that regaining confidence and a sense of self through sexual intercourse is a common strategy for dealing with the suppressed anxiety implicit in the colonial situation. Yang Zhao, whose contribution to the special issue will be discussed in the following section, gives an account not of the Chinese versus Western colonial dynamic, but of Taiwan's "internal colonialism." In his 1993 novella, "Memorandum of the Past," we meet a male protagonist who is recalling a past affair for a female psychoanalyst:

In this game [of caressing], I could feel that she was fully prepared; she was so wet that her moisture had dripped onto my groin. But when I tried several times to move my body to penetrate her, she intentionally resisted. Suddenly, she pressed her palms against my chest and asked, "Do you love me?" Of course I said, "I love you." She pressed her lips together, and after thinking for a while, said, "But I hate you." I was confused and asked, "How can you hate me?" "Of course I hate you," she said. Meanwhile she moved my hesitating hands toward her nipples and in a gentle voice ordered, "Tell me you are a mainlander."[22] I followed her order, "I'm a mainlander." She closed her eyes and guided my hands toward more sensitive areas, saying, "Say that again." "I'm a mainlander," I repeated.

All of a sudden, she jumped up and jammed my swollen penis painfully into her vagina, and began to shake her butt up and down violently. I wasn't prepared for her to get into it so quickly, and almost erupted. I clenched my teeth, and breathed deeply, and luckily I was able to hold it. At that moment, she closed her eyes, and then, while continuing her rocking, looked up and murmured, "I hate you mainlanders who have ridden on top of [us] Taiwanese for forty years. I hate you mainlanders who have raped this land . . ." Even in her orgasm, which electrified her entire shivering body, I could still hear amidst her heavy breathing, her sexy sweet crying for "Taiwanese victory . . ." (Yang 1993a, 88–89)

In this violent war of sexual intercourse, the reader is invited to identify with the male narrator. Yet the writer puts the woman in the dominant position, and it is with her that he identifies. In other words, Yang uses the woman to express Taiwanese antagonism against the mainlander. Orgasm is not enacted by the "I" but by the "electrified . . . shivering body" of the "Taiwanese." The male author's double identification is first with the "Taiwanese" (but not women), and secondly with the object of the Taiwanese woman's desire—the male mainlander whom he wants to replace. But why identify with a male mainlander? In the following episode, which continues the protagonist's narration to the psychoanalyst, Yang writes:

It's a pity that some old habits just won't die. I put her on the bed, trying to launch a new round of play with a kiss, but she couldn't help screaming. She still couldn't accept my being on top. She still couldn't help saying, "But I hate you." When I sensed a moment of hesitation, I entered her. After a fit of unexpected spasms, she regained the habit of swaying her butt to my rhythm. Her breath was becoming heavier, but she still made the effort to say, "But you are a mainlander, and I hate mainlanders." I hated this clichéd topic. It was preventing me from concentrating on the pleasure of the physical touch between our hips. I tried to snap her out of it, "That was your old excuse. You don't really hate mainlanders." She slowed down the pace with which she pressed her vagina around me and looked at me with suspicion. "I really hate mainlanders. That's why I do this with you. I like reversing the world. I like the feeling of the Taiwanese riding the mainlander." This remark made me feel awkward—I didn't know whether to laugh or to cry. I thrust strongly several times to make her feel the real touch of physical intercourse, then stressed, "Our relationship is based on love, not this Taiwanese and mainlander stuff." The word love did calm her down. She swayed gently and foiled my forceful attack. But she still insisted, "Love is one thing, but I'm still on top of a mainlander."

Her stubbornness was becoming really unbearable. With my anger swelling, I couldn't help pricking the lie and telling her: she was actually riding a Taiwanese, not a mainlander. What followed was our first fight since getting to know each other. At last I even pulled out and went to grab my ID card to show her, all the while with no clothes on. This really was a ridiculous contrast — that the naked me should need an irrelevant little card to prove his existence, and that the card clearly recorded the fact that I was from Changhua, Taiwan.

Having resolved this quarrel, we returned to bed and continued where we had left off. But I could feel her turning absent-minded. After we finished, I couldn't help asking her, "You didn't like it?" She shook her head. Tears trickled down and she murmured softly, "I feel you are a tyrant today . . ."

From then on, we never tried to see each other again. I couldn't find any excuse to approach her. Yet strangely, the experience of making love like that, of being tightly pressed underneath her in bed, has always fascinated me . . .

Can you explain to me what's going on? (Yang 1993a, 90)

The male protagonist is at a loss, but he hopes that the psychoanalyst can deliver an answer. One explanation of what is going on might be as follows: in this scene, the first-person narrator has become more active than in the last episode, no longer willing to shoulder the Taiwanese resentment toward mainlanders. When the Taiwanese (the female protagonist) attempts to reverse the world so that the Taiwanese can ride the mainlander, the male protagonist, in order to maintain his dominant position as a real Taiwanese male, has to prove that he was from Taiwan by resorting to the authority of the state apparatus, the official identification card being the most basic instrument by which the nation-state constructs one's identity. The female protagonist then fully realizes that Taiwanese women are actually dominated by Taiwanese men. When she says, "I feel you are a tyrant today," it is because the man is no longer a mainlander but has become instead the dominant Taiwanese man; the Taiwanese woman becomes governed by one of her countrymen (*tóngzú rén*). It is precisely their realization that they are both Taiwanese that causes the two protagonists to end their relationship. They cannot find any reason to see each other because the pleasure of reversal no longer exists. When a Taiwanese is on top of a Taiwanese (no matter if it is the man or the woman who is on top), the pleasure of conquering the former rulers is lost, and there is no longer the mainlander's superior position to be usurped. Once the narrator's "Changhua, Taiwan" identity is revealed, the woman becomes "absent-minded," losing the desire to go on exercising violence, even shedding tears as she recognizes the tyranny of the Taiwanese man who can no longer be the object of her desire.

Both Yang Bo and Yang Zhao demonstrated a clear identification with the subject position of the Taiwanese man. Through their interaction with women, Taiwanese men (the colonized) were attempting to fulfill their historical mission — that is, resolve their desire to overthrow and supplant the mainlander colonial man. Their use of sexual intercourse was a metaphor for a general social and political anxiety, and for power struggles among politicians at the highest levels of the state. Given the political mood in Taiwan when the novella was published, a time when the mainlander and Taiwanese factions of the KMT were vying for control of the state, Yang Zhao seems to be documenting a prevalent psychic condition.[23] It is not incidental that the novella touches on the problem of what happens after these battles are fought — which is to say, what happens at the stage of replacement. Despite the insightfulness of his novella, by the time of his 1994 piece in the southward-advance special issue, Yang's critical awareness was no longer evident, and he had become an active supporter of the ruling regime.

If we push the analysis a bit further, it is possible to read the novella as the writer's unconscious projection of the Taiwanese man's need to have his identity recognized by the mainlander man through intercourse with the mainlander woman. The inferiority complex of the colonized is thus dissolved by identification with and assumption of the dominant position occupied by the mainlander man. The direction of this politics of desire follows the same logic in Yang Bo's essay, where the writer's identification with the Chinese man is what allows him to usurp the position occupied by the colonial subject (Duras). In both instances, the purpose is to win the colonizer's recognition and then to replace him. Yang Zhao disguises this relationship by reversing it — from Taiwanese male versus mainlander female to Taiwanese female versus mainlander male — a writing which projects an androgynous autoerotic anxiety.

The psychohistory of self-affirmation through the violence of sexual conquest, using sex as a means of alleviating politically generated male anxiety, is a topic which requires further study. If we imagine a triangular framework made up of the colonized male, the female colonizer, and the male colonizer, the male colonizer — representing the patriarchal colonial regime—would be on top. At one of the bottom corners would be the colonized man, who seeks to identify with the father at the top and then replace him. At the other bottom corner is the female colonizer, who serves as an intermediary between the colonized male and the colonial father. To borrow a term from Ashis Nandy's psychology of colonization, this relation between the two males positioned so differently in colonial culture is one of "intimate enemies" (Nandy 1983). In the light of Eve Kosofsky Sedgwick's queer theory, we can also read it as the desire for homosocial bonding between heterosexual males (Sedgwick 1985). Standing at the intersection of these two theories, we are able to see that in contemporary "colonial culture," the colonizer and the colonized male live out their intimate love-hate power relations through the mediation of women.

The analysis in this section points to a deeper layer of psychological mechanisms displayed in the southward-advance discourse. In Yang Bo's "Mysterious Chinese," the subimperial subject attempts to reverse the colonial order of subjugation to reclaim self-identity. The intense desire for recognition that is evidenced by this work can be satisfied only by entering the space of an earlier colonial cultural imaginary, and by sexually dominating the other gender, the other race, and the other class. It is in this structural formation of desire that class, race, gender identity, and the positioning of the imperial subject are projected. It is also on the level of desire formation that the southward-advance discourse reveals the overlapping relations of imperialism, colonialism, ethnocentrism, chauvinism, and capitalism.

From Periphery to Center: The Imperial Desire of the Nativist Left

The backbone of the special issue is the long essay by Yang Zhao titled "From the Periphery of China to the Center of *Nanyang*: A Neglected Episode of History," which appeared in three installments over the issue's three-day run. Compared with Wu Micha's academic position, Yang Zhao's is more diversified. Gu Xiuxian (1993, 3) categorizes his work as belonging mainly to the field of cultural criticism. Tan Shi (1994) positions him in literary criticism, specifically as part of the literary tradition of Ye Shitao and Chen Fangming that favored Taiwanese independence. Yang was also a member of the writing team that produced *Newly Rising Nation*, a book published under the name of Xu Xinliang, then chairman of the DPP. Yang himself claims to hold a "nativist left" position (Li Guangzhen 1994; Yang 1993b, 6–18). This is suggestive in the context of our analysis. One might expect that a self-proclaimed leftist would come forward to register an alternative voice, and to critique rather than support the implications of the right-wing southward-advance policy.

Like Wu, Yang begins his reading and writing of history with Lee Teng-hui's visit to Southeast Asia to evoke a sense of the contemporary political reality. Unlike Wu with his objective historical style, Yang performs in a rather exaggerated mode. As he puts it, Lee's visit did not simply "popularize the southward advance as a topic for discussion, but suddenly caused all of Taiwan to turn its eyes toward the South with strong hope, eager to find its future there." Yang's own inflated desire has become the desire of "all of Taiwan" to seek a future in Southeast Asia. Throughout his essay, Yang's "we," "Taiwan," and "Taiwanese" are lumped together without any mention of the social diversity those terms embody. Yang opens his argument by positing the southward advance into Southeast Asia as an alternative to the ongoing westward advance into mainland China. But whose choice is this to make? Capital? The state? "Native leftists"? Is Yang suggesting there is unanimity of opinion among these various actors? If not, what differences between them does he assume?

Yang's analysis focuses on capital accumulation and flow, though he never questions the price paid for that accumulation or mentions the hard labor that made it possible. He argues that Taiwan was once only the recipient of capital investment; but now, "in its late-capitalist period, the country has risen to become capital owners and exporters." According to Yang, the difference is that "under the conditions of low autonomy, we had to accept a world outlook arranged by others, and had very limited choices. Now we must produce our own understanding, construct our own worldview, and be confident enough to find our own answers." Here Yang urges his readers to take a nationalist position, enlisting our devotion to the nation. Framed by a discussion of the direction of the flow of capital, Yang's view seems to be that of a state policymaker. But what is the content of the worldview that Yang puts forward, and what is its function?

Yang constructs his worldview through negation, and what he negates is the notion of a "Greater China Economic Sphere," composed of Chinese communities in Taiwan, Hong Kong, and Singapore, with mainland

China at the center. Because "Greater China" is the dominant framework, it has to be dealt with before Taiwan can attempt to construct a new worldview. Yang attributes the cultural basis of the existing mainstream notion to long-standing "Chinese nationalism," shaped and promoted by the KMT state, as well as to the lingering effects of "anti-feudalism" and "anti-imperialism," artifacts or earlier moments of resistance against Japan and the West. In practice, Yang notes, Chinese nationalism has produced two serious problems: first, the Greater China economic sphere is controlled by the authoritarian Chinese Communist Party (CCP), which will fail to sustain economic growth and therefore fundamentally "cannot be trusted"; and second, Chinese nationalism evokes hostility in neighboring countries. It is because of these two problems, Yang argues, that "Taiwan has finally been forced to entirely rehash the old worldview."

If we place Yang's argument in the political context of mid-1990s Taiwan, it becomes clear that he was making a real effort to create a different worldview. The China-centered worldview, long held by the KMT as its version of Chinese nationalism, had lost its authority. After the end of the cold war, Taiwan was no longer able to isolate itself from Communist China. At the same time, both the Taiwanese nationalist faction within the KMT led by Lee Teng-hui and the newly formed DPP were struggling to capture power. Both of these new political forces required a new vision to further their political goals, and the Taiwan-centered worldview implied in the southward advance, "restoring Taiwan to Southeast Asia, returning to Nanyang," was something both camps could share. Here Yang Zhao echoes Yang Changzhen, Wu Micha, and the two Lees in designating the function of the southward advance as "a step toward resolving Taiwanese society's collective anxiety and ambivalence over westward advance." As Yang Zhao puts it, the "real significance" of the southward advance is not so much to further Taiwan's economic interests, but to declare that the "Greater China economic sphere is not our inescapable fate."

But Yang's point of departure differs from Wu's. Whereas Wu claims to know where Taiwan's "true location" is, Yang regards the positioning of Taiwan in the South as a cultural construction, not an objective scientific truth. Yang argues for Southeast Asia over China as Taiwan's rightful place of return on the ground that it is "the product of collective psychology," without noting that this argument is itself a cultural construction. Collective psychology has no a priori essence but is constructed under specific historical conditions. Yang's essay—and the special issue in general—is an example of the process of making such a collective psychology.

Yang's projection of "anxiety and ambivalence" should be understood in terms of the debate over Taiwan's future, specifically the question of re-unification or independence. To those in the reunification camp, includ-ing both officials and people outside the government, the logic of capital "naturally" leads westward and will end in the unification of Taiwan and mainland China. To those in the independence camp, the same economic logic produces collective "anxiety and ambivalence" and leads inevitably to the loss of the nation. Thus, for those who favor Taiwan independence, the possibility of a southward advance brings a great sense of relief. This is also why Yang can proclaim that its "real significance" does not lie in eco-nomic gain, but in asserting that unification "is not an inescapable fate." What both positions have in common, in fact, is exactly what Yang criti-cizes as Chinese "nationalism." Yet he does not mention that if Chinese nationalism is the ideological basis for Taiwan's westward advance, then Taiwanese nationalism is the basis for its southward advance. The pairing of the southward and westward cultural discourses forms a binary opposi-tion that mirrors on the ideological level the reunification-independence dichotomy, but this hegemonic squeezing out of other positions is defi-nitely not a "leftist" move.

If the southward advance represents a new Taiwan-centered world-view, the return to Southeast Asia is meant to reverse the fatalism result-ing from Taiwan's marginalization and to materialize the escalating desire for self-centeredness. The title of Yang's essay, "Moving from the Periph-ery of China to the Center of *Nanyang*: A Neglected Episode of History," could not have been clearer. The discursive effect of his rewriting and re-mapping is to interpellate the reader into a collective national imaginary: with our horizons no longer limited by our marginal position, and our past repopulated with episodes of glory, we can now recenter ourselves and thereby satisfy our deep psychological needs.

Yang combines his spatial center-periphery framework with a chrono-logical narrative similar to Wu Micha's. Yang recounts how, with the sole exception of the final years of the Japanese occupation, "when Taiwan ap-peared to be the cultural and economic center of Southeast Asia," Taiwan was consistently marginalized under a long series of imperial regimes. But as he goes through the familiar list of Taiwan's colonizers—the Dutch, the Ming and Qing Dynasties, the Japanese, and the U.S.-backed KMT — there is a moment when his writing of history takes an important turn. In the previous discussion of Wu's Taiwan-centrism, I suggested that his mapping was derived from an earlier imperialist cultural discourse. Here I would like to push further by noting that in the geographical imagination of the 1930s, the "center" of Taiwan-centrism was not Taiwan (or its capital, Taipei), but the Japanese empire (and its capital, Tokyo). Taiwan was viewed by the Japanese as little more than a transitional centering point. If Taiwan-centeredness was simply a matter of situating Taiwan in the center of the map, then Taiwan was, is, and will always be the center, as soon as the map is drawn the way one wishes. What matters is the psychological map of the nationalist imaginary. It is precisely for the purpose of constructing a Taiwan-centric national imaginary that native leftists are willing to "make a painful concession" (Yang's own term) and rewrite history. In Yang's case, the concession is painful indeed. He argues that since the latter part of the Japanese occupation, Taiwan has not been a colony but a part of Japan's (extended) national territory.

In this writing of history, Yang's strategic purpose is to establish the legitimacy of Taiwan-centrism from the Japanese imperialist perspective, which he views as a precondition for constituting the southward-advance worldview. He develops his argument by first taking issue with Yanaihara Tadao's 1929 authoritative historical text, *Taiwan under Imperialism*, the first book ever produced on the subject, and one which is still influential today. On the one hand, Yang agrees with Yanaihara's simple factual claim that the Japanese invaded and exploited Taiwan. On the other hand, Yang declares that "we cannot ignore the fact that Professor Yanaihara's famous work dealt only with the early phase of colonization, and that all the data [he used] were collected before 1927." Yang takes great pains to emphasize that 1927 was a watershed in the history of the Japanese occupation of Taiwan. After 1927, due to "inland extensionism," which was the imperial policy of extending and incorporating colonies into Japan's national territory, colonial Taiwan became the center of the southward advance and subsequently underwent rapid industrialization. Japan concurrently "relinquished its colonial exploitation of Taiwan in exchange for a condition which allowed more effective control over Southeast Asia." With the gradual implementation of the Japanese southward-advance policy, Yang concludes, "Taiwan was elevated from a typical colony to an extension of the Japanese homeland and the center of Southeast Asia; this [elevation] influenced both the daily life and consciousness of ordinary people, which indirectly weakened the intensity of their [anticolonial] resistance."

This is the move Yang makes in order to rewrite history. We have to ask: is it true that the elevation of Taiwan to the status of "national territory" and the change in Japan's governing techniques gave rise to a new form of Taiwanese subjectivity? To put it even more plainly, is it true that Taiwan was no longer a colony of the Japanese empire? Yang does not provide any definitive answers, but the logic of his argument implies that the answer to both questions is yes. If this were true, however, former British or American colonies should also not be considered to have been colonies, because British and U.S. rule was less harsh than that of the Japanese. In this light, the "nativist left" rewriting of history has the effect of exonerating the Japanese empire from its historical transgressions. This is indeed a huge sacrifice and a high price to pay, simply to establish Taiwan as the imaginary center of Southeast Asia. Does the 1927 "historical rupture" that Yang identifies suggest that by that year, Taiwan had finally emerged from the oppression of the earlier era? The fact is that the Japanese suppression of the Taiwanese left did not stop but even intensified after 1927, and the suppression of leftists in Taiwan was also more severe than it was in the "home country." According to Zhang Yanxian, a historian in favor of Taiwan independence, in 1931 a number of Taiwanese Communists were arrested and imprisoned by the colonial government, and various other resistance movements were actively suppressed, rather than spontaneously "disappearing," as Yang suggests was the case (Zhang 1994, 36).

Yang's move is a costly and painful one, but it may not be surprising. Driven by a powerful desire for recognition, the colonized is often sucked into the colonizer's worldview. In *The Wretched of the Earth*, Fanon writes, "The settler makes history and is conscious of making it. And because he constantly refers to the history of his mother country, he indicates that he himself is the extension of that mother country. Thus the history which he writes is not the history of the country which he plunders, but the history of his own nation in regard to all that she skims off, all that she violates and slaves" (Fanon 1968 [1961], 51).

The colonized's adoption of the colonizers' historical perspective is not just attributable to colonial indoctrination, but involves an unconscious psychological mechanism. As Fanon notes, "the native never ceases to dream of putting himself in the place of the settler—not of becoming them, but of substituting himself for the settler" (ibid., 52). Under these conditions, the rewriter of history accepts and adopts the imperialist perspective, and exemplifies again the imperialist horizon flowing in "Taiwanese blood," delimiting the historical basis for constructing a new worldview. A tragedy!

Yang interestingly begins his conclusion by noting that some people in the period immediately after the Second World War believed that "if Taiwan is ambitious enough, it should take over Japan's former trading position in Southeast Asia." Without commenting on the origin of this desire to continue the cause of imperialism, he argues that this historical episode is a "very unique moment in that [it shows Taiwan had] rid itself of the fatalism of the periphery and consciously moved toward the center." Yang himself adopts the perspective of what he calls a "revisionist historian of Japanese colonial history." His purpose is no less than to prove that Taiwan was a part of Japan and of Southeast Asia, and is therefore not necessarily on the periphery of China. Only through a southward advance can Taiwan leave its marginal status and emerge once again as the center of Southeast Asia. Yang goes on to argue that even though the theoretical basis for the southward advance is derived from Taiwan's experiences during the Japanese occupation, Taiwan at the time was no longer a typical colony. Therefore, the adoption of the colonizer's perspective is acceptable, as long as the move from the painful margin to the triumphal center can be accomplished.

Yang's rewriting can be seen as part of a larger "movement for reaffirming the Japanese occupation" that gained popularity among historians and cultural critics in the 1990s. For instance, a 1994 special issue of the Taiwan publication *Japan Digest*, titled "Taiwan under the Flag of the Sun," consists of a series of essays reaffirming the positive contributions made by Japan's colonization of Taiwan. Li Hongxi, the editor of the journal's special issue and a respected law professor at National Taiwan University, lists the magnificent achievements of imperialist Japan in Taiwan in such areas as law enforcement, education, hygiene, and industry (Li Hongxi 1994). Li admits that the legal system imposed by the colonial rulers was obviously a technology of government used to control the colony's population. But from his perspective, to discuss, for example, the birth of the "modern" legal system in Taiwan is simply to "retrieve for the reader a lost history through an objective stance." If his logic stands, it could just as easily be used to affirm the contributions to Taiwan's modernization made by the American imperialist incursion and the KMT rule after 1949, which those in Li's camp would be much less likely to condone. This selective rewriting is based on a separatist position: emphasizing Taiwan's close ties with Japan while downplaying the relations with mainland China has the effect of extracting Taiwan from the Chinese sphere of influence. Taiwanese nationalism has become the mirror image of the KMT's "Great China" (*Dà Zhōngguó*) discourse, the exact ideology that it is attempting to resist.

All the essays in the southward-advance special issue refer in one way or another to the imperialist and colonialist past, but not one of them mentions Taiwan's southward-advance policy as a reproduction of that colonial imperialist past. Yang Changzhen's and Liu Kexiang's naturalism, Wu Micha's Taiwan-centrism, Yang Bo's ethnocentric desire for recognition, and Yang Zhao's construction of an imaginary margin-to-center trajectory have to be placed in the Taiwanese nationalist context, so that the complicity between this set of cultural discourses and the southward-advance policy of the state can be properly understood.

Taiwanese Nationalism Co-opted

There are many differing views of the historical formation of Taiwanese nationalism, each a reflection of a particular ideological position. Most such discourses give greater or lesser weight to some combination of race, ethnicity, nationality, or the state as constitutive of nationalist feelings. This diversity of views, however, belies a fundamental similarity. They all hold that "Taiwan consciousness" (*Táiwān yìshì*), a precondition for the emergence of Taiwanese nationalism, was formed in interaction with — and in resistance to — Taiwan's many colonizers.[24]

The Pitfalls of the "Taiwan Consciousness" Narrative

Most histories of Taiwan repeat this common refrain: "Taiwan's history is a history of colonization" (Qiu 1992, 1). This Han-centered line of historiography argues that "Taiwanese history is four hundred years old," and by extension that the five-thousand-year history of Taiwan's aboriginal people is only a prehistory (Shi 1980, 11). The brushing aside of over

90 percent of Taiwan's history to focus on the Han Chinese and their colonizers amounts to a denial of aboriginal peoples' subjectivity. This is the position held by the aboriginal critics Ichiang Barluer and Lawagau Ligelaker in their essay "A History of Aboriginal Nations in Taiwan." As late as the seventeenth century, before the Dutch and Spanish invasions, "Taiwanese aboriginal people were still the masters of the island" (Ichiang and Lawagau 1992, 33). Only later does Taiwanese history become a history of domination by successive colonial regimes coming from the outside. From the perspective of the aboriginal people, one would assume, the colonization of Taiwan would come to an end only when they are once again masters of the island. Likewise, for people in the working class, homosexuals, and women, only when they acquire enough power to be masters of their own fates can decolonization be said to have been achieved.

The slighting of racial, class, gender, and other marginal perspectives, combined with a fixation on ethnicity, is the Taiwanese nationalists' most tragic blind spot. Once ethnicity becomes the only concern, all other discourses are marginalized, sometimes to the point of nonexistence. Take Shi Ming's celebrated text, *The Four-Hundred-Year History of the Taiwanese*, for example. On the one hand, Shi adopts a class perspective. He criticizes the leaders of the national liberation movement during the Japanese occupation as coming primarily from landlord, bourgeois, or petit bourgeois backgrounds (Shi 1980, 688) and deplores the division of Taiwanese society into exploiting and exploited classes that occurred under the post-1949 KMT regime (ibid., 1059–64). On the other hand, he is still able to reach the following conclusion: "In the February 28 revolutionary struggle[25] against the mainland Chinese . . . the connections in our consciousness with the Chinese due to common descent were finally broken. Since then, Taiwanese nationalism has been striving for Taiwanese national independence and liberation, defending its nationalist interests, and being concerned with the nation's fate and future. This coherent set of national ideals at last emerged as the single and highest principle" (ibid., 1096).

It is under this single and highest principle that pan-class politics faded into the background and became a minor footnote on the national agenda.

Shi Ming writes as a revolutionary, but similar narrative directions are also evident in academic studies of ethnicity and nationalism, which likewise fail to maintain any critical distance from the official construction of ethnic categories. Wang Fuchang's sociological study of ethnic integration follows, in his words, the "commonly accepted official categorization" (Wang 1992, 2–9). The commonly accepted official categorization is based on place of birth and entirely disregards the issues of class, gender, and aboriginal status, and these perspectives are conspicuously absent in Wang's analysis. The sociologist Zhang Maogui explores Taiwanese nationalism by drawing on Benedict Anderson's (1991) notion of the nation as an imagined community, and uses the notion of the "tribal idol" to explain the rise of the Taiwanese independence movement in the late 1980s (Zhang 1992, 6–14). He adopts Shi Ming's class perspective without asking some fundamental questions: Who is constructing the tribal idol? Who are the ones building the imagined community? What are the articulating agents for class, gender, ethnicity, and race? One expects critically minded sociologists to ask such questions, and to exercise caution when their analyses have the discursive effect of legitimizing power.[26]

To confront nationalism seriously, rather than naively attributing it to an irreducible "collective desire," we must identify the characteristics of its articulating agents, as well as the class, gender, and racial affiliations of those groups who benefit from the nationalist agenda. We must question the rhetoric of singularity (such as "Taiwanese" or "the Taiwanese people") and ask who constructs, appropriates, and co-opts nationalism and nationalist identity. As James Blaut argues in his seminal work, *The National Question: Decolonising the Theory of Nationalism*: "National struggle is indeed class struggle. It is a form of class struggle for state power and is not an autonomous force" (Blaut 1987, 24). He suggests that nationalist struggle can be the resistance of the colonized against the colonizer, but can also be a strategy of the proletariat to obtain state power, or of the national bourgeoisie to ease internal conflicts or manage crises. In a different context, Ernesto Laclau has cited Nazism as an example of the populism of the dominant class (Laclau 1977). Stuart Hall has described Margaret Thatcher's neoconservatism as authoritarian populism (Hall 1980).[27] In a similar vein, the Singapore feminists Geraldine Heng and Janadas Devan have criticized the Singaporean nationalist suppression of women and minorities, boldly asserting that "women, and all signs of the feminine, are by definition always and already antinational" (Heng and Devan 1992, 356).[28] The formulation of a "queer nation" has been a challenge to the exclusionism of a "national identity."[29] And a Taiwanese lesbian feminist has declared that "we live in different countries, in different lands."[30]

The Theoretical Structure of Taiwanese Nationalism

By multiplying the number of subject positions, a different history can be articulated. Taiwanese nationalist history can indeed be charted from a subaltern perspective, with its content and form, as well as its agent and subject, changing over time.

Starting with the 1635 aboriginal rebellion against the Dutch invaders, called the Great Struggle in Madou (Shi Xinyi 1988, 83; Lin 1992, 45), there has been a rich history of resistance in Taiwan against economic, political, and ethnic oppression, but these were mostly isolated instances. Not until the early twentieth century did anything resembling a national liberation movement appear. In the years leading up to the First World War, Japanese colonialism strengthened its hold on Taiwan, but it did not enjoy an ideological monopoly. Ideas such as national self-determination and socialism, which were then spreading rapidly around the globe, inspired Taiwanese communists to press for an independent Taiwan. Grounded in class and anticolonial struggles, this movement marks the beginning of the theorization of Taiwanese nationalism.

After the KMT's defeat at the hands of the CCP in the Chinese civil war, the KMT moved its government to Taiwan and undertook a project of "internal" colonization.[31] Ever since that time, the Han Chinese in Taiwan have been divided into two groups: běnshěng rén, or "native" Taiwanese, and wàishěng rén, the mainlanders who came to Taiwan with the KMT. The state violence of the 228 Incident was later articulated as the symbolic basis of the long-lasting conflict between the two groups, and an important catalyst for the intensification of Taiwan consciousness. Ethnic conflict remained a strong undercurrent in Taiwan society, but it did not fully emerge until the 1980s, when ethnicity was mobilized as a political strategy by the opposition DPP in its bid for power. The central discourse of the Taiwanese nationalist movement is now premised on this běnshěng-wàishěng or us-Other division.

While Taiwan consciousness was being formed in the decades after the Second World War, the KMT was legitimizing its power through its own ideological project. Through its construction of "Chinese nationalism," which among other things held that the KMT was the legitimate government of all of China and that it would one day retake the mainland, the KMT cast the Chinese Communists as the common enemy. Anticommunism became both the fundamental national policy and the common sense of the dominant ideology. The KMT's projection of Red China as the imaginary enemy lasted for the forty years during which the two states refused to officially communicate with each other. As mainland China opened up economically and diplomatically in the 1980s, Taiwan became increasingly marginalized, and the futility of its dream of retaking the mainland was increasingly obvious. Internally, Taiwan consciousness was strengthening, as were demands for democracy and an open civil society.[32] The KMT response to these external and internal pressures was to transform itself by "nativizing." Under the direction of President Chiang Ching-kuo, the emphasis of the party changed from anticommunism to "national unification." Martial law was suspended in 1987, and Taiwanese elites began to be incorporated into the party. In addition to becoming president in 1988, the Taiwan-born Lee Teng-hui became chairman of the KMT as well, marking the start of the transition from the "Chinese KMT" to the "Taiwanese KMT."[33] The process was challenged by old-line KMT mainlanders, but they were unable to wrest power from the nativist bloc led by Lee Teng-hui. Shi Huimin, vice director of the KMT's propaganda division, called the shift a "silent revolution." When the building that housed the KMT's Central Party Committee was demolished in 1994, it symbolized the end of an era.

Forty years of anticommunist ideology did not simply vanish after the KMT adjusted its political strategy. Since the 1950s, tens of thousands of people—intellectuals, political activists, and others—had been imprisoned or killed by the state in a horrific White Terror campaign. One of the many legacies of this era was that the leftist movement in Taiwan was completely wiped out, which left the Taiwanese nativist movement without any progressive elements. Ruthlessly suppressed at home, the nativist movement developed overseas, mostly in Japan and the United States. It was the KMT that wrenched Taiwan from Japan, and then fixed it in the American neocolonial structure, but both the KMT and the Taiwanese nationalists saw the Japanese and American imperial powers not as enemies but as friends. When the KMT turned away from its anticommunist ideology, anticommunism became available for the Taiwanese nationalists to adopt and extend into a more general anti-China ideology. Events in mainland China facilitated this expansion: the Tiananmen Square Massacre in 1989 and the Qiandao Lake Incident in 1994[34] are moments when the imaginary enemy became real. Both events triggered widespread outrage in Taiwan, and the CCP's authoritarian handling of them was taken as revealing the true nature of the evil communists. In short, anticommunist and anti-Chinese sentiments inherited from the Chinese nationalist KMT era, strengthened by American neoimperialism, and exacerbated by CCP authoritarianism have allowed mainland China and the mainland Chinese to be defined as the Other and the imaginary enemy of Taiwanese nationalism.

In reviewing the development of Taiwanese nationalism, we see it was the ethnic difference between mainlanders and Taiwanese that led to the five-year so-called silent revolution (1988–93) and intensified the struggle over national identity. At the same time, the factional split over these issues within the KMT power base was diffused downward, reinforcing this ethnic complex. Taiwanese nationalism, constructed through years of Taiwanese consciousness, was at this time identified with Lee Teng-hui. Chen Fangming, a Taiwanese nationalist historian and then in charge of culture and propaganda for the DPP, acutely commented on the "Lee complex" in criticizing the KMT move toward "independence" (*Táidú*): "The only thing that makes Lee into the nodus of the complex is that he was born Taiwanese. Other than this, he has nothing to do with Taiwanese society or the people's sentiment. Lee can successfully curry the favor with Taiwanese people simply through his being a native Taiwanese. This is indeed the sorrow of the Taiwanese" (Chen 1990, 140).

After several hundred years of colonial experiences, the desire of those possessing Taiwan consciousness to replace their colonizers is exceptionally real and intense. For years, the government had largely been run by mainlanders. The emergence of Lee Teng-hui as the head of state was symbolic of being one's own master. In the absence of class consciousness within Taiwanese nationalism, ethnic politics became the central premise. Lee Teng-hui—Han Chinese, Taiwanese, bourgeois, heterosexual, and male—swallowed up the energy that had been building in the nationalist movement for decades. As the articulating agent of Taiwan consciousness, he was able to enact significant reforms. Lee oversaw the revision of the constitution, the transition to direct elections of the president and members of the Legislative Yuan, and the attempt to rejoin the United Nations—all steps along the road to the building of a new nation. But he was also building a new structure of sentiment. When Lee famously stated that "the KMT is an external polity," and when he employed rhetoric such as "the sorrow of the Taiwanese," it was further evidence that the oppositional aspect of Taiwanese nationalism had been entirely co-opted by mainstream political forces. As chairman of the KMT, it was Lee Teng-hui who brought Taiwanese nationalism to the center of politics, which is why the fundamentalist wing of the Taiwan independence movement regards him as the founding father of the Republic of Taiwan.

Looking back on Taiwan's political history in the second half of the twentieth century, we see that the decades-long buildup of Chinese chauvinism begun by Chiang Kai-shek and carried on by his son Chiang Ching-kuo caused great harm to Taiwanese society. It imposed a party-state fascist culture throughout the state apparatuses of ideology (such as the education system and media) and radically distorted Taiwan's modernity (Chen T. 1994). In their effort to eliminate Japanese colonial culture in Taiwan and replace it with their own Chinese nationalist mythology, both Chiangs intervened in all social realms. Their method—White Terror totalitarianism—led to appalling mutilation of the collective psychic structure, mutilation that can be seen in today's warped modes of communication, suspicion of other people, and alienation. Such fascist cultural forms as the patriarchal mind-set, whisper campaigns, dividing others into either friends or enemies, and surreptitious defamations still operate in Taiwanese society. Even progressive social movements in the civil society are not exempt from these fascist currents. All these cultural effects cannot be disassociated from Chiang Kai-shek and Chiang Ching-kuo's brand of Chinese nationalism.

Such authoritarian practices inevitably resulted in increasing feelings of discontent, deepened the paranoia of those already being suppressed, and finally triggered the onset of Taiwan consciousness in reaction. This consciousness gradually changed from personal rebellion to a more organized form as it contested and won spaces in the public sphere. As the opposite of Chinese chauvinism, Taiwanese nationalism had its progressive moment in the 1990s when it led the resistance against authoritarian state power. But in that resistance, it also learned and imitated the structures and methods of its opponent. By attempting to build a new national culture through the top-down operation of the state apparatus, rather than encouraging—or simply allowing—more autonomous space for subaltern groups, the Taiwanese nationalist movement forfeited the opportunity to establish a democratic social and cultural subjectivity, as opposed to a nationalist one.

The Chiang family's Chinese chauvinism collapsed, but it was inherited by Lee Teng-hui's Taiwanese nationalism. The ethnic chauvinism of Lee's Taiwanese KMT is exemplified in the adversarial relationship between native Taiwanese and mainlander that he promoted. From a historical-theoretical perspective, it put an end to antiestablishment nationalism. The cultural discourse of the southward advance embodied that historical shift. After years of holding antiestablishment positions, Taiwanese nationalist intellectuals were now formally announcing their enthusiastic support of the state policy.

For the first time in history, Taiwanese nationalism had become the weapon of the dominant ruling class. From the "sorrow of Taiwanese people," oppositional consciousness was converted into the affective basis for the elite's new nation-building project. To put it more crudely, the Taiwanese KMT co-opted the Taiwanese consciousness developed over the past hundred years, and was able, in the context of the 1990's, to transform those energies into ideological forces, winning the power struggle within the KMT and winning popular consent from the Taiwanese people. This critical moment has defined the political agenda in Taiwan until the present day.

The Imperialist Eye and Beyond

The meaning of the "imperialist eye," the title of this chapter, should by now have become clear. The Taiwanese subimperialist eye, a role performed by the cultural discourse in question, was constructed to see the world according to a new southward-advance worldview, but its role was mediated through the eye of the old Japanese empire. Our analysis has identified an angle of vision shared by the old empire and the new subempire. What is most striking is that the strategic map for the new southward advance was an embodiment of the old imperialist eye. The old eye had been internalized and resurfaced after some sixty years, in the 1990s, as the eye of the new subempire.

In addition to this temporal shift, there is also a spatial dislocation between the new eye and the old one. The eye that views the world presupposes the location of the body and implies the I of the viewing subject. The geopolitical location and subject positions of the I determine both the world that exists within the horizon of its view and the cultural imaginary constituted by that world. The old empire's I refers to 1930s Tokyo, headquarters of the first southward advance, and its subject positions were located within the Japanese military state. The subempire's I, however, was located in 1990s Taipei—the headquarters of its southward advance was the office of the president of Taiwan, in a building that had housed the office of the Japanese colonial governor—and the subject positions of President Lee as the articulating agent were ruler, Han Chinese, Taiwanese, heterosexual, and male. The differences that emerged during the transition between the two were geopolitical location and ethnic identity: Taipei replaced Tokyo, and Han Chinese and Taiwanese replaced Japanese. But the political unconscious of the two shared a common projection of an ethnocentric imperial desire. This has forced us to recognize the historical inheritance from the old in the new, an inheritance with both rupture and continuity: the cultural imaginary constructed by the old imperial I is internalized in the body of subempire, forming its self, worldview, and imagination.

The Trinity of Nation, State, and Empire: A Hegemonic Project

At this point, we are in a better position to answer the questions posed in the first section of this chapter, regarding the ideological implications, sources, genealogy, and operation of the southward-advance discourse. First, what are the cultural and political implications of the discourse? The southward advance was a manifestation of a subimperial formation and received full support from the cultural discourse of the special issue of Human Space in the *China Times*. The essays there drew on natural, scientific, historical, and literary resources to provide the southward-advance discourse with theoretical and ideological validation.

Second, by what mechanisms did the discourse operate? What were their contents and forms? The strategy used to recruit the imperial subject was to establish historical, geographical, and cultural connections with the object of colonization (Southeast Asia) as well as with its previous colonizers (Holland, China, Japan, and, tangentially, the United States).

This enables a self-definition—that is, through redrawing the map and rewriting history, Taiwan's geographical and historical connections with others can be established in relational terms, so that the new identity and status of Taiwan can be discovered.

Third, what are the historical resources employed by the southward-advance discourse? The discovery of Taiwan's new identity comes from the imperialist cultural imaginary constructed during an earlier historical era. The colonized's research makes full use of the colonizer's worldview to justify the move from colonized to the new colonizer. This appropriation involves accepting the former colonizer's perspective: the Wallace line, Duras, and Taiwan as the center on the old southward-advance map all bear the obvious imprint of the colonial imagination. This reproduction means that decolonization is still far from unfolding. This strikes me as the saddest and most painful result of my analysis.

Fourth, what is the ideological structure of the southward-advance discourse? The reservoir of discontent that the colonized had for years been accumulating was co-opted by the ruling bloc. The co-optation made possible intimate links between Taiwanese nationalism, statism, and colonial imperialism, while ideologically constituting the desire for the formation of the Taiwanese subempire.

It is essential to position the southward-advance discourse in the politics of its time. In the early 1990s, the Taiwanese nationalist faction of the KMT was facing pressure on multiple fronts, from the integration of mainland China into the network of global capitalism to the growing strength of oppositional political parties and social movements at home. The regime responded to these pressures by undertaking a grand political and economic restructuring project, which was composed of three integrated axes: nation building, state making, and empire formation. The articulating agent of this trinity of hegemonic politics is the patriarchal, Han Chinese, Taiwanese, and chauvinist national bourgeoisie. Its unifying principle was to fundamentally reposition Taiwan, by recruiting and co-opting the social forces released after the dissolution of the old KMT dictatorship and the 1987 suspension of martial law. Though it eagerly attempted to erase all the Chinese signs and trappings of the old-line KMT government, the Taiwanese nationalist movement inherited much from the Chiang era. Like its predecessor, it targeted the CCP as the Other, so as to unify Taiwan by covering up class, gender, racial, and other differences. The Taiwanese nationalists were also adept at maintaining, if not deepening, Taiwan's position in the American neocolonial structure, which placed them in a position to better exploit labor, natural resources, and the environment in places at the subaltern end of the global capitalist hierarchy.

In this context, the southward advance and its cultural discourse constitute a clear plan to set in motion the hegemonic regime's project of building nation, state, and empire. One stone was able to kill many birds: (1) the discourse co-opted Taiwanese consciousness, which had been forged over a period of decades; (2) it recruited the desiring subject into a nationalist subject position, which encouraged pride in Taiwan's southward expansion; (3) it reinforced the authority of the state, which was necessary for the remaking of the state machine; and (4) it formed a subimperial consciousness, which was intended to facilitate economic development and help the regime gain a firmer footing in the international arena. Following these lines of interest, we can understand why opposition political forces, led by the DPP, had to not only endorse the project (which incorporated its ideological interests, specifically the move toward Taiwanese independence) but also actively aid it with theoretical weapons (in the hope of reversing the direction of economic integration resulting from Taiwan's westward capital investment—that is, lessening Taiwan's economic dependence on mainland China). The building of a new nation-state was, in short, the unifying desire of every group that aspired to power, oppositional or otherwise.

Inscribed within a condition of total war, the cultural discourse was dominated by the rewriting of history in various forms. This flood of history, both academic and popular, has been rising since the early 1990s. The field of Taiwanese history has grown quickly since previously forbidden topics such as the 228 Incident and the White Terror became available for investigation. A more pervasive but little-noticed movement was the emergence of local history groups, which work throughout the island at the village level to collect materials, chronicle local events, and in the process build a cultural identity. This massive writing is evidence of the current struggle over who has the power to interpret history. The interpretations are clearly oriented toward the future, not mere retracings of a suppressed past; most originate from a particular political position or ideology and are used to support political or ideological goals, including the dream of an independent nation, the consolidation of state power, and a combination of the two. The most important function of historical interpretation is to selectively organize popular memory. As critics of the society, we are fortunate to be able to watch these processes in action and see firsthand how collective memory does not just exist "out there," but is constructed and reconstructed through the writing of the past into the future.

Returning to the Third World

If there is anything to be learned from our analysis of the subimperialist southward-advance discourse, it is that there is a pressing need to deepen the recognition and understanding of Taiwan's third-world structural location.

The ubiquity of the postcolonial trajectory, in which decolonization is followed by recolonization or neocolonization, shows that the ideological condition that permits the subimperial desire to take shape exists precisely because there has been no critical reflection on decolonization. This is what makes it possible for the imperialist cultural imaginary to be so effortlessly inherited by the colonized. Whether other potentially subimperial places, such as Korea and Hong Kong, have gone through their decolonization phases remains to be seen. What are the particular cultural and ideological mechanisms operating in these locales? In the 1980s, Korean scholars began describing South Korea as quasi-imperialist, in terms of its reproduction of imperialist expansion. Until recently, Hong Kong was still a colony, but like Taiwan, it has been sending capital to Southeast Asia, making it a new colonizing force. Hong Kong has also become an important center for the East Asian culture industry, and a major exporter of films, music, and television programs. What is the theoretical significance of this unusual historical phenomenon?

Rewriting history and redrawing the map are important strategies in the third-world nationalist imagination (Anderson 1991, 163–85). But third-world critical discourse, including cultural studies, need not follow the delimitations of the nation-state. It can start from a critical subject position and reach out to encompass common third-world experiences; it can produce a different set of histories and maps. Many border-crossing practices in Asia have shown that national boundaries can be ignored as instruments of mediation between oppressed subjects in the third world (Mutō 1998).

Finally, we need to learn not to repeat the mistake of an imperialist knowledge paradigm that maps an abstract and universal theoretical framework onto the earth. Third-world cultural studies, actively confronting the phenomena and problems of lived reality, can be more powerful and more liberating if, in our analysis, we can identify and act on points for intervention.

CHAPTER 2

DECOLONIZATION
A Geocolonial Historical Materialism

> In a sense, until it is possible to state who the subjects of independence
> movements are likely to be, and in whose names cultural decolonization is
> being conducted, it is not possible to complete the process . . . [Q]uestions
> of culture can never be discussed free from and outside of power . . . Without
> the others there is no self, there is no self-recognition . . . Identity is always a
> question of producing in the future an account of the past.
> STUART HALL, "NEGOTIATING CARIBBEAN IDENTITIES"

The Problematic of Decolonization: Rediscovering "Our" Culture?

In this chapter, I propose geocolonial historical materialism as a framework for analyzing the problematic of decolonization in relation to cultural formation in formerly colonized spaces.

The previous chapter, on the southward-advance discourse, concluded
that the absence of a reflexive decolonization of thoughts and practices
is a condition which fosters the perpetuation of the imperialist cultural
imaginary. The decolonization question, therefore, has to be reexamined.
Why has decolonization work on the level of the cultural imaginary not
been more thoroughly developed? Is the case of Taiwan exceptional?
Have other third-world nation-states, formed after the Second World
War, been confronting similar crises? After the old colonial regimes
yielded power, did the newly independent regimes devote all their energies and resources to the political and economic arenas, effectively ignoring reflexive cultural decolonization? What has gone wrong with nativism,
which could have been a form of decolonization but has turned out to be
a movement uncritically supportive of the ethnocentric nation-building

project? Has decolonization only meant anticolonial? Has the struggle to oppose the colonizer reproduced the frame and limits defined by the enemy, and therefore allowed the imperialist cultural imaginary to persist uninterrupted?

To answer these questions, a methodology specific to the colonized third world is needed. The formulation proposed here is based on historical materialism, an approach which informs much cultural-studies research, but locates historical materialism in geographical space. To highlight the importance of geographical space is to emphasize the specificity of dynamic local histories — that is, how local history, in dialectical interaction with colonial and other historical forces, transforms its internal formation on the one hand, and articulates the local to world history and the structure of global capital on the other hand. In many contexts, colonial history mediates the histories of the local and the global. The question of modernity cannot be addressed without accounting for the history of colonialism and modernization as products of the structural transformation from the colonial to the neocolonial. Through the international system of nation-states, global capitalism unifies the plurality of geographical spaces and histories into a single, measurable structure. In this context, the formation of postcolonial discourse is intended not to announce the happy arrival of a postcolonial era, but rather as an attempt to foreground the deep-seated forces of colonialism in history. If there is a shared impetus to move from the colonial to the postcolonial and beyond, this can be done only through decolonization, by constantly rethinking our routes and strategies. In this era, what are the critical tasks of locally grounded cultural studies? In what ways can cultural studies more effectively challenge the cultural imaginary formed by capitalism, imperialism, and colonialism?

The first task of the geocolonial historical materialist framework proposed in this chapter will be to work through the third-world discourse on colonial identification in order to first situate geocolonial historical materialism within cultural studies, and then to make the theoretical move to connect it with the spatial turn, a move inspired by radical geography. This chapter is a theoretical exercise that aims to connect and reconnect with these discursive traditions by tracing selected responses to colonialism immediately after the Second World War; it is concerned essentially with the problems within former colonies. Decolonization today takes at least three forms: nationalism, nativism, and civilizational-ism. All three forms have been recognized as necessary for the success of the decolonization movement, but they have also been evaluated more cautiously and critically by earlier analysts. Fanon's critique of national-ism at the peak of the third-world independence movement in the 1950s and 1960s, Memmi's questioning of nativism during the 1950s and 1960s, and Nandy's revitalization of a critical traditionalism (what I shall later describe as civilizationalism) in the early 1980s all emerged in response to problems of decolonization. But why, decades later, are we who live in the formerly colonized world still deeply enmeshed in these problems? In East Asia, it is partly because of the neocolonial structure that we have been made to identify with intellectual formulations coming from the imperial centers, and hence have been completely blind to the powerful interventions proposed by Fanon, Memmi, and Nandy. This is a sad story. If we had listened carefully to these thinkers, we might have been better equipped to escape the trap of the colonial politics of resentment. But it is never too late to listen. The question is whether we have the desire to reconnect to this line of thought so as to empower others and ourselves.

This desire to retrieve the forgotten tradition of cultural studies as practiced and produced outside the imperial center has materialized at an intense moment in this so-called post–cold-war era, when all of us are forced to emerge from our own geographical isolation and disciplinary ghettos in order to more adequately respond to neoliberal globalization and subsequent regionalization, and answer questions which were sup-pressed, suspended, and closed off during the cold-war era. Under the rubric of cultural studies, we might be able to do this necessary work, work which cannot be done in other fields. At the same time, we might also be able to change the terrain of cultural studies itself.

In this historical context, the long-term structural transformation from territorial colonialism to neocolonialism and the neoliberal call for the end of the cold war also signal the movement of capitalism, which has shifted from Western Europe across the Atlantic to North America, and now across the Pacific to Asia. As the Asian continent emerges as a central site for political and economic struggle and a focus of global attention, it inevitably triggers among Asians suspended recollections of being conquered. Throughout the East Asian region, there is now a sense of anti-Western triumphalism: the twenty-first century is ours; we are finally (once again) the center. Wherever in Asia one is geographically positioned, a syllogism is emerging: Asia is becoming the center of the world and we are at the center of Asia, so we are the center of the world. This is where history comes in. Contrary to the now-fashionable claim that we have entered the postcolonial era, the mood of triumphalism, which is a clear reaction to colonialism, indicates that we still operate within the boundaries of colonial history.

Critical discourses of decolonization have diverse intellectual ancestries. Among the rich body of anticolonial cultural works in Chinese, perhaps the most representative are Lu Xun's *The True Story of Ah Q* and *Diary of a Madman*. These two stories from the early twentieth century might well be the first psychoanalytic self-criticisms of the feudal elements of a Chinese culture confronted by imperialism. The tradition of Lu Xun has been continuously influential in critical circles in China, and it has frequently been rediscovered in South Korea and Japan. During the Japanese colonial period in Taiwan, Lu Xun, along with the socialist movement, influenced Yang Kui's novel, *Paperboy*. Although Lu Xun's works were prohibited by the KMT regime, Chen Ying-zhen's social-realist novels and critical writings on Asia and the Third World inherited much from the critical tradition initiated by Lu Xun. This line of critical thought, interestingly enough, has never been framed in terms of decolonization, mainly because the term was not central to intellectual analysis until the 1990s.

In addition to these East Asian discourses, there have been a number of intellectual projects related to decolonization coming out of the third world. Indian subaltern studies has probably been the most influential. The decolonial project of the Latin American "modernity/coloniality" program is another.[1] As the first step in formulating a geocolonial historical materialism, rather than engaging with all these alternative intellectual formations, I have chosen to link together an indispensable set of discourses on colonial identification. Not surprisingly, the central figure here is Frantz Fanon. But to identify Fanon's problematic, we have to situate him both within the polemical context against which he formulates his thesis and in a moment of late colonial history, the context within which he brought his formulations to higher levels of abstraction. I will begin with Octave Mannoni (1990 [1950]), mediating through Fanon's articulation of "colonial identification," and then move on to reread Fanon,

Memmi, and Nandy in light of their critiques of nationalism, nativism, and civilizationalism. This reading forms a genealogy of critical traditions in third-world cultural studies.

It will become clear that, in positioning cultural studies as a decolonization movement, my purpose is to analyze and disarticulate colonialist and imperialist cultural imaginaries that are still actively shaping our present. By questioning the objects of identification, theoretical discourse on colonial identifications offers a way to address pressing contemporary issues. But this reading is a critical exercise, not a blind appreciation. As we move along, the limits of these positions will also be identified.

Marxism, Identity Politics, and Decolonization

Before establishing the theoretical trajectory of colonial identification, I want to clarify the relevance of Marxism to the project developed here. It is probably fair to suggest that the intellectual impulse to initiate a global decolonization movement had its origins in Marxism. For critical intellectuals in different parts of the third world, and also in places like Paris and London, theoretical resources did not emerge solely from the violence of colonial experiences, but also grew out of oppositional thinking within the empire. Marxism has been indispensable both in terms of political practice and intellectual thought.

It was at the high point of European colonial imperialism, when the industrial revolution was helping engineer the rapid expansion of markets overseas, that Marx realized the importance of capitalism and its historical agent for change—the working class. This was the founding moment of modern identity politics, in the critical and oppositional senses of the term. The words "socialism" and "communism" themselves presuppose a speaking position outside capitalism. This future-oriented, political-cultural imagination made empire the target of a radical critique, analyzing and revealing its working logic, and going further to posit a blueprint for a utopian alternative. For the next century and a half, this alternative theory and a desire for a different world slowly became stronger within the imperial center. The Russian revolution of 1917 pushed this imagination forward. Marxist revolutionary theory, for the first time, had proven to be more than a daydream. The perceived practical success of Marxist theory gave hope to the forces promoting decolonization from within the centers of the capitalist world. More importantly, Marxism offered anticolonial movements in the colonies an alternative to capitalism. For better or worse, most nationalist independence movements had to negotiate with the Marxist seduction. Although the statist politics of the First and Second Internationals ended up reproducing the rigid hierarchical structures of feudal capitalism, the cultural vision of internationalism remained.

To evoke the Russian revolution today is somewhat ironic: after the long competition between capitalism and socialism, the formation of the three-worlds structure, and the end of the cold war, the few remaining socialist nations have been, to different degrees, drawn into the magnetic field of global capitalism. How is this episode of history to be written? The easiest way would be to erase the entire twentieth century and carry on as if it had never existed. But critical elements of Marxism have soaked into different geographical sites and can always be called upon to deal with difficult uncertainties. Simply put, the tradition of Marxism has established an imaginary discursive position outside capitalism from which to critique the internal logic of the latter. As long as decolonization is understood as a permanent cultural revolution, Marxism will be relevant. It can no longer be seen as something coming from the outside; rather, it has become part of the cultural subjectivity of intellectuals outside the imperial centers. It continues to survive precisely because of its heterogeneity and its articulation in local intellectual histories.

On a theoretical level, the Marxism of the nineteenth century was never able to rid itself of its Eurocentrism, but in practice, it generated a whole series of decentering movements, some of which are still active today. Historical materialism, in its battle with idealism, radically historicized social activities and institutions. It saw capitalism as a product of history, and hence able to be superseded. However, it also inherited the evolutionary view of history from the Enlightenment tradition, and consequently it used the narrative of a universal proposition to account for phenomena in all geographical spaces. It was precisely because of this contradiction that universalism started to crack, and confidence in the universal subject was lost. The gradual emergence of multiple resisting subjects on the historical platform was an inevitable conclusion of the theoretical trajectory initiated by Marxism. The series of epistemological breaks was unstoppable: the capitalist class, first-world subjects, men, whites, heterosexuals, and so on could not escape the fate of being decentered. In terms of geopolitics, these shifts parallel the historical trajectories of decolonization movements internal to the imperial centers. But once the trajectories of identity politics are linked to emerging globalization movements, different forms of identity politics generate symbolic impacts and alliances that, despite local differences, transcend geographical boundaries and national spaces. The feminist, gay, lesbian, bisexual, and transsexual movements staged in the centers, which in some ways parallel the earlier class movements of international communism, have affected decolonization globally.

After a century, in many places the practices undertaken in the name of Marxism have been declared finished. But precisely because it was practiced in different local formations over long periods of time and in a variety of concrete ways, Marxism has become the common property of all critical intellectuals, though in different locations and at different times, there are different emphases and concerns. Intellectual circles, whether located in capitalist zones or in the former socialist world, cannot really afford to abandon this intellectual tradition (which is our own), but have to critically reexamine and reevaluate our heritage of socialist practices. For those of us living in the capitalist world, the most serious intellectual challenge is that capitalist liberal democracy (as a set of normative discourses) has been adopted to criticize the undemocratic practices in the former socialist regimes, but our theoretical discourses, developed during the cold-war era, cannot adequately explain the social and historical logic of the postsocialist formation in its present form. For example, in East Asia, intellectual circles in South Korea, Japan, Hong Kong, and Taiwan cannot use their own existing analytical tools to understand the structural operating logic of the state and society in mainland China, Vietnam, and North Korea. The simple notion of the market does not suffice to explain the social and political formations there. Elements of the socialist era are still operating. To quickly abandon the analytical language of Marxism would not produce a proper understanding of ongoing transformations. In the end, we also have to question the understanding of our own society. Can an imagined universality be separated from knowledge produced during the cold-war era?

In this era of neoliberal globalization, to insist on the intellectual relevance of Marxism is more than a simple gesture of resistance. It is to preserve a common global language as common property for critical intellectuals. The real question is to what extent an open-ended Marxism can set aside historical baggage, such as class determinism and the teleology of historical imagination. To what extent can it accept that social formations are made up of multiple, coexisting structures, which makes it necessary to analyze different structural axes together, and to embrace new forms and subjects of struggle? For our purpose, which is to revitalize historical materialism, we will have to recognize the immanent complexity of colonialism. Its larger historical effects cannot be understood in relation to the capitalist system only, as if the colonial question were simply an extension of class struggle.

In this context, the problematic of decolonization will be formulated by linking together seemingly disconnected discursive spaces, and cultural studies will be the strategic site where the entangled trajectories will be articulated. The theoretical route of the chapter begins by tracing the shifts in the practices and meaning of colonial identification in the genealogy of psychoanalytic discourses on decolonization. There are two reasons for this delineation. First, it seeks to mark out an alternative line of cultural studies, one which evolved in the geographical space of the colony and follows the critical tradition begun by Fanon. Second, it attempts to identify the limits and crises of contemporary cultural identities formed after the overwhelming practices of colonialism have taken their toll. I then propose the ethics of a critical syncretism as decolonization's strategy of identification, to avoid reproducing colonialism and to go beyond the politics of resentment that bind colonizer and colonized together. On this basis, the connection with geographical historical materialism will be drawn.

A Theoretical History of "Colonial Identification"

If "decolonization is always a violent phenomenon," as Fanon (1968 [1961], 35) argues, the emergence of multiple subjects can also bring violent effects. On the one hand, the emergence of multiple subjects challenges the unifying imperialization of the subject. On the other hand, such a challenge forces the emerging subject groups to shoulder the pressure of the intense confrontation. In relation to their opponents, the cultural resources and historical traditions of the subaltern subjects are indeed rather shaky. Although much of the historical writing about the emerging subaltern subjects aims to reclaim the past, it cannot in the short run accumulate enough power to compete with the established mechanisms of colonial domination. Language, institutional dispositions, habitual rituals, the hierarchy of cultural categories, and so forth cannot be quickly transformed. The subject in struggle still has to operate within the existing rules of the game, in effect reproducing, at least in part, the existing structural relations. Once the desire for insertion in the social space prompts an attack on the symbolic order, the psychic condition of the subaltern subject in question becomes extremely fragile, and she or he is forced to either activate psychological defense mechanisms or face the possibility of breakdown.

To emphasize the importance of the psychoanalytical space presupposes that power and resistance work in the domain of the psychic. Political struggle does have an irreducible psychic dimension. Only when we have sufficiently dealt with the internal mechanisms of the psychoanalytic space can a strategy be cautiously advanced without endangering the self. The well-documented experiences of contemporary social movements suggest that the pain of struggle is always inscribed on the psychic body. Regarded as a personal and sometimes a shameful matter, the issue of recurring psychic suffering is rarely openly discussed, but if lessons about this psychic realm are not learned and shared, the problems will continue to return. Similarly, to fully understand the violence of the colonial condition, we need to enter this same psychic space. Hence, the psychoanalysis of colonization and decolonizing psychoanalysis are one and the same process.

Another point needs to be stressed: in the third world, it has become obvious that the personal is always linked to the group (though not necessarily to the collective). Psychic symptoms are often shared ones. The psychoanalytic space and the social space are directly linked, and desiring production cannot be separated from social production (as Deleuze and Guattari have shown). This is one of the lessons we learn from Fanon.

From Colonial Psychology to the Colonizer's Self-analysis

Understandably, the initiating proponent of the psychology of colonization could not have been the colonized subject. In order to effectively control, govern, and carry out the civilizing mission in the colony, the colonial empire had to first develop this field of knowledge. The richest achievement in the area of the psychology of colonization is to be found in the old colonial empire of France.

In her fascinating Ph.D. thesis, "Monsters and Revolutionaries: Colonial Family Romance and Metissage" (1995), Françoise Vergès argues that Fanon's "decolonization of colonial psychology" has to be juxtaposed against the French tradition of "psychology of the people," which had its genesis in the nineteenth century. The motives of the psychology of the people were to clarify the relationships among race, culture, and psychology. Its problematic was set in place to deal with the disorder of the "dangerous classes": the working class, the poor peasants, and the vagabonds. Toward the end of the nineteenth century, the psychology of the people was expanded to the colony. Briefly stated, the epistemological foundation of colonial psychology was the political unconscious of family romance: the relationship between parents and children. The colonized subjects were essentialized as being poor in linguistic expression and lacking the capacity for clear conceptualization: they believed in supernatural powers; they were fatalistic; all their knowledge came from blind faith in their ancestors' superstitions; and therefore, these natives could not mature unaided into adulthood. The colonizer's mission was to guide them. Of course, this entire formulation hid behind the name of science, and the validity of the psychologist's observation was backed by the guarantee of scientific neutrality.

A major epistemological break in colonial psychology came into being around the end of the Second World War, when the third-world decolonization movement began to unfold. According to Vergès, the turning point came in 1950 when Mannoni's *Prospero and Caliban: The Psychology of Colonization* (1990 [1950]) was published. Mannoni brings the colonizer into the picture of colonial relations and starts to address the psychological condition of the previously concealed master. Unlike the colonial psychologist, whose central concern was the colony and whose enunciative position was left unexamined, Mannoni had the colonizer as his target, and his analysis presupposed a relationship of mutually constituted subjectivity. From this point on, colonial relations came sharply into focus. Fanon's landmark 1952 *Black Skin, White Masks* further radicalizes psychoanalysis as a weapon in the anticolonial struggle. Albert Memmi's *The Colonizer and the Colonized* (1991 [1957]), George Lamming's *The Plea-*

sures of Exile (1992 [1960]), Ashis Nandy's *The Intimate Enemy: Loss and Recovery of Self under Colonialism* (1983), and Ngugi wa Thiong'o's *Decolonising the Mind: The Politics of Language in African Literature* (1986) have expanded on the colonizer-colonized problematic first brought up by Mannoni. One can easily criticize the theoretical dangers of binarism and essentialism in these works by evoking sliding hybridity and performativity, but doing so also risks analytically abandoning the subject positions produced by the colonial structure, and erasing historical antagonisms as engines of struggle.

Reading Mannoni half a century after he wrote, we must position his discourse symptomatically; it is as much a text about the psychology of colonization as it is a self-analysis of the colonizer. Even though Mannoni was obviously against colonial exploitation and racial discrimination, in his position as a colonial information officer—who attempted to account for the 1947 anticolonial revolt in which more than a hundred thousand Madagascans were killed—he could not escape the epistemic limits of Eurocentrism. Figures borrowed from Shakespeare, Prospero and Caliban, frame his entire analysis. The foreword to Mannoni's book, written in 1950 by Philip Manson, then the director of studies in race relations at the Royal Institute of International Affairs, in London, is full of racist and stereotypical language and reveals the epistemological limits of research at that time in history.

The question to be posed is this: why did the analysis of the colonialist self happen at this particular moment? Certainly, uneasiness about the postcolonial situation and nostalgia for lost colonial privileges during the transitional period paved the way for Mannoni's examination of the colonizer's situation. In short, his analysis prepared the colonizer to face the anxiety of having to leave the colony. Mannoni's work can be located within the wave of writings and practices that constitute the postwar decolonization movement, but his particular contribution was to document the psychological struggles of that specific historical moment, which prepared the way for later psychoanalyses of the colonizer. In this regard, Mannoni's book can be positioned as a text that, while clearly produced under tumultuous historical circumstances, still made the first, courageous attempt to decolonize the colonizer.

The central thrust of Mannoni's argument is that the psychology of colonization can be explained as an encounter between two types of distorted personalities. The colonizer suffers from an inferiority complex and the colonized from a dependency complex; the two are thus perfectly complementary. Mannoni's analysis, founded on evolutionism, is a universal history modeled on a person's life history. The different stages of personality development are mapped onto the entire world. After a child is born, Mannoni argues, the material conditions of existence, the processes of socialization, and affective development all create a relation of dependency on the parents. The turning point of this gradually forming dependency complex comes with the child's fear of being abandoned by the parents. On the one hand, this fear or anxiety can move the child toward a rational individualism and lead to a more mature and autonomous personality; on the other hand, it can erode self-confidence and lead to an inferiority complex. The latter is then transformed into an abandonment of the parents, accompanied by a form of repressed, unconscious guilt that can be remedied by dominating others. For Mannoni, the colonizers who are sent to the colony express this form of inferiority complex, while the natives remain stalled at the child's dependency stage. Upon meeting, they quickly develop a symbiotic relationship. Throughout the book, Mannoni constantly evokes this founding narrative. The act of colonial revolt is explained as an expression of the anxiety about being abandoned, and the natives' lack of gratitude toward the white colonizers is understood to be a reflection of a dependency complex.

The discursive effect of Mannoni's theory is the justification of colonialism. In this regard, it is not very different from the colonial psychology mentioned earlier, which was grounded in the story of parents guiding children into maturity. Although he drags the colonizer into the mix and points out that individual's distorted mentality, Mannoni cannot explain the specific historical conditions within which the two different mind-sets were formed. One does not have to debate the Eurocentric view of history wherein Europe has reached adulthood while the rest of the world remains in a childish state, because to do so would be to fall into the reductionist and evolutionist view of the singularity of history. Once this simple picture of development is challenged, Mannoni's explanatory framework crumbles.

Turning at the end of his book to practical matters, Mannoni proposes that if the French were to leave their colonies, political power should be handed over to the tribal council (*fokon'olona*), symbolizing the parents, so as to avoid abandoning and traumatizing the natives. Whether Mannoni had any direct influence on the policy of decolonization is uncertain. Nevertheless, his mode of thinking was inextricably linked to the colonial regime.

Fanon's critique of Mannoni focuses on the position and worldview of the colonized.

The Psychoanalysis of Decolonization

Fanon's writing is much angrier than Mannoni's. It is at the same time passionately reflexive. His writing style is closer to that of his mentor, Aimé Césaire. Césaire attacked Mannoni's Eurocentric superiority in his *Discourse on Colonialism* (1972 [1953]),[2] a text that served as an inspiration for Fanon's intervention. If one reads Mannoni as a self-analysis of the colonialist personality, then Fanon's *Black Skin, White Masks* can be said to do the same for the colonized.[3] For Fanon, neither the dependency complex nor the inferiority complex describes the essence of the colonial relation; both symptoms were imposed on the body of the colonized as a result of economic control and exploitation (Fanon 1967 [1952], 11). The alienation of the black cannot be reduced to the question of individual psychology. It is the social structure that conditions the collective psyche; hence, to use his words, "the black man must wage his war on both levels" (ibid.). Fanon's emphasis on the historical conditions of power relations is what distinguishes his basic analytical stand from Mannoni's.

In the opening pages of *Black Skin, White Masks*, Fanon lays out his crudely stated but enormously important discovery: "At the risk of arousing the resentment of my colored brothers, I will say that the black is not a man . . . The black man wants to be white . . . Black men want to prove to white men, at all costs, the richness of their thought, the equal value of their intellect . . . For the black man there is only one destiny. And it is white" (ibid., 8–10). The colonized wants to displace the colonizer; he identifies with and wants to be "him." That is to say, the black's self-worth can be validated only through recognition of him by the whites. Fanon sees this demand for recognition as impossible to satisfy, and therefore the source of a permanent crisis: the foundational logic of colonialism is racism, and essentialized racialist differences cannot be overcome. He declares: "I believe that the fact of the juxtaposition of the white and black races has created a massive psycho-existential complex. I hope by analyzing it to destroy it" (ibid., 12). Language, sexual encounters, everyday constructions of blackness, mental disorders, and questions of recognition become his sites of analysis.

Fanon's simple discovery has revolutionary implications. His painfully straightforward description of the colonized's psychoanalytic identification with the colonizer had a shocking, unprecedented impact on the colonized subject. Proponents of anticolonial discourse, such as Césaire and others in the negritude movement, were forced to see the colonized self in a new light. The colonized had to clarify where the projected object of their own desire lay and to examine what the achievement of such a desire in relation to the formation of the self-subject could be. The attack on white colonialism (its discourse, practice, and mentality) and the inverse celebration of all aspects of black cultural tradition are expressions of an unconscious yearning for the colonizer's recognition. For Fanon, "black" is imposed by the white colonizer and is a reactive construction. His reservation about the negritude movement is that the object of identification has not shifted but remains the same: i.e., the colonizer. Without radical self-analysis, the change from "whitening" to "blackening" cannot be located in the direction of the unconscious flow of desire: on the surface, "blackening" leads toward self-identification, but the (white) colonizer does not disappear from the scene and still conditions the self. This Fanonian problematic has enabled us to locate the core complex of the colonizer and the colonized. After half a century, this complex has not dissipated and continues to frame postcolonial trajectories.

In other words, the Fanonian problematic is: How is the black's colonized subjectivity formed? Why does the black skin have to wear white masks? In a footnote, Fanon explains: "When one has grasped the mechanism described by Lacan, one can have no further doubt that the real Other for the white man is and will continue to be the black man. And conversely. Only for the white man the Other is perceived on the level of the body image, absolutely as the not-self—that is, the unidentifiable, the inassimilable. For the black man, as we have shown, historical and economic realities come into the picture" (ibid., 161).

Here Fanon puts Lacan's "mirror stage" theory in the colonial context. Although subjectivity is always mutually constituting, the colonial history of economic domination has put the entire symbolic order in the hands of the white colonials, making them the defining agents of the ideological structure. The position occupied by the whites reduces blacks to the level of biological color alone. For the white subject, this bodily difference marks the boundary of the white subject. It has nothing to do with history or economics but is a "universal" difference. Only when the black man leaves his body and enters the white symbolic order, can he become a "man." In this way, the black's self-understanding is defined through the eyes of the whites. He is only a half-man, a partial subject, and only by whitening himself can he become a man. In this structure of oneness, the defining agent is above the categorization of racial differences: "white" is not colored, but above colors. This makes it impossible to ask certain troublesome and challenging questions. Within this symbolic system, "the negro symbolizes the biological" (ibid., 167): he is phallus, athlete, boxer, soldier, animal, devil, etc. Wherever he goes, the black is black. Only by wearing a white mask can he relieve his anxiety. Suffering a permanent lack and a permanent self-doubt, the black is permanently locked into the white jail.

Unlike Mannoni, Fanon proposes a politically charged psychoanalysis. He argues, "as a psychoanalyst, I should help my patient to become conscious of his unconscious and abandon his attempts at a hallucinatory whitening, but also to act in the direction of a change in the social structure" (ibid., 100). For Fanon, to look for a solution within the existing structure is a dead end. The black subject's psychic condition is always on the edge of collapse, since the unconscious desire to be white is a dream that cannot be realized. Only with the refusal to be the slave can the master disappear.

To consider Fanon's proposal in concrete political terms, one feels compelled to ask: is it possible to apply his collective analysis to the public space under the colonial regime? That is evidently difficult. Does this difficulty suggest that cultural decolonization of the psychoanalytic sort is possible only after the collapse of the empire? After the departure of the colonizer, can a critical self-analysis change the implanted psychoanalytic structure? Is there enough of a support system in place to protect the subject from breaking down during the decolonization process? Does not the structural shift from colonial to neocolonial entail a corresponding shift in the psychic structure? Is the colonial condition simply a racial divide based on economic differences?

A crucial theoretical and methodological question also emerges from

Fanon's account. When Fanon refocuses the psychoanalytic analysis on the social structure and the need to change it, is "social structure" singular or plural? In arguing with Mannoni, Fanon realizes that there are multiple structures of domination. Mannoni argues that "colonial exploitation is not the same as other forms of exploitation, and colonial racialism is different from other kinds of racialism" (quoted ibid., 88). Fanon counters that "colonial racism is no different from any other racism," and that "all forms of exploitation are identical because all of them are applied against the same 'object' man" (ibid.). If this is the case, why does the removal of colonialism have priority? Fanon's immediate concern was territorial colonialism, but his analysis forced him to consider the existence of multiple structures of domination. This is an important question to think through. Many postcolonial theorists focus on a singular structure of domination—along the continuum of race, ethnicity, nation, and civilization—and are unwilling to bring other structures into the picture. But if structures of domination have historically always been interlinked and mutually referencing, then colonial structures are necessarily entangled with other structures of power.

During and after the postcolonial revival of Fanon's discourse in the mid-1980s, Fanon was sharply criticized for blind spots such as male chauvinism and homophobia, but none of his critics have been willing to abandon the problematic he opened up. His work has been used in the analysis of third-world national independence movements and postcolonial societies, but it has also been expanded to analyses of multiple structures of domination, reconfiguring the meaning of "colonization" itself. After Fanon, "colonization" as well as "colonial identification" can no longer be understood simply in terms of race relations. The various strains of identity politics that have emerged in the postwar era—gender, sexuality, ethnicity, even class—can also be conceptualized in terms of the Fanonian problematic.[4]

Nationalism, Nativism, and Civilizationalism

Fanon made his analysis right after the end of the Second World War. What distinguishes his work from that of his contemporaries is that he moved beyond unqualified celebration and gave a critical depth to the analysis of third-world national independence movements. After the withdrawal of the colonial master, is the psychoanalysis of decolonization still useful? If so, what new problems are encountered? In this section, our analysis will focus on three different effects that have emerged during the decolonization process: nationalism, nativism, and civilizationalism. I want first to clarify my position. As historical products of decolonization, these three responses and challenges to colonialism are widely spread throughout formerly colonized spaces. We, as critical intellectuals living in former colonies, have to recognize the power and legitimacy of these forms of decolonization, each of which have had their respective moments in history. Nationalism had an active, unifying function during the anticolonial struggles. Nativism brought people's focus from the imperial centers back to their own living environments; in the process of reclaiming tradition, it tilted the balance away from the previous, sometimes worshipful embrace of the modern. Civilizationalism, in providing a cultural-psychic cure for the colonized, challenged the superiority of Western-centrism and produced the ideal of mutual respect in a multicultural world. At the same time, we cannot afford to ignore the problems these decolonization effects have caused. Unlike those living in the imperial centers, our own existence is internal to the decolonization movement. We do have to take analytical note—and have a sympathetic understanding—of the huge power exercised by third-world nationalism, nativism, and civilizationalism. We also have to keep a critical distance from these effects in order to go on thinking reflexively, resist the temptation of resentment, and thereby arrive at a more balanced subjectivity.

Fanon's Critique of Nationalism

Algeria declared its independence in 1962. Fanon had participated in revolutionary activities there since the mid-1950s, and shortly before his death in 1961, he published his most influential work, *The Wretched of the Earth*. Participation in the Algerian independence movement gave him an opportunity to see the emergence of new problems caused by the decolonization process. In a chapter called "The Pitfalls of National Consciousness," Fanon painfully forecasts the most pressing complication: the colonizer leaves the previous colonial structure unchanged, and the new condition "puts on the mask of neo-colonialism" (Fanon 1968 [1961], 152). He argues, "if it [nationalism] is not enriched and deepened by a very rapid transformation into a consciousness of social and political needs, in other words into humanism, it leads up a blind alley" (ibid., 204). When the colonizers leave, they hand the government over to the native bour-geois elites, who have identified with and internalized the culture of the colonial power. In this way, the original colonizers use old colonial link-ages to control the former colonies.

Predicated on the inside-outside metaphor—or, to use Fanon's ex-pression, the Manichaean divide—colonialism, driven by the expanding forces of capital, established in the colonies the structure of the nation-state as its mediating agent to unify internal differences. Once the sys-tem of the nation-state was imposed around the globe, the most viable mechanism for colonies to use in evicting the outsiders (colonizers) was, ironically, the nation-building and state-making project. Third-world nationalism, as a response and reaction to colonialism, was therefore seen as an imposed but necessary historical choice, a choice made in order to affirm the new nation-states' autonomy from the colonizing forces. In territories divided and occupied by colonial powers throughout Africa, Latin America, and Asia, colonialist governments saw the rise of nation-alist independence movements not as a threat, but as a moment of re-adjustment, an opportunity to shed their responsibilities and reduce their costs while still maintaining colonial linkages, markets, and political influ-ence. "Self-determination," a slogan heralded by the younger generation of imperialist powers such as the United States, proved to be not so much a humanist concern, but a political strategy on the part of the imperial-ists to scramble the already occupied territories in order to secure for themselves a larger piece of the cake in the name of "national interests." J. A. Hobson, as early as 1902, had remarked on the close ties between nationalism and imperialism: the latter, he argued, cannot function with-out the former (Hobson 1965 [1902]). By the 1940s, it had become clear that neoimperial nationalism was in good shape. Césaire's *Discourse on Colonialism* warned third-world intellectuals not to be deceived by this rising new power. He argues that the rise of the United States signals a transition from colonialism to neoimperialism, from territorial acquisi-tion to "remote control." Occupied by their struggle to grasp state power, third-world nationalists did not seem to be bothered by the formation of U.S. hegemony; in fact, they prosecuted their struggle for independence with financial and military "help" from the United States. The nation-state structure, finally implemented everywhere, proved to be the funda-mental constituent of the neocolonial system. With no better choice to counter an offensive nationalist-based colonialism, a defensive nationalism became the only unifying force opposing the colonizer.

In recognizing the almost inevitable historical necessity of nationalism, one should not lose sight of its problems. Shaped by the immanent logic of colonialism, third-world nationalism inevitably reproduced racial and ethnic discrimination, a price that was paid by the colonizer as well as the colonized. Fanon identified the problem in 1961, writing that "from nationalism we have passed to ultra-nationalism, to chauvinism, and finally to racism," and "we observe a permanent seesaw between African unity, which fades quicker and quicker into the mists of oblivion, and a heartbreaking return to chauvinism in its most bitter and detestable form" (Fanon 1968 [1961], 156–57). The ruling elites, struggling against each other to replace the colonial regime and gain state power, mobilized preexisting ethnic and regional differences to their advantage.[5] It is in this context that Fanon calls for a change in the nationalist agenda. Fearing that the postcolonial situation would otherwise become even more reactionary, chaotic, oppressive, and selfish, Fanon calls for the radical revolution to be continued on all levels, and urges it to be grounded in social and political justice.

How true was Fanon's critique of nationalism? How accurate was his forecast? In 1985, a quarter-century years after *The Wretched of the Earth* was published, *The South* (a journal concerned with third-world issues) and the Vienna Institute for Development organized a conference called "Decolonization and After: The Future of the Third World," to review the diverse practices and experiences of decolonization forty years after the inception of many national independence movements. Among the scholars and government officials from Africa, Asia, Latin America, and the Caribbean who were invited to attend, it was Altaf Gauhar, a Pakistani writer and the editor of *The South* and of the *Third World Quarterly*, who best summarized the situation in this often-cited passage:

It did not take long for the people to discover that all that had been changed was the color of their masters . . . independence brought little change and they remained chained to the same British-style institutions which the ruling elites manipulated and controlled to perpetuate their own advantages . . . For the masses the achievement of independence was the end of their struggle and also the end of their dreams

... nationalism could not serve either as a cover to conceal economic and social disparities nor hold back the tides of regional autonomous pressures ... when cultural homogeneity and truly national consciousness failed to evolve, people began to revert to the security of their traditional parochial and class identities ... The seeds of disintegration in the sub-continent [of India] were all sown in the colonial period. They are now coming to bitter fruition. (Gauhar 1987, cited in Kreisky and Gauhar 1987, 4–5)

By no means does this bitter commentary from the third world express nostalgia for the colonial regime, nor does it aim to legitimize the history of colonialism, but it does put into sharp focus what has happened since the foreign powers left. Internal colonialism began with essentially the same logic as external colonialism. As Nandy forcefully puts it, "the rhetoric of progress uses the fact of internal colonialism to subvert the cultures of societies subject to external colonialism," and "internal colonialism in turn uses the fact of external threat to legitimize and perpetuate itself," but one has to understand that "neither form of oppression can be eliminated without eliminating the other" (Nandy 1983, xii). This is exactly where the difficulty lies. After the colonial era, the strong connection between the inside and outside makes the distinction difficult to sustain. The national bourgeoisie continues to govern by exercising colonial tactics, dividing and ruling, for example, by exploiting ethnic differences. The situation has forced us to question the legitimacy of using color, racial, and ethnic distinctions to justify any form of government. To put it crudely, is it more legitimate to be ruled by an insider than by an outsider?

Memmi's Critique of Nativism

Nativism, which like nationalism emerged as a byproduct of the national independence movement, operates deep inside the social structure. For the nationalist movement to succeed in capturing state power, it requires the nativist movement's wider cultural support. For centuries, colonizers had carried out what they called a civilizing mission to replace backward local traditions with more-advanced practices via state-sponsored modernization programs. After nationalist governments assumed control, nativist self-rediscovery movements were called upon to replace cultural imaginations deeply contaminated by colonialism with authentic traditions and a pure self.

If, as Fanon and Nandy argue, colonialism is enabled by the mechanism of identification with the colonizer—both through the aggression that binds the colonizer and the colonized together, and by establishing the colonizer as the embodiment of modernity for the colonized to emulate—then nativism works by identification with the self. But the Other, the opponent of the self-recovery movement, is still the colonizer, who has now left the colony. In the process of reconstituting the subject, nativism must constantly keep moving away from the narcissistic self, or risk being dragged once again into the colonial framework.

Defined in relation to the nonnative colonial master, nativism operates on every level of social formation. Official posts are nativized first, followed by changes to the national flag, dress, language, curriculum, textbooks, food, and so on. But at the gut level, colonial elements still permeate the society; they cannot be eradicated overnight. Colonial values unwittingly become the common standard of measurement. They condition the course of nativization: if the colonial situation is A, then nativization is not-A. The irreducible difficulty is that the colonial imagination has always been part of the native activist's body, thought, and desire.

In the last two chapters of his seminal work, *The Colonizer and the Colonized*, Albert Memmi documented and analyzed this nativist "self-rediscovery movement." Although Memmi never used the word "nativism," the phenomenon he described is what I understand today to be the nativist movement. The book was originally published in 1957, five years after the first publication of *Black Skin, White Masks*, and four years before that of *The Wretched of the Earth*. But unlike Fanon's work, Memmi's important statement about nativism was neglected by the third-world nativist movement, and it has not received enough attention in contemporary postcolonial studies. If Mannoni's text can be understood as a colonizer's confession, and Fanon's as a self-analysis of the colonized, then Memmi's occupies a position closer to that of the subject with a split identity. As a Tunisian Jew living in a French colony, he was treated like a second-class citizen. Although he did not belong to the majority Muslim population, his actual living conditions were closer to those of the colonized Muslims than to those of the French colonizers. But his training and desires were products of France and Western civilization. As Memmi frankly puts it,

"I know the colonizer from inside almost as well as I know the colonized" (Memmi 1991 [1957], xiii). This peculiar point of view allows him to analyze how colonialism restrains nativism.

Tunisia declared its independence in 1956. Living through this transition enabled Memmi to capture the changing psyches of the colonizer and the colonized. Unlike Mannoni, Memmi does not essentialize the colonizer. The first half of his book focuses on the differences between those who refuse and those who accept the role of colonizer, and he acutely depicts the dilemma of the French leftist living in colonial conditions. The second half of the book is concerned with the colonized. His critique of nativism appears in the last two chapters, where he begins to pinpoint solutions for the colonized.

For Memmi, the revolt of the colonized is caused by the inescapable internal contradiction of the colonial framework. In the process of the revolt, he argues, "we then witness a reversal of terms. Assimilation being abandoned, the colonized's liberation must be carried out through a recovery of the self and of autonomous dignity. Attempts at imitating the colonizer required self-denial; the colonizer's rejection is the indispensable prelude to self-discovery. That accusing and annihilating image must be shaken off; oppression must be attacked boldly since it is impossible to get around it. After having been rejected for so long by the colonizer, the day has come when it is the colonized who must refuse the colonizer" (ibid., 128).

For Memmi, the revolt is also inevitable. The internal contradiction of colonial "assimilation" is implied in its aggressive attack. It requires that you admit to the inferiority of your own culture. It forces you to abandon your existential dignity. It then wins over your active consent to learning and acquiring everything that belongs to the governing colonizers. To do this presupposes a painful process of self-negation. Once you have done that, you are told that your imitation is not quite right: you are still not like "us"; you are, in essence, inferior. In this sense, assimilation has become the internal contradiction of colonialism. Paradoxically, one effect of assimilation was that it supplied a language of revolt. Memmi argues that "the colonized fights in the name of the very values of the colonizer, uses his techniques of thought and his method of combat. It must be added that this is the only action that the colonizer understands" (ibid., 129). When the culture of the colonizer's mother country is challenged, the retaliation against the colonized becomes quite unbearable. This is the key moment in the birth of nativism, which—expressed in the xenophobia of the colonized—is indeed a return to colonial racism. But the racism now embodied in the colonized is complicated by the fact that the xenophobic protest cannot uproot the seeds planted long ago by the colonizer: "while modern European racism hates and scorns more than it fears, that of the colonized fears and also continues to admire" (ibid., 131). The admiration cultivated for the civilizing mission was based on a negation of the self; the new xenophobia requires a corresponding confirmation of the self.

In Tunisia, the nativist movement first reaffirmed the value of religion, which had been negated by the colonizer. Through religion, different social classes were unified to "reinforce their bonds, verify and recreate their unity" (ibid., 133). Next, the nativist reaffirms language: "in recovering his autonomous and separate destiny, he immediately goes back to his own tone" (ibid., 134). Language is unequivocally the foundation of all nativist movements because the integration of nationalist feeling can be achieved only in one's own language. Religion and language have become the core expressions of cultural tradition, the Other of the colonial modern.

Observing the process of the revolt, Memmi notices the exclusionary aspects of ethnic nationalism: the colonized "will be nationalistic but not, of course, internationalistic. Naturally, by so doing, he runs the risks of falling into exclusionism and chauvinism, of sticking to the most narrow principles, and of setting national solidarity against human solidarity—and even ethnic solidarity against national solidarity" (ibid., 135). Memmi points out the danger of this self-centered exclusion of other groups: "the colonized accepts being separate and different, but his individuality is that which is limited and defined by the colonizer" (ibid., 136). A constant struggle for essentialist difference constitutes the fate of nativism.

This is how Memmi documents the process of nativist revolt:

> But to go all the way with his revolt, it seems necessary to him to accept those inhibitions and amputations. He will forgo the use of the colonizer's language, even if all the locks of the country turn with that key; he will change the signs and highway markings, even if he is the first to be inconvenienced. He will prefer a long period of educational mistakes to the continuance of the colonizer's school organization. He will choose institutional disorder in order to destroy the institutions

built by the colonizer as soon as possible. There we see, indeed, a re-active drive of the profound protest. He will no longer owe anything to the colonizer and will have definitely broken with him. But this also involves a confused and misleading conviction: everything that belongs to the colonizer is not appropriate for the colonized. This is just what the colonizer always told him. Briefly, the rebellious colonized begins by accepting him as something negative. (ibid., 137–38)

This passage contains the genesis of Memmi's critique of nativism. The existence of the colonized is a long chain of negation. He had to accept being negated by the colonizer and now has to accept that he himself is the negative Other of the colonizer; negating the colonizer is therefore necessarily a self-negation. For Memmi, the deep hurt of the colonized cannot be completely cured: "we must await the complete disappearance of the colonization—including the period of revolt" (ibid., 141). Indeed, the period of revolt is a moment of pure negation. Nativist movements will have to move beyond this negativity to reconstitute the self. And it is in that moment of overcoming that nativism can be transformed.

In his last chapter, Memmi makes this appeal:

The liquidation of colonization is nothing but a prelude to complete liberation, to self-recovery. In order to free himself from colonization, the colonized must start with his oppression, the deficiencies of his group. In order that his liberation may be complete, he must free himself from those inevitable conditions of his struggle. A nationalist, because he had to fight for the emergence and dignity of his nation, he must conquer himself and be free in relation to that nation. He can, of course, assert himself as a nationalist. But it is indispensable that he have a free choice and not that he exist only through his nation. He must conquer himself and be free in relation to the religion of his group, which he can retain or reject, but he must stop existing only through it. The same applies to the past, tradition, ethnic characteristics, etc. Finally, he must cease defining himself through categories of colonizers. (ibid., 151–52)

I have quoted these long passages because I believe it is worth listening to the advice that Memmi issued in 1957. Listening to his exhortations half a century later, we cannot but admit the limits of even the most prescient analysis. Nativism is still burning. The contemporary nativist movement in the present context is mixed with a reactive response to the imposed pressure of globalization. Fanon's critique of nationalism may have been ahead of its time, but we still live under the shadow of Memmi's critique of nativism.

The rediscovery of the self is in no way bounded by the nation-state. It can go in different directions when a tradition of difference from the colonizer is discovered. The contemporary movements of Asianization (against the West), Africanization (again, against Western hegemony), and even Europeanization (against America) can be described as nativist movements. The assertion and reclaiming of Asian, African, or European values and identities are not necessarily products of nationalist interpellation. They form a part of the ultimate nativist ideal: civilizationalism.

Nandy and Civilizationalism

In *The Intimate Enemy* (1983), Ashis Nandy builds on the problematic identified by Fanon and Memmi by shifting the site of analysis to post-colonial Indian society.[6] Compared with Fanon, who was writing as the national liberation movement was unfolding, Nandy has had more time to reexamine the deeply implanted forces of colonialism. For him, the saturating power of colonialism lies in its ability to impose a whole set of hierarchical categories onto the traditional order. When the colonial regime left, the structure installed by the colonizer remained, paving the way for local society to confront what Nandy calls the "second form of colonization" (Nandy 1983, xi). No longer presenting itself as the face of the colonizer, but instead relying on the superior imaginary of the West, the second wave of colonialism was able to exercise its power to change the cultural priorities in the formerly colonized society. The West was no longer a geographical and temporal entity, but a universal psychological category: "the West is now everywhere, within the West and outside; in structures and in minds" (ibid.). Nandy's main agenda is to combat the hegemonic West by rediscovering cultural practices and traditions uncontaminated by colonialism.

Nandy's notion of the second wave of colonization roughly parallels the discourse of cultural imperialism, which emerged in the 1960s. In an earlier period, a whole set of metadiscourses (for example, progress, science, rationality, and enlightenment) were adopted to justify colonialism.

Decolonization has unfortunately not worked on this level to challenge the assumptions behind the justifications, and in fact has helped facilitate their development. This set of discourses became the dominant psychic and material basis for the second wave of colonization. Nandy's critique challenges these unquestioned assumptions in order to open up new possibilities.

Nandy's attitude toward the West is not one of total negation. His critique focuses on those elements and dimensions that support colonialism, though the discursive effect of his writing may create the impression that he is constructing two distinct entities, the West and the non-West. In the end, there does seem to be a competition between different forms of universalism, a battle over which version has greater moral legitimacy and is less complicit in the expansion of colonialism. Nandy's attempt to rediscover local cultural resources is "an unheroic but critical traditionalism which develops a sensitivity to new experiences of evil." His project "contributes to that stream of critical consciousness: the tradition of reinterpretation of traditions to create new traditions" (ibid., xvii–xviii). This rediscovery of tradition is an alternative myth making, and its sources come from the victims of colonial modernity. When faced with a choice between "modern master" and "non-modern slave," one can only choose the slave because "he represents a higher-order cognition which perforce includes the master as a human whereas the master's cognition has to exclude the slave except as a 'thing'" (ibid., xv–xvi). This form of universalism presupposes a subject who lives within the dominant West, but who operates in a space outside the framework defined by colonialism. As "non-players" and "outsiders," these thinkers and writers construct an alternative while resisting the "loving embrace of the West's dominant self" (ibid., xiv). Nandy includes the work of Kipling, Orwell, Wilde, and Charles Andrews as alternative responses to colonialism from within the West. The most subversive response to the West, however, comes from the critical traditionalism of Gandhi.

Gandhi's philosophy, according to Nandy, is an attempt to establish nonviolence as the core of Hinduism and the main virtue of Indian culture (ibid., 51). Under English colonial rule, identification with the aggressor bound together the colonizer and colonized. To use force to replace the colonizer would be to strengthen this psychic identification mechanism.

But Nandy argues that "Gandhi wanted to liberate the British as much as he wanted to liberate Indians" (ibid.). Gandhi's nonviolence is not passive: it is a courageous form of activism, intended to eliminate violence. If Western colonialism is the expression of "manhood," then Gandhi's nonviolence is an appropriation of "motherhood" and femininity. It is a strategy that claims the "femininity in man." As Nandy points out, the Indian tradition of femininity includes the intimate relation between female power and activism. He writes: "it also implied the belief that the feminine principle is a more powerful, dangerous and uncontrollable principle in the cosmos than the male principle" (ibid., 53–54). Gandhi's anticolonial methods were successful precisely because he was able to appropriate the universalist notion of femininity already existing in the tradition of Indian philosophy. In a sense, the highest form of universalism is motherhood. Here we cannot resist asking: in Gandhi's (or Nandy's) categories, is there a possibility of masculinity in women? The argument sounds strikingly familiar to the yin-yang logic in Chinese philosophy, yet another masculine appropriation of femininity and one which has the effect of hardening gender and sexual stereotypes.

Nandy's discursive strategy of rereading Gandhi's view of history to arrive at a higher level of universalism reappears eleven years later in *The Illegitimacy of Nationalism: Rabindranath Tagore and the Politics of Self* (1994), in which Nandy moves a step further in elaborating what he means by "Eastern universalism." He argues that nationalism is a by-product of colonialism, and that third-world nationalism buys into the belief that it is backward without the nation-state and nationalist sentiment. Nationalist independence movements are reactions against colonialism and are thus caught in a colonialist frame of mind, accepting that the formation of the nation-state is an inevitable stage in the evolutionary progress of mankind. Nandy attempts to retrieve from Gandhi's and Tagore's thoughts and practices the possibility of breaking away from the dilemma of nationalism. The crux of his argument is that:

> In both Gandhi and Tagore, the fear of nationalism grew out of their experience of the record of anti-imperialism in India, and their attempt to link their concepts of Indianness with their understanding of a world where the language of progress had already established complete dominance. They did not want their society to be caught in a

situation where the idea of the Indian nation would supersede that of the Indian civilization, and where the actual ways of life of Indians would be assessed solely in terms of the needs of an imaginary nation-state called India. They did not want the Indic civilization and lifestyle, to protect which the idea of the nation-state had supposedly been imported, to become pliable targets of social engineering guided by a theory of progress which, years later, made the economist Joan Robinson remark that the only thing that was worse than being colonized was not being colonized. (Nandy 1994, 3)

If Indian nationalism worked only on the level of the nation-state, then the larger historical entity—the "higher order" of the Hindu civilization—would resist being trapped in the colonial framework. The concrete implication of this recognition is that Gandhi's freedom movement ceased to be defined by a nationalist agenda. It redefined itself as a universalist struggle for political justice and cultural dignity.

In Nandy's reading, Tagore's and Gandhi's philosophies cannot be defined as a form of Indian nationalism; civilizationalism is a more precise way to characterize the universalist sentiment they expressed. Nandy's 1994 construction of civilizationalism can thus be seen as a departure from his 1983 critical traditionalism, and a theoretical advance made in response to an evolving postcolonial condition. Having experienced the making of the nation, the formerly colonized has woken up to discover that nationalism is really not the solution. It is clear, once we look at it in the global context, that the hierarchical structure of the nation-state more or less continues the established order of colonialism, and within the context of that order, it is impossible to compete with the originators of the form, the Europeans. At this moment, perhaps only by bringing out a higher and larger category—civilization—can we the formerly colonized psychically rediscover ourselves and compete with the West. The inventing and reinventing of signs familiar to the popular imaginary, and the subsequent articulation of those signs as a higher form of universalism, is a way to regain confidence in the civilization and to beat the West in cultural terms. This form of psychological identification is unquestionably a part of the postcolonial imagination.

At the opposite end of the spectrum from civilizationalism is the postcolonial complex of little subjectivity. The Sri Lankan anthropologist S. J.

Tambiah's ethnographic abstraction from a position marginal to a "great civilization" is a useful point of entry:

> Notwithstanding their genial qualities, Sri Lankans are also apt to be proud and arrogant abroad: they feel superior to the Indians, the Malays, the Chinese, perhaps even the Japanese. For their eyes are set on the West, particularly Great Britain, which was their colonial ruler from the early 19th century until 1948. They are proud of their British veneer: their elites acculturated more quickly than their Indian counterparts; their island enjoyed a prosperity owing to its plantation economy that was the envy of its Asian neighbors; and the British raj established a school system and a transportation system that, because of the island's size, was more efficient than any could possibly be in the vast subcontinent of India. And therefore, although India is undeniably their parent in many ways, all indigenous Sri Lankans — Sinhalese, Tamil, Muslim — become visibly annoyed, if not outraged, if Sri Lanka is mistaken physically to be part of India (as many people in distant parts of the world innocently do), or if it is thought culturally to be part of "greater India" (as some Indians patronizingly do). (Tambiah 1986, 2)

Tambiah's psychic geography reveals a general complex of sentiments that resonates in other geopsychic relations. If one replaces the name Sri Lanka with Taiwan or Canada, and India with China or the United States, the same logic holds true. It follows, then, that "China," "India," "Islam," and "the Orient" are not necessarily nationalist concepts, but emotional signifiers. To proudly reclaim a four- or five-thousand-year history is a postcolonial response. The downside is that these larger, non-Western civilizations may fall into the logic of colonial competition and struggle over which represents the Other of the West. Does this not reproduce the structure of ethnocentrism? Is the center not still the opposing West? Surrounding the self-claimed civilizational entities, how do the little subjectivities — which do not have a larger civilization to hang onto, or which are now forced into an identification with one — handle their comparatively diminished destinies and sense of marginalization?

There is, of course, a range of civilizationist positions, and I am not attempting here to erase the many important differences between them. Nandy's left-leaning populist civilizationalism is radically different from both Samuel Huntington's statist civilizationalism and from certain Neo-Confucian attempts to link the Chinese civilization with state ideology. Nandy's approach is nonstatist and counterhegemonic; Huntington's is a reflection of an anxious, declining empire, and is really a form of imperial nationalism; and Neo-Confucianism has emerged as common ideological discourse increasingly deployed by state machines across East Asia. Huntington's "The Clash of Civilizations?" (1993) has generated widespread antagonism in China and Southeast Asia, but all the nationalist-civilizationalist reactions it inspired do not challenge his framework as a whole but rather are absorbed into it.[7] Those geographical spaces that do not clearly belong to bigger civilizations are now forced to take sides and are boxed in by Huntington's categories; sites with the potential to be more syncretically multicultural may change their orientation. Australia, for example, used to claim to be "a multicultural nation in Asia," but in the 1990s, with a conservative government in power, the state presented itself instead as a multicultural Western nation in Asia.

The Politics of Resentment

By now it must be clear that nationalism, nativism, and civilizationalism are interconnected movements. If nationalism is a general form of decolonization which targets the nation-state at the political level, then nativism is a downward cultural movement operating in everyday life, and civilizationalism is an upward version of nativism, often formed in physically larger geographical spaces with relatively long histories, and usually set against the imaginary West. These three forms cannot be reduced to a single plane of analysis. Much like the interrelated terms "imperialism," "colonialism," and "ethnic nationalism," they cannot be understood in isolation, only in reference to each other. What reconnects and unifies nationalism, nativism, and civilizationalism is what Memmi, using the language of psychoanalysis, calls "resentment." This is also exactly what binds the colonizer and the colonized together (Memmi 1991 [1957], 132). The object of resentment for anticolonial nationalism is always the colonizer, who after independence becomes the absent presence of the imaginary Other. Nativism denies the legitimacy of things "foreign," but with the former colonizer as the central concern, the nativist's own subjectivity is defined and conditioned by the nonnative. For civilizationalism, the object of resentment is always the West, against which the self is measured. The inside-outside, self-other logic of colonialism lingers on in these three forms of decolonization. A constant resentment against the colonial outsider or the imaginary Other is still at work, often expressing itself in the form of ethnocentrism or racism.

As Memmi points out, the colonizer's racism is always offensive, but the racism of the colonized is reactive and defensive in nature. As he puts it, "though xenophobia and racism of the colonized undoubtedly contain enormous resentment and are negative forces, they could be the prelude to a positive movement, the regaining of self-control by the colonized" (ibid.). We certainly hope that Memmi's optimism is justified, and that formerly colonized subjects can move away from a primarily reactive way of being. But practices on the ground do not seem to signal any departure from the politics of resentment. We have to recognize that Memmi's discussion of the role of self-rediscovery is still relevant today; it is the reactive politics of resentment that still keeps us in the trap of colonial history.

Colonial Identification and Identity Politics

In thinking through the problematic of colonial identification, our discussion cannot operate outside the context of the conditions of existence that the colonial structure created. This structure produces two theoretical subject positions, the colonizer and the colonized. Recent postcolonial studies have criticized the tendencies of binarism and essentialism implicit in these two subject positions. The notion of diaspora, popular in the 1990s, stressed the fluidity of identity, but this and other similar theoretical moves run the risk of denying the relevance of the colonial structure, or indeed of any form of stable identity. Most of the important issues in colonial history cannot be discussed without having the colonial structure in mind. At the same time, we need to remember Fanon's point about other structures coexisting in the same social formation. The colonial regime is a "structure in dominance" (in the Althusserian sense) that intersects with other structural forces.

The homologous relation between colonial identification and other structural identities can be heuristically charted. Table 1 shows that the structure or regime produces identity and subject positions, not the reverse. Until the structure breaks down, the identities it produces will always exist. Here lies the homologous logic: the colonized, like other

Table 1. Structural Homology of Identity Politics

Structure or Regime	Opposing Identities and Subject Positions		
colonial regime	colonizer	vs.	colonized
capitalism	capitalist	vs.	worker
patriarchy	male	vs.	female
heterosexual regime	heterosexual	vs.	homosexual, bisexual, transgender

subaltern subjects who are in the process of self-recovery (those at the right of each pair), are seeking self-identification and self-affirmation. But until the structure breaks down, the object of identification for the subaltern subjects is always bound up with the subject in power (those at the left of each pair), and the result is the reproduction and strengthening of the structure or regime. Colonial identification theory indicates that it is through violence and a politics of resentment that the colonizer and the colonized are bound together. The same logic applies to the relations within other forms of identity politics. The danger implicit in these relationships is that the subaltern subject can easily be locked within a single structure, noticing only the existence of the opponent and indulging in struggles internal to that structure, never stepping out of the structure to see the existence of other subaltern subjects. Hence, the worker's movement is preoccupied with capitalist and does not sympathize with women's conditions, while the feminist struggle is concerned only with patriarchal issues and does not take class issues into account. Although the colonial regime, capitalism, patriarchy, and the heterosexual regime are different structures, the alliance between colonizer, capitalist, male, and heterosexual is always and already formed. However, the subaltern subjects are divided by the different structures and have their own concerns and priorities; cooperation and alliances between the groups are difficult to achieve.

A Critical Syncretism: Decolonized Subjectivity

The previous section traced the discursive shift from the psychology of colonization to the psychoanalysis of decolonization. In the process, we have understood the interpenetration of psychoanalytic identification and the political-economic structure, and subsequently the structural transformation from colonial to neocolonial conditions, which entails a psychoanalytic movement toward a new object of identification. If assimilation, as the archetypal desire of the colonial cultural imagination, has proved to be an oppressive, violent, and impossible operation, is multiculturalism a viable alternative?

From "Multiculturalism" to "Syncretism"

One of the most self-conscious adoptions of multiculturalism as state policy took place in Australia, so a critique of Australian practices will be suggestive here. As pointed out by Ghassan Hage, multiculturalism, as practiced in the dominant Anglo-Celtic nationalist-republican discourse, is in effect a collection of other cultures deployed for national if not nationalist window dressing: "this exhibitionary multiculturalism is the post-colonial version of the colonial fair" (Hage 1993, 133). For Hage, the fact that multicultural policy "allows" others to "maintain their cultures" does not mean that it is "not a fantasy of total control" (ibid., 135). Like zoological taxonomy, the language of multiculturalism classifies others and constructs hierarchical orders. Minorities are displayed like rare animals in a zoo: "all ethnic cultures within the Anglo-Celtic multicultural collection are imagined as dead cultures that cannot have a life of their own except through the 'peaceful co-existence' that regulates the collection" (ibid., 133). Hage powerfully argues that "if the exhibition of the 'exotic natives' was the product of the relation of power between the colonizer and the colonized in the colonies as it came to exist in the colonial era, the multicultural exhibition is the product of the relation of power between the post-colonial powers and the post-colonized as it developed in the metropolis following the migratory processes that characterized the post-colonial era" (ibid.).

To mesh Hage's theoretical articulation with our concerns here, it may be useful to sum up the differences between assimilation and multiculturalism as follows: if the cultural basis of colonialism is racism, and its cultural strategy is assimilation (which generates an identification with the aggressor-colonizer), then the cultural basis of neocolonialism is multiculturalism (which recognizes differences but conceals the dominant ethnic position of the agent who classifies and divides), and its cultural strategy is peaceful coexistence (which generates an identification with the self in the form of nativism and identity politics). If this accurately describes our current situation, the incomplete project of decolonization must move beyond the territorial politics of peaceful coexistence.

Hage's insight pushes us to question the structural positions of the state apparatus and the dominant culture in the handling of problems related to identity. One may have good intentions but still prolong the logic of neocolonial domination. The rhetoric of multiculturalism inherits colonial categories that divide a population along the dominant axes of race and ethnicity, covering up the privileged position of the subject of articulation, and excluding other cultural differences such as class, gender, and sexuality. In the end, multiculturalism is not as multifarious as it claims to be, and the culture it refers to is limited by its nationalist inspiration. If multiculturalism has reached its political and theoretical limits, how do we envision new possibilities?

In *Chiao Hung and the Restructuring of Neo-Confucianism in the Late Ming* (1986), the late Edward T. Ch'ien deploys the concept of syncretism to explain the emergence of a consciousness that mixes elements of Buddhism, Taoism, and Confucianism to combat the orthodoxy of the dominant Neo-Confucianism. According to Ch'ien, in Chiao Hung's mode of thinking, the three systems of belief no longer maintain a relationship of peaceful coexistence and compartmentalization. Instead, they "intermix" (Ch'ien 1986, 15) and are "mutually explanatory and illuminating" (ibid., 14). On a theoretical level, syncretism not only emphasizes the process of mixing but also produces a much more active and reflexive consciousness, which is the real justification for the practice (ibid., 2). Further, syncretism implies the active participation of the involved subjects: the practices of the subject are not imposed and unconsciously accepted, but are reflexive processes that engage the interlocutors. Understood in this way, the difference between syncretism and hybridity is that syncretism denotes a subject who is highly self-conscious when translating the limits of the self, whereas hybridity is simply a product of the colonial machine's efforts toward assimilation.

In this framework, subjectivity is composed of three historically grounded sites of interaction and interarticulation: body (*shēn*), mind (*xīn*), and desire (*qì*) — the classic Taoist philosophical cosmology. Individuals and cultural subjectivities are constituted by, and operate on, these three historical axes. The implication is that unless these three elements are liberated simultaneously, subjectivity remains colonized.

Here I want to insert Ch'ien's concept of syncretism into the ethics of decolonization to suggest a way to break free of colonial identification. I shall call this alternative strategy of identification *critical syncretism*. The key issue here is the object of identification. The formation of the colonized subjectivity has always been passive, reactive, and imposed, and the colonizer has been its only object of identification. In the decolonization movement, nativism and identity politics shift the object of identification toward the self. This self, however, is still conditioned by an active disidentification with the colonizer. If a critical syncretism presupposes a subject position emerging out of progressive decolonization movements, who and what could be its objects of identification?

A Critical Syncretism

The direction of identification put forward by a critical syncretism is outward; the intent is to become others, to actively interiorize elements of others into the subjectivity of the self so as to move beyond the boundaries and divisive positions historically constructed by colonial power relations in the form of patriarchy, capitalism, racism, chauvinism, heterosexism, or nationalistic xenophobia. Becoming others is to become female, aboriginal, homosexual, transsexual, working class, and poor; it is to become animal, third world, and African. Critical syncretism is a cultural strategy of identification for subaltern subject groups. Here "others" refers not just to racial, ethnic, and national categories but also includes class, sex and gender, and geographical positions.

Viewed in light of the homologous relation between colonial identification and identity politics, critical syncretism provides two clear imperatives. First, critical identity politics needs to shift and to multiply its objects of identification so that structural divisions can be breached, making it possible to seek alliances outside one's own limited frame. Second, the articulating agent, critical for building connections across structures, needs to be especially conscious of cultivating and even occupying identities defined by multiple structures. By operating simultaneously within different structures, the articulating agent is able to link different subject positions into an overarching struggle.

In *Culture and Imperialism*, Said argues that "imperialism consolidated the mixture of cultures and identities on a global scale. But its worst and most paradoxical gift was to allow people to believe that they were only, mainly, exclusively, white, or Black, or Western, or Oriental" (Said 1993, 336). Imperialism has indeed produced hybrid subjectivities, which made impossible a return to an uncontaminated self. And it has further pushed the world structure toward neoliberal globalization, deepening the hybridity of the already hybrid subject. Confronting the various forces of globalization, national identity has emerged at this moment of history as a privileged axis of identification. Where are you from? How long are you going to stay here? When are you going back to your country? Global bureaucracy, through the universal apparatus of ID cards and passports, constructs one's identity according to the nation-state one belongs to. In the essay "The Question of Cultural Identity," Stuart Hall proposes a list of the contradictory effects of globalization:

1. Cultural homogeneity and the global-postmodern breaks down national identity.
2. Resistance to globalization has deepened national and local identity.
3. National identity is in decline, but new forms of hybrid identity are gaining their positions. (Hall 1992a, 330)

Hall's first proposition is indeed happening. The autonomy of national sovereignty and territory has been challenged by the worldwide flows of capital, technology, and people. But the second proposition is also true: the global rise of nationalism is in part a response to the formation of global capital. Hall's third proposition points to the emergence of new identities, represented by the identity politics of new social movements, including the formation of new immigrant communities that challenge dominant ethnic compositions.

Under such conditions, if the contemporary decolonization movement is to escape both from identification with the colonizer and from the nativist movement's narcissistic tendency toward the splitting of the subject, what decolonized or postcolonial object of identification remains? What would such a liberating form of subjectivity look like? The proposal for a critical syncretism does not pretend to provide a conclusive answer, but it does honor and reflect the need for a change from passivity to an active shifting of the objects of identification. Critical syncretism attempts to push this possibility in a more liberating direction. Said's conclusion to *Culture and Imperialism* is instructive:

No one can deny the persisting continuities of long traditions, sustained habitations, national languages, and cultural geographies, but there seems no reason except fear and prejudice to keep insisting on their separation and distinctiveness, as if that was all human life was about . . . It is more rewarding—and more difficult—to think concretely and sympathetically, contrapuntally, about others than only about "us." But this also means not trying to rule others, not trying to classify them or put them in hierarchies, above all, not constantly reiterating how "our" culture or country is number one (or *not* number one, for that matter). For the intellectual there is quite enough of value to do without *that*. (Said 1993, 336)

What Said points to, in my reading, are the sentiment and horizon of nationalism, both nearly impossible to transcend. It is neither possible nor necessary to ask people to give up their national identity and pretend to be world citizens, or to cultivate a privileged position of cosmopolitanism. But only through a constant suspension of national interest as the first and last priority can we begin to become others.

Critical syncretism takes an alternative understanding of subjectivity as its starting point. Only through multilayered practices can one become others. The aim is not simply to rediscover the suppressed voices of the multiple subjects within the social formation, but to generate a system of multiple reference points that can break away from the self-reproducing neocolonial framework that structures the trajectories and flow of desire.

Geocolonial Historical Materialism

Cultural studies developed in different parts of the world in line with local trajectories. The field is not a unified discipline. The Birmingham tradition of cultural studies, exemplified by the work of Stuart Hall, can be traced back to the decolonization movement after the Second World War and the formation of the British New Left in the 1950s. The movement was a mix of at least two components: E. P. Thompson and Raymond Williams represented the dissident side of the British Communist Party, whereas Hall belonged to a group of intellectuals from the Caribbean and other colonized locations. These two groups came together after the Soviet Union's invasion of Hungary and the United Kingdom's involvement in the seizure of the Suez Canal. Both groups were highly critical of imperialism. Beyond England, cultural-studies practices in Africa, Asia, and Latin America have maintained a productive tension between research and academic discourse on the one hand, and social and political movements on the other. The driving energy of cultural studies has been its connection with forces of social transformation and its engagement with historical reality. For these reasons, cultural studies should be understood not simply as an academic discipline, but as a field of intellectual practices connecting with various other forms of struggle.

If cultural studies can be repositioned as an integral part of the global decolonization movement, then its assumed methodology—historical materialism—must also be renewed and reworked in the new context of globalization. In the previous two sections, we traced the genealogy of the discourse on colonial identification and made a proposal to move forward by means of a critical syncretism. At this point, we are ready to make the next move, which is to reconnect with the analytical framework of historical materialism via radical geography.

Decolonizing Historical Materialism

In its attempt to fill a gap in the decolonization project, the formulation of a geocolonial historical materialism presupposes that to understand contemporary cultural formation and subjectivity, it is necessary to return to the encounter between specific local histories and the history of colonialism. Historical materialism was proposed at the moment of high imperialism in the nineteenth century. Its epistemological principle of historicization (of any analytical object) fundamentally transformed classical political-economic analysis. But its actual writing of world history took Europe as its reference point, and it was from Europe that it combined disconnected spaces into a coherent narrative. This has been known as the problem of Eurocentrism. One way to rewrite world history is to not assume unity and singularity, but to see the world through the historical convergence and interaction of geographical spaces. After the decolonization movement that followed the Second World War, radical geographers involved with the journal *Antipode* began to develop a geographical historical materialism, which reached its theoretical rigor in the late 1980s. As we shall see, to spatialize historical materialism is a necessary theoretical move.

Prior to the formulation of geographical historical materialism, there was an attempt to develop a geographical materialism. It is now out of fashion to talk about geography as nature. At the same time, it is refreshing to bring nature back into historical analysis, to remind us that global history cannot be properly understood without taking the natural environment into account. Climate, natural resources, rivers, and mountains do shape specific forms of and relations within human society. The debate, and indeed the earliest moment of synthetic encounter between historical materialism and geographical materialism, can be found in the early work of Karl A. Wittfogel, a member of the Frankfurt School.

In an important essay, "Geopolitics, Geographical Materialism and Marxism" (1985 [1929]), Wittfogel considers the central problematic for the early German geographical materialist tradition to be the relation between nature and human society. By nature, he means the environment, ecology, weather, natural resources, and topography. Bringing the issue to the framework of historical materialism, the question posed at the time was: "which factor ultimately determines historical development, the natural or the social?" (Wittfogel 1985 [1929], 54). Wittfogel's main point is that in the process of production, labor mediates between the human and the natural. The relation between human and nature is crucial for historical materialism, as the mode of production cannot be understood without it. Using the method of dialectical materialism, Wittfogel faults the geographical materialists for asking the wrong question. Choosing between the natural and the social should not be an either-or question: there is a dialectical relation between the two. Wittfogel writes: "If the totality of the powers of production determine the character of the mode of production at any given historical moment, it is the social aspects which (being the actively motivating agents) determine change, whereas the naturally conditioned agents determine whether and if change is possible and accordingly the direction of this change. *Even as man puts nature to his 'service,' he thereby submits himself to nature* (Plekhanov) *and follows her*" (ibid., 55; emphasis in original).

In his subsequent analysis, Wittfogel follows Marx in advancing the notion of an "Asiatic mode of production," which he subdivides into Egyptian, Japanese, and Indian types to demonstrate the relevance of the natural environment to historical development. The problem here is obvious. European modes of production are the referents, the ideal types, and the unconscious contrasting points against which the rest become meaningful. This epistemological framing was later named Orientalism. Operating within the limits of his time, Wittfogel subsumes geographical materialism under historical materialism, and hence the possibility of departing from Eurocentrism is closed off. The breaking away from this loyalty to historical materialism would only come with a later historical movement.

Decolonizing Spatial and Geographical Materialism

An important epistemological break from historical materialism occurred in the 1970s, when a group of scholars within radical geography proposed that "space" be substituted for "nature." In earlier forms of geographical materialism, geography had been understood as nature, but the new wave of radical geographers conceived of geography as space (which includes nature). In "Between Geographical Materialism and Spatial Fetishism: Some Observations on the Development of Marxist Spatial Analysis," Edward Soja and Costis Hadjimichalis (1985 [1977])[8] sum up the theoretical and methodological developments that have taken place within radical geography and put forward a programmatic shift: "the materialist dialectic applied to history remains incomplete without the simultaneous development of a spatial or geographical materialism as its necessary complement" (ibid., 60). This desire for completeness takes up and pushes further what has been censored by Wittfogel: the spatial is no longer only subsumed as an important element of the historical, but is now understood as one pole of the dialectic.

Inserting a spatial problematic into materialist analysis, according to Soja and Hadjimichalis, is not a struggle for power and recognition (i.e., the claim that geography is indispensable to Marxism), but the result of a growing consciousness of space expressed in various forms: the organization of urban space, the politics of regionalism, the expansion of the state into the social space, the formation of an interlocking international economic system, and the emergence of corresponding themes in critical discourses surrounding the urban political economy, such as urban social movements, the ideology of urban design, regional development, the relation between the center and the periphery within the global economy, the concentration of capital within specific locations, and national (territorial) independence movements. These discourses produced a concept of the spatial that went beyond the concept of nature in the earlier tradition of geographical materialism. From this point on, space displaced the notion of geography (defined by nature) and opened the entire field of geography to the spatial problematic.

To establish the legitimacy of such an attempt, "the spatial problem" is defined in Marxist terms: "The production of space, human geography in its fullest sense, is thus rooted in the mode of production and is shaped by the same contradictions between the forces and relations of production, between reproduction and transformation, that permeate all modes of production. Stated somewhat differently, every mode of production produces its own space, or perhaps more accurately, its own socially organized space, which becomes particularized and concrete within a given social formation" (ibid.).

Having connected spatiality to the mode of production, Soja and Hadjimichalis immediately suggest that "it is primarily the *reproduction* process, however, which lies at the center of the spatial problematic" (ibid., 61). Here they turn to the three levels of the reproduction processes identified by Henri Lefebvre (biophysiological, labor power and means of production, and social relations of production) to locate the sites of the spatial problematic. Soja and Hadjimichalis use Lefebvre's authority to push spatial analysis to the center of the capitalist formation: "the class struggle itself is seen as embedded in the structure and contradictions of socially organized space. No social revolution can therefore succeed without being at the same time a spatial revolution" (ibid.).

After Soja and Hadjimichalis establish the legitimacy of space, they argue that although the spatial problematic has been rather marginalized in Marxist thought, there indeed exist partial and disconnected discourses and practices which can be added to a coherent line of concerns that paves the way for a mature geographical-historical materialism. They point to the attempt by Russian geographers and city planners in the 1920s to achieve a "new socialist spatial organization," and to Gramsci's analysis of urban and regional problems (the Southern question), which places the ideological at the center of social formation. Lefebvre's groundbreaking books *The Production of Space* (1991 [1974]) and *The Survival of Capitalism* (1976 [1973]) were critical transitional works, linked to the earlier moment while opening the way for work such as that of Manuel Castells and David Harvey. The formation and consolidation of this tradition of radical geography, manifested in the journal *Antipode,* was then connected to the work of world-system theory of Samir Amin, Immanuel Wallerstein, and Andre Gunder Frank.

In *Postmodern Geographies: The Reassertion of Space in Critical Social Theory,* Soja tells a different story by placing Marxist geography alongside the history of critical social theory, from structuralism to postmodernism. He concludes: "Marxist geographers such as Harvey, [Neil] Smith and others cut through their former ambivalence to join together in developing a transformative historical materialism, a much more radical project than the earlier call for a spatialized urban political economy" (Soja 1989, 70). What is radicalized is in the temporal-spatial dialectic, which is much more fundamental, inclusive, and abstract than an urban political economy would allow. Whether Soja has successfully "postmodernized" Marxist geography and transcended its internal factionalism is not our concern here. But the trajectories that Soja maps out do help us to push the issue further along and to articulate the epistemic shift in the decolonization question.

On the surface, Soja's theoretical problematic gives equal weight to space and time, but in practice, the obsession with space reinscribes the priority of the geographical over the historical. Overwhelmingly concerned with the spatial question, *Postmodern Geographies* displays only a very thin historical consciousness. One can read this discursive effect as a reaction against the long-term hegemony of historical materialism, or as the author's desire to elevate his own disciplinary territory. Nevertheless, geographical-historical materialism differs from Wittfogel's defensive incorporation of the spatial into the historical in that it generates the methodological effect of decentering historical materialism. To spatialize historical materialism is not only to remove Eurocentrism, but also to launch another round of spatializing (after historicizing) epistemology. For instance, the analysis of the Asiatic mode of production can no longer take the European mode of production as the ideal model or point of comparison. It is no longer a question of explaining why a Chinese mode of production cannot develop into a real (European) capitalist mode of production. Instead, the question becomes: within the imminent historical-geographical formation, how does a geographical space historically generate its own mode of production? I would like to emphasize that I am not arguing for the abolition of comparative analysis, nor that only internal history matters. On the contrary, comparative points of reference are at the heart of the type of analysis I suggest. But we have to be careful not to make the mistake of setting up just one referent as the ultimate point against which to measure the self and others. It is only through a comparative, inter-referencing strategy that certain questions about local history can be formulated and adequately responded to. What changes took place in China as it became linked to the world economic system during the Ming and Qing Dynasties? After forty years of delinkage in the twentieth century, what forms and transformations have come into being in China's contemporary encounter with global capitalism?

Soja devotes the final two chapters of *Postmodern Geographies* to a discussion of Los Angeles, but it is important to note that spatializing does not mean a shift from Eurocentrism to American-centrism. However, without problematizing such a move, the choice of Los Angeles as a point of reference could reproduce that danger. One could also push the question further and ask why postmodern geography, as a general theoretical development, did not originate in Cambodia or Burma, or why Seoul and Hong Kong were not the reference points of the postmodern urban space. If they had been, what differences might have been produced? One has to be quite self-conscious and reflexive to ensure that geographical-historical materialism does not reproduce the singularizing tendency of historical materialism and thereby sacrifice its radical critique. More seriously, for Soja and other geographers of the post-1960 generation, the triumph of the spatial and the downplay of the natural is not only a paradigm shift, but also a potential theoretical liability. Without highlighting the critical importance of the natural, divergent cultural formations cannot be fully explained. Once global history is examined over a longer time span, natural factors have to be brought to the foreground within the explanatory framework. Weather, climate, geographical location, and so forth are all determinant of earlier forms of cultural subjectivity, and those early forms are integral to the cultural subjectivities of the present.

Toward a Geocolonial Historical Materialism

The decentering and decolonization of the problematic of space (geography) and time (history) does not mean opting for a postmodern and poststructuralist destiny of fragmentation and random flow. The two forces driving world integration are still the international system of the nation-state and the globalization of capital. We have already seen how globalization emerged out of colonial imperialism. In its five centuries of operation, colonialism has fundamentally transformed and linked together relatively unconnected geographical spaces. To fully understand the cultural formation of any specific geographical space, one has to be able to grasp the interarticulation of local history and the history of colonialism.

Colonialism has transfigured the inner structure of the cultural imaginary in both the colony and the imperial center. To consider the colonial question on the same level as historical materialism and geographical-historical materialism is (1) to politicize the epistemological grounding of historical materialism, so that colonization is necessarily placed at the center of analysis; (2) to remove the hidden Eurocentric elements, so that a more balanced account of the formation of different regional spaces of the world can surface; and (3) to emphasize the relative autonomy of local history and to insist on grasping analytically the specificities of the historical and the geographical. In centering the colonial question, however, one should guard against the reverse essentialist tendency: acting as if only the history of colonialism matters. To put it simply, the contemporary shape and the structure of the cultural imaginary in a specific space and time both result from the dialectic articulation of the colonial, the historical, and the geographical.

According to Blaut's (1993) highly persuasive argument, prior to 1492, Europe, Africa, and Asia were more or less equally developed, and there was no indication that Europe would take the lead in capital formation. In the early sixteenth century, however, Europe gradually emerged as the epicenter of capitalism, which then shifted to North America in the late nineteenth and early twentieth centuries. Europe's relative proximity to North America made it easier for European powers to "discover" and occupy the "new world." This acquisition sped up the process of capital accumulation and gave Europe a stronger material basis for acquiring the resources it needed to expand, giving it an advantage over other world regions. The 1688 Glorious Revolution in England symbolically announced the rise of the bourgeoisie and the defeat of the feudal landlord class; the move toward commercial capitalism had begun. The Industrial Revolution of the eighteenth century marked the next advance. By transforming the means and relations of production and accelerating capital accumulation, it propelled the world to the high point of colonial imperialism. Blaut's analysis concludes: "Capitalism arose as a world-scale process: as a world system. Capitalism became concentrated in Europe because colonialism gave Europeans the power both to develop their own society and to prevent development from occurring elsewhere. It is this dynamic of development and underdevelopment which mainly explains the modern world" (Blaut 1993, 206). Blaut's political, economic, and geographical analysis is set against the myth of Eurocentric diffusionism. The visionary scope of his analysis brings out a much clearer picture of the earliest historical trajectories of colonialism, and their power to shape global culture.

The theoretical implications of Blaut's analysis defeat the universalist claim on world history. If before 1492 the world was composed of world regions that interacted with each other but maintained a high degree of relative autonomy, and each region had its own inner logics in the domains of politics, economics, society, and culture, then no single analytical framework could possibly grasp the diversity of world history without falling into reductionism. To use the relations and mode of production to analyze the transformation of all the world's regions in an attempt to arrive at a single explanatory view of world history is an exercise in pure fantasy. To understand the world prior to the existence of nation-states and colonialism, one has to return to the original conditions of each region. This understanding recognizes that after 1492, interactions and mutual influences among the world regions began to speed up, partly mediated through European colonialism's forcing of different regions of the world to connect and integrate. But the basis of interaction among the regions was the organic condition formed in each region before 1492. Even though European imperialism exported its institutions to its colonies, it could not fully impose its will and had to adjust to preexisting conditions. This explains why, although the world today is much more extensively integrated than it was before 1492, the globe remains heterogeneous.[9]

Harry Magdoff's classic study, *Imperialism: From the Colonial Age to the Present* (1978), offers some relevant statistics. From the start of the Industrial Revolution to 1800, European colonialism effectively occupied 35 percent of the earth's surface. The number had jumped to 67 percent by 1878; it reached 85 percent in 1914, the high point of imperialist expansion and a time of unprecedented amalgamating of different regions into one world (Magdoff 1978, 29, 36). Historians have still not persuasively explained the quick demise of colonial empires in the decade following the Second World War. How can we explain the sudden collapse of this five-century effort? One way to come to terms with the question is to argue that unless one accepts an empiricist, positivistic, or formalist understanding of the world, imperialism in fact has not collapsed; rather, the direct territorial mode of control has given way to direct or indirect political and economic maneuvering. This is precisely what Fanon described as "neocolonialism" (Fanon 1968 [1961], 152). As Miyoshi (1993) and Said (1993), among others, have argued, colonial imperialism is still actively exercising its power. Even nations such as Thailand, which has never been territorially colonized, or Finland, which has never been a colonizing power, cannot escape the global forces of colonialism. To understand contemporary social formation, colonialism is thus an indispensable site of analysis.

The actual exercise of colonialism is always mediated through the cultural imaginary, which is reason enough to establish its importance as a site of investigation, but the cultural imaginary also has two important methodological implications. First, historical materialism and geographical-historical materialism have concentrated on the level of the mode and relations of production, and therefore the cultural imaginary enters the picture as part of the material condition. In the previous chapter and the next two chapters, we found and will continue to find that the cultural imaginary is really the mediating category linking structure and agency. Without the analytical category of cultural imaginary, the specificity of the international relations of production between the colony and the imperial center cannot be adequately addressed. To bring the notion of cultural imaginary to the center of geocolonial historical materialism is to produce a dialectic between political economy and cultural studies. Second, in East Asian scholarship, the domain of the cultural imaginary is a strategic but underexplored area. Unlike other world regions, where the physical distance between the imperial powers and the former colonies is relatively great, in East Asia, contemporary international politics is conspicuously mixed with colonial history; it is a region where the old colonial power, Japan, and the postcolonial power, the United States, remain a visible part of daily life. As we will see in the next chapter, the cold war mediates the continuity between the colonial and postcolonial history of East Asia, and it is in the space of the cultural imaginary that the resulting unresolved issues are contested. Because issues within this site actively prevent various levels of regionwide reconciliation from taking place, the cultural imaginary is where the political intervention of cultural studies in East Asia can make a difference.

On one level, geocolonial historical materialism can be seen as a shifting site of analysis that was first developed in Said's *Culture and Imperialism* (1993). In his chapter on "Empire, Geography and Culture," Said points out that his analysis attempts to address how imperialism generates a whole set of "cultural forms and structures of feeling" (Said 1993, 10). What he calls cultural forms and structures of feeling are the spaces that comprise what we call the cultural imaginary. The cultural imaginary is, once again, a result of the encounter between colonialism and local historical and cultural resources. Through discursive articulation, the cultural imaginary is disseminated to different social fields, shaping the imaginations of both colonizing and colonized subjects. Operating on the terrain of the popular, the cultural imaginary structures the system of ideology, links to the concrete experiences of daily life, and forms the direction and boundary of the psychological space. Its discursivity saturates popular subjects, official discourse, and anticolonial discourse. Academic analysis appears to be more neutral, but its problematic is always the result of the cultural imaginary. For instance, "East" and "West" are colonial categories but have also become dominant frames of academic discourse. In this sense, the notion of the cultural imaginary intersects with the Althusserian concept of ideology, in that it too is an unconscious system of representation. The difference is that the Althusserian attempt is a general theory establishing the relation between the subject and its living world, whereas the cultural imaginary refers to an operating space within a social formation, in which the imaginary perception of the Other and self-understanding are articulated. In this domain, the structure of sentiment is the link and mediator between the colonizer and the colonized. It is through the domain of the cultural imaginary that the psychoanalytic tradition of decolonization opened up by Fanon becomes a constitutive part of geocolonial historical materialism.

The Meanings of Decolonization

This chapter has attempted to reposition cultural studies as an integral part of the counterhegemonic decolonization movement. The cultural imaginary is the site targeted for the work of a geocolonial historical materialism. After decentering both history and geography, we bring the colonial question to the analytical framework. The chapter has implied a cultural politics that analytically moves beyond nationalist epistemology, using geographic space to displace the nation-state as the unit of analysis. The study of colonialism and imperialism is not simply a return to history in order to deconstruct the colonial cultural imaginary and colonial identification, but, operating with the principle of a critical syncretism, it is an active intervention against the triumphalist sentiment of the imperialist desire.

I hope it has become clear that decolonization operates on different levels of the social formation and has different meanings. If decolonization, at this historical conjuncture, no longer simply means the struggle for national independence but a struggle against any form of colonization, then we have to recognize both that neocolonialism, neoimperialism, and globalization are structural continuations and extensions of colonialism; and that colonialism is not yet a legacy but is still active in geocolonial sites on the levels of identification and cultural imaginary, and it continually reconfigures itself amid changing historical processes to reshape the colonial cultural imaginary. To further the progress of decolonization, the task of cultural studies is to deconstruct, decenter, and disarticulate the colonial cultural imaginary, and to reconstruct and rearticulate new imaginations and discover a more democratic future direction. In imagining a new line of flight, one possibility is to leave behind the obsession with colonial bondage and seriously practice a critical syncretism—that is, to multiply and shift the existing sites and objects of identification. In order to multiply the reference points, the analysis in the next two chapters will more self-consciously bring in historical experiences from different parts of East Asia.

Decolonization no longer refers only to the objective structure of the historical movement, but also to action, subjectivity, thought, cultural forms of expression, social institutions, and global political-economic structures. The argument presented here is not an attempt to define the mission of cultural studies simply as decolonization. But to decolonize the colonial cultural imaginary so as to free colonizing and colonized subjects from the limits imposed by colonial history is an important task for a politically committed cultural studies. As practitioners of cultural studies, we are the articulating agents and linking points of decolonization; our research and discursive practices can become critical forces pushing the incomplete project of decolonization forward. At the very least, we must strive to decolonize ourselves.

CHAPTER 3

DE–COLD WAR
The Im/possibility of "Great Reconciliation"

In the 50s, anticommunist cleansing radically eradicated intellectual thought and knowledge on anti-imperialist national liberation. For a long time, in Taiwan, anyone who criticized the U.S. would be labeled a "communist spy," which would destroy one's life and family. Unlike other progressive intellectuals in the Third World, those in Taiwan lost the knowledge, ideas, and ability to criticize the hegemony of U.S. neo-colonialism. Under the Cold War structure in East Asia, the anticommunist security regime deeply penetrated the social body and educational institutions. In the minds of young intellectuals, the image of America as a powerful, civilized, developed, and wealthy country was solidly established. Until today, "the best will study in the U.S." has become the highest value for young students in Taiwan.

CHEN YING-ZHEN, "THE MAKING OF TAIWAN'S AMERICANIZATION"

De–Cold War, or Modernity and Its Tears

Since the early 1990s, I have visited Seoul every so often, and I feel that the more I go to Seoul, the better I understand Taipei. For me, South Korea has become an important reference as I think about the political history of Taiwan. My understanding of South Korea comes less from books than from conversations with friends and from physical impressions and subjective involvements.

In August 2000, while doing research in Seoul, I was surrounded by the emotional scenes of family reunions between North and South Koreans that were being broadcast at the time. Although it was obvious that the South Korean state was staging the televised reunions for political purposes, the tears and sorrow were overpoweringly real, overshadowing or even transcending the symbolic power of the state: the scenes cut into the affective space of the collective social. As an outsider who could not understand Korean, I had to rely on *The Korea Herald*, an English daily newspaper published in Seoul, to get a sense of what was happening. Despite the language barrier, I could not help feeling deeply moved. Here are some excerpts from that newspaper:

> "Mother, you are still alive to see me," shouted Li Jong-pil, 69, when his 99-year-old mother, suffering from Alzheimer's disease, appeared to recognize him. But she then spoke incoherently: "Where do you live? In Seoul? How old are you?" Li's brothers and sisters wept continuously. (Chon 2000)

> Choi Tae-hyon, 70, gave a golden ring to his 72-year-old wife in the North when the outpouring of emotions died down. "My wife in the South bought a couple of gold rings, one for me and the other for my wife in the North," Choi said. "I feel very sorry for the suffering my wife in the North underwent, and I thank my wife in the South for embracing my heart," he said. (ibid.)

> Kim Dong-man was at a loss for words when he saw his brother from the North for the first time since the outbreak of the Korean War 50 years ago. It took a moment before the two could recover from their emotion. "How are you, brother?" said Kim Dong-man, 68, breaking the silence as his 74-year-old brother, Kim Dong-jin, held back tears. "Mother left these things with me to give you," he added, presenting a necklace, ring and bracelet left by their deceased mother as gifts before she died in 1992. Kim Dong-jin broke into tears, screaming "Mother, mother!" "She told me to bury her on a hillside looking toward the North so that she could see you again," said Kim Dong-man, adding that he had built a mock tomb for his brother alongside their mother's resting place. (Joint Press Corps 2000)

In these situations, when critical analysis becomes superfluous, tears seem to be the only language capable of communicating the unspeakable, and gifts the only objects that might somehow represent the unrepresentable. It is like the opening of a floodgate: at the moment of reunion, all that suffering and pain, historically condensed and compressed, is suddenly released. It comes with such speed and force that it is impossible for those involved to slow down enough to tell all the sad stories that have happened since the separation—all the flashing images of the suffered events are conflated and entangled in the mind so that one is rendered speechless.

Flooded by tearful scenes during those three days—15–18 August 2000—of organized family reunions, the whole of Seoul was, in the words of the feminist anthropologist Kim Seongnae (2000), turned into a space of "mourning Korean modernity." The resurfacing of this overwhelming sentiment was all too familiar to me; it echoed the situation in Taiwan in the late 1980s and early 1990s, when one-way visits to mainland China were officially made possible. Loaded with gifts and longing for home, groups of travelers passed through the old Hong Kong airport, eager to reunite with their relatives. In the early 1990s, after my mother died, my father, escorted by my older brother, was one of these travelers. He came home to Taipei silent, not even mentioning the living conditions of his children there. He never went again, dying in 1995.

I did not go to the mainland, the formerly prohibited zone, until the summer of 1997. Since the late 1980s, a group of us in Taiwan had taken what we called a "popular democratic" stand in an attempt to move beyond the rigid binary structure that demanded a choice between unification with mainland China and independence from it. Before that time, declaring oneself to be on the Left was simply not a viable position, as it would have immediately caused one to be linked to the CCP. If one of us had actually gone to mainland China, that would have been read as an even stronger expression of political identification.[1]

My trip in 1997 was officially organized by the editorial collective of *Taiwan: A Radical Quarterly in Social Studies*, in order for the journal's board members to begin to acquire a feel for mainland China and to search for counterparts and possible allies there.[2] Unexpectedly, it also turned out to be a personal mission for me. I decided to pay a visit to Beijing, the city where my mother had gone to college. I had picked up a bit of a Beijing accent from her, and I felt that I could quickly tune into that linguistic environment. Although my foreign clothes made me conspicuous,[3] I could almost pass as a local, and I was not treated as an outsider.

Having spent a difficult life bringing up three sons, my mother had had a breakdown after her children left home. She was diagnosed with schizophrenia, and indeed she had created an imaginary world to liberate herself from the sad life she had led. For each meal, she insisted on setting our dining table with a full bowl of rice and a pair of chopsticks for the invisible "Father Chiang" (Chiang Kai-shek). She swore she would never go back to her homeland while it was "occupied" by the Communists. I am still uncertain whether her hardcore anticommunism was rooted in her work as a student activist in the KMT, which at the time conducted patriotic activities against the Japanese invaders of China, or from the simple fact that she taught Chinese cultural history. When she got sick, she scolded the Communists for their savage inhumanity, while at the same time blaming Lee Teng-hui, Taiwan's president, for his pro-Japanese, pro-separatist line. After her condition worsened, she was moved in and out of the hospital several times and occasionally had to be strapped down, depriving her of her basic dignity as Professor Chen. In 1991, she died in a nursing home from a sudden heart attack. I was very close to her in the latter part of her life, and as I retraced her footsteps during my trip in 1997, I missed her very much. The convoluted images conjured up by my memories of her were mixed up with the official purpose of the visit.

In the case of North and South Korea, as well as that of Taiwan and mainland China, the historical experiences of nation and family clearly intersect. For subjects encountering these experiences, the emotional plane of affective desire seems to be the most prominent, overshadowing all other aspects of the reunions. Nor does it matter if the bodily experience (*tǐyàn*) of the event is real or imaginary. These moments of intensity are an ineradicable part of subject formation.

Can we say, then, that instances like these reunions and returns are evidence that the cold war is finally behind us in East Asia? Widespread claims to the contrary, I argue that this is not yet the post-cold-war era. The effects of the cold war have become embedded in local history, and simply pronouncing the war to be over will not cause them to dissolve. The complex effects of the war, mediated through our bodies, have been inscribed into our national, family, and personal histories. In short, the cold war is still alive within us.

The end of the cold war was repeatedly announced during the late 1980s. There can be no doubt of the reality of changes in Europe and America at the time. The Soviet Union crumbled, Germany was unified, and Eastern Europe had once more drawn safely to the bosom of the capitalist West. Ideologically, the triumph of capitalism and the end of socialism has become the dominant narrative in the West, and it is now confidently included in the ongoing saga of globalization, which since the second half of the 1990s has offered a framework for a new structure of sentiment, rallying North American academics who had previously toyed with ideas of the postmodern or postcolonial, and comforting European intellectuals bent on nostrums of a so-called third way (in this sense, one has to insist that the ideological precondition for globalization is the announcement of the end of the cold war).

In East Asia, the situation has been very different. Cold-war structures in East Asia have been weakened, but by no means dismantled. Chinese Communism has not been overthrown, and Indochina has not gone the way of Eastern Europe. Korea remains divided, and Taiwan a garrison state. There is still no peace treaty between Japan and Russia. Of course, Sino-American relations are relatively stable, the two Kims leading North and South Korea have met, and the KMT was defeated in a democratic election in Taiwan. But the very excitement generated by the 2000 summit in Pyongyang and the jubilation at the downfall of the KMT regime in Taiwan speak to the extent to which the dead weight of the cold war is still a source of tension and frustration in East Asia.

As happened during the tensest moments of the cold war, the U.S. military continues to operate in Japan, Okinawa, and South Korea. As allies of the United States, the Japanese, South Korean, and Taiwanese states are still spending huge amounts of money on American weaponry. These are undeniable markers of the continuation and extension of the cold war. Chalmers Johnson argues in his well-documented book, *Blowback: The Costs and Consequences of American Empire* (2000), that even after the so-called end of the cold war, the United States has continued to rely on the same basic military strategy that it has deployed for the previous forty years. He warns that if the United States does not demobilize its empire, it will become an enemy to the rest of the world.

Just as the formal end of colonialism did not lead overnight to a dissolution of its cultural effects, so the subjectivities formed during the cold war remain within us. Our worldview, political and institutional forms, and systems of popular knowledge have been deeply shaped by the cold-war structure. During the past fifty years, issues surrounding the flows of people and knowledge have become so divisive that their accumulated historical effects demand careful analysis. But this work has not been taken up in East Asia.[4] To cite some examples: before the 1990s, a great number (close to 90 percent) of postwar South Korean and Taiwanese intellectuals were trained in the United States,[5] and these people, deeply imbued with an American outlook, are now in power in their countries, where they are implementing another round of modernization. Knowledge production in the region has been heavily influenced by the U.S. academy ever since the end of the Second World War. One would expect that China's relations with the United States would be less intimate than they are with the rest of East Asia. But starting in the 1980s, there was an overwhelming turn to America by intellectuals in mainland China; since the late 1990s, China has had more citizens studying on U.S. campuses than any other country.[6]

With the cold-war structure loosening up, the moment has arrived to undertake the critical work of confronting the ongoing problematic of the cold war; to put it simply, it is time to "de–cold war." To de–cold war at this point in history does not mean to simply rid ourselves of a cold-war consciousness or to try to forget that period in history and naively look toward the future (the approach most state leaders and other politicians have called for). It means to mark out a space in which unspoken stories and histories may be told, and to recognize and map the historically constituted cultural and political effects of the cold war.

To de–cold war in East Asia, it will be necessary to reverse the trend of leaving Asia for America, which has been the dominant tendency during the postwar era. Now, the trend must become leaving America for Asia. At this historically critical time, to de–cold war is to de-Americanize. This means to examine the consequences of the United States' role as a central component in the formation of East Asian subjectivity. Whether de-Americanization can really unfold depends on the extent to which regional integration, autonomy, and peace have really been achieved. The particular topic of the current conditions of knowledge production, which is also a part of this process, will be taken up in a more focused way in the final chapter.

On various levels of abstraction, to de–cold war is a task parallel to and connected with the historical project of third-world decolonization. These two historical trajectories have intersected, but what is the relationship between the two? The obvious link is that, like colonialism, the cold war contributed to U.S. global hegemony. Beyond this simple fact, I shall argue that decolonization movements on all fronts, since the end of the Second World War, have been intercepted, interrupted, and invaded by the cold-war structure. The far-reaching psychic and cultural effects of colonialism have not been properly and thoroughly addressed, and a full-fledged reflexive politics has been suppressed by the formations of the cold war. The war divided Asia into capitalist and socialist blocs, and as a result, capitalist East Asia was pressured to avoid conflict within the anticommunist camp. Historical issues of Japanese colonialism in Taiwan and Korea could not be tackled because the Japanese, South Korean, and Taiwanese states were locked into the pro-American side; to address such historical issues would have entailed confronting internal contradictions within the capitalist bloc.

In earlier East Asian regionalisms, including Sun Yat-sen's pan-Asianism and Japan's Greater East Asia Co-Prosperity Sphere, national differences were the politically dominant frames and the bases for strategic alliances, while Western imperialism was positioned as the invader and the racial Other. For instance, according to the fine analysis done by Luo Zhi-tian, there was a general sentiment among Chinese intellectuals in the 1930s that they should prepare for the death of the country (*wáng-guó*). Modernist nationalists such as Hu Shih shared a global view, anticipating that a future world conflict would be between "the yellow and the white," and that a "total war" was inevitable. Hu Shih went even further, suggesting that "Japan should not conquer China by military forces, but by winning the heart of the Chinese people" (quoted in Luo Zhi-tian 1998, 207). He argued that, because China was so weak, Japan should take the responsibility to lead the preparations for a total war.[7]

Further complicating the de–cold war process is the discursive tradition of Japanese exceptionalism. Like the United States, Japan was a relative newcomer to the colonial enterprise, but it was also a non-Western imperialist power.[8] The Japanese occupation (in East Asia, "occupation" is used more often than "colonization" in connection with Japan) of Taiwan, Korea, Manchuria, and other territories in Southeast Asia before and during the Second World War has made the story of imperialist conquest more complex—and the ambivalence longer lasting—because the racial aspect of colonialism did not quite apply. In fact, the slogan "same script, same race" (*tóngwén, tóngzhŏng*) was used as a strategy to unite Japan with the neighboring countries it colonized. Because of this added layer of complexity, the discussion of a number of critical issues has been fore-closed in this case. For instance, to prove that they were not just different from Western colonial powers, but could be better than them, Japanese colonialists mobilized talented people and enormous resources to launch large-scale developmentalist experiments of various kinds. After just ten years of Japanese occupation, Taiwan became financially self-sufficient and began to ship products and natural resources to mainland Japan. As part of Japan's southward-advance strategy, the industrial infrastructures in Taiwan, Korea, and Manchuria were put in place, a policy that went far beyond what most Western colonizers had done for their colonies. One of the effects of this deployment of Japanese resources was the accelerated industrialization that took place in these former colonies after the Second World War. If we rid ourselves of our nationalist baggage, we clearly see that colonial history can help explain how Taiwan and South Korea so quickly achieved newly industrialized country (NIC) status, and why the northeast is still the most advanced industrial area of China. However, once a simplistic anti-Japanese moral stance is taken, potentially useful avenues of discussion such as this are quickly closed off.

Like the question of Japanese exceptionalism, the Greater East Asia Co-Prosperity Sphere is an issue that has also prevented intellectuals from working through crucial cold-war concerns. As an ideal, it mobilized Japanese intellectuals who opposed Western imperialism; at the same time, it produced a split in the intellectual circles of the Japanese-occupied zones in Asia. Once the concept was actually deployed by the Japanese military, any discussion of Asian unity was essentially ended. The major consequence is that whenever an alliance in the region is proposed, there are objections that it would be a reproduction of the Greater East Asia Co-Prosperity Sphere, a charge that has effectively undermined numerous attempts at promoting regional solidarity.

The replacement of the worldwide colonial system of power with the cold-war structure has prohibited the colonizing powers and the formerly colonized from undertaking critical reflection, and this has led to the re-production of the problems of colonialism. In the first chapter, I discussed how the Japanese expansionist southward-advance discourse of the 1930s became the foundation for the Taiwanese southward-advance movement of the 1990s. Similarly, the rhetorical tropes used to justify the Greater East Asia Co-Prosperity Sphere of the 1930s are the same as those used in the contemporary Asian-values debate in the late 1980s: anti-West, anti-individualism, anticommunism, and Confucianism.[9]

The leading Korean activist and political sociologist Cho Hee-yeon (2000a) succinctly describes the characteristics of the South Korean political regime after the Second World War as authoritarian, developmentalist, statist, and anticommunist—one could add that it was pro-American. These terms also accurately characterize the Taiwanese state of today, although authoritarianism and anticommunism are now in decline. In order to secure state power and to further nationalist modernizing projects, the right-wing regimes in Japan, Korea, and Taiwan pledged their allegiance to the democratic camp and formed close alliances with the United States to combat the evil communist enemies. This calling up of anticommunist fear has meant that it is prohibited to ask questions about U.S. imperialism and made it more difficult to address the problematic consequences of the nationalist modernizing project's identification with the United States.[10] The economic modernization project has used anticommunism to justify both statist authoritarianism (for efficiency) and developmentalism (for economic growth). These characteristics are the result of the intersection of the third-world nationalist struggle for power, postcolonial imperialism, and the cold war. Within this triangular relationship, nationalism has played a critical mediating role in that it allows for the projection of an imaginary enemy, which in turn is used by the state to justify its suppression of the internal drive and desire for democracy.

To urge that the de-cold-war process be a priority on the intellectual agenda is to insist on the continuity of the process with the work of decolonization. The purpose of this chapter is to establish the historical links between the two through concrete analysis. I hope to show that they are two aspects of the same historical project, and to indicate the type of transformative work that has to take place if we are to move out of the shadow of colonialist and cold-war structures.

Historical structural conditions have a direct bearing on living subjects and groups. Kim Seongnae's "Mourning Korean Modernity in the Cheju April Third Incident" (2000) analyzes the relationship between South Korean state violence and the rhetoric of anticommunism during the 1948 Cheju Uprising (which bears striking similarities to both the 228 Incident and the White Terror in Taiwan). Her ethnographic work documents the painful suffering of the survivors and the victims' families. Inspired by her analysis, I want to concentrate on two Taiwanese films to demonstrate how the structural effects of the cold war not only shape national spaces but also work on the body, consciousness, and desire of ordinary people. Much like the Korean family reunions cited above, the tensions that give rise to emotional encounters is the focus of analysis. These two films, *Dou-sang: A Borrowed Life* (1994) and *Banana Paradise* (1989), are strategic sites chosen to illustrate how in contemporary Taiwan the entanglements of colonialism and the cold war have produced different "emotional structures of sentiment,"[11] which have become the affective material basis of ongoing ethnic conflicts.

These two films cover roughly the same period in postwar Taiwan, from the late 1940s to the late 1980s and early 1990s, and focus on two subject positions: Dou-sang, a Minnanese (see below) member of the working class, who was predominantly shaped by colonial history; and Menxuan and Desheng, lower-class wàishěng rén molded mainly by the cold war. I wish to show that, because living subjects inhabit different historical structures, these two axes, colonialism and the cold war, have produced different affective experiences, which have in turn constituted different identities and subjectivities. This split explains the impossibility of constructing a shared imagined community, and therefore the great difficulty faced by advocates of a great reconciliation between běnshěng rén and wàishěng rén, and between Taiwan and Mainland China.[12] It is the divergence of these emotional structures of sentiment that we need to bring into our analysis, so that the projects of decolonization and de–cold war can converge and the transformative work can begin.

A word is in order here to clarify that—unlike gender, sexuality, class, race, and ethnicity—běnshěng and wàishěng are not analytical but living concepts, politically constructed in the concrete historical processes of everyday life. The years 1945–49 are a dividing line: those who came to Taiwan from China before then are called běnshěng rén (which literally means "people who come from the province" of Taiwan), and those who came after are labeled wàishěng rén (literally, "people who come from outside the province" of Taiwan). Within the category of běnshěng rén, Minnanese (who speak the language of southern Fujian province) are the largest population; Hakkanese and aboriginal people do not necessarily identity themselves as běnshěng rén.[13] These simple classifications cannot account for the entire range of identities of those who have lived in Taiwan. For instance, there is no common language or customs among the wàishěng population,[14] and the term "wàishěng rén" is meaningful only in relation to the term "běnshěng rén." Similarly, there is much diversity among běnshěng rén. Some came to Taiwan much earlier than others; there is no unified language; and the extent of their relationship with mainland China also varies. The analytic construction of these categories is not my purpose here. Throughout the chapter, rather than using the categories as they are typically rendered in English — Mainlander and Taiwanese — I have opted to use the local terms. Likewise, instead of "ethnic conflict," the local term "provincial register contradiction" (shěngjí máodùn)[15] is preserved to connote the central clash between běnshěng rén and wàishěng rén.

I will now analyze each film so as to bring out the differences in the emotional structures of sentiment of běnshěng rén and wàishěng rén. The discussion then moves on to explain why reconciliation between the two groups is impossible at present, and to sketch the conditions that are necessary to make it possible. The concluding section argues that the problems of colonialism and the cold war cannot really be overcome within the framework of a single nation-state, which is limited by the narcissistic logic of nationalist self-centrism. In order to push the projects of de–cold war and decolonization forward, a necessary step will be to compare or relate historical experiences throughout third-world Asia.

Dou-sang, or the Logic of Hierarchy: Japan › Taiwan › Mainland China

Dou-sang (the English translation adds a subtitle: "A Borrowed Life") was written and directed by the well-known Minnanese scriptwriter and novelist Wu Nian-chen (whose name sometimes appears as Nien-Jen Wu). Released in 1994, it was the first film to address the effects of colonialism in Taiwan after the Second World War. Dou-sang is a Taiwanese term for father that comes from the Japanese otosan. The narrator of the film, Wenjian, uses it to refer to his father, the film's protagonist. Lian Qingke is Dou-sang's Chinese name, but friends and neighbors of his own generation more often use Seiga, his Japanese name. He was born in 1929, thirty-four years after Taiwan became a Japanese colony, and he received a Japanese education. The film begins in the late 1940s, right after the end of the Second World War. Dou-sang supports his wife and three children with the meager salary he earns working in a gold mine. When the mine closes down, his wife supports the family by doing construction work, while Dou-sang plays mahjong to kill time, and his sorrow. Five years later, Wenjian goes to the city to work and study, and Dou-sang takes a job as a coal miner. Dou-sang becomes the head of the village—not, according to Wenjian, because of his leadership skills, but because so many of the villagers have moved away to look for jobs. In 1984, at the age of fifty-five, Dou-sang begins to suffer from illnesses brought on by his work in the mines. He retires two years later, receiving a modest pension. He gives the little money he receives to his younger son, Wenjian's brother, to start a small business. At the age of sixty, Dou-sang is hospitalized and needs constant oxygen treatment to survive. One year later, in 1990, on a windy evening with the rain pouring down, he is put in an intensive-care unit to wait for the final moment to arrive. Dou-sang takes his own life by jumping out of the hospital window.

Despite the simple story line, *Dou-sang* is a rather complex film. The linear development of the film parallels the historical changes in postwar Taiwan: the KMT took over state power from Japan, rural community life was changed by economic development and urbanization, and rural working-class populations lost control over their own lives. Beyond the dominant dynamic of the father-son relationship, two central lines of tension are presented in the film. First, there is an intergenerational conflict between Dou-sang and his children: in contrast to Dou-sang's Japanese-ness, the children's patriotism has been shaped by the KMT state's nationalist education policies. Second, Dou-sang struggles to defend his masculine dignity as the head of the family. As a man who married into his wife's family, normally something done only by men from very poor families, Dou-sang does not have enough social capital to perform the expected patriarchal role. Wenjian, the first son, had to adopt the mother's family name, Chiang, as was often the case in such marriages. Dou-sang's style of masculinity is a form of self-defense, a way for him to try to maintain some dignity. Even when he is finally hospitalized and can barely stand, he refuses to urinate in the bed. "A man," he says, "has to stand up to pee." He also refuses to let his grandson visit him because he does not want his pain to be seen; he does not want to lose his dignity as a grandfather.

The languages spoken by the different characters in the family also serve to crystallize large-scale social changes. Dou-sang uses mainly

Minnanese and Japanese, though he picks up a little Mandarin late in his life. The eldest son, Wenjian, speaks Minnanese with his father but narrates his story in Mandarin, and Dou-sang's daughter argues with him in Minnanese and Mandarin. The grandson, Wenjian's child, is educated completely in Mandarin and can neither speak nor understand Minnanese. In three generations, the daily mixing of Japanese and Minnanese gives way to the mixing of Minnanese and Mandarin, and then to the exclusive use of the official Mandarin. By the 1980s, after thirty years of official Mandarin education, a younger, urban generation of the Minnanese population, including people like Dou-sang's grandson, can no longer speak the native language of their country. The language shifts that accompany the change of political regime are a source of intergenerational conflict and miscommunication. Even worse, just as in the colonial era, when languages other than Japanese were prohibited, Mandarin is the only legitimate national language (*guóyǔ*). Schoolchildren were punished if they spoke other languages, and people of all ages could advance economically if they mastered Mandarin. The hierarchy of languages that emerged therefore has clear class implications as well.

Having lived his formative years in the colonial era, Dou-sang uses Japanese and takes Japan as a reference point in his daily life, just as his children, who are forced to use Mandarin, necessarily adopt the Republic of China as their point of reference. When a language enters a society and becomes a popular referent like this, it also becomes internal to the formation of cultural subjectivity. In Taiwan, these multiple referents have become codified into a highly hierarchical system that has become the primary way of understanding the self. Reasoning like "Japan also has this..." or "America also has that..." to justify one's own positions is widespread.[16] Today, the imaginary America has become the dominant system of reference in Taiwanese society, very much as the imaginary Japan was throughout the prewar period. That China became a basic point of reference during the period covered by the movie was the work of the KMT, which selectively created an imaginary China that fit its own anticommunist and Chinese nationalist agenda. In the era of Mandarin dominance, Dou-sang's generation is deprived of using Japanese and has become a silent generation. Not only the working class suffered: intellectuals who were trained during the Japanese occupation and could not quickly learn Mandarin have become, to use the critic Zheng Hong-sheng's (2002, 109) expression, a "generation of no language," and hence, no power. Could a great reconciliation really rehabilitate this entire generation?

References to Japan occur throughout the film. Dou-sang listens to Japanese-language radio broadcasts, watches Japanese movies, likes to sing with his mine "brothers" at Japanese-style bars, prefers Japanese female bodies (to the Western ones displayed in *Playboy*), swears in Japanese, and dreams of going to Japan to see the Imperial Palace in Tokyo and Mount Fuji. In one scene, the tension between his worldview and the emerging one explodes. After Dou-sang sends Wenjian to buy some noodles from the neighborhood grocery store, Dou-sang's daughter asks for help with her homework. She needs to draw the national flag. When Wenjian comes home, he witnesses the fight.

The daughter complains to Wenjian: "You see, Dou-sang paints the national flag in such an awful way. How can I hand this [the drawing shows a twelve-pointed white star on a red background] in?" Dou-sang tries to explain: "I'm helping you out. How can you complain? If the sun isn't red, what color can it be? Only the devil would see the sun as white." The daughter replies: "Lu Hau-tung painted it white, originally."[17]

Dou-sang starts to get angry: "He's illiterate, and are you as stupid as he is? You are really stupid. Look closely at the color of the sun on the Japanese flag. Is it white? Nonsense." The daughter cannot accept his response and yells in Mandarin: "For you, everything is Japanese! Are you Wang Jingwei?"[18] Dou-sang, unable to understand Mandarin or what Wang Jingwei means, gets angrier: "Don't think that I don't understand *Bagin Huei* [Minnanese for Mandarin, literally "Beijingese"]."

Noticing that Dou-sang cannot understand her, the daughter speaks in Mandarin again, this time yelling in a high-pitched voice: "You are a Han traitor, a running dog. You are a Wang Jingwei!" Dou-sang turns to Wenjian for help and scolds the daughter in stronger terms: "What is she saying now? *Bakayarou* [a rude Japanese term for "idiot"]!"

Wenjian tries to cool things down by saying to Dou-sang in Minnanese, "Nothing." But Dou-sang utters the dirty word again — "Bakayarou!" — and leaves the scene.

For the daughter, molded by her nationalist education, it is probably irrelevant whether the sun is red or white; red just doesn't correspond with her knowledge of the national flag. For Dou-sang, however, it is common sense for the sun to be red, just like it is on the Japanese flag. To support her argument, the daughter brings up the flag's original designer, Lu Hau-tung. To maintain his authority, Dou-sang belittles Lu as stupid and illiterate. His daughter feels these charges are unjust. The disagreement escalates. The daughter is scolded for being stupid, but what really angers her is Dou-sang's invocation of the Japanese flag as an assumed referent, which is antithetical to the anti-Japanese education she has received from the state, whose negative feelings toward the Japanese are overwhelming. Without any sense of Dou-sang's historical experience — that things Japanese have been firmly established as fundamental orienting points in his life — her comment "For you, everything is Japanese!" becomes a nationalist as well as a personal attack.

In this context, it is not accidental that she instinctively switches to Mandarin and charges her father with being a traitor by citing Wang Jingwei, the archetypal turncoat she most likely learned about from the nationalist historiography in her elementary-school textbook. She has to issue the attack in Mandarin, largely because it is the language of the system of resources she draws upon to see the world, and also because it is probably difficult for her to revert to Minnanese at such an emotional moment. Also, she may not really want to hurt her father directly. Whatever the reasons, her sudden resorting to the outsider's language further upsets Dou-sang. Knowing that her father cannot understand her, the daughter utters the insult again. Not understanding, but sensing that his daughter is saying something quite nasty, Dou-sang becomes furious and turns to his son for help. Wenjian then tries to mediate; he knows if he translates accurately, the situation will really explode, so he only says, "Nothing." The intense episode ends with Dou-sang cursing in Japanese.

It would be too simplistic to reduce this intergenerational encounter to a case of competing nation-state identifications. The hybridity of the languages used already indicates the complexity of the situation. For Dou-sang, the red sun on the Japanese national flag is unquestionably the authoritative reference point. Although it is unclear exactly what he knows about the KMT national flag, he apparently reads the twelve-pointed KMT symbol as equivalent to the sun on the Japanese flag. The desire to map one onto the other, even if it is a conflation of different signs, expresses his will to maintain continuity in the trajectories of his life. If that referent constitutes part of his subjective knowledge, and hence part of his subjectivity, it is only natural for him to mobilize that system of knowledge to defend himself. The same applies to the daughter. She cannot understand the huge difference between the two reference systems, Dou-sang's and hers, and therefore concedes nothing to her father. Her education has been conditioned by the cold war, as evidenced by her references to iconic figures such as Wang Jingwei and Lu Hau-tung. The disjunction of the father's and daughter's living systems of knowledge opens an emotional space that can be filled only with aggression and defensiveness. It is impossible to close the gap, for both sides to recognize the generational differences formed by the changing totality of the society. This is a situation that cannot be resolved, and that can end only with dirty words from the mouth of the powerless patriarchal father.

The basic conflict persists. In a later scene, the family is watching television in their small living room. A basketball game between Japan and "us" is on.

Dou-sang asks: "Is this a Japanese team? Who are they playing?" The younger son replies: "Us."

Observing that the Japanese side keeps scoring, Dou-sang murmurs: "No point in watching. If they play against us, there's no point in watching. If they weren't good enough, they wouldn't dare to come. [Our team] will be killed." Annoyed by Dou-sang's condescending remark, the younger son raises his voice: "You never know . . . cheer up, cheer up, score, hurry, hurry, pass, pass, good, score!"

Irritated by his son's high spirits, Dou-sang picks a fight: "You see, you see, they are a country playing in the Olympic Games. Will they lose to us? If they lose, I'll ask each of them to commit suicide. You'll see. Eat your damn meal. Don't yell like a devil." The younger son fights back by shouting Dou-sang's own words even more loudly: "Watch, score again, suicide, suicide, suicide."

Wenjian senses Dou-sang's rage, and sends a warning signal to his brother: "Others eat their meal. You watch with burning heat." After another brief exchange, it is clear that the younger son will not heed Wenjian's warning. He goes on shouting: "Two points again, suicide, suicide." Losing face as his prediction goes unrealized, Dou-sang gets impatient and starts to shout: "What the hell are you yelling for? Calling a ghost? It's the middle of the night, very late."

Wenjian sees the fight is escalating and sends another warning to his brother: "All right, all right, don't get too excited." The mother overhears the unfriendly exchange between Dou-sang and the younger son from the kitchen and comes into the living room to find out what is happening. She demands: "What are you quarreling about?"

The daughter intervenes at this point, shouting in Mandarin: "You do this every time! You, a Han traitor and a running dog!" Dou-sang fights back: "If I had known you'd be like this, I would've drowned you when you were small."

Taken aback by Dou-sang's violent attack, the younger son plays innocent. "What's wrong with watching TV?" he asks, as he gets up and walks toward the door.

The mother asks: "Where are you going?" Escaping from home, he now dares to launch his final attack: "To watch the Japanese being killed [at the neighbor's house]!"

Dou-sang is deeply hurt and shouts with anger: "Evil wife, devil children!" The mother also gets furious: "Strange, haven't you had enough? You're an adult, but still quarrel with kids while watching TV!"

Dou-sang too storms out of the house. As he walks away, he says hopelessly to himself: "Evil wife, devil children. Nothing can be done!" The mother yells: "Don't bother with him! That madman!" Dou-sang starts to sing a slow, sad song: "Pitiful, my youth. Sorrowful, my fate."

"Evil wife, devil children" are what cause Dou-sang's sadness. In this scene of family tension, Dou-sang stands all by himself. He feels his youngest son, his daughter, and his wife are all against him. This time, the innocent younger son is placed at the center of the confrontation with the father. The daughter is not so involved in watching the basketball game, but, reminded of the previous quarrel, she seizes the chance to attack again: "You do this every time! You, a Han traitor and a running dog!" When the younger brother gets excited about the possibility of "us" beating "them," Wenjian asks him to calm down, trying again to avoid an escalation of the conflict. Meanwhile the mother, who has been working in the kitchen, has no idea what the quarrel is about. She cannot understand Dou-sang's childish behavior and calls him a madman. Feeling betrayed and misunderstood by everyone close to him, Dou-sang can only escape, walking away from the house, his last refuge, to release his sadness and self-pity on the street by singing that chilling song. "Evil wife, devil children" is an expression not so much of Dou-sang's discontent with his family, but of an unspeakable sense of loneliness and powerlessness: "Pitiful, my youth. Sorrowful, my fate."

As with most international sports events, the issue of national identification is forced upon the audience; choosing to support "us" against "them" allows us to project our desire to win. But we have to be cautious: in this scene, the use of "them" and "us" is more nuanced. The younger son is overtly identifying with "us" and "our team." Dou-sang clearly separates "them" from "us," treating the Japanese team as "them," so he does not take "their" side. But his forecast that "we" will lose is based upon the contention that "they" played in the Olympic Games, and so "they" are much stronger than "us." How does one understand the hierarchical nature of the us-versus-them relationship?

Dou-sang's intuitive judgment cannot be properly understood unless it is situated in the wider context of his life. For him, a Japanese radio works better and lasts longer than a Taiwanese one, Japanese tools are sturdier than those produced in Taiwan, and so on. There are abundant details of this sort in the film. It is very much like the situation in the 1960s and 1970s, when Taiwanese people traveling to the United States would bring back gifts like soap, perfume, and cosmetics to distribute among friends. The common consensus was that American products were simply better. Since the Second World War, Japan has been displaced by America as a symbol of the modern. Pushing further, one could thus read Dou-sang's denunciation of Lu Hau-tung as illiterate to mean that mainland Chinese are more backward than both the Japanese and "us." But for Dou-sang, the arrival of the American era cannot keep him from viewing the Japanese as the pinnacle, for his use of Japan as a standard for comparison is not limited to things local or Chinese, but also includes those from the United States. In one scene, having quarreled with his wife, Dou-sang escapes to visit Wenjian in the city. While Wenjian is away at work, Dou-sang finds a copy of *Playboy* on his son's desk. He thumbs through it with interest, evidently never having seen the magazine before. Wenjian later explains that he uses the magazine for learning English.[19] Looking at a sexy, nude blonde, Dou-sang remarks, "How come the hair color is gold, but below it's black? They [the breasts] are too big. The Japanese [female body] is better, more delicate." In Dou-sang's system of thought, things Japanese are always stronger, subtler, more valuable, better.

Indeed, Dou-sang relies on a hierarchical structure to make judgments and comparisons, with the Japanese at the top, "us" in the middle, and mainland Chinese at the bottom. The cultural imaginary that engendered such a hierarchy was not at all unique to Dou-sang, but was a widely shared structure of sentiment for his generation of běnshěng rén. Of course, we should not oversimplify the operation of this hierarchical logic. There are hierarchies within the imaginary Japan, Taiwan, China, and America, and different social classes have different imaginations and consensuses. In the colonial period, for the Japanese and Taiwanese elites, Europe, France, and Paris were the pinnacles of civilization. This traditional view is still held among the intellectual elite of the postwar era. Those who had studied in Europe would secretly look down on those who had studied in the United States. Scholars who had studied in Paris would see those who had studied in London as more conservative and less up-to-date because England could not truly be counted as a part of European culture. Such colonialist and postcolonialist productions of the hierarchy of modernity reside in the body, mind, and desire of the intellectual elite.

Dou-sang's embodiment of the colonial aspiration for modernity, for things that are better, more advanced, more modern, and more civilized — desires that explain how colonialism was able to operate in the colony — indicates that such a structure of sentiment was not limited to intellectuals and other social elites of the colonial period. Japan, as the symbol of modernity, penetrated deep into the social strata, reaching even the rural working class, who had also tasted the fruits of modernization. The complex passion for Japan intensified when it was set in sharp contrast with the even harder life in the immediate postwar, Kuomintang era. Nostalgia for the good old days surfaced almost immediately. "We'd probably be better off if we were still living under Japanese rule" has been a general sentiment shared by the older generation of běnshěng rén.[20] Such a sentiment is not without material basis, given the fact that Dou-sang's generation had lived through the modernization undertaken during the Japanese occupation and personally experienced elements of the modern. By the 1970s, Japan had also become globally recognized as an advanced country. Thus Japan's position as the archetype of the modern was further consolidated, and to Dou-sang's generation, the perception was simply not open to challenge. The extent to which the older generation of běnshěng rén feels proud to have shared in the glory of a rising

Japan is difficult to measure, but the fact that Japan became the model for Taiwanese modernity does have this traceable historical trajectory. For the běnshěng population, who lived in a Taiwan that had not had ties with mainland China since the island was ceded to Japan by the Qing Dynasty in 1895, the desire to live under Japanese rule is a commonly shared sentiment. The Japanese modernizer moved Taiwan forward, whereas the KMT regime, as the symbol of China, is unbearable in its backwardness: "they" are worse than "we" are, so how can they govern us?

The third-world nationalist desire for the modern and the colonialist civilizing mission are complementary; together they form the horizon of the popular structure of sentiment. This is, indeed, the core assumption that has to be questioned and challenged, especially when the ideology of the modern is adopted by the powerful to suppress subaltern subject groups.

Returning to the two scenes from Wu's film, we can see that it is only through such emotional confrontations that Dou-sang's painful sadness and his Japanese structure of sentiment can be felt, and hence shared with and handed down to the next generation. Unlike his younger sister and brother, Wenjian is in his late teens, more grown up, and better able to understand and sympathize with Dou-sang's passion. In the end, he becomes the inheritor of Dou-sang's emotional structure of sentiment. After Dou-sang's death, Wenjian is sent to Japan by his mother to carry the picture of his deceased father to the Imperial Palace and Mount Fuji, fulfilling Dou-sang's final wish. The film ends with sad music in the background, while Wenjian utters in a moving voice these words which are shown against a black screen: "1991, January 11. Dou-sang finally sees the Imperial Palace and Mount Fuji. It is the day of the first snow in Tokyo. Dou-sang is speechless."

The mood of the final scene is a mixture of fulfillment and chilly sadness. It's the fulfillment of a long-held dream, but without any sense of achievement. The Imperial Palace and Mount Fuji stand in the cold of winter, covered by the first snow, and can no longer symbolize the sublime power of the Japanese empire. Finally arriving in Tokyo, Wenjian's comment, "Dou-sang is speechless," is the culmination of a lifetime of sadness. What can he say? Members of the speechless generation had to jump out the window, committing suicide to maintain what little dignity they could muster. Can the posthumous fulfillment of his wish make up for a lifetime of agony? Throughout the film, Wenjian—the son, heir, and empathetic narrator—never negatively judges Dou-sang's endorsement of Japaneseness. His sympathy for his father's suffering is evident when he attempts to help him in the workplace and when he offers him money, though to maintain his dignity, Dou-sang constantly refuses these offers. Wenjian's sympathetic identification with Dou-sang is a recognition of his father's borrowed life, of the desperate desire to move beyond it, and of the hopelessness of trying to change its course.

A borrowed life, once it is set in the contemporary context, can be understood as the drive to find the life lent to others. It is an attempt to stand on one's own, to be independent, to be in charge of one's destiny rather than going on living under the shadow of the outsider. This drive is precisely the basis of the structure of sentiment for all national independence movements in the third world.

Unfortunately, this collective drive for independence in all senses of the word was mobilized, subdivided, and appropriated by the political elites among the formerly colonized, who fought against each other for state power—a battle which has led to long-lasting ethnic conflicts. It was also cruelly intercepted by the cold-war structure, under which anticommunism was adopted as an alibi by authoritarian governing powers to suppress all other ideological positions. The social forms that have emerged from these processes have perpetuated the basic logic of colonialism, from racial discrimination in the colonial period to ethnic nationalist hatred in the era after independence.

Banana Paradise:

Trajectories: Anti-Japan → Anticommunism → Returning Home

Banana Paradise, directed by Wang Tung and written by Wang Shiao-di, was released in 1989, not long after contacts between Taiwan and mainland China became possible. The film is told from the point of view of "old soldiers" (*lǎobīng*)[21] from mainland China. The opening scene is set in Shandong, in the winter of 1948. Menxuan is a naive teenage boy from a peasant family in a rural village. His father sold all of the family's property to raise money to send Menxuan to join Desheng, a slightly older man from the same village, who was serving as a cook in the Kuomintang army; the two consider each other like brothers because of their shared origin. Defeated by the People's Liberation Army, their unit retreats to

Taiwan. The two do not have the slightest idea of the island's location; they believe it is nearby and are told it is known for its natural beauty, and for growing the best bananas. They are happy to leave the horrible battlefield behind and, for the moment, to enjoy this new banana paradise. They expect to go home as soon as the war is over.

Having moved to Taiwan during the anticommunist red purge there, they both find themselves in trouble because they naively picked the wrong false names while still on the mainland. Because his adopted feminine name, Jiumei (meaning "ninth sister"), was laughed at by other soldiers, Menxuan changed his name to Zuo Fugui (literally "left prosperity"), which was seen by the KMT authorities as procommunist. Desheng selected the name Liu Jinyuan from a list of soldiers in his military unit. Because the real Liu did not come to Taiwan, Desheng thought he could simply inherit his colleague's identity. Unfortunately, back on the mainland, Liu was suspected of being a communist spy. This was a time of panic in Taiwan, when it was common to hear the warning, "Watch out! A communist spy is right next to you!" Tortured by the security forces, Desheng escapes to another army unit, adopts a new name — Liu Chuanxiao — and is put in charge of the kitchen and food supply. There he makes friends with a local peasant family, headed by A-Xiang and his wife, Banana Sister, thus named by Desheng because they grow bananas. A-Xiang's entire family treats Desheng like a member of the family, and he takes refuge in their kindness. Perhaps not surprisingly, Desheng himself gets caught up in the red scare fever and accuses his own commanding officer of being a communist. The attack backfires, and Desheng is once again severely beaten by security forces. At this point, he begins to lose touch with reality.

Meanwhile, in a parallel development, Menxuan too is suspected of being a leftist. In the process of escaping from the security forces he happens to meet a dying man, Li Qilin, who is accompanied by his wife, Yuexiang, and their newborn son, Yauhua (literarily, "glorifying China"). After Li dies, in order to support Yuexiang and her son, Menxuan takes over Li's identity and attempts to capitalize on his status as a university graduate with a degree in English to take an air-force job that had been arranged for Li before he died. Menxuan is illiterate and cannot do the work, so his "family" has to leave the air-force base to join Desheng, the only "relative" he has. With sympathetic support from A-Xiang's family,

Menxuan learns to read and write and is able to finally pass the civil-service examination, become a low-level bureaucrat, and support his "family," including Desheng—who by then has gone completely mad.

Years later, when contacts between Taiwan and the mainland are once more officially permitted, Yauhua goes to Hong Kong to meet his mainland Chinese grandfather. He goes enthusiastically, not knowing that Menxuan is not his real father, and thus not the real son of the mainland Chinese man. Anxiously awaiting news about the reunion in Hong Kong, Yuexiang reveals to Menxuan that she is not actually Yauhua's mother. Like Menxuan, who took over Li Qilin's identity, she also has an assumed identity: she was not Li's real wife, but someone who promised Li to take care of his son. Having had no physical relationship despite having pretended to be married for so many years, she and Menxuan finally embrace each other, in tears, for the first time. When Yauhua finally calls home, Menxuan has to talk to the grandfather on the phone and bursts into tears. He calls the stranger "Dad," as if he were speaking to his real father.

Unlike *Dou-sang*'s unsentimental storytelling, *Banana Paradise* is full of black humor. It was also the first film produced in Taiwan that was critical of the Kuomintang regime (interestingly, the film was produced by Central Studio, an organ of the KMT). The sympathetic portrayal of these innocent nobodies—Menxuan, Desheng, Yuexiang, Banana Sister, and A-Xiang—stands in sharp contrast to the depiction of the security forces as cruel representatives of a violent state. The film was released only two years after the 1987 lifting of martial law, when the political mood was still darkened by the shadow of the police state. Those decades of fear and violence inflicted by the state may account for the film's use of black humor, which was probably a textual strategy to soften the film's critical stance toward the state.

Throughout the story, drama is generated through a number of underlying ironic tensions. The nobodies are suspected of being communist spies but prove to be the most apolitical and innocent characters, while the depiction of the security forces—supposedly the good guys—is in line with the stereotypical image of sneaky and brutal communist spies (*fěidié*). The banana "paradise" turns out to be an anticommunist, White Terror hell. Desheng, whose name literally means "winning victory," has never won anything. He teaches Menxuan all the little techniques for surviving in that turbulent era, but eventually he is the one who goes crazy and has to be taken care of by the supposedly useless younger "brother." Menxuan does not know how to handle any of the difficulties he encounters and always has to count on others to survive. In the end, though, he is the one who ends up supporting them.

During that tumultuous era of civil war, many people had to take on false identities by creating fake records. Like Menxuan, some pretended to have a college degree, and many more altered their identities in subtler ways, like changing their birth date so as to be old enough to take a particular job. Desheng, Menxuan, and Yuexiang are all forced to adopt multiple identities, but by adopting new names, they were either mistakenly identified as communist spies or forced to assume another's identity for the rest of their borrowed lives. Eventually, all these necessary, well-intentioned lies are exposed. As the story slowly unfolds, it emerges that nobody is who they are supposed to be: the father is not the father, the mother is not the mother, the son is not the son. The audience does not know the real name of Desheng, who becomes Liu Jinyuan and then changes his name to Liu Chuanxiao. Menxuan is simply a nickname, and the man who is called that becomes He Jiumei and then Zuo Fugui before settling on Li Qilin. He is not the father of Yauhua, nor the husband of Yauhua's supposed mother. And Yuexiang is neither the wife of her dead husband, nor Yauhua's mother; in the end, we are not even sure whether the name Yuexiang belonged to her or to Li's real wife. To be denied an identity—or, more precisely, to not be able to claim one's real identity—constitutes the central problem of the film. However, it would be incorrect to deploy a theory of split or multiple subjects to suggest that these people are displaying multiple identities as a consequence of living in the postmodern era. And it would be equally incorrect to use ethnic or nationalist political language to claim that they do not love Taiwan and therefore do not want to identify with their new home. Such careless explanations do not do justice to the real historical conditions forced upon these nobodies.

In *Dou-sang*, the wàishěng population does not directly enter the sphere of Dou-sang's everyday life, but they are always there in the background. Their absent presence is marked by the KMT regime's conscription of Dou-sang's younger brother and neighbors into the army, by Dou-sang's conflict with his state-indoctrinated daughter, and by the basketball game, which is broadcast in Mandarin. Dou-sang's only direct statement about the wàishěng population appears in an ironic remark about his grandson: "Two Taiwanese [Wenjian and his wife] gave birth to a wàishěng child." The grandson cannot understand Dou-sang's Minnanese; he can speak only Mandarin, which for Dou-sang is the language of wàishěng rén. In contrast, encounters between běnshěng rén and wàishěng rén are in the foreground of *Banana Paradise*.

After Desheng is suspected of being a communist, he is tortured by the military police. He manages to escape and find work with another military unit under the name of Li Chuanxiao, but by then he has begun to act abnormally. As a result of his victim's complex, he imagines that strangers are communists who want to entrap him. When Menxuan and Yuexiang finally find him staying with A-Xiang's family, he suspects that Yuexiang is actually an undercover agent sent by the security forces. Taking Desheng in, the peasant family treats these wàishěng rén warmly. In time, Desheng becomes attracted to Banana Sister's teenage daughter, A-Zhen. In one scene, Desheng loses control, embraces A-Zhen, and caresses her, saying that he wants her to marry him. This rather unexpected behavior scares A-Zhen. She yells for help from her father, and A-Xiang chases Desheng away with a stick. Unable to find Desheng, A-Xiang comes home and discusses the matter with his friends, condemning Desheng's dishonorable betrayal. Suddenly, they hear a gunshot. A group of soldiers is tracking Desheng down in a nearby field. At this critical moment, Desheng desperately seeks refuge in his adopted home, and A-Xiang and Banana Sister intervene to save his life.

A low-ranking officer says to A-Xiang and some other villagers attracted by the commotion, "Sorry to bother you." A-Xiang looks anxiously at Desheng: "Sergeant [Desheng's military rank, and also the name the family calls him] is bleeding so much! What happened to him? What happened?" A soldier explains: "He's out of his mind. He accused our lieutenant of being a communist spy, and of having poisoned his food. At dinner he pulled out a gun and threatened to shoot him . . ."

A-Xiang seems to have forgiven Desheng's earlier betrayal and begs the officer in charge not to shoot him: "Officer, please spare his life for now, and decide what you want to do with him later." The officer thinks for a moment and replies, "OK, let's carry him over there and wait for the major to come and decide."

Seeing Desheng injured, Banana Sister, who has consistently treated Desheng warmly, thinks A-Xiang was the one who beat him. She yells, "A-Xiang, what the hell are you doing? Beating him up and making him bleed so much!" A-Xiang replies innocently, "I didn't do that." Banana Sister does not believe her husband: "If you didn't do it, who did?"

The major arrives and speaks to Desheng in a northern Chinese accent: "Li Chuanxiao, what happened? Li Chuanxiao, what's wrong with you?" Crying, Banana Sister begs the commander pitifully, "I beg you, if you want to arrest him, wait until he finishes this meal. Please." She had brought food for Desheng and now understands that this could easily be Desheng's final meal. The major replies, "All right."

Banana Sister holds Desheng in her arms and says, "Sergeant, don't be scared. These are all your favorite foods. Hurry and eat. I will ask A-Zhen to come to eat with you. Hurry and eat." A-Zhen comes and helps. Desheng looks toward Banana Sister and, holding her tightly, breaks into tears, shouting hopelessly: "Ma, Ma, I miss you so much! Ma, I want to go home! Ma, I miss you!" Desheng seems to treat Banana Sister as if she were his mother, and as if this were their last meal together. Banana Sister cries and gently reassures Desheng: "Don't be scared. It's all right."

A-Xiang also humbly begs the major for mercy: "Commander, this person is very pitiful. He's already gone crazy, and it's useless to arrest him . . ." A-Xiang continues his attempt to talk the major into allowing the family to keep Desheng at their house, so that they can take care of him.

Meanwhile, Menxuan is told about the situation, and he rushes out of the house shouting: "Desheng, what happened to you? You cannot go mad . . . I have eaten enough bananas here [in Taiwan]. I don't want to eat any more! Damn, you brought me here, and now you have to take me home. I don't want to eat any more! Take me home."

A soldier says to Menxuan: "Little brother, let him [Desheng] finish the meal." Banana Sister turns to A-Zhen and says, "A-Zhen, bring more food. Hurry and eat. Finish it, we'll bring more."

The commanding officer makes up his mind to accept A-Xiang's proposal and announces his decision to the other soldiers: "All right, all right. Let's go back. Let's go." But a sneaky-looking security officer waves his hand at Menxuan, asking to have a word with him on the side: "Who is he [Desheng]?" Menxuan innocently replies in his Shandong accent, "My big brother."

Following the security officer, Menxuan disappears from the scene. He is later brutally questioned and beaten. The next morning, A-Xiang brings him home in a cart used for transporting bananas. Menxuan, who has not yet recovered from his nightmare interrogation, lies completely motionless, with a blank look in his eyes. At the lunch table, however, he suddenly jumps up and attacks Desheng, who has become a madman and is destined to be taken care of by Yuexiang and Menxuan for the rest of his life.

In these emotionally charged scenes, *Banana Paradise* presents an image of support and solidarity between two lower-class ethnic groups in contrast to the violence of state power. For the peasant family and Desheng, language differences are not a barrier to establishing friendship. Banana Sister, A-Xiang, and their children all like Desheng's outgoing personality and generously take him in as a member of the family. When he is not working at the military base, Desheng is always at their home, eating, drinking, and chatting with the family, and at night he shares a bed with the children. When Menxuan, Yuexiang, and Yauhua come, the family also welcomes them, kindly offering them a separate room to live in. When Desheng is in trouble, they forgive his misconduct and save his life.

One may argue that this is an exaggerated and romantic representation of relations between ethnic groups. But there were a large number of intermarriages between lower-ranking soldiers and běnshěng women, which indicates that such friendly relations did exist among these nobodies. Even during the intense conflict of the 228 Incident, many běnshěng rén protected wàishěng rén in their houses. Although there is a tendency to romanticize the open-mindedness of working-class people, the film does not cover up the real conflict that existed. The moment of tension arrives in Desheng's uncontrollable desire for A-Zhen, resulting in his act of sexual aggression. His desire for A-Zhen is a mix of passion, lust, and loneliness. Though they feel betrayed by his conduct, the family does not ask Desheng and his friends to leave. And though shamed, Desheng still has to come home to find support when he is persecuted. Banana Sister, A-Xiang, and A-Zhen generously forgive him.

Desperate and powerless, Desheng's longing for home is projected through his desire to see Banana Sister as his mother, his shelter. Patriotic, anticommunist, resentful of his harsh treatment, and with no real home or mother to return to, he can express this desire only in hysterical terms. In tears, he shouts, "Ma, Ma, I miss you so much! Ma, I want to go home! Ma, I miss you!" One hears the suffering in his voice as he desperately searches for the right words to say to his mother before he is killed. This is an emotional moment, a convergence of overwhelming feelings of love and loss. But what do the hysteria and tears in this scene entail? In this emotionally conflated moment, is he adopting Banana Sister as his new mother in this new home? Yes, but not quite. At this critical turning point, the suffering Menxuan, who will later experience a similar vicarious projection, quickly reminds Desheng of his responsibility to take him home: "You cannot go mad . . . I have had enough bananas here. I don't want to eat any more! Damn, you brought me here, and now you have to take me home."

Why has Desheng's generation of wàishěng rén been unable to adjust and adopt Taiwan as their new home, or their only home? This is the question at the heart of the provincial register contradiction. The image of home evokes an entire set of structured feelings about "Ma," "missing you," and "going home." The going-home sentiment has been a persistent desire for lower-class wàishěng rén like Menxuan and Desheng, who have no resources or capital and who have suffered much as a result of their forced migration. They never thought they would stay in Taiwan, much less make a new home here. And even though a new home is later established, it is seen as temporary; the prevailing sentiment has been and is still that "we will return eventually."

Parallel to the nationalist state's diminishing will to recover the mainland, the mind-set of those desiring to return home has been changing gradually since the 1970s. But the deep drive to return has never completely disappeared. For that generation of wàishěng rén, to adopt Taiwan as their true home or to say to a běnshěng rén "I am also a Taiwanese" is difficult, if not impossible. But the truth of the matter is that Taiwan has been, and is, their only home. Many accepted this harsh reality only after the political changes of the late 1980s made it possible for them to return to their supposed homes on the mainland. In the 1960s and 1970s, for Desheng to give up his identity as a person from Shandong and occupy the position of Taiwanese would have been unacceptable not only to him, but also to Banana Sister. How would she see herself in relation to Desheng? While many in Desheng's generation have visited mainland China, very few have stayed there; most have come back to Taiwan. In part, this is because mainland Chinese consider these wàishěng rén, especially the second generation, Taiwanese. For the second generation, like Yauhua, having been born or having grown up in Taiwan, it is much easier to say "I am a Taiwanese, and my home is in Taiwan, but at the same time I am a Chinese," whereas it is simply not possible to force those in Desheng and Menxuan's generation to become Taiwanese.

The defeated KMT regime and the people who followed it to Taiwan could never see themselves as outsiders who had occupied an overseas colony, or as exiled migrants who had established a base in a foreign country. Like the innocent Desheng and Menxuan, who originally did not even know where Taiwan was, most lower-class or low-ranking wàishěng rén were simply swallowed up by political tides beyond their control. They thought that they were retreating to Taiwan, a province of China, on a short-term basis and that, once the war was over they could just go home. Many of the old soldiers were drafted by force into the military. They sacrificed their youth and risked their lives to fight for their country. This gave them a feeling of entitlement to be in Taiwan, which was often expressed in careless ways and later proved to be the psychic foundation of political, cultural, and provincial conflicts.

For běnshěng rén, the feeling is that Taiwan is our past, present, and future home: We have no other home to go back to. We are the hosts, you are the guests; Taiwan is ours, not yours. Such a sentiment is expressed very clearly in Banana Sister and A-Xiang's interaction with Desheng and Menxuan. At the lunch table, after a few rounds of liquor, Desheng communicates his sincere gratitude: "Banana Sister, you've been too nice to me. When I go home, I will hire a sedan chair to take all of you, one by one, back to Shandong. There, we will drink [liquor] out of a big bowl." Banana Sister replies, "Going to Shandong, I will definitely take with me a big basket of bananas, so that you will have enough to eat." A-Xiang seems to be a bit embarrassed and interrupts, "Bananas are too cheap [to bring as a gift]." Banana Sister insists, "They're a very famous thing [from here]." In the course of this exchange, the friendly relations between host and guest are obvious. Later, when Menxuan expresses his anger and fear to Desheng in the scene cited above about having had enough bananas and wanting to go home, sympathetic friends such as Banana Sister and A-Xiang understand his desperation, suffering, and desire to go home.

But if such overt expressions were made at the peak moments of the provincial register conflict in the 1990s during the election campaigns, what would have been the response of most běnshěng rén? Would these sentiments not have hurt their feelings? How would enthusiasts of the Taiwanese independence movement, with their strong Taiwanese consciousness, have responded to Menxuan's statement? Would they not think that wàishěng rén like Menxuan and Desheng, having had enough bananas, felt they could leave at any time, coming and going at their will without any obligation or commitment to Taiwan?

With no chance to go home and lacking any means to contact relatives in what was often called the communist bandit's territory for over forty years, wàishěng rén had to find ways to keep themselves psychologically healthy. Finally, in the 1980s, cold-war tensions eased, mainland China opened its doors, and the KMT lifted its travel ban. This sudden breakdown of previous taboos produced a huge movement called "return to the home village" (fǎnxiāng).[22] Very much like the Korean stories addressed at the beginning of this chapter, but mainly operating through the social sector rather than that of the state, this movement brought to light countless buried—sometimes secret—stories, and new problems soon followed. Back in the 1940s, some soldiers had had patriotic slogans such as "exterminate the devil communist" or "recover the Mainland" tattooed on their shoulders or chests. They were desperate to find ways to erase these historical records from their skin, worrying that they would be arrested by the people they still called communist bandits when they went home. Some soldiers who had married before the war and later remarried in Taiwan had to find ways to deal with these suddenly complex relationships.

In some ways, this should have been an exciting moment. It coincided with the lifting of martial law, and it was a time when people could finally rediscover their hidden selves and acquire new lives. But life is never ideal. How would people who had officially adopted different identities confront these new challenges? In what names, with what identities, could they possibly go home? Could they go at all?

After tirelessly searching for what he believed to be his father's relatives on the mainland, Yauhua finally finds them and prepares to go to Hong Kong to meet his grandfather and aunt.[23] In order to surprise Menxuan, he does not tell his parents about the reunion before he leaves, and they think he is simply on a business trip. At the airport, he tells Shuhua, his wife, to keep the parents at home in the evening and says that he will call, with the grandfather, at around 8:00 p.m. In the late afternoon, in order to prevent Menxuan and Yuexiang from going out to see friends, Shuhua has to tell them that their son and his grandfather are going to call. Completely unprepared, the supposed parents retreat to the bedroom to discuss in private what to do. Menxuan begs Yuexiang to tell him more about Li Qilin's family, so that he can avoid having his secret exposed. After a long silence, Yuexiang finally reveals her own secret.

"Menxuan, I'm not Li Qilin's wife either." Forced to confront deep scars she had not wanted to face again, Yuexiang tells him what happened: "In trying to escape the war, I lost touch with my family. It was like calling out to the heavens and receiving no response, hailing the earth, but to no avail. I had to run back to my old home. But as I traveled, I learned that the old home had already burned down. I had no place to go. I just had to get back. I desperately ran and ran, but I bumped into these local gangsters. They grabbed me, used metal hooks to dig at me, separated my hands, pulled my legs apart. I lay on the ground. They tore apart my clothes. The wounds were very painful, very painful!"

In tears, she tears at the buttons on her cheongsam, as if she were reliving the traumatic scene. Menxuan too starts to cry and kneels on the floor, sharing her pain, wanting to protect her. Yuexiang continues: "Luckily, Mr. Li and his classmates were passing through, and they saved me. I feel so . . . I did not know it could last until now. Later, his wife died of an illness. A big man, holding a baby, crying so sadly! From that moment, I swore I had to raise the child of this man who had such a good heart. I would treat him like my own kid and love and protect him. I did it."

Menxuan helps Yuexiang button her clothes. They break into tears again and, for the first time, embrace each other.

Yuexiang gradually recovers from the painful memory, telling Menxuan, "I also feel grateful to you. It's you who helped me to make it. We have finally brought him up. I cannot imagine that we have lived our entire lives like this."

If the unexpected family reunion had not been organized by Yauhua, Yuexiang might have kept her painful secrets buried forever. But she does tell what happened to Menxuan, the man with whom, despite their lack of any physical contact, she has lived as husband and wife for the majority of her life. The pain of being gang raped explains why she could never let Menxuan touch her. She is hurt once again in reliving the memory, but perhaps she can now begin to be liberated from it.

In the film, Yuexiang is presented as a tough woman with her own character and agency, which is indeed an accurate representation of many of the women of my mother's generation. They are inherently persistent, driven, and decisive, though they often come across as being soft. An untraceable, grievous past lies behind the polite front they project. In their struggle to survive the Chinese civil war, they came to Taiwan, often on their own. They had to live with—and put up with—men like Menxuan, those who had no social or economic capital but still attempted to uphold their role as the family patriarch. Fortunately, most of these courageous women had no mothers-in-law to rule over them and tell them what to do, as they would have had on the mainland. In raising their families, they could bring into play their own survival instincts, to an extent they had probably never expected. If they were lucky, they could finally free themselves after their useless husbands had passed away and their children were grown up; if they were unfortunate, like my mother, after fulfilling their duties, they might have a breakdown, succumbing to the lack of material necessities, social resources, and psychic support that characterized their lives.

As expressions of a shifting patriarchal structure, the toughness of the wàishěng female (Yuexiang), and the conservative cowardliness of the wàishěng male (Menxuan) demand analysis. Like the men in Dousang's generation, who have been deprived of a language to speak and are hence silenced, these older generation wàishěng men have also been castrated, but in a socio-political sense, rather than a psychoanalytic one. The shallowness of their patriarchal power is directly linked to the characteristics of the state. As a defeated regime, the KMT had no strong material or psychic basis for its legitimacy to govern. Lacking economic resources, expertise, and confidence, it was nevertheless inconceivable for the KMT to allow the colonized běnshěng elites to run the state. Authoritarian suppression covered up this powerlessness, and that form of state power produced a whole generation of psychically distorted people. Most men in my father's generation had no resources at their disposal, but they pretended to be the head of the family to maintain their male dignity; often, they elevated their own status by looking down on the běnshěng population, which had been educated by the Japanese and were hence culturally inferior. These wàishěng men could never have imagined that, in the eyes of many běnshěng rén, it was due to the incompetence of the mainland Chinese (and, by extension, wàishěng rén) that Taiwan had been ceded to Japan in the first place.

In the film, when the phone call from Hong Kong finally comes, Menxuan and Yuexiang walk hesitantly out of their bedroom. Shuhua picks up the phone. Watching their eye contact, we know that Menxuan hopes Yuexiang will talk to his supposed father, but finally it is Menxuan himself who takes the receiver.

In tears, the grandfather speaks in a trembling voice: "Qilin, you have suffered, you have suffered!" Menxuan does not quite know what to say and reluctantly replies: "Dad, no, it was not so miserable. Dad, please do not feel bad." Menxuan turns to Yuexiang, telling her, "He's crying . . . Dad, how is your health? . . . Yes, Dad, I do remember, yes, I remember everything you told me. Your son is not filial. Dad . . ." Menxuan bursts into tears.

The grandfather goes on: "When your Ma died, she would not close her eyes, she would not close her eyes . . ." Menxuan is shocked to hear this news, and shouts: "What? Ma died? When did she die? Ma, Ma, your son is not filial, your son doesn't deserve to live, Ma . . ." Menxuan is no longer able to control himself at this point.

The grandfather keeps on crying: "I'm almost dead and buried. But you did not come to visit me once, you could not visit me even once." Menxuan responds: "Dad, don't say that. It makes me feel even more guilty. Dad, you must look after yourself, you must look after yourself. Dad! . . . Ma! . . ."

Menxuan cries and shouts. He is overwhelmed by his emotions and cannot talk further. Yuexiang takes the phone from him. Menxuan continues to cry: "Dad, Ma, your son is not filial. Ma, how could you die? Ma, your son is not filial."

Yuexiang holds the phone as if she's going to speak to the grandfather. But after hesitating for a few seconds, she hangs up.

In the scene discussed previously, Desheng takes Banana Sister as his substitute mother. Now Menxuan is forced to take on the role of the son, Li Qilin. But he feels as if he were talking to his real father. When he learns his "mother" has died, he cries with real emotion. In this intense moment of "reunion," tears conflate the real and the imaginary. What are not spoken are the miserable histories of suffering on both sides, the guilt, and the mourning; but in one sharp moment, all this pain converges and is released. The grandfather regrets not being able to take care of his son. He revisits the memory of the death of his wife, who could not peacefully close her eyes. Menxuan repeats "your son is not filial" not simply to release his own guilt at not being able to take care of his parents, but also to live out his own long-suppressed grief. Overcome with sorrow, Yuexiang, Yauhua, and Shuhua are also in tears. One can imagine that Yuexiang's tears are not just an expression of sympathy for Menxuan and the Li family, but also an outpouring of grief over her own sorrowful past: the loss of her family in the war, the rape, and the long, difficult years spent supporting these two men, Yauhua and Menxuan.

Like Wenjian in *Dou-sang*, the tears of Yauhua and Shuhua signal recognition by the younger generation of the lives of suffering led by their parents. By participating in the mourning of family history, they also inherit their parents' emotional structure of sentiment. It is in such moments that the postwar generation of wàishěng rén more or less partakes of the structure of sentiment handed down by the earlier wàishěng generation, and the postwar generation of běnshěng rén receives an analogous inheritance from the earlier běnshěng generation. These feelings have now become the emotional bases of the two populations.

The film ends with yet another piece of black humor. Menxuan's petition to delay his retirement is turned down by the personnel office. He claims that the official record of his age was a mistake and that his real age is much younger, which may well be true. However, because Li Qilin was about ten years older than he was, once he adopted Li's identity and used Li's university diploma to find a job, Menxuan's real age is no longer of any consequence. The officer in charge tells him that if the age on his petition is correct, he must have received his university degree at the age of 11. Menxuan cannot respond, and it becomes a big joke in the office. As he approaches the end of his career, he is thus insulted once again, this time by losing the respect of his colleagues. His failure to reclaim even his own age means that he has to go on living indefinitely with the identity of Li Qilin superimposed on his body. Isn't this also a borrowed life?

The Entanglements of Colonialism and the Cold War

Though Dou-sang and Menxuan followed very different paths, they were both forced to lead borrowed lives, and in this way they are very much connected. The preceding analyses of the conditions highlighted by the films have prepared us to account for the formation of divergent structures of sentiment during Taiwan's complex postwar period.

Dou-sang is about the effects and "representations" of Japanese colonialism,[24] and *Banana Paradise* deals primarily with the effects of the cold war, but by juxtaposing the two films one cannot help but identify "tears of suffering" as an affective trope common to the historical experiences of both wàishěng rén and běnshěng rén. But, as the effects of two very different emotional structures of sentiment, the two groups' tears of suffering have very different historical trajectories. In *Dou-sang*, the intersection of colonialism and the cold war is shown in the tense scenes in which Dousang, who has been molded by Japanese colonialism, is in conflict with his own children, who have been shaped by their nationalist education, the obligatory use of Mandarin as the official language, and other cold-war policies intended by the KMT to eradicate Japanese influences.[25] In *Banana Paradise*, on the other hand, colonialism has been completely supplanted by the cold-war structure and is not touched on at all.

In my view, the key to understanding the difference is this: for wàishěng rén, colonialism does not exist as part of the historical memory, just as the cold war does not occupy a central place in the historical memory of běnshěng rén. This does not mean that the wàishěng population has not been touched by the history of colonialism. On the contrary, the wàishěng population—who were never directly ruled by the Japanese, but who either suffered through or were educated about the war with Japan, particularly the Nanking Massacre—is generally anti-Japanese. My point is that for běnshěng rén, it is the fifty-year colonization of Taiwan that informs the historical memory and fundamental perception of Japan. No matter whether it is couched in positive or negative terms, an intricate love-hate relationship with the former colonizer, who had been the archetypal symbol of the modern, is the standard form of subjectivity for the formerly colonized third world. However, for wàishěng rén and mainland Chinese, the dominant historical perception of Japan begins with the Mukden Incident of 1931 and includes the Marco Polo Bridge

Incident that started the eight-year war between China and Japan, which became part of the Second World War, and China's eventual victory in 1945.[26] For these groups, Japan has had no positive value for many years. One can even argue that this anti-Japanese sentiment, shared by the KMT and the CCP, and by wàishěng rén and mainland Chinese, is the most essential element in the formation of the contemporary Chinese nationalist subject. A double resentment is at work, as the Chinese think: Japan has learned from us for centuries, but they humiliated and attacked our nation when it was in crisis; we will never forget this. What is crucial to understand is that the anti-Japanese sentiment of wàishěng rén is not informed at all by the Japanese occupation of Taiwan because they did not experience it themselves. Colonialism and 1895—the year the Japanese occupied Taiwan—two deeply meaningful signs for běnshěng rén, never became part of the wàishěng rén's historical memory, probably in part because of the nationalist versions of history written in the postwar era.

The divergence of these living memories has resulted in the emergence of two different emotional structures, which themselves are mediated through different imaginations of Japan and Japanese colonialism.[27] The existence of these two structures also renders mutual understanding between Taiwanese and mainland Chinese impossible. The dichotomy of attitudes toward Japan—the Japanese are either modern and progressive, or devils—colors the emotional logic of other relationships. In reality, many běnshěng rén do express anti-Japanese sentiments, and it is impossible to claim that they all share a fundamentally pro-Japanese stance; but comparatively speaking, anti-Japanese sentiments among wàishěng rén are more deeply felt and more frequently expressed. The controversy over Kobayashi Yoshinori's manga, *Thesis on Taiwan*, which triggered a clash of opinions when a Taiwanese edition was published in 2001, clearly expresses such structural differences. Some běnshěng rén (who tend to favor Taiwan independence) felt that Kobayashi was affirming many of Taiwan's achievements, while many wàishěng rén (who tend to favor Taiwan's unification with China) understood their praise of the book as a fawning gesture toward the Japanese. To fully account for these reactions, we have to return to the historical memory of the prewar era.

Despite the fact that the modern history of China before the end of the Second World War has to be understood through its reactions to colonialism and imperialism, mainland China, in contrast to Taiwan and other third-world spaces, was never subjugated by a single colonial power. Parts of China were indeed carved up by different imperial powers, and China can therefore be considered a sub- or quasi-colony, but the Chinese population was not completely conquered or colonized. None of the colonizing forces was able to generate a unifying experience among the population. Although imperialism and anti-imperialism are familiar elements in the Chinese worldview, people on the mainland do not recognize, as Taiwanese do, what colonialism means, culturally and psychically. The nationalist formulation of a strong Chinese civilizationalism is a tough imaginary resource with which brutal foreign invasions could be culturally and psychically resisted: you can conquer our territory, but never our hearts. This defensive strategy is evident in common expressions such as "foreign devils," "Eastern foreign devils," "Japanese bandits" (Rìbĕn wōkòu), "expel barbarians, renew China," and "we lost material, but not spiritual, civilization."

If indeed there is any unity in the popular memory of nationalist anti-imperialism, it may be found in this condensed narrative of popular phrases and slogans: "Western powers partition our territory," "resistance to foreign invasion," the possible "death of the nation" and the subsequent "rescue the nation and ensure its survival," "build strong fleets and cannons," "move forward to catch up," and finally the adoption of modernizing projects to "build a New China." In this grand narrative, Western powers, Japanese imperialists, and their collaborators—Han traitors and running dogs—are the enemies. Such sentiments reflect a difference with the typical colony, where collaborators are ubiquitous and there are no indications that the colonizers may one day be defeated. The lasting emotional drive to rebuild a strong nation is at the heart of contemporary Chinese nationalism and is shared by actors across the political spectrum—Left, Right, CCP, and KMT.

The civil war between the CCP and the KMT was not just a factional struggle for political power, or a simple reflection of the global ideologies of socialism and capitalism. It was also an ideological struggle over China's road to modernity. When the defeated KMT withdrew to Taiwan, it felt a sense of entitlement. To the new arrivals, the base they were building to eventually recover the mainland was part of their own territory. The KMT and wàishĕng rén never thought of themselves as invading outsiders, and never imagined they would stay for the long term. Dreams of recovering the mainland were sustained by the global cold-war structure and nurtured by U.S. military and economic support. The dreams later became memories of a loss, a wound that could no longer be healed. After half a century, the KMT still cannot quite bring itself to publicly acknowledge that its right to participate in deciding China's destiny was lost forever when it was defeated in 1949 by the CCP, or that its survival would have been impossible without the support of a Western imperialist power.

In the collective historical memory, the key terms framing the Chinese nationalist narrative were anti-imperialism and resisting foreign power, rather than colonialism. This framing is an obstacle that makes it difficult for wàishěng rén to understand the suffering and sadness of the colonized population. An example of this misunderstanding is the "betraying the ancestor" (shùdiǎn wàngzǔ) criticism leveled at běnshěng rén. Wàishěng rén and mainland Chinese think that China has been oppressed for two hundred years, and that the Japanese took advantage of China's weakness to launch their attack; they believe běnshěng rén have been brainwashed by the Japanese to the point that they have given up the notion of rescuing the nation, and have even become pro-Japanese. To wàishěng rén and mainland Chinese, this is just not acceptable.

On the other side, the 1980s "Orphan of Asia" narrative expresses for the běnshěng population an unforgettable historical wound: Taiwan was abandoned to Japan by China in 1895. The sentiment that mainland Chinese, the KMT, and the wàishěng rén who followed the KMT to Taiwan can simply never be trusted has been constitutive of běnshěng subjectivity. This has been the unspoken and unspeakable consensus. Although modern infrastructure projects, such as railways, had been started during the Qing Dynasty, the subjugated population that lived through the early phase of modernization under Japanese rule was the first to enjoy the fruits of colonial modernity. They developed a hierarchical worldview, with "modern" Japan on top, then "modernizing" Taiwan, and finally "backward" China. For fifty years, there was no indication that Taiwan would ever be liberated from Japanese colonialism; the colonized population had no alternative but to struggle to survive under the colonial regime. Being forced to learn the Japanese national language was in some ways no different than later being forced to learn Mandarin, the national language of the KMT regime, at a time when it was difficult to imagine that the KMT could also one day be pushed out of power.

The 228 Incident of 1947 signaled the start of a long period of fascist military rule and, together with the subsequent White Terror era, it became a symbol used for political mobilization. The KMT's authoritarianism intensified the will among many of the běnshěng population to become independent, to stand on their own two feet, and to defend their home. Further complicating the situation was the KMT's successful anticommunist and pro-American education of the entire population, wàishěng and běnshěng alike. The enemy was defined as communist bandits, and this fear of communism has contributed to the pro-American, pro-Japanese politics of the Taiwan independence movement. The emotional drive for independence found its first official expression in the era of Lee Teng-hui, who, although coming from the KMT, was the first běnshěng president. A second and fuller expression of Taiwanese triumphalism came when Chen Shui-bian, representing the běnshěng-dominated Democratic Progressive Party, was elected president in 2000. His election ended the KMT's monopoly on state power and ended the series of outsider governments that had ruled Taiwan since 1895.

The year 1895 is a crucial marker. For wàishěng rén and mainland Chinese, the concession of Taiwan to Japan was caused by the corruption of the Qing court, whose long abuse of power had ruined China. This is commonly expressed in formulations like: "the Manchus should be blamed for the concession, not us Han Chinese." This ideology of avoiding responsibility for the Taiwan question causes consternation among běnshěng rén. If this sort of argument is accepted, they argue, there are no legitimate grounds for demanding an apology from the Japanese government, since its postwar regime was not the same as the previous military government and therefore, need not shoulder responsibility for the war with China. Without the will to shoulder responsibility for the past, historical wounds cannot be healed, and reconciliation is impossible.

Several important questions underlie the present discussion. First, how do we, in analytical terms, understand the 1949 forced immigration of the wàishěng population? How do we position the KMT regime? Besides a few examples found in Chinese history, such as the Southern Song Dynasty—which, as the remnants of the defeated Northern Song, "temporarily resided on the left bank of the river" (*piānán jiāngzuǒ*), or controlled only the south side of the Yangtze River waiting for the right moment to fight back—it is difficult to find similar instances. The 1947 partition of India and Pakistan split up huge numbers of families who were forced to choose between the two new countries, but that conflict centered on religious differences.[28] After the Korean War, neither the North nor the South was forced to abandon the Korean Peninsula and move to another territory, such as Cheju Island. The lack of a precedent or analogous situation makes it difficult to determine how best to conceptualize the plight of wàishěng rén in Taiwan. Are they settlers, migrants, immigrants, refugees, or people in exile? Are they part of a diaspora, to use the fashionable academic term? Is the KMT regime a government in exile (which would mean that it resides abroad), a regime from another province, a defeated regime, or simply a cold-war regime? None of these common terms accurately describes the complexity of this history.

Given the context provided in this chapter, it seems reasonable to describe the KMT as a defeated, exiled regime existing under the global cold-war structure, and to describe wàishěng rén as those who came to Taiwan with that regime. Even if these complexities can be clarified in theoretical terms, people holding different political positions or those of other ethnic identities may insist on other understandings. One thing is certain: to call the KMT a "regime from the outside" or a "colonial government," as is commonly done, only partially accounts for the historical characteristics of the regime.

A second concern that arises from the analyses of the films is the plight of the nobodies (*xiǎo lǎobǎixìng*), both běnshěng and wàishěng, who have been innocently caught up in larger political currents, and who have to endure much pain and suffering. Not being able to maintain their basic human dignity, some have gone mad (Desheng), some have committed suicide (Dou-sang), and still others have been stigmatized for either willingly making themselves slaves (*núxìng*) to the Japanese, or not fully identifying with Taiwan. In my view, the twin ideologies of statism and nationalism must shoulder much of the responsibility for this suffering. Blaming outside forces, such as colonialism and imperialism, actively and facilely conceals the effects of statism and nationalism on the population. We cannot equate innocent nobodies such as Menxuan and Desheng to the KMT regime, just as we cannot equate the warm-hearted Banana Sister and A-Xiang to the regimes of Lee Teng-hui or Chen Shui-bian. We have to carefully sort through these complex emotional realities so that we can properly explain—and potentially intervene in and break—the logic of various complexes, such as the provincial register contradiction. This is precisely why the KMT regime in Taiwan needs to be analyzed in a new light. The KMT is similar in many ways to the right wing, pro-U.S. regimes in Japan and South Korea, but it is substantially different from cold-war regimes in other parts of the world. This is especially true in the East Asian context, where states not only exercise political power but also have had extraordinary success using their strong symbolic and cultural power to produce popular subjectivity. If we ignore these powerful forces and fail to clarify the formation of the postwar KMT culture, we cannot fully explain the culture of the KMT's reactive counterpart, the DPP, or other oppositional political and social movements.

It is also necessary to reopen the question of patriarchy, as the analysis of Yuexiang in *Banana Paradise* reveals. One of the factors affecting how the patriarchy is expressed in a society is its relation with state power. The nature of the state-patriarchy alliance encourages the development of particular forms of femininity, masculinity, gender relations, and other related oppositional positions. Let me suggest a hypothesis: homosexual cultures are internally related to, or evolve in response to, specific forms of patriarchy. If we compare the patriarchal structures of Taiwan, South Korea, and Japan, I would argue that the weakest is Taiwan, because the political regimes of both the KMT and later the DPP have both been symbolically castrated. The stereotypical views of Japanese women as soft on the outside but tough on the inside, and Korean women as tough on the outside but soft on the inside, need to be explained within the larger historical context. Without addressing the specificity of a particular expression of patriarchal logic, it is difficult to intervene and change it.

To sum up: experiencing the war against Japan on the mainland made it impossible for wàishěng rén to have a sympathetic understanding of the suffering of běnshěng rén under Japanese colonialism or of the mind-set engendered by that experience; at the same time, běnshěng rén cannot empathize with the suffering that wàishěng rén endured as a result of their forced migration with a defeated regime. Conditioned mainly by colonial structures, běnshěng rén cannot really understand the wàishěng structure of sentiment, which was shaped primarily by cold-war structures, just as wàishěng rén cannot truly understand on an emotional level the cultural effects of Japanese colonialism. What makes things worse is that each side uses its own suffering to ignore the possibility of acknowledging the other's grief. Therefore, subjectively, the two structures of sentiment have run parallel to each other, never intersecting, and yet from an objective historical-social perspective, both běnshěng rén and wàishěng rén have been living in a space where these two axes overlap.

Why Is a "Great Reconciliation" Im/possible?

Given the preceding analyses, we are now better prepared to address the issue of the so-called great reconciliation. In the wake of the cold war, the question of reconciliation emerged in many places around the world; it is not unique to Taiwan. And it is not just nations, races, or ethnic groups within a nation that can be reconciled. Reconciliation also refers to the resolution of conflicts among family members, such as those between left- and right-leaning brothers and sisters, or between a father and son who have taken opposing political stands. I was fortunately able to have a reconciliation with my father right before his death in the emergency room of a hospital. Throughout the postwar era in Taiwan, political rivalries over state power, ethnic mobilizations, and struggles over identity and cultural priorities have had real emotional impacts on the population, and all are entwined with the encounters between the two structures of sentiment analyzed in this chapter. Reconciliation between these two segments of the population will be made possible only by establishing mutual recognition of each other's history of suffering. This cannot be done in the very superficial way attempted by those politicians who have called for a temporary suspension of the controversy over unification versus independence. If reconciliation is to be possible, repressed historical memories have to be reopened and confronted. We have to be able to see the provincial register contradiction as a historical-structural question, one that dwells within everyone living in Taiwan. From here we must all recognize the different histories suffered by both běnshěng rén and wàishěng rén, to bridge the gap of understanding and initiate a process of reconciliation.

Likewise, if reconciliation between Taiwan and China is to be possible, it cannot be discussed simply in political or economic terms; nor will nationalist sentiments, which do nothing but cover up real differences, be of any use. The process has to begin with a mutual effort to understand each other's emotional and psychic terrain. The election of the DPP signified the end of the civil war between the KMT and the CCP, and the cold war is also coming to an end. This conjunction of historical forces represents a new political possibility for a reconciliation of the two sides separated by the Taiwan Strait. Old understandings must be adjusted and reformulated, and the old mind-sets of the civil and cold wars need to be changed. The CCP has in reality defeated the KMT; it has won the competition to decide China's road to modernization. There is no need for mainland China's leaders to treat Taiwan highhandedly. The 1996 Chinese missile exercise in the Taiwan Strait and the aggressive statements made during the 2000 Taiwanese presidential elections have gone far beyond simple contradictions between two political regimes and have inflamed the feelings of people on both sides. These actions renewed anticommunist fears in Taiwan.

The articulations of colonialism and the cold war that are proposed here to explain the provincial register contradiction are just one form of narration. The painful historical experiences of běnshěng rén and wàishěng rén are much more complex than the story told here, but I hope that this historical-theoretical explanation will inspire other forms of storytelling and imagination. Unless more stories are honestly and reflexively told, it will be impossible to start the reconciliation process. I am uncertain whether the present historical conditions are conducive to the formation of a politics of mutual recognition, but the changing political environment in the wider domestic and regional contexts does seem to make it possible that a more reflexive politics could emerge.

In terms of international relations, engaging with the historical memories of Japanese colonialism is key to advancing reconciliation and peace in East Asia. In reality, it is still too early to reconcile Okinawa, Taiwan, Korea, and China with Japanese colonialism. Mizoguchi Yūzō (2001, 6) poses some questions for Japanese intellectuals: "What kind of apology should we Japanese pay in terms of the war? What are the boundaries of the apology? Is it an apology only for the violence and crimes, for the military invasion in China, or for the entire modernization process after the Meiji era?"[29] What Mizoguchi means is that if the fundamental question of modernity is necessarily connected to imperialism, then a formulaic apology by the Japanese government is absolutely not enough;

instead, the government has to confront the violence implanted in the very structure and formation of modernity.

Mizoguchi's urgent desire to seek reconciliation comes too early. In East Asia, as Sun Ge (2001a) suggests, intellectuals, governments, and the public in general have not yet openly discussed the issue of the region's historical memory in any meaningful way. So how do we respond to Mizoguchi's sincere invitation to collectively deal with the question of apology? The history suppressed by the cold war has not yet been opened up for critical reflection, so how can we talk about regional reconciliation?

From our experiences of addressing painful historical memories, such as the 228 Incident in Taiwan or the Gwangju Uprising in Korea,[30] we have learned that the rewriting of history textbooks, apologies from the state, compensation funds, and the erection of monuments have real meaning, but it is limited and largely symbolic. None of these actions can fully heal the wounds of the victims, their families, and everyone else who suffered as a result of the events. These painful memories can easily be revived by the eruption of a new controversy, and they are sometimes actively summoned up for purposes of political mobilization. Most efforts to deal with the history of East Asia have been appropriated by the state (which is never politically neutral or trustworthy), partly because of the lack of credible groups in the popular sectors (most of which are divided ethnically or by their positions on national issues). As a result, there is no one who can deal patiently with the topic of reconciliation and address it in depth. The difficulty is further compounded by the fact that, under the new conditions of globalization, increasing the pace of development has become the state's national and nationalist priority. Historical questions are relegated to a secondary status, if they are considered at all.

The move toward reconciliation cannot happen in isolation. The reality is perhaps best expressed by the Chinese saying that "whoever tied the bell to the tiger should be the one to untie it." To be able to overcome the difficulties facing regional reconciliation, we have to go back to the historical harms that Japanese militarism, colonialism, and imperialism produced in the region. Quite unlike other colonial powers that are geographically remote from their former colonies, Japan is right next door. The fact that no country in Asia has yet accepted an apology from the Japanese state reflects the general sentiment that much of this history has not been forgotten. The lack of forgiveness is partly due to the fact that these historical questions have not yet been adequately thought through within Japan.

Let us be reminded again that the new historical moment we share does not permit us to take politically correct positions, nor does it allow us to endlessly rehash the well-worn oppositions between the Left and the Right. We must also think beyond purely theoretical terms and deal with the real tensions internal to our history. Thus, we have to recognize the limits and possibilities provided by the current historical conditions, while keeping in mind the fact that the energy to drive this work forward lies in people's historically rooted structures of sentiment. From experiences in Japan and elsewhere, we have learned that evading the question of nationalism or confronting it directly only diverts this real emotional energy toward unsophisticated popular nationalism, toward the Right, and toward the state machine. How to properly analyze and harness popular energy and transform it into a motor of change working in the interests of the subaltern population is a difficult challenge. Imperialism, colonialism, and the cold war are inherently international forces. In the era of globalization that has emerged in the wake of the cold war, it is even clearer that these questions can no longer be addressed inside any national border. If attempts to engage these questions are locked within national boundaries, we will never break out of the imposed nation-state structure. If critiques remain within the limits of the nationalist framework, it will not be possible to work toward regional reconciliation.

CHAPTER 4

DEIMPERIALIZATION
Club 51 and the Imperialist Assumption of Democracy

Over the past fifty years, through training, exchange, and the policy of study abroad, Taiwan has "successfully" fostered numerous elites with American values. They widely and deeply occupy the political arena, the bureaucratic system, the production sector, and educational institutions. American ideologies and value systems have become the common will and thinking among Taiwanese elites, whether in power or in opposition. I am certain that in the global context, no other society is like Taiwan, which falls completely to the U.S.

CHEN YING-ZHEN, "THE MAKING OF TAIWAN'S AMERICANIZATION"

In the middle of the 1996 Taiwan Strait missile crisis,[1] a document called "An Open Letter to the Social Elite of Taiwan" was distributed to the media and much publicized. The letter was signed by Chou Wei-ling on behalf of a group named Club 51. Next to the signature was a circular drawing featuring a map of Taiwan in the center and a series of slogans in English: "Statehood for Taiwan — Save Taiwan — Say Yes to America."[2]

Club 51 was unknown at the time, but since then, whenever there has been a chance to disseminate its ideas, Club 51 has made its views known. In early 1999, when Lee Teng-hui redefined relations between Taiwan and mainland China as "a special relationship between two countries," Club 51 took to the streets in front of the American Institute in Taiwan (AIT), the de facto U.S. embassy on the island, to protest Washington's ambiguous position on Taiwan's status.[3] After September 11, 2001, Club 51 was one of the leading supporters in Taiwan of the U.S. government's aggressive response. In 2004, Club 51 advocated sending Taiwanese troops to Iraq in support of U.S. military intervention there.

If the seven-page letter of 1996 had appeared at any other time, one would have thought that Club 51 was merely being ironic, but in the context of the missile crisis Taiwanese immediately understood why Club 51 had been formed: to demand American intervention in the Taiwan Strait to counter the threat of an attack by mainland China. This was undoubtedly true, but it was only part of the story. The letter spelled out a much more radical program: Club 51 called for Taiwan to join the United States as its fifty-first state, so as to "guarantee Taiwan's security, stability, prosperity, liberty, and democracy."

Founded on the Fourth of July, 1994, by fifty-one intellectuals and businessmen with strong ties to the United States, Club 51 had grown to some five hundred members by 1996. In addition to its headquarters in Taiwan, it opened a branch office in Los Angeles to promote the idea of "Taiwan state building" in the United States. Anticipating resistance from various groups, Club 51 issued a series of memorandums from 1995 to 1998 addressed to different sectors of the Taiwan population, including the lower-middle class, businessmen, and physicians. In March 2000, Club 51's sister organization, the Foundation for Establishing the 51st State, released "A Report on the Public Opinion Survey of the Will to Build a Taiwan State," a thirty-page analysis of data gathered by a public-opinion research firm.[4]

Club 51 has not expanded into a mainstream movement, but it has nonetheless enjoyed a significant media presence. Its chief spokesman, Chou Wei-ling—also known as David C. Chou—was born in 1949 in Huwei, Taiwan. Often wearing jeans and a T-shirt sporting the American flag, his public persona is that of a hippie, but he holds law degrees from institutions in Taiwan and the United States. A former activist for the Taiwan independence movement, Chou is an articulate writer and speaker. Taiwan's leading newspaper, the *China Times*, devoted a full-page interview to Club 51 on 29 May 1996, and *The New York Times* published a profile of Chou on 4 August 1999.[5] Chou has appeared on various call-in shows on television and radio to offer Club 51's perspective on current affairs.

In mainstream Taiwanese politics, Club 51's 1996 proposal did not initially receive the same serious attention that it garnered in the media. Nevertheless, over the past ten years, its position has slowly become a point against which other positions on the political spectrum are measured. Club 51's seeming pragmatism has, for example, embarrassed the fundamentalist faction of the Taiwan independence movement because it raises an unspeakable dilemma: to become independent, Taiwan must depend on the United States militarily, diplomatically, and economically, but to openly admit this fact is contrary to the very idea of independence.

In 1998, encouraged by sympathetic as well as antagonistic reactions to Club 51's program, Chou published a highly imaginative work to substantiate his arguments and articulate his dream. *A Date with the U.S. — The Ultimate Resolution of Taiwan's Future: Taiwan Becomes a State of the U.S. in 2013; Say Yes to America* advocates a two-stage strategy. First, Taiwan becomes a U.S. territory, along the lines of Puerto Rico, then it seeks full statehood, as Hawaii did. Then, on 1 January 2013 — naturally, a splendid, sunny day — Taiwan officially becomes the fifty-first state of the United States of America. All Chinese surnames are changed forthwith: Yuan to Adams, Kung to Cohen, Chen to Dunn, Ding to Dean, and Chou to Jefferson. All Taiwanese cities and districts acquire new place names. Eight pages of the book are devoted to the renaming: Taipei is renamed as Cambridge, Taichung as Dalton, Kaohsiung as Farfax, Hsinchu as Talcom, and Makung as Malcolm. Among the forty-six newly elected members of Congress from the state of Taiwan, twenty-two are fluent in English. Of these, fourteen are second-generation mainlanders and eight were educated in the United States. These eight also happen to be children of the leading politicians of the time, including the son of the former Taiwan provincial governor James Soong, Soong Chen-yuan, who will change his name to James C. Stevens; and the son of the former vice-president and KMT chairman Lien Chan, Lien Sheng-wu, who will rename himself Vincent W. Lane. On this day, the Taiwanese will finally have "the sense of belonging, the sense of certainty, the sense of direction, and the sense of security" denied to them by Taiwan's former ambiguous geopolitical position (Chou 1998, 324).

One might assume that Club 51 is a uniquely Taiwanese phenomenon, but the impulses that gave rise to the organization are not confined to Taiwan. There have been similar movements in the Philippines and Okinawa, kindred but more subdued sentiments in Korea,[6] and similar appeals by groups in other parts of the world.[7] More nuanced explanations of this competition over who gets to be the fifty-first or fifty-second state obviously require detailed analyses of specific local histories and their interactions with various global configurations of power. Though the theoretical structure of this America complex might be quite similar in various countries, the relationships between the locales' material and imaginary connections to the United States will necessarily have different trajectories.

I wish to make clear that I have no personal investment in Club 51 or its position, and I do not want to be read as taking a stand simply for or against either one. The moralizing tendency found on the nationalist Left and nationalist Right in both Taiwan and mainland China is not helpful in analyzing the issues at stake here. In Asia, there has been a frequent practice of quickly jumping to moral judgments whenever controversy arises, but this forecloses the possibility of critical reflection, which is a precondition of understanding the psychological forces at work in our societies. To either quickly cast Club 51 aside as politically irrelevant or readily endorse its position misses the point. The real political significance of Club 51 is that it opens an alternative discursive space for Taiwanese statehood, one that lies beyond the banality of separatism versus integrationism that has been the dominant discursive mode shaping Taiwanese politics for the past thirty years. Club 51's radicalness lies in its move away from any form of independence or national sovereignty by proposing to become a state of another entity—the United States. This switch from "state building" in the sense of building a nation to "state building" in the sense of building one more part of the United States is a sea change in the parameters of the anticolonial imaginations that have powered third-world independence movements to date. Its form of identification and affiliation may remind us of France's so-called foreign departments such as Martinique or, indeed, of the case of Hawaii, but its emergence shortly before the beginning of the twenty-first century seems to indicate the existence of a new historical condition markedly different from earlier moments of decolonization.[8] How does one describe this new historical juncture? To what extent can globalization account for this change? What are the historical conditions in which such a political position could emerge? What can we learn from Club 51?

Determining the extent to which the sentiments expressed by Club 51 represent current popular desires in Taiwan is not the purpose of this discussion, but Club 51 does provide an ideal vantage point from which to address the question of deimperialization. More concretely, Club 51 penetrates a layer of issues related to what I call the interiority of the imaginary concept of America in East Asia—or, as the Japanese put it, Americanism. America is now an integral part of Asia, as a result of the culture of U.S. imperialism that emerged in the wake of the Second World War. But this crucial problematic also needs to be understood in the wider context of what can be described as an insecurity born of global uncertainty, a new structure of sentiment that is the direct product of neoliberal globalization.[9] The emergence of this sentiment of insecurity cannot be explained except in the context of the currently emerging reconfiguration of imperialism and capitalism, of which globalization is a form of expression.

If the problematic is situated in the analytic and discursive plane of postcolonial cultural studies, we can see there is an urgent need to bring the issue of imperialism back to the center of debate, but we must approach it in new ways. While recognizing the tremendous extent to which the present historical moment has been shaped by anti-imperialist struggles, we must insist that the new direction of the study of imperialism avoid two pitfalls: a return to the old anticolonial nationalist and nativist positions, which often operate within the hierarchical logic of civilization, race, nation, and ethnicity, while placing other social contradictions on the sideline; and advocating a globalist position, which often endorses forms of transnationalism or cosmopolitanism that ironically perpetuate the same racial, national, and ethnic mind-sets. Setting aside these two unacceptable approaches, how do we begin to imagine an alternative? To stake out a new position, we must first recognize that imperialism exercises its power not simply through an imposition of force from the outside, but also from within. The drive for modernization is just as strong among the colonized as it is among the colonizers. If we accept this proposition as the point of departure for rethinking the question of colonial subjectivity, we not only return agency to the colonized subject, but we also come closer to describing real historical conditions.

In East Asia, the United States has always been regarded by critical intellectuals and others on the Left as an outsider—simultaneously outside the territory and the cultural psyche. But after a century of insinuating itself as the dominant point of reference in East Asia, it no longer seems analytically accurate to say that the United States is exterior to the histories of the region. As Shunya Yoshimi has pointed out, Americanism is no longer composed of unsystematic and free-floating signs but has evolved into a dominant system of reference (Yoshimi 2000). There is, therefore, an urgent need to find new critical languages and positions to overcome the platitudes of the nationalist framework. With perhaps the exception of the Philippines, U.S. imperialism as an integral part of the cultural forces interior to Asia has not been sufficiently studied.

The problematic of U.S. imperialism in Asia is not new. By confronting the United States as an insider to the region, one runs the risk of being read as a postcolonial nationalist. Indeed, advancing nationalist interests in the name of the postcolonial has become the standard intellectual practice in both colonized and formerly colonized spaces. But in this chapter, I attempt to shift the direction of the postcolonial paradigm toward the horizons of decolonization and deimperialization, both of which are directly connected to the reconstitution of subjectivity, and neither of which can be understood from within the closed space of nationalist ambition.

Reading Club 51

Since its inception, Club 51 has maintained a perfectly consistent position. In facing different events, it always responds from the same political stance, and through this process, it deepens and renews its discourse and beliefs. During the 1996 Taiwan Strait missile crisis, the main arguments of Club 51 were highlighted, point by point, on the first page of its open letter. The first point reads:

> If Club 51 cannot awaken the elite sector of the population of Taiwan in time to give up such selfish and short-sighted practices as individual immigration, and to support instead the proposal of the Taiwan State Building Movement for collective identification and naturalization into the U.S., within a few years Taiwan will not be able to escape the appalling fate of Hong-Kongization. Even if it can avoid this, it will be constantly beset by Beijing's psychological warfare, plunging it into economic recession, falling confidence, and social unrest. (Club 51 Open Letter, 1)

Conjuring up the specter of Hong Kong on the eve of its return to China in 1997 was calculated to trigger fear and insecurity, but Club 51's appeal does rely not just on demonizing the communists and hammering home the threat they pose to Taiwan. It also offers an alternative for the many elite individuals who were thinking about joining the panicky exodus abroad. Club 51 proposes to the Taiwanese elite that they need not selfishly emigrate, but rather collectively change their nationality. No one even has to leave home. The letter states: "once Taiwan becomes a state of the U.S., we will be in America right here, and Taiwanese will not have to dwell in other places throughout the world as a minority of minorities in local societies." The ingenuity of Club 51's proposal is this radical resolution to the impasse of Taiwanese independence. The message is clear: Let us give up our own nation-state, with its hopelessly ambiguous status, and instead join another nation of our choice. State building would then no longer require endless unsuccessful efforts to join the United Nations. Our partial Americanization over the past fifty years can expand to fully embrace a new nationality — one allowing Taiwanese to say of their island "this is America."

This vision is pitched not only to the elite, but to everyone living on Taiwan, which makes Club 51 an ambitious political project. Club 51 articulates the people's desire to be at home and envisions that the impending economic success of the island as part of the United States would not only make those currently in Taiwan willing to stay, but would also encourage emigrants and their children to return. Underpinning this craving to be at home is an overwhelming sense of insecurity. The closing words of the paragraph — "economic recession, falling confidence, and social unrest" — can be understood as either a strategy for mobilizing popular fear and hence support for Club 51's position, or as an expression of such fear. Either way, the fear of communism cultivated by the KMT is deeply rooted in the same cold-war discourse that later produced Club 51. Despite the rhetoric of globalization that it employs, Club 51's approach is based on a cold-war sensibility.

Having triggered a sense of crisis, the open letter continues: "When Beijing announced its 'missile rehearsal' to threaten the presidential election in Taiwan, our Deputy Minister of Foreign Affairs called upon the AIT Director, begging the U.S. to uphold justice for Taiwan. Any clearsighted person knows that Taiwan cannot survive without U.S. protection. If the United States does not uphold the principle of justice, 'the Republic of China in Taiwan' might soon become 'the Republic of China in Los Angeles'" (ibid.). The United States is perceived as an international police force whose mission is to maintain the principles of global justice, and without whose protection the Republic of China would devolve into something else. In the Taiwanese context, Club 51's gesture is provocative, even iconoclastic. Although everyone knows that the island is under U.S. protection, this has never been publicly admitted by any member of the government. It simply remains an unspoken assumption, but one that frames the activities of both of Taiwan's major political parties, with the KMT typically seeking "help" from the U.S. Republicans, and the DPP "assistance" from the Democrats. Questions of whether or not Taiwan can survive without the U.S. military shield, or without the mainland Chinese market, have never been debated in the public arena.

Club 51's blunt use of the word "begging" reveals the hierarchical nature of the Taiwan-U.S. relationship and Taiwan's subcolonial status — or, as Club 51 imagines it, Taiwan's quasi-state status, similar to the relationship between the suzerain and vassal states in the classic tributary system. Club 51's pragmatic realism cancels out all rhetorical pretensions of national dignity. It does so in the name of survival, a consideration that overrides any theoretical claim to state sovereignty. Herein lies the real difficulty: Club 51 speaks the reality that cannot otherwise be openly discussed because it is a slap in the face of nationalist sentiment. But once this taboo subject is brought to the surface, there is no way to circle around it any longer. It must be confronted. This is the reason why Club 51 has persistently attempted to bring to light the reality of Taiwan's dependence on the United States, which Taiwan independence supporters want to hide. Only by recognizing and accepting the hard facts can state building proceed.

Particularly striking in this respect is the scenario projected in the last sentence of the paragraph. If Taiwan were forced to become a part of China, then something like a refugee government would be set up in Los Angeles. By what chain of equivalents could the quasi-nation-state of Taiwan somehow effortlessly shift categories and borders to set up shop in the city of Los Angeles? But this idea is by no means ungrounded. From the 1960s to the 1990s, the United States, in particular Los Angeles, was the destination of choice for Taiwanese emigrants, and the city is now home to the largest concentration anywhere of middle-class immigrants from the island. In the Taiwanese imagination, Taiwan has long been inside Los Angeles and is an integral part of that city. The large residential community of Monterey Park just east of downtown Los Angeles is widely known as Little Taipei, and several other communities in the area could also vie for this distinction. At the same time, Los Angeles has also been inside Taiwan and is an integral part of its life. The pop group LA Boys, all of whose members grew up in greater Los Angeles, has "returned home" to Taiwan, and become one of the most popular "local" pop acts in Taiwan. It is not difficult to imagine Los Angeles hosting a Republic of China government in exile.

During the Taiwan presidential election campaign in March 2000, all of Taiwan's satellite news channels set up call-in programs to boost ratings and advertising revenue. One popular station, TVBS, set up its call-in center across the ocean, in Los Angeles. This was a rather natural choice. Supporters of each of the three presidential candidates, their affiliations clearly identifiable by the colors of their campaign vests, were brought into the studio and divided into groups. Each group enthusiastically proclaimed that its candidate best represented the real "new Taiwanese" (*xīn Táiwānrén*), and that his rivals were fakes. Yet when asked by the television host who constituted the real "new Taiwanese," the participants all agreed that the real "new Taiwanese" are the ones who live in Taiwan and have a commitment to Taiwan. How can we explain this paradox?

Overseas supporters were in fact probably more involved in the election battle than most of those who actually live in the geographic space of Taiwan. The overseas Taiwanese spared no effort to further their respective causes by donating money, arranging debates with opponents, and persuading expatriates to go home to Taiwan to vote (airlines supporting a particular candidate offered discounted tickets to his supporters). The overseas supporters acted as if they were the real "new Taiwanese." In fact, Los Angeles was already imagined as part of Taiwan. The physical distance between Taiwan and Los Angeles was negated by the television screen and the imaginary it sustained. It is typical for immigrants to live in communities in different parts of the world, but in every other respect to live "at home." They read newspapers published at home, watch satellite news broadcast from home, consume goods and foods from home (exported to supermarkets and restaurant chains run by enterprises from home), and worry more about changing the government at home than about the one they are subject to abroad. They split and form new alliances when political parties at home do the same.

How does Club 51 handle possible objections to its program? The open letter states: "If you hear an accomplice of the Chinese communists cursing Club 51 as 'the slaves of a subjugated nation,' 'traitors to the country,' 'traitors to the Han people,' 'the running dogs of American imperialism,' please argue back that national identity is based neither on blood descent nor threat of military force. Like the Chiang family, which has German, Russian, and Japanese blood, we have the right to choose to be American or German, and to live in New York or San Francisco" (ibid.). Club 51 is well prepared for the kinds of rude reactions it is likely to attract and has prepared lines of response for each of them. The phrases in the letter are derogatory Chinese terms that were used in different historical moments and during various nationalist wars against foreign invaders. Anticipating likely directions of attack, Club 51's letter instructs the reader how to debate with the "accomplices of Chinese communists." Its counterargument is impeccably anti-essentialist, rejecting common descent as the basis for national identification. Boldly, it invokes the international marriages of the supposedly evil Chiang Kai-shek family as a point of reference to legitimize the free choice of nationality. It is slightly unclear why American and German are mentioned as identities of preference, and why Russian or Japanese are silently discarded. Indeed, German itself seems little more than a rhetorical flourish when the choice of cities is confined to the United States. Why this selectivity?

The answer is offered a little later when the letter quotes Professor Lee Hsiao-fung, a professor of history at Shih Hsin University: "We would rather be stuffed to death by the hamburgers of American imperialism than shot to death by machine guns of Chinese Communist imperialism." Of special note here is the phrase "American imperialism," which appears only once in the letter. Even so, its mention is a further indication of Club 51's willingness to openly address issues considered anathema in mainstream politics. The letter continues: "all of us try desperately to stay out of China's reach, and all of us nourish a deeply hidden 'American dream' in our mind" (ibid., 6–7). Hamburger heaven is the outward expression of an implicit dream: America is the pinnacle of human civilization; a powerful, prosperous, democratic society; a land of certainty and security. Here, courageously displayed, is a window into the psyche of nouveau riche Taiwanese who harbor a "deeply hidden 'American dream'" and long for an impossible assimilation into the U.S. middle class.

This leads us back to what I suggested earlier: the great imperial dream of becoming American is never simply imposed from the outside. On the contrary, it is also cultivated within the local milieu—and in our particular case, within the "new Taiwanese" middle class. The longing to become an American imperial subject occupies a prominent and intimate position in the Taiwanese psyche. My analysis will show how, in the aftermath of September 11, Club 51's imperial desire was transformed into an imperialist desire.

However, it would be a mistake to essentialize this American dream. Near the end of the open letter, this paragraph appears: "If the Chinese break everyone's glasses [confound expectations] and build a free, democratic, universally prosperous, happy land on earth, while America becomes a poor, devastated inferno, the people of the state of Taiwan can always peacefully promote a movement to 'unite Taiwan and China,' without any fear of suppression by American military force. In short, once Taiwan becomes a state of America, the door to either 'Taiwan independence' or 'reunification with China' will not be closed, because America is a democratic and free country" (ibid., 7). The logic of the choice could not be clearer. Economic success is the primary criterion for selecting national belonging. Club 51 claims Taiwan can keep the door open to China or any society rich and powerful enough to guarantee freedom, democracy, and wealth, since the American state is such that if one day Taiwan changes its mind and wants to leave the United States, it will make no objection. Club 51 appears never to have heard of the American civil war, but that hardly matters. The point is that its proposal dispenses with national loyalty and replaces it with a calculation of pure self-interest.

Despite this rhetoric of openness, Club 51 is really demanding that Taiwan make a choice between the United States and China. If in fact wealth is the fundamental criterion, why is Japan, which is much closer to Taiwan, not also an option? Unlike mainstream Taiwan independence groups, Club 51 considers only the United States and China. The absence of Japan reveals Club 51's unconscious identification with the Chinese empire, an empire with a worldview that looks down on Japan as a small country on the periphery of East Asia, a country that can never compete culturally with China. And herein lies a major clue to Club 51's logic: whether it is the United States of today or the China of the past, Club 51 wants to identify with the strongest empire.

The open letter is aware of the kind of resistance it may provoke: "although you cannot immediately accept our case at an emotional level [*qínggǎn shàng*], we believe that on a rational level [*lǐzhì shàng*], you cannot deny that our new proposal for Taiwan's future is the only solution to the real crisis of our society" (ibid., 1).

To be effective, Club 51 must take account of nationalist sentiment, which is deeply rooted in historical experience. It understands that the intended readers of its letter are likely to feel uneasy "at an emotional level" about the idea of becoming American. Although in practice many Taiwanese have, as individuals, become naturalized as American, Australian, or Canadian citizens, to demand that every Taiwanese immediately become American is likely to offend collective pride. Club 51 thus urges its audience to operate rationally and cast aside their irrelevant emotional, moral, and historical baggage. Of course, Club 51's appeal to rationality has its own emotional bottom line, evident in its strong desire for prosperity and security. The group's appeal also plays upon feelings of nostalgia. The sentiment that Taiwan would be better off if it were still under Japanese rule is quite widespread, especially among the generation that lived through the Japanese colonial period in Taiwan. Club 51's tacit message to these people is this: Let's not miss our chance again. We can make the rational choice to substitute the Americans for the Japanese.

After establishing these key arguments, the open letter moves into a detailed narrative. It begins with a description of the military threat facing Taiwan in an attempt to elicit a mood of insecurity, and it suggests that even if there were no immediate danger of Taiwan's being occupied by communist forces, the island still lacks the means to defend itself. The letter then raises a critical question: whom can we count on to protect the lives and freedoms of the Taiwanese people—Taiwan's own armed forces? This narrative relies on the logic of fear: threats lead to war, and war results in the destruction of life, security, and accumulated wealth. There is, therefore, a need for a mechanism that guarantees protection, which can be provided only if Taiwan becomes part of the United States. This basic argument underlies all of Club 51's claims.

If we consider the overall tenor of the letter, what we find at work is a "radical plural opportunism."[10] I use this term without any derogatory connotation. What it denotes is a nonessentialist, pragmatic, and open-ended position whose adherents will seize any opportunity to further their self-interest. The phrase embodies an imperative to abandon whatever moral baggage one may be carrying and jump onto whatever vehicle promises the quickest route to individual wealth and security. Operating within an overwhelmingly conservative political society, critical forces in Taiwan lack the strength to propose radical alternatives such as this, yet the outlook can nevertheless be found in many parts of mainstream Taiwanese society — in nongovernmental organizations, civil society, and business. One might even say that it is a general characteristic of Taiwanese capitalism, or perhaps of any brand of capitalism.

There is little doubt that current global conditions provide particularly fertile soil for such opportunism. The emergence of Club 51 in the 1990s was symptomatic not only of specific anxieties about Taiwan's status vis-à-vis mainland China and the United States, but also of a general uneasiness about the direction of the world as a whole. The protests against the World Trade Organization in Seattle in 1999 and Hong Kong in 2005, and other reactions against globalization, contributed to the apprehensiveness felt by Taiwanese already unsettled by mainland China's military threats. While no analysis can confidently predict the exact nature of the changes that globalization will bring, it is clear that gaps between countries and classes are likely to widen. In this environment, a strategy of leaning on the strongest party — "the watermelon tilts toward the bigger half," as the Taiwanese expression has it — makes sense to Club 51's middle-class constituency. Club 51's nostalgic desire for empire, energized by the pressures of globalization, strongly marks the continuity of imperialism even after the Second World War. The decolonization movement has not yet undertaken the cultural process of deimperialization, and thus it has not yet examined the problem of imperial imagination. This old desire to be part of the empire has spilled over into the present. Rather than illustrating any epochal decline of the nation-state, Club 51 is evidence of the rise in identification — imaginary, symbolic, and real — with the strongest state, that single superpower we coexist with today.

How to Understand Americanism

The presence of the United States in East Asia as an imperial power has not been seriously taken up as an object of study, and we must try to account for this lack of analysis. The easiest and least satisfying explanation is to deny the imperial status of the United States altogether, which is to argue that U.S. hegemony has been established by virtue of its global leadership and the consent granted by other nations rather than through military force, economic domination, or other means. This argument immediately crumbles if we consider the conspicuous military presence of the United States in East Asia (where people's movements have struggled to have U.S. bases removed),[11] the first Gulf War (conducted under the guise of liberating Kuwait), the U.S. missile attacks on Iraq and Kosovo (which lacked sufficient international consensus), or the U.S. military intervention in Afghanistan and Iraq in the aftermath of September 11. The imperial status of the United States is also sometimes obscured due to methodological failings. In her introduction to *Cultures of United States Imperialism*, an important work in the national tradition from an earlier moment in American studies, Amy Kaplan succinctly explains the denial of contemporary U.S. imperialism: "Most current studies of imperial and postcolonial culture, however, tend to omit discussion of the United States as an imperial power. The history of American imperialism strains the definition of the postcolonial, which implies a temporal development (from 'colonial' to 'post') that relies heavily on the spatial coordinates of European empires, in their formal acquisition of territories and subsequent history of decolonization and national independence. How would this Eurocentric notion of postcoloniality apply to the history of American imperialism, which often does not fit this model?" (Kaplan 1993, 17). Kaplan's analysis suggests that because the dominant paradigms used to understand imperialism are based on European experiences, and that there exist no models that can properly account for U.S. imperialism.[12] This assumes an epistemological break between Eurocentrism and American-centrism: as we entered the era of American hegemony, the issue of imperialism conveniently dissolved, allowing the American empire to escape the same kind of scrutiny that European imperialism has been subjected to.

The neoimperial form of U.S. postcolonialism mixes military force, international diplomacy, intervention in other countries' domestic affairs, and cultural exports. And the active importation of American ways of doing things by nationalist elites who worship at the altar of American modernity certainly suits U.S. national interests. The United States does not have to invest capital to occupy and develop colonies, yet it still manages to achieve its strategic and economic objectives. Furthermore, the local modernizing elites save face, since they are not seen as the running dogs of the imperialist master, while at the same time the United States can maintain the facade of American idealism. This complicit arrangement is the distinguishing characteristic of the U.S. model of postcolonialism.

A third reason that the U.S. role as an imperial power has not been adequately addressed can be attributed to the formation of an enduring cold-war logic. In East Asia, after all, there was a direct connection between the traditional form of colonialism and the cold-war structures that emerged after 1945. Ever since the bombing of Hiroshima and Nagasaki, the Japanese state has lived under the permanent shadow of American rule. In many parts of East Asia, Japanese imperial holdings were handed directly over to the United States. Meanwhile, authoritarian anticommunist regimes in South Korea, Taiwan, and South Vietnam were strongly supported by the United States as part of its effort to establish a vast arc of strategic protectorates to defend against the spread of communism. All of these imperialistic developments have ironically served to displace the question of U.S. imperialism.

While the cultural impacts of the cold-war structure are indeed significant and underanalyzed, we must resist the temptation to accept a determinist worldview in which the feelings for and against the United States engendered during the cold war are seen as natural and inevitable. Automatically distancing ourselves from the United States would once again deprive us of the critical distance needed to analyze the open secret of the American dream as internal to national and nationalist identity in Asia. This has been a problem for the nationalist Left in East Asia because it complicates attempts to hold U.S. imperialism fully responsible for dividing our countries. This type of reductionism does little to explain the desire for America cultivated in East Asian societies and exaggerates the discontinuity between politics during and after the cold war.

In documenting the 1948 Cheju Uprising, the feminist anthropologist Kim Seongnae describes the momentum and resilience of anticommunism:

> Although the Cold War has ended, anti-Communist ideology continues to dominate state politics in South Korea and has effectively silenced much of the memory of the 4.3 Event . . . Since the end of

World War II, it could be said that Koreans have lived under "the state of emergency" for national unity and identity. This profound sense of emergency has served to justify state violence in both separate regimes of South and North Koreas . . . As it is described as "a microscope on the politics of postwar Korea," the 4.3 Event remains stigmatized as a primal scene in the acceleration of Korean modernity that is closely related to political violence of the state. (Kim 1996, 8)

Kim reminds us of the continuity between the cold war and the post-cold-war "state of emergency," as well as the role of the state and critical intellectuals in perpetuating it. To these often-overlooked points we must add the importance of imperial identification, a cold-war product which is absent from studies of U.S. imperialism in East Asia. Cultural studies of U.S. imperialism in the region are only just starting to emerge, and it is important to caution against counterpositioning one (subaltern) nationalism against another (paramount) nationalism.

Due to the complexity of the sixty-five years of U.S. hegemony in East Asia, a comprehensive laundry list of the deep American impacts in the region is impossible to produce (Chen 1998). It is important to note that the fact of U.S. hegemony does not imply its acceptance; in fact, resistance to U.S. hegemony is evidence of its presence. To see the strength of the American complex in East Asia, one need only look at the popularity of the "X Can Say No" phenomenon. After the big success in 1990 of Ishihara Shintaro and Morita's Akio *The Japan that Can Say No* came the popular *China Can Say No* (Sung 1996) and *Taiwan Can Say No* (Ker 1996). Unmistakably, the United States is what these countries are saying no to. What this implies, of course, is the preexistence of an indisputable yes. These texts are signs of deep and continuing identification with what their titles deny but are unable to displace.

East Asians' profound identification with the United States also raises a crucial methodological issue. The study of the culture of U.S. imperialism needs to move beyond the frame of cultural imperialism that was formulated in the 1970s. The earlier argument holds that newer forms of imperialism operate through an external imposition of cultural products and ideologies that brainwash third-world societies, or create a false consciousness in them. Frequently cited examples are McDonald's, Hollywood, and American Top 40 music, but the effects of these symbolic objects have been exaggerated. Since the mid-1980s, several parts of East Asia have seen the emergence of local culture industries strong enough to compete with the American output. For some thirty years now, Hong Kong films have captured a significant share of the market in various East and Southeast Asian countries. By the 1990s, younger East Asians were no longer singing American pop songs in karaoke bars. The false consciousness thesis no longer has explanatory power. It cannot persuasively articulate these imported products to the internal logic of local cultural history. The theoretical turn from cultural imperialism to the culture of imperialism enables a more sophisticated understanding. We need to ask why imperialism produces such long-lasting effects when the local cultural machinery is not, or at least is no longer, mediated through transnational media. We need to carefully investigate the specific mechanisms through which imperialism links up with local political and economic forces.

Before more historical research is done to address these questions, we can only put forward a tentative proposition. In East Asia, colonial identifications and disidentifications since the Second World War have set the boundaries of the local cultural imagination, consciously and unconsciously articulated by and through various institutions of the nation-state in alliance with capital and even sectors of the civil society. The power behind the culture of U.S. imperialism comes from its ability to insert itself into a geocolonial space as the imaginary figure of modernity, and as such, the natural object of identification from which the local people are to learn. Throughout the region, U.S. institutional forms have been copied, American English has become the first foreign language to be studied, and the United States was practically the only foreign space available for advanced education until the 1980s. For the elites of both the state and the opposition, American experiences have become reference points that reinforce their own legitimacy. In the popular imagination, the extent of the unconscious identification with America can be seen in the use of the Mandarin word *guówài* (abroad, foreign) which is very often used interchangeably with *Měiguó* (America).

To evoke this identification is not so much to add a psychological gloss to history, but to suggest that the material history of imperialism has created identifications and disidentifications through which neocolonial systems of representation and modes of living have infiltrated the space of the national popular imagination. The flow of psychic desire and energy is confined within the boundaries of the colonial and neocolonial cultural imaginary, and this network stretches to every corner of the social body. It would be inappropriate to directly apply Fanon's famous thesis to suggest that Japanese, Korean, Chinese, and Taiwanese want to be American just as "the black man wants to be white." However, it is difficult to deny that a similar theoretical logic is at work. The twist in the post-cold-war era of globalization has been the leaving behind of the limited theory of colonial identification, and the new articulation of identity under a condition of global uncertainty.

The complexity of the situation is the complexity of history. The past is inevitably appropriated to explain and respond to the present, a case in point being the emergence of civilizationalism as the latest form of nativism. Cho Haejoang (1999) has succinctly analyzed the Confucian revival movement in Korea; Chua Beng Huat has taken up the Singaporean redrafting of Asian identification (Chua 1998); and Japan is also undergoing a re-Asianization phase. These self-rediscovery movements are obviously connected to the regionalization of global capital, but the psychological drive at their core is once again grounded in colonial history. The implicit Other that defines this new Asian civilizationism is America, and the regionwide anti-Americanism that has surfaced is a return of the repressed desire for empire. Even the pro-American Club 51 is an example of this trend.

The preceding analyses have no ironic motive; I do not wish to ridicule any of these movements, only to point out that both the pro- and anti-American modes operate within a space defined by the same object. Disidentification assumes the existence of a prior identification. I believe this is one reason why the question of U.S. imperialism has not been adequately addressed. America as an object of identification has not only been with us all along, but it has been so thoroughly integrated into our thoughts and practices that we have lost the ability to critically engage with the issue of U.S. imperialism at all. America exists and thrives at a level deeper than most analysts have explored. If we wish to honestly understand the subjectivity of the self in East Asia, we have to recognize that the United States has not merely defined our identities but has become deeply embedded within our subjectivity. And it is precisely by occupying this position as the dominant system of reference that America constitutes our subjectivity. When the United States, rather than the Philippines or Korea, has been consistently adopted as our default point of reference, it means that we are Americanized, if not American. This basic recognition is the necessary starting point if Taiwanese subjectivity is to be transformed.

Americanism after September 11

The reconfiguration of global politics that followed September 11, 2001, compels us to think about the U.S. neocolonial military-industrial complex in a wider context, beyond that of Club 51, Taiwan, or East Asia. Most responses to the attack from around the world could be divided into two types. The first strongly supported U.S. military action to combat terrorism, which was Club 51's position. The second reflected the anti-American sentiment that rapidly surfaced throughout the world on an unprecedented scale. Among the responses in this type, a consensus emerged: "*Yes*, we condemn the inhuman aggression and express our great sympathy for the victims, *but* we also think this attack is the result of the U.S. government's unacceptable conduct toward other countries. We hope the American people will be prompted by the attack to reflect on the harm their government has inflicted on the rest of the world and work to change their government's brutal foreign policy." The development of the Internet made it possible for the first time to have an extremely focused global discussion of America's role in the world; in the wake of September 11, "yes, but" was the rhetorical mode of many of the critical commentaries that emerged. The sympathetic expressions in the first half of these utterances were largely negated by the condemnations in the second half. If this rhetoric accurately represents the sentiment of a significant segment of the global population at the time, it shows that the United States was losing legitimacy in the eyes of the world, and that the singular hegemonic superpower was in decline. Indeed, its leadership had been questioned long before September 11, and the event was really a touchstone for preexisting antagonisms. This being the case, the question becomes: how can this intense, global anti-American sentiment be properly explained?

A theoretical mode of interpretation will not be useful in this instance. To understand how the United States has been perceived, especially in East Asia, we need to return to history. Since the mid-nineteenth century, America has never been outside Asia. Japan was opened to the United

States in 1858 when the treaty-port system was established. The impact on Japan of the subsequent economic and cultural interactions, continuing through the period between the world wars, cannot be overstated. By the 1930s, some Japanese intellectuals felt that America had become a constitutive element of Japanese identity. A startling passage from Takanobu Murobuse's *America*, published in 1929, makes this quite clear: "Where could you find Japan not Americanized? How could Japan exist without America? And where could we escape from Americanization? I dare to even declare that America has become the world, Japan is nothing but America today" (quoted in Yoshimi 2000, 202–3). The presence of the United States on the Korean Peninsula also had significant cultural impacts. Yoo Sun-young's important analysis of 1930s Korea highlights the role American modernity played in combating Japanese colonialism (Yoo 2001). For the elite in Korean society at the time, a command of things American in everyday life allowed them to express a modernity that surpassed that of Japan.

The studies by Yoshimi (2000, 2003), Yoo (2001), and Chen (2001a) suggest that the emergence of America as the dominant symbol of the modern had to do with its image as a liberator in East Asia and elsewhere. The rise of the United States as a global power after the First World War was felt not only in the imperial centers of Europe and East Asia, but also in their colonies. The United States was a relative newcomer to imperialist power politics, and led by President Woodrow Wilson, it proposed a strategy of self-determination for colonized spaces, which proved to be effective not only in U.S. competition with established imperial powers in already occupied territories, but also in leading colonized nationalist subjects to collaborate with the United States. Ideologically, self-determination was difficult for the imperial powers to oppose, and it held tremendous appeal for colonial elites. National self-determination was quickly propagated as the meta-language of anticolonial independence movements. The image of the United States as a liberator in the imagination of nationalist elites continued after the Second World War and contributed to the postwar formation of the global cold-war power structure.

The historian Bruce Cumings has traced a direct transition from Japanese to U.S. imperialism throughout East Asia in the years following the Second World War (Cumings 1984). In addition to occupying the

Japanese mainland, the United States assumed control of Japan's colonial apparatus directly from the defeated Japanese empire. The KMT's retreat to Taiwan and the Korean War finally consolidated the cold-war power structure in East Asia. The United States had built its anticommunist boundary against China and North Korea. The East Asian capitalist bloc was different from its counterparts in Europe and other parts of the world. In East Asia, old colonialism was immediately replaced with new militarism, and mainland China, which had not directly been under U.S. influence, began to view America as the negative Other, the idealized representative of the West.[13] In short, since the 1950s, America has gradually become East Asia's "inside outsider" or "outside insider"—in either case, an important element in the formation of identity and subjectivity in East Asia.

In the past fifty years, Japan, South Korea, Taiwan, and Okinawa have become semicolonies of the United States. The domains of economic development, military management, and international politics are all subject to American influence. With the exception of Taiwan, where military bases were removed after the United States established formal relations with mainland China, these locations still host operating U.S. military bases. American military aircraft take off and touch down continually in the suburbs of Tokyo. Itaewon, in the center of Seoul, is the site of an American base. U.S. bases occupy nearly twenty percent of the island of Okinawa. Should hostilities break out in East Asia, these bases are sure to be among the first places targeted for attack.

The U.S. cold-war strategies of balance of power and containment depended on military force, but this began to change in the late 1970s. The reform and reopening of mainland China was the starting point. The Chinese hatred of the United States slowly gave way to open admiration of American modernity. The American dream was no longer exclusive to the capitalist zone of East Asia but had finally unified the collective imagination of the region.

The end of the cold war was marked by the collapse of socialist regimes in Eastern Europe, and then the collapse of the Soviet Union itself. By the late 1980s, it was clear that the bipolar global competition was over, and that the United States had become the sole military superpower. But the spectacular growth of capitalism in East Asia at the end of the 1980s made that region symbolically, if not in reality, the center of the world's economy. The Reagan administration could not claim world hegemony. However, by the early 1990s, with the bubble economy in Japan about to burst and the slowing of economic growth in the remainder of East Asia, America had unequivocally become the sole global superpower. Militarily and economically, no other nation-state or regional bloc of nations could compete with or even serve as a counterbalance to the United States. It was in this context that the "end of the cold war" rhetoric ushered in the neoliberal globalization movement. With its promise of a fresh start and new economic opportunities, the discourse of globalization was in some ways a throwback to the old Wilsonian call for self-determination.

In 1991, the first President Bush initiated the first Gulf War, which can be seen as an attempt to reclaim America's national honor after the defeat in Vietnam—but after the collapse of the Soviet Union, it also signaled the selection of the Islamic world as America's new enemy. This choice was later explored by academics such as Samuel Huntington (1993), whose "clash of civilizations" theory describes a shift from the cold-war opposition between the Left and the Right to a confrontation of civilizations. The selection of the Islamic world (among the seven or eight civilizations identified by Huntington) was clearly evident in the U.S. response to September 11, which was not to bring the guilty to justice by following international law or even U.S. domestic law, but instead to unilaterally select Afghanistan and Iraq as the objects of its vengeance. Ironically, the heavy-handed American reaction fostered an overwhelming anti-American sentiment and helped unify the diverse Islamic world by bringing it to the center of global politics.

Like his predecessor, President Clinton also ordered a military attack on Iraq, albeit on a much smaller scale, and the Clinton administration also oversaw NATO's bombing campaign in Kosovo, which was conducted without the backing of the United Nations. American authoritarian militarism ended any hope that the regional balances of power achieved during the cold war would be maintained, and it radically weakened the U.N.'s ability to fulfill its core mission, which is to mediate conflicts in the global system of nation-states. By the time of the 1999 World Trade Organization protests in Seattle, which involved a large-scale transnational alliance, the legitimacy of U.S. world leadership was already in doubt. In East Asia, however, Clinton dealt with mainland China as a strategic partner rather than as an adversary, and he did not intervene in the summits between the two Kims in Korea. These real and symbolic choices contributed to hopes for a long-lasting regional peace.

After the 2000 election, however, the second President Bush began to reverse the Clinton administration's East Asia policies. Mainland China was redefined as a competitor, if not an enemy. On the Korean Peninsula, negotiations between the North and South were blocked, and Kim Dae-jung's 2000 Nobel Peace Prize quickly faded from memory. Beyond East Asia, Bush antagonized the entire world by refusing to submit the Kyoto Protocol to the U.S. Senate for ratification (following Clinton's precedent). These positions betrayed a disregard for the changing global political situation. The neoliberal globalization project spearheaded by the United States in the early 1990s had also ramped up the formation of regional alliances: the European Union was already in place; Latin America was slowly integrating economically; ASEAN Plus Three, which added mainland China, Japan, and South Korea to the Southeast Asian group, was moving forward; the booming mainland Chinese economy gave rise to thoughts of a Greater China; and the reintegration of the Koreas had become a tantalizing possibility. Furthermore, there were direct interactions among the various regional blocs. The creation of regional economic entities and superstate organizations signaled the emergence of multipolar nexuses of power and laid the foundation for the development of regional subjectivities. The mood of the time differed strongly from that of the early 1990s, when the United States was universally hailed as the sole superpower. In a very short period of time, a global sentiment had surfaced in response to the reactionary policies of the Bush administration: the United States had done its best to tear apart the international consensus and had become the global enemy.

The shift from liberator to global enemy was what enabled the explosive critique of the United States that emerged in the run-up to the 2003 invasion of Iraq.[14] Rather than implement the democratic ideals that the nation ostensibly stands for, the United States acted just like the imperialist powers of old. The current fierce anti-Americanism is part of a necessary historical process. It is an important step in dismantling and moving beyond the myth of American singularity and ushering in a more pluralistic and heterogeneous global future. The multifaceted contradictions unleashed by September 11 have given rise to the delinking of politics and culture, state and society. Democratic political regimes have their own internal logics and do not necessarily represent the will of the populations they were elected to serve. Though we have long been fed the propaganda that the cold war is over, many state leaders have in fact not yet discarded the cold-war paradigm and continue to embrace what are now in effect alternative cold-war positions. The Iraq invasion was fully supported by Tony Blair in the United Kingdom, John Howard in Australia, Junichiro Koizumi in Japan, Kim Dae-jung in South Korea, and Chen Shui-bian in Taiwan. Many legislatures have become nothing but rubber stamps. Voices of opposition from the civil society were loud but ineffective. The gap between the operating logic of the state and peace movements in the civil society is painfully obvious.

Democratic Movements under Imperialism

September 11 and its aftermath changed the political dynamic in the Taiwan Strait. Because the Bush administration needed mainland China's participation in the so-called global war on terror in order to contain North Korea, part of what Bush referred to as the axis of evil, the U.S. anti-China policy was recast as a strategic partnership. Not long after that shift, mainland China, emboldened by its new relationship with the United States, for the first time openly tried to counter the DPP's line on Taiwan independence.

In March and April 2003, Anglo-American military attacks in Iraq provoked spontaneous global antiwar movements that were unprecedented in scale. Even in Taiwan, where the tradition of anti-Americanism is relatively weak, there were multiple rounds of street demonstrations and protest rallies. In public forums, the Taiwanese government's support of the U.S. invasion of Iraq was fiercely debated. Those in favor of the government, the United States, and the war formulated a chain of equivalents: antiwar = anti-America = anti-Taiwan = pro–mainland China ("Disclosing the 'Anti-war, Anti-US, Anti-Taiwan' Syllogism of the Pro-China Force's Conspiracy" 2003). In contrast, the movement that formed to protest the first Gulf War in the early 1990s had no such formula — being antiwar then was merely a universal humanitarian value. Ten years later, some of the opponents of the earlier war became supporters of the new war (King 2003).

Though public-opinion polls in Taiwan indicated that a majority opposed the war in Iraq, the antiwar movement was much weaker in Taiwan than in the neighboring countries of Japan and South Korea.[15] Nevertheless, the movement managed to gain sufficient momentum to raise the taboo issue of Taiwan-U.S. relations.[16] In some of the discussions on Taiwan's interest and involvement in the war, Club 51 began to be cited as a point of reference. Club 51 had finally entered the arena of public opinion as the proponent of an extreme but viable position.[17]

In April 2004, a controversy was sparked when Taiwan independence groups lobbied the U.S. Senate to pass a resolution calling for Taiwan to send troops to Iraq as an expression of solidarity. Given the U.S. relationship with mainland China, it was of course impossible to believe that the United States would entertain the notion, but within the DPP, support for the measure was strong. If Taiwan had still been in the old KMT era, we could easily understand this eagerness to support the U.S. intervention in Iraq, but the DPP was supposed to represent the democratic opposition movement, and previously it had shown little interest in international affairs of any kind, let alone aggressive military adventurism. How can we explain Taiwan-U.S. relations in the new era of antiterrorism?

Growing out of the same democratic opposition movement as the DPP, Club 51 was not absent from this round of political events. The group, now also known as the Taiwan State Building Movement, announced:

> The Taiwan State Building Movement posted an essay to call for the Taiwan government to send troops to Iraq to join together with the multinational forces in action there . . . Saddam Hussein's evil regime has to be overthrown and his two ferocious sons have to be prevented from taking over his position [as head of the state]. Unless a stable democratic regime is established in Iraq, the Middle East will not find peace, and the U.S. itself will not be secure . . . Taiwan has to send troops to assist the U.S. in establishing a new order in Iraq. Under such a democratic and free new order, different ethnicities and political factions can coexist and prosper together. After stable development, starting from Iraq, the whole Muslim world can be gradually democratized . . . Under American guidance, the Taiwanese people have moved toward democratization. Now it is our responsibility to assist the U.S. to eradicate the evil empire . . . To respond to Little [George W.] Bush's demand, Taiwan's action to send troops to Iraq

is the first step for we Taiwanese to learn to assume responsibility for the world.[18]

This statement brings to light a dimension of Club 51 that goes beyond lobbying for U.S. statehood. In the eight years between the Taiwan Strait missile crisis in 1996 and the controversy over sending Taiwanese troops to Iraq in 2004, Club 51 internalized and solidified its position; members of the group began speaking as Americans to defend what they perceived to be American national interests. In 1996, America stood for democracy, freedom, wealth, and power. But after September 11, Club 51 justified the U.S. invasion of Iraq in a manner that was perfectly consistent with U.S. government propaganda. It was necessary to overthrow Saddam Hussein's evil regime for the sake of establishing political democracy in Iraq, and to further democratic development in the Islamic world. Club 51 is advocating an imperialist democracy.

If Club 51's attitude toward the United States had not been one of absolutist American patriotism, if it had instead selectively endorsed America's democratic freedom and criticized its authoritarian militarism, then we could have understood Club 51's approach as radical, plural opportunism. However, given Club 51's support of the war, the label does not seem to apply. Where did this imperial desire come from? How did Club 51, a group born out of the democratic opposition movement, end up as a supporter of imperialist action? And since this mentality was also widely shared by the so-called democratic movement in Taiwan, including the DPP, we can also pose a more fundamental question: what is the relationship between democracy and imperialism?

In order to address the issue of democracy and imperialism, allow me to shift our points of reference to contrast sentiments toward the United States in Taiwan and South Korea. Even if we accept the argument that anticommunism and pro-Americanism are major elements of Taiwanese subjectivity to explain Taiwan's relatively weak opposition to the U.S. invasion of Iraq, the depth of pro-Americanism in Taiwan is still difficult to acknowledge. Being anti-American is like opposing ourselves, and to love Taiwan is to love America. This is why we cannot oppose U.S. imperialist intervention. Taiwan's popular culture has a long tradition of Japanophilia; the Korean Wave (Korean popular culture circulated widely during the last decade) that swept through Asia has created its share of Taiwanese Korea-philes; and there are even groups of Taiwanese Shanghai-philes. But no one speaks of Americaphilia. The desire for America is so deep that we have no easy way of addressing it. For Taiwanese, America still provides the default models to follow in the areas of critical intellectual thought, alternative culture, and even oppositional political movements.

Once as anticommunist and pro-American as the democratic movement in Taiwan, the democratic movement in South Korea underwent a major change in the 1980s after the Gwangju Uprising. The South Korean democratic movement not only liberated South Koreans from an authoritarian military regime, but it also radically questioned U.S. support of the South Korean government. Anti-authoritarianism and anti-imperialism became the same political agenda. South Koreans originally thought that the United States would, in the name of human rights, intervene to stop Chun Doo-hwan's violent suppression of the popular protest, and the joint-command agreement between U.S. and South Korean military forces certainly would have made intervention possible. But the United States did not intervene, and the Korean government's crackdown was widely understood to have been approved by the Reagan administration. Later, President Reagan invited President Chun to visit the United States, which intensified popular discontent in South Korea. Koreans realized that the United States had a double standard: domestically, it claimed to support democratic values and respect for human rights; but internationally, it practiced imperialism and supported authoritarian military regimes for its own benefit. This recognition formed the basis of anti-American sentiment in South Korea. By 1985, progressive activists there had determined that the fundamental condition allowing for the survival of the authoritarian military regime was U.S. imperialism. The struggle for Korean democracy therefore had to also eradicate external imperialist forces.[19]

Because of the affinity established between anti-authoritarianism and anti-American-imperialism, South Korea's democratic movement has accumulated a solid anti-imperialist, anti-U.S. sensibility. This explains how huge rallies protesting the U.S. invasion of Iraq after September 11 simultaneously occurred in nineteen Korean cities. It further explains how Roh Moo-hyun, proclaiming a strongly anti-American position, could have been elected president (restrained by equally strong conservative forces, he was unable to remove the U.S. military from South Korea). By celebrating South Korea in this way, I do not mean to belittle Taiwan. The South Korean desire for Americanization may even be stronger than its Taiwanese counterpart. My point is that in Korean political culture, U.S. imperialism is regarded with a critical distance that is absent in Taiwan.

In light of this discussion, it is clear that Taiwan's democratic opposition movement as led by the DPP has not done the necessary work of reexamining American complicity in the authoritarian rule of the KMT. Though exercising considerable political control over the KMT, the United States did nothing to stop the atrocities of the White Terror or the suppression that followed the Formosa Magazine Incident.[20] In its eight years in power, the Democratic Progressive Party did not disassociate itself from the imperialist policies of the United States. Instead, the DPP's pro-American tendencies became even more pronounced than those of the KMT regime under martial law. If anti-imperialism is a defining feature of third-world democratic movements, then Club 51 and the DPP are not such movements, never having even critically reflected on the relationship between U.S. imperialism and Taiwan. And once an opposition movement assumes power, the desire to maintain that power, and the opportunities to further the movement's self-interest that come with it, make it all the more difficult to overturn the status quo.

On the evening of 20 March 2004, with the results of the presidential election in, Chen Shui-bian addressed his supporters by emphasizing that his reelection was a victory for Taiwanese "subject-consciousness," although he did not clarify what he meant by this. In terms of the history of representative democracy in Taiwan, the most important result of the election was the open revelation that Taiwan was a U.S. protectorate. Prior to 1987, the KMT maintained that the whole of China was its territory, which had been temporarily occupied by communist thieves. The KMT regime in Taiwan presented itself as the government of a large and dignified country, even though in reality it led only a small state under U.S. military protection. To save face, the KMT never openly acknowledged that Taiwan was a protectorate of the United States. In the eyes of the Taiwanese public, the United States was simply Taiwan's most intimate ally. Although this ally deserted Taiwan in 1979 and formally recognized the Chinese Communist Party as the legitimate government of China, Taiwanese justified this abandonment by thinking that because the United States was a global power, it had no choice but to work with mainland China. And even so, the United States was still our loyal ally in defending the Taiwan Strait.

But the political situation quickly changed after the DPP assumed power. All the embarrassments hidden in the past now had to be put on public display, and when mainland China took issue with these actions, President Chen would have to send senior members of his staff to Washington to report. It became increasingly clear to the public that Chen needed permission from the United States to make political decisions, and three events surrounding the 2004 presidential election in Taiwan spelled out the nature of the countries' relationship in no uncertain terms. First, because the United States opposed the use of a ballot referendum, Chen was forced to edit the content of the referendum in a way acceptable to the United States. Second, because of the controversy surrounding the failed election-eve assassination attempt on Chen,[21] the U.S. government postponed congratulating him. Annette Lu, Chen's vice-president, immediately demanded an official acknowledgement from the United States recognizing the election's result. Third, Chiu Yi-ren, the general secretary of the Taiwan National Security Council, flew to Washington to seek approval for Chen's inauguration speech.[22] As the public became aware of these events, the perception grew that sending Taiwanese troops to Iraq was like paying the Mafia a protection fee, or like the ancient tributary system in which the vassal state had to offer tribute to the emperor of the suzerain state. If the United States and Taiwan have long been engaged in a protectorate relationship, one that is commonly understood to exist by the political elite of both parties, but one that each side was unable or unwilling to acknowledge, then the major shift here is that the public now saw the exact nature of the relationship. What was the effect of this public recognition?

For proponents of Taiwan independence, that is a sacred ideal that cannot be compromised. Recognizing Taiwan's status as a protectorate of the United States is a move that could never be accepted. As Chen Shui-bian has frequently said, "Taiwan is an independent sovereign state and its name is the Republic of China." If you add what he has left out — "under U.S. protection" — does the independence movement still have legitimate appeal? Of course, a reliance on U.S. imperialism is what has allowed the movement to exist in the first place. If it is to stake out a legitimate position, its first mission must be to clarify its position vis-à-vis the United States. The reality, however, is that none of the factions within the independence movement have dared to challenge U.S. imperialism.

Compared to the independence fundamentalists, Club 51's position is much more courageous. Club 51 is willing to honestly face the political realities of the present; its problem lies with its obviously fantastic vision of the future. What makes it think that American citizens will accept Taiwan as a state, or that mainland China will accept that arrangement?[23] Nevertheless, Club 51 relentlessly pushes its views: Taiwanese must choose whether they want to be Chinese or American. This is how the group framed its position in 2003 in relation to the existing political spectrum: "We will make and seek a new basis of support beyond the life and death struggle between green and blue, beyond ethnic confrontation, and beyond the impasse of unification and independence. This white space will be established to be different from red China, and the blue and green camps in Taiwan."[24] There is no need for a critical reading to unpack the meaning of this statement: the "white space" that Club 51 identifies with is nothing other than the United States.

We have come full circle. Anticommunism and pro-Americanism built over the decades following the Second World War are constitutive of Taiwan's subjectivity. In the mid-1980s, Taiwan's so-called democratization movement began to focus on conflicts over ethnic and national identity. By exploiting the politics of ethnic difference, the opposition movement accumulated the energy to finally grasp state power in 2000. The 2004 presidential election continued and deepened these rifts. The sturdy ideological structure of anticommunism has effectively delegitimized any thought of unification with mainland China under the rule of the Chinese Communist Party. Now, although the KMT's Ma Ying-jeou has won the 2008 presidential election and economic integration has pushed forward, the old-line anticommunist stand is still alive.

To put the issue in a wider context, democratic opposition movements in Taiwan and other parts of Asia need to rethink our history. Through this process, we need to face the long-term damage that Japanese colonialism inflicted throughout Asia. We also need to investigate the impact of U.S. support of pro-American authoritarian regimes on contemporary democracy. But we must abandon the habit of treating imperialism as a force external to regional discourse. For a very long time, imperialism has not just operated on East Asian politics, societies, and economies but has also slowly shaped our Asian bodies, thoughts, and desires. The critique of subjectivity needs to begin with the self if we are to entertain any hope of true independence.

Asia's Independence

In March and April 2005, large-scale anti-Japanese protests broke out in South Korea and mainland China in response to Japan's bid for a seat on the United Nations Security Council. Underlying the protests was a mix of unfinished historical business and new political developments. The main driving force behind the changing dynamics in East Asia is the peaceful rise of China, but the anti-Japanese demonstrations were also energized by Roh Moo-hyun's attempt to move away from the anticommunism, pro-Americanism policy of the past, and toward independence and autonomy on the Korean Peninsula. Roh's policy was a calculated one: Korea hopes to play a key role in what some Seoul-based analysts call the Northeast Asian century, a dream that could never be realized with Korea's continued reliance on the United States. Driving the U.S. military out of Korea would bolster Korean independence, but even more important, it is a precondition for Korea's assuming a position of leadership in the region.[25] In contrast, Taiwan's Chen Shui-bian and Japan's Junichiro Koizumi were still confined within a structure inherited from the cold war, which bound their countries to continued dependence on the United States.

During the wave of anti-Japanese protests in China and Korea, reactions in Taiwan were low-key, but Taiwan was engaging a different regional dynamic. Before 2005, no Taiwanese politician dared pay a friendly visit to mainland China, because doing so would be seen as "cozying up to China and selling out Taiwan" (*qīn Zhōng mài Tái*). Chen Shui-bian's razor-thin and heavily contested reelection victory, and the DPP's huge losses in the 2004 legislative elections marked a major shift in Taiwan's political climate. In this context, the opposition KMT and the People First Party felt they had enough popular support to bypass the elected DPP government and deal directly with the CCP. Lien Chan, chairman of the KMT, undertook a visit to China in the hope of easing tensions across the Taiwan Strait, which he called "a journey of peace." His direct talks with Hu Jintao, chairman of the CCP, symbolized a reconciliation of sorts between the two parties. Had the fifty-year Chinese civil war come to an end? Such a scenario would not have been imaginable before 2005.

Lien's visit may have suggested to some that reconciliation between Taiwan and mainland China was inevitable, but in reality, the contradictions and conflicts accumulated over the previous decades have made neither unification nor independence possible for Taiwan in the short run. Without the possibility of internal consensus, any hasty move toward either extreme runs the risk of igniting a civil war in Taiwan. Maintaining the status quo is the probable reality, while interaction between China and Taiwan continues. The question becomes whether the two regimes on either side of the Taiwan Strait will be able to reach a peace agreement, temporarily postponing the issue of independence or unification. Doing so demands that Taiwan stop seeking independence and that China renounce its threats to invade Taiwan to force unification. Only in this way can communication at other levels continue. Whether such an agreement can be reached, however, remains to be seen.

If peaceful interaction between Taiwan and China is to continue, the biggest remaining obstacle to the integration of East Asia is Japan. Neither the Japanese state nor Japanese society seem prepared to debate Japan's postwar relations with the United States. On 22 April 2005, the fiftieth anniversary of the Bandung Conference, Prime Minister Koizumi once again apologized on behalf of his government for Japan's invasions of different parts of Asia during the Second World War. This type of apology has become frequent and formulaic. The victims have not yet accepted these apologies because Japan refuses to stand with the rest of Asia, where most people would say to Japan: "You say you are not a military power, but your weaponry is the most advanced in Asia, and since you rely on your security alliance with the United States, how can you function as a truly independent nation?" If the question of Japan's status as an independent nation is still debatable, then how can it be a member of the United Nations Security Council? If Japan were given a seat, that would essentially give more voting power to the United States. Thus, many Asians believe Japanese apologies to be insincere, and made only for the sake of Japan's national interest. For the victims of Japanese fascism, the apologies carry no emotional resonance. Japan is respected for its economic prowess, but it has yet to win political or cultural respect from its neighbors. To accomplish this, Japan must reexamine its identity, identifications, and position in the region as a whole.

This situation stems from a consensus established after Japan's defeat in the Second World War. The U.S. military mandate brought Japan democracy—known as God's gift in some circles—and economic promise. Almost overnight, Japan went from being a colonizing power to being a U.S. colony, from victimizer to victimized. This mutually negating shift dissolved any momentum Japanese society had had to reflect on its relations with its former colonies and colonial subjects. The arrival of the cold war soon after further diminished the possibility of deimperialization. The result was a postwar national consensus in Japan in which economic development took priority over politics, the promise of a peaceful and prosperous future replaced a tragic history, and military matters were left entirely to the United States.

In the early postwar years, South Korea and Taiwan were also incorporated into the U.S. defense network. Like in Japan, economic development was the priority, and colonial histories were ignored. But in both Taiwan and South Korea, military expenditures siphoned off half the national budget, and authoritarian rule suppressed democratic energies. The implications are clear. First, the rapid recovery of the postwar Japanese economy was made possible in part by Japan's passing defense spending along to the United States. Japan now declares itself to be a world power, but at the same time, it is unwilling to relinquish its reliance on the U.S. military. The trade-off is immense: on the surface, Japan is an independent country, but in reality, it subordinates itself to U.S. military power. Culturally belonging to the third world, Japan refuses to position itself accordingly and stand with its Asian neighbors. Second, democracy in South Korea and Taiwan was achieved through difficult and persistent struggles against authoritarian regimes. Problematic as they are, the democracies in South Korea and Taiwan were not gifts from a U.S. military government, but achievements won in spite of American strategic interests.

If Japan is an independent country, how does it justify maintaining a U.S. military presence on its soil? One could argue that this is merely the historical legacy of a postwar political arrangement, but both U.S. and Japanese officials have publicly acknowledged that the cold war is now a thing of the past. The eruption of protests against the presence of U.S. bases in Japan and on Okinawa clearly indicates that opposition is strong at the societal level, and that the Japanese state has little democratic justification for its policy of keeping the bases. While the likelihood of American troop withdrawal in the short term is low, a first step toward achieving that goal is considering the implications of such a move. If, for example, U.S. military withdrawal means an increase in the Japanese defense budget, then in what ways would Japan's military affairs with its neighbors have to be readjusted for peace and stability in the region to be maintained? Does the AMPO Treaty have the goal of keeping the U.S. military in Japan permanently?[26] If not, when and under what set of conditions will the U.S. military leave Japan? These sensitive questions must exist in the minds of many critical intellectuals in Japan and elsewhere in Asia. If the consensus among Japanese is in favor of allowing the U.S. military to remain, then Club 51's approach seems to be the appropriate model to follow. However Japan proceeds, it is clear that the postwar political arrangement formed in the context of the early cold war is now in need of adjustment.

Takeuchi Yoshimi's penetrating reflections in 1952 on the U.S. military mandate offers a relevant perspective. In his essay "Independence and Ideal of the Nation," Takeuchi argues:

> What we should be concerned with is to not become entangled in the legal and political surface meanings of independence, but with the substantive meaning of independence, or what I think can be called cultural independence. Since the Meiji era, the formation of the mainstream spirit in the Japanese state has only emphasized independence in its external form, but has not reflected on its real substance. The result is a failure. Everyone is puffed with pride when the international political arena recognizes Japan as an independent nation and calls us a first-rate country. But seen today, it is not real independence. Today, those who were educated in the Meiji era can still consider prewar Japan the model of an independent country. But I do not recognize it as that model. At that time, it looked as if Japan acted in accordance with its own will, but actually it did not. Conscious or not, in sum, it was manipulated by international imperialism and was blindly used as cannon fodder for imperialism. Independence in name was actu-

ally being another's slave. Today's occupation is really a logical result, and not because defeat in war led to the loss of independence. Our generation understands this point through physically experiencing it. (Takeuchi 2005b [1952], 279–80)

Reading this passage today, one cannot help but be disappointed by the fact that not only Japan, but East Asia as a whole, has not yet achieved the independence imagined by Takeuchi. His notion of "cultural independence" can be understood as an attempt to build a more penetrating critical subjectivity at the societal level. In Takeuchi's view, this is a level deeper than that of law and politics, and without reaching it, true independence cannot be realized. As with the present situation in Taiwan, changing the name of the country or the national flag will do nothing to achieve this type of independence.

The urgency of dealing with the U.S. military occupation did not spur even highly self-reflexive thinkers such as Takeuchi to break through their own epistemological limits and reflect on the pain Japan had caused by depriving its former colonies and colonial subjects of their independence. If, even in discussing the issue of independence, the Japanese cannot recognize the suffering caused by their country in Asia, then Japan's defeat in the Second World War was not just a military loss, but also a cultural failure. Because Japanese intellectuals were not pushed to think through the meaning of depriving others of their independence, it is difficult for them to understand the importance of achieving their own independence. I concede that it is not fair to expect Takeuchi to have thought along these lines. After all, Takeuchi was one of the few scholars who, despite overwhelming national shame, could self-reflexively address Japan's historical problems in the years immediately following the Second World War. He demanded that in the struggle for independence, Japan's citizens not fall once again into the trap of formalism, which would result in their once again becoming slaves of imperialism.

Japan's evolution in the half-century since Takeuchi's essay confirms the prescience of his concern. On the surface, independence seems to have been achieved, but in reality the choices that Japan made were just taking the easy way out. In the end, Japan did not avoid becoming a slave of imperialism. Being a slave is not necessarily shameful. What is embarrassing is when a slave adopts the superior attitude of the master.

Takeuchi's thoughts on independence force us to ask what independence really means. For him, a crucial component of true independence is the presence of an ideal to pursue. Without this ideal, independence is meaningless. In the same essay, Takeuchi suggests that to have a genuine impact, the formulation of the ideal has to result from collective involvement of the body politic. For him, the "wealthy country, strong military" ideal of the Meiji era was not a meaningful ethical practice and was proved by history to have been a fantastic dream. Defeat was a logical necessity. Learning from this failure and moving toward substantive independence is the way forward. Takeuchi suggests that Japan has gone in the opposite direction of India and China, since both of those countries "did not immediately gain formalistic independence, but have firmly acquired a non-conformist ideal" (ibid., 281). He attempts to guide Japanese citizens to imagine what that ideal could be by quoting Sun Yat-sen on his Three Principles of the People (nationalism, democracy, and socialism):

> After all, what responsibility should China have for the world? World powers at present are destroying other countries. When China becomes strong and prosperous, if it learns from the imperialism of world powers to destroy other countries, China would be repeating their mistakes. Therefore, we need to make a policy to support the weak and to help the ones in trouble [*zhìruò fúqīng*]. That is our nation's natural duty. We have to support weak nations and resist world powers. If all citizens of our nation have this firm ambition to stand on, then the Chinese nation can develop. If this position is not established, there is no hope for the Chinese nation. Before we are fully developed, we have to establish this will to support the weak and to help the troubled today. (Quoted in Takeuchi 2005b [1952], 281; my translation)

Takeuchi is heavily influenced by Sun Yat-sen's ideals, but he knows full well that it will not be easy to adopt them in the Japanese context. Nevertheless, he hopes Japanese citizens will be inspired by Sun's ethics to collectively consider the future of Japanese independence.

Rethinking the problematic of independence through our reading of Takeuchi's account of Sun Yat-sen, it is clear that half a century later, we face drastically different conditions in Asia. Japan and the Four Little Tigers (Hong Kong, Singapore, South Korea, and Taiwan) now have formidable economic resources. China is not yet "strong and prosperous," but is in the process of a peaceful rise. In formulating an ideal of Asian independence today, we should at the very least strive to answer Sun Yat-sen's call: supporting the weak, helping the troubled, and resisting imperialism should be not just slogans, but actual practices. The resource-rich countries of East Asia need to think beyond the basic considerations of national interest. To reach multilateral consensus, resources — material and otherwise — need to flow freely between different groups and locations.

Resisting imperialism can no longer be reduced to the simple gesture of resisting outside forces. Chinese intellectuals need to transcend the lingering master narrative of the tragic Western imperialist invasion. Our shared consciousness of suffering should not prevent us from critically reflecting on the immense political, military, and cultural pressures that the Chinese empire has exerted on its neighbors throughout history. The anxiety over the rise of China in the region today does not stem only from contemporary China's economic and military growth or the authoritarian policies of the CCP, but also from the historical China — the China of the tributary system. Intellectuals in mainland China, Hong Kong, Taiwan, and even the Chinese communities in diaspora need to reflect on the historical identity and positioning of the Chinese empire in the premodern era. Doing so preempts the possibility of falling back into the imperial dream, the desire to become a superpower that can compete with the United States.

In Asia, the deimperialization question cannot be limited to a reexamination of the impacts of Western imperialist invasion, Japanese colonial violence, and U.S. neoimperialist expansion, but must also include the oppressive practices of the Chinese empire. Since the status of China has shifted from an empire to a big country, how should China position itself now? In what new ways can it interact with neighboring countries? Questions like these can be productively answered only through deimperialized self-questioning, and that type of reflexive work has yet to be undertaken. In my view, it would be a huge mistake to think of a return to empire as a way to resist U.S. imperialism, though this sort of dangerous thinking has already begun to emerge in mainland China. Instead, Chinese intellectuals need to self-consciously recognize that by positioning itself as a big country, China needs to shoulder a commensurate responsibility—not to fight to achieve world domination, but to make contributions to the integration of Asia. China must not become an imperializing force in Asia.

Following Sun Yat-sen's insights, we must recognize that the first step toward the elimination of imperialism is the lessening of our own imperial desire. Only by radically reflecting on our own past imperial identity can we acquire a new subjectivity, and only then will we be able to extend the deimperialization question to rethink Euro-American imperialism and Japanese colonialism. In this context, debating whether Japan is an independent country is, in fact, a type of self-questioning. The Japanese problem is also ours. The worship of America in Chinese and Taiwanese intellectual circles is due to our inability to recognize our own imperial identification with the Chinese empire. To peel back the layers of history and expose imperial desire is a precondition for moving toward regional reconciliation, integration, and independence.

Deimperialization and the Global Democratic Movement

On 21 September 2005, a news item with the headline "Political Advertisement Published in Washington D.C.—'Taiwan Defense Alliance' Calls for the U.S. to Take over Taiwan," written by the senior journalist Fu Jianchung, was published in Taiwan's *China Times*. Given the extraordinary nature of the subject, the tone of the article is matter-of-fact:

> An organization called the "Taiwan Defense Alliance" bought a full-page advertisement today in *The Washington Post* urging the U.S. government and Congress to take over Taiwan, include Taiwan as part of the U.S. defense system, dissolve the government of the Republic of China, and terminate the operation of the Ministries of National Defense and Foreign Affairs.
>
> The argument put forward by Lin et al. justifying a U.S. takeover of Taiwan was that after World War II, the taking over of Taiwan by Chiang Kai-shek (of the Republic of China) was conducted under the order of Gen. Douglas MacArthur, the commander of the Allied forces. Therefore, legally speaking, Taiwan is still under U.S. military government rule, and the U.S. is still occupying Taiwan. Hence, to dissolve the Ministry of Defense and Ministry of Foreign Affairs is only

to return Taiwan to the status of the immediate postwar situation. As for defense affairs, the U.S. Congress should authorize its Ministry of Defense to be responsible.

The U.S. Congress should also come up with a timetable to retire the current President, Vice President, Heads of the five Yuans [branches of government], the Grand Justice of the Supreme Court, and so on, and then the U.S. will assist Taiwan to establish a transitional government and to hold meetings for making a new constitution, national flag, national emblem, etc.

After the analysis of Club 51 earlier in this chapter, this news item may not come as much of a surprise. It reflects the despair about Taiwan's indeterminate status felt by many Taiwanese after the country's bids to rejoin the United Nations are denied year after year. It also reflects anxiety over the steady rise of China. In fact, policy statements posted on the website of the Taiwan Defense Alliance (TDA) indicate that its position is quite different from that of Club 51.[27] Club 51's agenda is to completely give up on the idea of Taiwan independence and have the country join the United States, whereas the TDA's position is that Taiwan's being taken over by the United States is only a necessary first step toward eventually achieving independence. Where Club 51 and the TDA overlap is in their calculation that because of the international power structure, reliance on the United States is the only option for Taiwan in the short term.

To return to the question posed earlier in the chapter, what has been the relationship between local democratic movements and imperialism in the former colonies of the third world? Owing to the structural conditions of the capitalist bloc during the cold war, democratic movements became entangled in the culture of U.S. imperialism, and the result was that the democratic movements that emerged were right-leaning, anticommunist, and pro-American. These movements were driven by a yearning for American modernity, an uncritical acceptance of an imagined U.S. conception of democracy, and, as a consequence, subordination to the United States in the arena of international politics. These assumptions are being questioned in the post–September 11 era. The American mode of democracy is now viewed with suspicion around the world, and the wider consensus is that the brutality of U.S. imperialist interventions has destroyed its symbolic status as a paragon of modern democracy. In my

view, the issues that Club 51 embraces are the products of conflicting desires and pressures that have been accumulating throughout the history
of imperialism. To unravel these issues, we will now focus the discussion
on the political and theoretical meanings of deimperialization.

In the first chapter, I argued that the process of imperialization is wider
in scope than the process of colonization because imperialist expansion
is always based on domestic mobilization, which is itself a process of imperialization. As an overall process of mobilization and integration, imperialization is the basis of colonization, not the reverse. If this is the case,
then any decolonization movement cannot be completed without a corresponding deimperialization movement in the imperial center. Without
a dialectical arrangement, decolonization will be unidirectional and incomplete. Gandhi wanted to liberate India and at the same time liberate
England. Fanon thought likewise: he argued that there is a symbiotic and
intimate relation between the colonizer and the colonized. The colony
not only has to decolonize, but it must also pass through a deimperializing process to undercut its loyalty to the empire and undo imperial desire.
This reflection and critique in the colony cannot move forward without a
corresponding consciousness in the imperial center from which to radically question and examine imperialist tendencies.

I assert that there is one key issue at the heart of contemporary global
politics: third-world decolonization has not unfolded as it could have because deimperialization movements did not take place in the homelands
of the former empires. The former empires have not actively thought
through the history of their imperialism and hence could not respond
properly to the living historical issues in the former colonies. Consequently, decolonization and deimperialization movements could not
successfully advance in the third world, and they were unable to build
enough momentum to drive the former imperial powers to take on the
historical responsibility of self-reflection. This seems to be a hopeless, self-
perpetuating loop, but we must recognize that, in contrast to the former
empires, the third world has developed a tradition of large-scale decolonization movements, which can now be mobilized to drive the next round
of deimperialization.

In *Becoming "Japanese": Colonial Taiwan and the Politics of Identity Formation*, Leo Ching argues against the unquestioned presupposition in
Japanese studies that there is a continuity between "assimilation" and the

"imperialization of the subject" (kōminka in Japanese; huángmínhuà in Chinese). According to Ching, the conflation of these two different colonialist ideologies results in the acceptance of an official discourse that justifies the "equality and benevolence" of colonial policy (Ching 2001, 91). In this view, the imperialization of the subject cannot be understood as the ultimate stage of assimilation but must be analyzed as its own historical process. When this is done, not only can the specific characteristics of each mode be identified, but through detailed analysis, Ching discovers that the internal contradictions inherent in assimilation are covered up by the process of imperialization. At the same time, imperialization changes the way colonial subjectivity is represented, especially on the level of identity formation. In so doing, it ushers this unresolved postcolonial issue into the contemporary fold (ibid., 132). To use my own terms, the conflicts and contradictions of today's identity politics in Taiwan presuppose a historical subject that has not yet been deimperialized.

The way in which Ching historicizes the imperialization of the subject is different theoretically than the way I have approached it in this book. Nevertheless, his analysis provides inspiration for alternative approaches. If, for example, we massage Ching's analysis of the imperialization of the subject a bit, different and more general theoretical questions emerge: How does imperialization work through the "bodily practice of everyday life" in the colony and in the imperial home (ibid., 90)?[28] By what specific practices, for example, were colonized subjects mobilized to fight for the imperial center? These types of questions are as relevant as ever. Cold-war subjects are similarly enveloped in the totality of imperialist strategic deployments and conditioned to serve the objectives of the center. Will decolonization, deimperialization, and de–cold war not require the same degree of intensity to reform, reshape, and rearticulate the body, desire, and thought of the subject?

Former colonies in East Asia, specifically Taiwan, South Korea, Hong Kong, and Macao, have not yet adequately reconciled their historical relations with their former colonizers. What has complicated the issue is that in the postwar period, Taiwan and South Korea became U.S. protectorates, which makes the work of deimperialization more layered and more difficult. In the late 1990s, Hong Kong and Macao were handed over to mainland China, itself a former semicolony that had gone through a socialist revolution before becoming caught up in the cold war. Busy with resisting the U.S.-led capitalist bloc and focusing on ensuring its own survival, mainland China set aside the question of its historical relations with imperialist powers and has not yet returned to it.

At the center of the international dynamics in East Asia is the question of the legitimacy of the U.S. presence. If a deimperialization movement does not first unfold in East Asia, are there legitimate grounds to address the issue of deimperializing the United States? If one pushes even further to argue that there must be a dialectical process in any deimperialization movement, then what conditions need to be created in the United States to bring about an effective movement there? What would the concrete forms of such a movement be? In addition to marching in the streets to protest the invasion of Iraq, what other actions should be taken? What are the appropriate methodologies for making deimperialization a reality in the neoimperial center?

In the second half of 2005, a curious book appeared in East Asian bookstores: *Modern History of the Three Countries in East Asia: Learning from History, Facing the Future, Building a New Peaceful and Friendly Framework Together.* The book was edited and written by scholars and teachers from China, Japan, and Korea.[29] According to the afterword, the book was conceived at the first Forum on Historical Understanding and East Asia Peace, in March 2003 in Nanjing, and plans were further developed at later forums in Tokyo and Seoul. In August 2003, the committee charged with writing the book met in Korea, with four later meetings in Japan and China, and two in Korea. Seventeen members of the team were from universities and research institutions in China; thirteen were from Japan, including university professors and high-school teachers; and twenty-three were from universities, independent research institutions, and the national archives in Korea. The book took three years to complete.

The introduction lays out the general conditions in each of the three countries in the premodern era, with special focuses on the countries' interrelations and the formation of civil society in each. The first chapter narrates the general historical processes of modernization in the countries, with an emphasis on the Euro-American powers' invasions and the responses to that aggression. It describes how the First Sino-Japanese War in the 1890s and the Russo-Japanese War in the 1900s reconfigured East Asian relations, and how the reform movements those wars brought about spurred social change and affected people's lives. The second chapter, "The Expansion of Japanese Imperialism and the Resistance of China and Korea," starts with a discussion of international relations in East Asia before and after the First World War. It describes the Japanese imperialist attempt to annex Chosen (an earlier name for Korea) and the resistance movement there, colonial conditions in Taiwan, the 1911 revolution in China, and the founding of the Republic of China. The analytical focus is on colonial rule in Korea, and the resistance and social movements in the three countries. The third chapter reexamines the violence inflicted upon individuals due to Japanese conquest. It includes discussions of such familiar topics as the Nanjing Massacre, the movement to imperialize the subject, so-called comfort women, and the atomic bomb, as well as of less frequently addressed issues like biological warfare and the brutality of the Battle of Okinawa. The fourth chapter, "Postwar East Asia," focuses on issues of historical assessment, including the Tokyo war-crimes trials, postwar reparations, and the social problems produced by the legacy of colonial rule. The chapter ends with a description of the establishment of diplomatic relations among the three countries. The final chapter discusses the direction East Asia is heading and the possibility for peace through open discussion on several unresolved controversies: for example, individual war reparations, the comfort women, history textbooks, and the Yasukuni Shrine.[30] It also outlines some positive aspects of current regional integration, such as the transnational flow of youth culture and the networking of civil-society groups, including East Asian peace movements.

The book is not without its problems. An emphasis on the Japanese colonization of Korea at the expense of investigating the situation in Taiwan and Manchuria, the absence of any detailed treatment of Okinawa, and the relative invisibility of locations at the peripheries of the region are among the shortcomings of the work. But as a whole, the book is a step toward regional reconciliation, and we must applaud the immense effort made by the many writers who worked together to produce such a landmark text. From the analytical standpoint of deimperialization, the fact that authors from Japan are willing to use imperialism to frame Japan's expansionist invasions is commendable indeed. The position of the former imperial power is crucial here. In light of the denial of imperialism that has been part of Japanese historiography for more than sixty years, we can imagine the difficulty the Japanese authors may have faced in dialogues with their counterparts from Japan's formerly colonized regions. In my view, it is this human dimension that is one of the most challenging tasks of deimperialization. The writing of this book proves that collectively facing difficult historical issues is possible. Furthermore, the fact that the writing committee included members from a former empire as well as others from former colonies means that a common will to take on the history of imperialism does exist. Reflecting on the past from the unidirectional perspective of a single country can be supplemented with the understandings and perceptions of others. Deimperialization is a double process. Mutual understanding is a necessary step for the dialectic to move forward.

Although *Modern History of the Three Countries in East Asia* cannot be considered a model for the work of deimperialization, its method should be appreciated. Addressing imperialism is a necessary first step toward deimperialization. With the emergence of this concrete practice, we can begin to imagine historians in the Philippines and the United States working together to write a history on the lasting impacts of American imperialism in the Philippines. Intellectuals from the United Kingdom can work with their counterparts in India, Malaysia, Singapore, Burma, and Hong Kong to write the history of British imperialism in Asia. Scholars in Indonesia and the Netherlands can work together on the problems that Dutch imperialism brought to Indonesia. French historians can collaborate with scholars in Vietnam, Laos, and Cambodia on the legacies of French imperialism in Indochina. Simply because Japan is a defeated empire and is located in Asia does not mean that it has had to deal with its neighbors. The lack of substantive communication between former imperial powers and their former colonies is a general problem of imperialism, neither diminished nor increased by geographic proximity.

In Europe and America, despite the postcolonial turn, an intellectual movement with the desire and energy to reexamine the legacy of Euro-American expansion at the level of theory and methodology, and simultaneously address the issue of how the historical responsibility of imperialism should be shouldered, does not seem to exist. Euro-American studies on decolonization in Southeast Asia, for example, are mostly conducted in a mode that neglects the political impacts of past imperialism on the present. Through the cultivation of individualism, relationships between the individual (scholar) and the state (nation) are always fragmented; therefore, there is no imperative for the individual to assume responsibility for the actions of the state. As critical intellectuals (leftists, feminists, and antiwar activists), we have naturally maintained an internationalist position against aggressive expansion undertaken by our own states. Should we be held personally responsible for the violence of our own states simply because we have been too weak to stop it? Once again, an ongoing debate within Japanese intellectual circles is instructive.

The activist Hanasaki Kōhei's essay "Decolonialization and Assumption of War Responsibility" sums up the key issues involved in the debate. In criticizing Katō Norihiro's controversial *Discussing Post-Defeat Japan,* Hanasaki develops his own theory: "I would like to emphasize that Japan, in the postwar state reconstruction process, has ignored the settlement of its historical legacies of colonialism. I mean decolonialization proper, including, but not reduced to, the settlement of war responsibilities in the narrow sense. This essay is intended to discuss the two related topics in a single context—the question of subjects in the assumption of war responsibility and the problem of decolonialization in postwar Japan" (Hanasaki 2000, 72). After Japan's defeat and the collapse of the Japanese empire, decolonialization was commonly understood as demilitarization and democratization. Hanasaki argues that this interpretation is incorrect, and I agree. Such reductionism is a legacy of the cold-war power structure, which has frozen the resolution of historical relations between former colonies and former imperial centers. Now that the cold war is supposedly over, Japan has to resume its incomplete task. Hanasaki cites Mitani Taichirō's *Wars and Politics in Modern Japan* to argue that Japan should enter the second stage of decolonialization: "Decolonialization primarily means the liberation and independence of former colonies, but it also refers to the corresponding process of decolonialization of the colonial powers. Mitani mainly discusses this latter process, the process of Japan 'liquidating its empire and Japan freeing itself of its empire'" (ibid., 72–73). The most fundamental issue of deimperialization has been ignored: the "pre-war imperial consciousness was not liquidated, but survived in postwar Japanese society" (ibid., 73). This is a crucial point. The collapse of the empire does not mean the collapse of the former colonizing population's imperial consciousness.

The most challenging criticism Hanasaki makes of Mitani is that the latter's account of the current state of decolonization is merely descriptive, and does not put forward any solutions. Hanasaki asks, quite directly, who should be held responsible for undertaking the task of decolonialization. He considers Japan's general lack of national responsibility to be a result of the common postwar historical narrative of how the Japanese nation came to be: "Japan's modern past was never properly grasped as a history of empire building and the eventual failure of this project and, as Kang [Sanjung] points out, the exclusion of Koreans and other former subjects of the Japanese Empire has been obliterated" (ibid., 74). Hanasaki wants to remedy the situation by reassociating contemporary Japan with its former colonies so that the modern history of Japan can be properly articulated.

This task has been made particularly difficult by the wave of nationalism that rose in the 1990s, when the Japanese right wing pushed hard to erase what they called the "dark side" of the nation's recent history. Japanese nationalists wanted younger generations to receive a "healthier" education, to learn about Japan's national glory, and to cultivate a commensurate sense of patriotism. The denial of responsibility, however, does not only exist on the Right. Radical Japanese refuse to identify with their country, and feminists consider Japanese imperialism to be the sin of men, therefore claiming the crimes of the past empire have nothing to do with them. Facing difficulties on both sides of the political spectrum, how can the Japanese reclaim the responsibility for deimperialization that was made possible by the loosening of the cold-war structure? Hanasaki advances a simple — but, in my view, workable — proposal. He appeals to those living in Japan, as well as to intellectuals who do research on Japan, to adopt a temporary and transitional identification with Japan in order to actively accept historical responsibility:

> I take the stand that as long as I was born as a member of the colonizer nation-state, and am still positioned in a historical situation where the decolonialization of Japan is not complete, I would provisionally take upon myself the definition of being "Japanese," the definition that is given to me by other people and that puts me in the national Japanese

collective. I say "provisionally" because I do not think I would remain forever passively defined and bound by this given relationality. Japanese colonial rule as viewed from the colonized people's perspective presents itself as nothing other than national oppression by the Japanese as a race. The colonized peoples thus take the Japanese race to task for their colonial responsibility. In the context of decolonialization, this identification of the nation-state with the race is grounded in both imagery and reality. (ibid., 78)

Without at least provisionally identifying with the Japanese, there is no position from which to respond to the call made by formally colonized peoples for the entire Japanese nation and race to take responsibility for colonization. But the assumption of Japanese identity is not simply a passive response to an external demand. Hanasaki cites an argument made by the highly respected activist intellectual Mutō Ichiyō: "As Mutō says, we will only be able to cease being an accomplice to the crimes committed by the state—war, colonization, and cover-ups—when we have overcome the postwar Japanese state and transformed it into a political formation based on alternative principles. However, we take on this task not because we are named and urged to do so, but because we have an inner urge and sense of obligation to do so" (ibid., 79).

In this important intervention, "decolonialization" is the word used by Hanasaki to frame the political task at hand. The use of the term intersects with my own use of deimperialization. As I use the word, "deimperialization" includes the following aspects: demilitarization, democratization, the assumption of war responsibility, and critical reflection on both imperial consciousness and the victimization of the colony. What needs to be emphasized is that war responsibility is but one aspect of deimperialization. To use Mutō's classification, deimperialization includes self-reflection on "war, colonization, and cover-ups." Although his discussion was formulated in Japan, the wider political and theoretical implications are clear. From the subject position of the former colonizer, Mutō urges critical intellectuals in the former empire to take responsibility for past aggression and to be actively involved in deimperialization. The discourse and practices of activists and scholars like Hanasaki and Mutō inspire us to work on different aspects of deimperialization. Critical reflections need to be developed not simply in the former colonies, but also, and with equal emphasis, in the former imperial homelands. Otherwise, imperial desire of the type expressed by Club 51 will continue to manifest itself.

The Meaning of Deimperialization

Our analysis of Club 51 has allowed us to explore the central problematic of deimperialization in contemporary East Asia. The analysis finds that anticommunism and pro-Americanism have, through the processes of imperialization and colonization, become an integral part of our social subjectivity. These processes, driven by the engine of world capitalist expansion, were able to endure in the postwar era through the establishment of the global cold-war structure. Club 51 is symptomatic of the underdevelopment of a tripartite movement of decolonization, deimperialization, and de–cold war. At a deeper level, Club 51's desire for empire is rooted in the historical memory of a glorious Chinese imperial past.

Of the three movements addressed in this book, deimperialization is the most basic, as it encompasses the problematics of both decolonization and de–cold war. In the context of Taiwan, the task of deimperialization inevitably compels us to address the state's own imperial desire to expand into Southeast Asia (as discussed in chapter 1), and the layered forces that constitute Taiwanese subjectivity: postwar American imperialism, prewar Japanese colonization, and the premodern Chinese empire. Through analysis of concrete events, we have attempted to disentangle these complex relations at different levels of abstraction.

In the process of sorting out the theoretical and political meanings of deimperialization, we have discovered that, although there are common issues to be addressed, the urgency to be given to particular questions of deimperialization is different in different locations. For instance, war responsibility and colonial victimization are key issues confronting Japan's deimperialization, whereas these are not a priority for Taiwan and Korea. Demilitarization, democratization, and the critique of imperial consciousness are concerns common to all three locations.

In the final analysis, Club 51 exposes a fundamental contradiction at the heart of many global conflicts: there is an unbridgeable gap between the exercise of national democratic rule and the functioning of imperialism, which is inherently international. One may disagree with Club 51, but its political appeal is made in line with democratic practices in Taiwan.

That is, domestically, the success or failure of the movement is contingent upon the will of the public, however imperfectly that will is expressed. Its competitors in the marketplace of possible political futures for Taiwan — be they integrationist, separatist, or something else — do not use military or police violence to suppress Club 51. Beyond the boundaries of the nation-state, the situation is not so polite. September 11 exposed a global crisis: most governments are to some extent obliged to follow democratic principles at home, but internationally these same states can ignore public opinion and, for example, support U.S. imperialist invasions. States operate beyond representational democracy. National democracy has only a weak mechanism to counter the potential for authoritarian rule: if you're doing badly, we'll vote you out in the next election. What are the democratic mechanisms at the international or global level? Is there any way to vote a superpower out of office?

This is precisely the issue of global governance. The world is increasingly globalized, but there is no corresponding growth in global democracy. The crisis now is that no force can stop U.S. military aggression. Once leaving their national territories, the strong freely impose their will on the weak. This abuse of power is sometimes understood and justified as the principle of real strength, though more commonly it goes by the name of neoliberal globalization. In such a situation, one often hears: "Well, it's unfortunate. But they are stronger, and we are weaker." We know from history that the principle of real strength leads to war, and that unless a democratic mechanism can be put in place at the global level to check it, it may well move us all toward destruction at an unimaginable scale. If there is no global deimperialization movement, imperialism will continue to be the default mode of future global "democracy."

One effect of neoliberal globalization, however, has been regionalization, and I believe that regionalization may afford a means to move beyond earlier failed attempts to counter real strength. Although the United Nations has proved to be as ineffective as national democracy, a model built up organically from regional democratic forms promises to make a positive contribution to global governance. The question of what kind of democracy is needed to allow this to happen is discussed in detail in the next chapter.

CHAPTER 5

ASIA AS METHOD
Overcoming the Present Conditions of Knowledge Production

> This I have called "Asia as method," and yet it is impossible to definitely state what this might mean.
>
> TAKEUCHI YOSHIMI, "ASIA AS METHOD"

> The critical analysis of nationalist thought is also necessarily an intervention in a political discourse of our own time. Reflecting on the intellectual struggles of nationalist writers of a bygone era, we are made aware of the way in which we relate our own theory and practice; judging their assessment of political possibilities, we begin to ponder the possibilities open to us today. Thus, analysis itself becomes politics; interpretation acquires the undertones of a polemic. In such circumstances, to pretend to speak in the "objective" voice of history is to dissimulate. By marking our own text with the signs of battle, we hope to go a little further towards a more open and self-aware discourse.
>
> PARTHA CHATTERJEE, *NATIONALIST THOUGHT AND THE COLONIAL WORLD*

Knowledge production is one of the major sites in which imperialism operates and exercises its power. The analyses in the preceding chapters suggest that the underdevelopment of deimperialization movements is a significant contributing factor in local, regional, and global conflicts throughout the contemporary world. This underdevelopment, I submit, has to do with the current conditions of knowledge production, which have serious structural limitations. To break through the impasse, critical intellectual work on deimperialization first and foremost has to transform these problematic conditions, transcend the structural limitations, and uncover alternative possibilities.

Leaving Asia for America

To confront the long-lasting impact of "leaving Asia for America" (*tuōyǎ rùměi*) since the Second World War in East Asia in general, and Taiwan in particular, this chapter puts forward "Asia as method" as a critical proposition to transform the existing knowledge structure and at the same time to transform ourselves. The potential of Asia as method is this: using the idea of Asia as an imaginary anchoring point, societies in Asia can become each other's points of reference, so that the understanding of the self may be transformed, and subjectivity rebuilt. On this basis, the diverse historical experiences and rich social practices of Asia may be mobilized to provide alternative horizons and perspectives. This method of engagement, I believe, has the potential to advance a different understanding of world history.

At the same time, the formulation of Asia as method is also an attempt to move forward on the tripartite problematic of decolonization, deimperialization, and de–cold war. To briefly recap the analysis developed over the previous four chapters: the historical processes of imperialization, colonization, and the cold war have become mutually entangled structures, which have shaped and conditioned both intellectual and popular knowledge production. Through the use of Asia as method, a society in Asia may be inspired by how other Asian societies deal with problems similar to its own, and thus overcome unproductive anxieties and develop new paths of engagement. In proposing a means for self-transformation through shifting our points of reference toward Asia and the third world, Asia as method is grounded in the critical discourses of an earlier generation of thinkers, with whom we now imagine new possibilities.

For those of us living in Asia, Asia as method is not a self-explanatory proposition. Until the last decade, most intellectuals in Asia had multiple direct links to North America or Europe, but we had few contacts among ourselves. If we met at all, it was in New York, London, or Paris. At its most basic, Asia as method means expanding the number of these meeting points to include sites in Asia such as Seoul, Kyoto, Singapore, Bangalore, Shanghai, and Taipei.

As a theoretical proposition, Asia as method is a result of practices growing out of the *Inter-Asia Cultural Studies: Movements* journal project, which has been operating since the late 1990s. In this context, Asia as method can be considered a self-reflexive movement to examine problems and issues emerging out of our experiences organizing interventions in various local spaces.[1] Those of us who have been involved come from very diverse intellectual and academic backgrounds, not to mention regions with immensely varied local histories. Yet we all feel that something important and worthwhile is emerging out of the intense dialogues we are undertaking among ourselves and with others. Asia as method is my own attempt to think through some of these intellectual concerns, priorities, and processes.

The Inter-Asia project is not new. An earlier generation of intellectuals paved the way, and having learned of their struggles, we are now finding out for ourselves how difficult it is to initiate dialogues and links among critical circles in Asia.[2] The most obvious difficulty is the imbalance between big countries and small ones, evident in the relationships between India and the rest of South Asia, Indonesia and the rest of Southeast Asia, and China and the rest of Northeast Asia. What we now call international relations existed in each subregion of Asia before the formation of the modern nation-state, and the earlier imbalances were exacerbated by twentieth-century colonialism and nationalism. Each of these factors — size, colonial experiences, and nationalism — is evident in the major historical conflicts in the region: Japan's aggression in East and Southeast Asia, Indonesia's 1965 massacre of communists and reluctance to grant East Timor its independence, the division of Korea, the conflict between the CCP and the KMT, the partition of Pakistan from India, the separation of Singapore from Malaysia, and the unequal distribution of wealth between first- and third-world Asian countries. Dealing with these large-scale conflicts is made more difficult by recurring practical problems. For example, English is often seen as a colonial language in non-English-speaking parts of Asia, and those countries that have adopted it are viewed by others as much too colonized. As we interact, problems such as this surface repeatedly, and we have not yet found effective ways to handle them.

Before moving on, I wish to clarify a political motive of Asia as method—the use of Asia as an emotional signifier to call for regional integration and solidarity. In reality, due to historical constraints and current local differences, the general mood does not justify using Asia in this way quite yet. Nevertheless, the globalization of capital has generated economic and cultural regionalization, which has in turn brought about the rise of Asia as a pervasive structure of sentiment. As a result, both a historical condition and an emotional basis exist for new imaginings of Asia to emerge.

The rise of Asia is not simply an artifact of the evolution of global capitalism; it is also the manifestation of a number of local historical currents. First, in contrast to the standard narrative, the regional integration of Asian economies has not yet lived up to expectations. Besides the loose networks of ASEAN Plus Three and the South Asian Association for Regional Cooperation, there is little integrationist activity. Official and informal talks on the Asian common market and the creation of an Asian dollar as a way to counter U.S. hegemony bear witness to integrationist sentiments, but there are no such regional mechanisms in place to take advantage of them. Second, some Asian nation-states have begun to create links with each other based not on economic needs but in their own self-interest. For instance, in South Korea in the 1990s, an East Asia discourse began to emerge, which, according to Choi Wan Ju, was based on the sentiment that the Korean conflict cannot be resolved within the Korean Peninsula, and therefore requires the involvement of neighboring countries.[3] As the biggest country in the region, mainland China has a unique relation to the rest of East Asia (Baik 2002). To alleviate regional anxieties over the supposed China threat, China has had to develop a set of specific policies to win over the trust of its neighbors. Like South Korea and China, the other nations in the region are in the process of creating their own relation with the concept of Asia.

Under present historical conditions, with the economic, historical, and cultural meanings of Asia fluctuating and contradictory, members of critical intellectual circles in Asia are better equipped to move beyond the limit of the nation-state boundary, to develop discourses congruent with the new condition, to create a new discursive mood, and to imagine new possibilities. In the intellectual history of the twentieth century, the word "Asia" was in fact loaded with anxieties. As Wang Hui points out in "Imagining Asia: A Genealogical Analysis," the notion of Asia "is colonial, and is also anti-colonial; it is nationalist and is also internationalist; it is European, but also in turn has shaped the self-understanding of Europe; it is tightly connected to the question of the nation-state, and is overlapping with the perspective of the empire; it is a civilizational concept in relation to Europe, but is also a geographical category established in geo-political relations" (Wang 2002, 204). These anxieties, entangled and interrelated, have to do not only with the question of the West, but also with historical memories within Asia.

Inside the region itself, anxiety over the meaning of Asia arises from the politics of representation. For instance, in Japan and South Korea, Asia has referred mainly to China, and occasionally to India. This under-standing of Asia indicates how larger civilizational entities functioned historically. China, for example, considers itself to be the center of its imaginary Asia, so Southeast Asia, South Asia, Central Asia, West Asia, the Pacific Islands, Australia, and New Zealand have been pushed to the margins or have simply disappeared altogether. In East Asia, challenging this bias can open up new horizons and a broader regional system of ref-erence. There is certainly a need for subregional integration, but it would be a mistake with enormous consequences if East Asia were imagined as a replacement for the whole of Asia.

The anxiety over representation is also evident when Asia is seen as primarily a colonial imagination. If Asia is to have analytical value, it does indeed have to be placed within the frame of world history, but if world history is understood as Euro-American imperialism and capitalist ex-pansion, the agency and subjectivity of Asia are stripped away. It would be no different than saying that since the nation-state is a European or colonialist construct, it is therefore illegitimate. If the legitimacy of the discourse on Asia is discounted, we are left with the old binary opposition between the East and the West, which erases Asia's rich multiplicity and heterogeneity.

Asia as method recognizes the need to keep a critical distance from uninterrogated notions of Asia, just as one has to maintain a critical dis-tance from uninterrogated notions of the nation-state. It sees Asia as a product of history, and realizes that Asia has been an active participant in historical processes.

Building on the analyses developed in the previous chapters, this chap-ter presents a series of dialogues. The first dialogue takes up once again the old question of the West as it is rearticulated in several seminal post-colonial texts. The purpose here is to pinpoint the understandable but unnecessary obsession with the question of the West, and then to suggest a move toward Asia as a possible way of shifting points of reference and breaking away from the East-West binary structure. The second dialogue is with Partha Chatterjee's theory of political society. By analyzing how civil society can be translated or understood as what I will call *mínjiān* society, it argues that this translation provides a point of access into the organic shape and characteristics of local society. The third dialogue is with Mizoguchi Yūzō's *China as Method* ([1989] 1996). In this dialogue, Asia as method ceases to consider Asia as the object of analysis and becomes a means of transforming knowledge production.

The Question of the West

In the history of imperialism, diverse positions and discourses competing against each other in colonized national spaces have responded in various ways to the invasions of Western forces. The discursive formulations have continually resurfaced at different points in history, constituting intellectual traditions. These traditions of response to the West have in turn become the main heritage of nationalist thought. In various Chinese contexts, this heritage is evident in the evoking of familiar historical events such as the Boxer Rebellion of the late Qing Dynasty; formulations like "Chinese knowledge as the basis, western knowledge as the application" (*zhōngtǐ xīyòng*); and positions as diverse as modernist, nativist, and neo-traditionalist. Emerging in different historical contexts, each of these diverse modes of response became the leading nationalist discourse of its time. But whatever the label, the moral and emotional legitimacy of these discourses appeals to patriotic sentiments. The presumed consensus is that "we are doing this for the good of the country and the people." Such a sincere appeal has its emotional and material basis in the national history of suffering. But the Other, which has conditioned this nationalist self, has been and still is the West.

This imaginary West has performed different functions in nationalist discourses. It has been an opposing entity, a system of reference, an object from which to learn, a point of measurement, a goal to catch up with, an intimate enemy, and sometimes an alibi for serious discussion and action. For the past few centuries, "the West as method" has become the dominant condition of knowledge production. As Stuart Hall points out in his important essay, "The West and the Rest," the West performs a wide range of functions. It is a framework used to categorize different societies and their characteristics. It is a structure of knowledge, a series of images that form a system of representation that connects with other concepts (the West/metropolitan/developed/industrialized versus the non-West/rural/underdeveloped/agricultural). It is the basic criterion by which the backward and disposable is differentiated from the desirable and progressive (Hall 1992b, 277). Hall's account sums up the functions of the West within the geographical space of the West, but in the third world, the West has become the object of both desire and resentment. This fatal attraction—or, to use Arif Dirlik's (1997) term, "fatal distraction"—has become the backbone of third-world nationalism. In fact, the discussion has always been framed as a dichotomy: the East versus the West, China versus the West, South Korea versus the West, Japan versus the West, India versus the West, and so on. In this situation, we must ask: what is the subject of nationalist discourse, if not the West?

If this political unconscious has become the basis for the reproduction of the structure of desire, we need to reconsider this history and compare how the West has been imagined and reimagined in various local spaces over time. The task is not so much to conduct an ideological critique, but to discover ways to break through this analytical impasse. Before attempting this type of comparative work, it will be useful to analyze several earlier strategies of dealing with the West that have been formulated in postcolonial studies.

The first strategy is to disrupt the Other by deconstructing it. This strategy argues that the West has no essence and no unity; it is only putative, and therefore cannot become "our" Other. The more complex version of this argument can be found in Naoki Sakai's "Modernity and Its Critique: The Problem of Universalism and Particularism." Sakai argues that Habermas "takes for granted a parallel correspondence among the binary oppositions: pre-modern/modern, non-West/West, mythical/rational. Moreover, for him, the very unity of the West is a given; it is an almost tactile reality" (Sakai 1988, 478). But if the assumed unity never existed or has been dissolved, can that type of "epistemological confidence" still hold? The importance of Sakai's essay lies in its pointing out that the complicity between universalism and particularism is a result of colonial practices. In Sakai's view, Europe, along with its invented discourse, has the value of universality, whereas the rest are particularistic; such a perception cannot be understood apart from the history of European colonization.

The point is sharply put and well taken, but the problem lies elsewhere. While Sakai is desperately trying to unpack universalist pretensions, universalism still prevails. Sakai makes this move to argue that if the universalism of the West cannot hold, then the particularism of *Nihonjinron* (the theory of Japaneseness) also collapses. The implication is that all anticolonial nationalist discourses that take Western imperialism as the Other cannot stand. If we follow Sakai's argument and insist that the frame for both universalism and particularism is the construction of colonialism, then the legitimacy of the frame can no longer be granted. The urgent task then becomes to confront, displace, and move beyond this frame; otherwise, lacking an alternative, the move to deconstruct the West is still locked within the same theoretical space.

The second strategy is to de-universalize, provincialize, or regionalize the West, so that the experiences of the West are limited to only one part of the globe. According to this argument, although the West has been influential and has indeed become a part of the cultural resources of Asia, it is, like other parts of the world, a product of history and cannot claim universality. Here the most articulate voice is that of the historian Dipesh Chakrabarty, a member of the Subaltern Studies collective, which, since the 1980s, has attempted to rewrite South Asian history from below. In his often-cited essay, "Provincializing Europe: Postcoloniality and the Critique of History," Chakrabarty argues: "In the academic discourse of history—that is, 'history' as a discourse produced at the institutional site of the university—'Europe' remains the sovereign, the theoretical subject of all histories, including the ones we call 'Indian', 'Chinese', 'Kenyan', etc. There is a peculiar way in which all these other histories tend to become variations on a master narrative that could be called 'the history of Europe'" (Chakrabarty 1992, 337).

He goes on to point out the anxiety of third-world historians, who in various ways are pressured to refer to European history while knowing that the reverse is not true for Western historians: "They produce their work in relative ignorance of, say, non-Western histories and this does not seem to affect the quality of their work. This is a gesture, however, that 'we' cannot return" (ibid.). Chakrabarty explains this Eurocentric discursive structure as originating in "history," itself an important part of the modernization project, and in "Europe," which is often thought of as the "home of the modern."

What can be done to redress this inequality? Chakrabarty proposes: "let us call this the project of provincializing 'Europe', the 'Europe' that modern imperialism and (third-world) nationalism have, by their collaborative venture and violence, made universal" (ibid., 351). That is, European modernity comes from interactive relations with its former colonies. At the heart of Chakrabarty's project are these claims:

a. The recognition that Europe's acquisition of the adjective "modern" for itself is a piece of global history of which an integral part is the story of European imperialism, and b. the understanding that this equating of a certain version of Europe with "modernity" is not the work of Europeans alone; third-world nationalism, as modernizing ideologies par excellence, have been equal partner in this process . . . I only underscore the point that the project of "provincializing Europe" cannot be a nationalist, nativist or an atavistic project. In unraveling the necessary entanglement of history . . . one cannot but problematize "India" at the same time as one dismantles "Europe." (ibid., 352)

Chakrabarty's strategy is to wrest the ownership of modernity from Europe, making Europe no longer the home of the global modern.

The history of India is Chakrabarty's major concern (see Chakrabarty 2000a), and his dismantling of Eurocentrism has not addressed the global hegemony of the United States. In the contemporary context, the critique of Eurocentrism will also have to address the problem of Americancentrism. Moreover, after Europe is provincialized, can we directly talk to each other, bypassing Europe and America? To provincialize Europe is a process that will loosen but not change the structure of the dialogue. A more active process needs to be initiated in order for a dialogue among sites outside Europe to take place.[4]

A third strategy was proposed by Ashis Nandy in the 1980s. The way he framed the problem was to suggest that certain elements that appeared to be from the West had actually long been a part of Indian civilization. These elements, which had been situated at the margin of that civilization in the past, were now moving toward the center due to the colonial encounter. In his seminal work, *The Intimate Enemy: Loss and Recovery of Self under Colonialism*, Nandy puts it this way:

> Colonialism is also a psychological state rooted in earlier forms of social consciousness in both the colonizers and the colonized. It represents a certain cultural continuity and carries a certain cultural baggage. First, it includes codes which both the rulers and the ruled can share. The main function of these codes is to alter the original cultural priorities on both sides and bring to the center of the colonial culture subcultures previously recessive or subordinate in the two confronting cultures. Concurrently, the codes remove from the center of each of the cultures subcultures previously salient in them. It is these fresh priorities which explain why some of the most impressive colonial systems have been built by societies ideologically committed to open political systems, liberalism and intellectual pluralism . . . As a state of mind, colonialism is an indigenous process released by external forces. (Nandy 1983, 2–3)

To support his argument, Nandy describes how the discourses of sex and age operated in colonial England, and then demonstrates how, through the colonial encounter, they evolved in India, specifically with reference to Gandhi's thought and action.[5]

According to Nandy, the common understanding that modern concepts were simply imposed from the outside and disseminated to the third world through colonialism cannot stand. The top-down imposition of the modern cannot explain why certain concepts were accepted with such ease by the colonized. Nandy argues that this was because these concepts were already internal to Indian civilization, even if they had been marginal before being brought to the center by colonial ideology. Therefore, to negate the West entirely would run the risk of also negating India's plural traditions, and of denying that the West itself has become one of India's many subcultures.

Nandy's project was to delegitimize nationalism (Nandy 1994), but in practice his strategy also applies to the nationalist enterprise. Some attempts to mobilize or even essentialize the imagined resources of the nation so as to oppose the West took the nationalist impulse a step further and claimed that "our" civilization was more universal than that of the

West. This approach leads to a competition to be the hegemonic Other of the West. Is it Confucianism, Islam, or Hinduism? Each imagined civilization, including the West, is once again totalized. In effect, civilizationalism, in alliance with nativist triumphalism, perpetuates the imagined superiority of nationalist subjectivity.

A fourth strategy used to respond to the question of the West can be termed third-world nativism. It is often invoked to justify certain uses of Western concepts in dealing with local problems. One of the most articulate examples is Neil Garcia's award-winning *Philippine Gay Culture: The Last 30 Years* (1996). In the preface, Garcia formulates an opposition between nativism and universalism: "While homosexuality, as a specific form of sexual orientation, doubtless originates historically in the West and is therefore modernist, what should the cultural critic's attitude be toward its appearance in the post-colonies, for example, the Philippines? There are two possible positions on this issue: one may be called for the sake of convenience, nativist, and the other for the sake of diacritical contrast, universalist" (Garcia 1996, xvi–xvii). He goes on to indicate that since the 1970s, the University of the Philippines has become a base for the "indigenization movement." The developed nativist position makes use of concepts (such as homosexual) from the West, but insists that they accurately represent the native's understanding and practices, all the while recognizing, in Garcia's words, that "these labels remain cosmetic and colonial." Therefore, the nativist "either categorically denies the possibility, or at least qualifies the issue" (ibid., xvii). To deny categorically is the extreme expression of nativism. It fundamentally assumes that there is an indigenous consciousness and selfhood which has not been touched by colonial subjectivity. A milder nativist position sees that concepts from the outside have, in the process of modernization, become part of the local culture, and furthermore have had a greater influence on the more affluent strata of the population, such as urban middle-class elites. Garcia argues: "that I continue to ground my analysis on a specific local milieu, in any case, qualifies my approach as still somewhat nativist, although it is an approach that will not deny the presence of Western cultural hegemony and the colonial constitution of subjectivity" (ibid.).

Confronting the challenge of a wider indigenist intellectual movement that had been developing in the Philippines since the 1970s, Garcia developed his own revisionist nativism. He suggests that many contemporary cultural practices have existed since before the arrival of colonialism, and are still part of lived experience today. Through the historical process of Western colonialism, new elements from the outside had to negotiate their way in and become part of the local, the native. These two sets of knowledge have to be understood simultaneously; otherwise, one cannot really understand local practices. He gives a concrete example by contrasting homosexuality, which he views as a modern Western category, with traditional *bakla* practices. Whereas homosexuals are those who prefer reciprocal and more or less equal sexual relationships, bakla are feminized men whose masculine sexual partners are not considered bakla, and may not even be considered gay. In the Philippines, bakla existed prior to homosexuality, but because the two terms belong to different systems of knowledge, there is no relation of equivalence. In contemporary practices, both forms coexist and intersect, and both terms have to be adopted to fully grasp the reality of gay life in the Philippines.

Garcia reminds us of the analytical value of concepts that existed prior to Western influence. At the same time, we realize that Garcia's nativism is produced mainly in reaction to the nativist movement in the Philippines, where the West is the Other that conditions the anxiety of the nativist.

In a close reading of these postcolonial strategies of response, we cannot help but see that the West as the location of the Other is a perspective shared by all of the theorists discussed here. Locating the West as the point of opposition once again consolidates the formula: the West and the rest (Said 1979; Hall 1992b). The difficulty in moving beyond this framework reflects an undeniable condition: the global structure of power is uneven, and the geographical and imaginary site of the West is the most dominant and the richest in resources. The West has been able to enter and generate real impacts in other geographical spaces without experiencing the same type or intensity of impacts from the outside. "The West and the rest" has a historical material basis. Western-centrism has constituted a solid structure of desire and knowledge, a structure that is indeed difficult to shake loose. But must we stand still and wait for these material conditions to change all by themselves? Unless we can more actively challenge Western-centrism, the call among the rest to interact directly is an unrealistic demand.

This is the predicament of postcolonial discourse. But the situation is not as pessimistic as one might imagine. Global and regional changes have created conditions which allow for the possibility of a breakthrough. Rather than continuing to fear reproducing the West as the Other, and hence avoiding the question altogether, an alternative discursive strategy posits the West as bits and fragments that intervene in local social formations in a systematic, but never totalizing, way. The local formation of modernity carries important elements of the West, but it is not fully enveloped by it. Once recognizing the West as fragments internal to the local, we no longer consider it as an opposing entity but rather as one cultural resource among many others. Such a position avoids either a resentful or a triumphalist relation with the West because it is not bound by an obsessive antagonism.

Elsewhere I have attempted to formulate an internationalist localism (Chen 1994c), which moves beyond the unconditional identification with the nation-state. Internationalist localism acknowledges the existence of the nation-state as a product of history but analytically keeps a critical distance from it. The operating site is local, but at the same time internationalist localism actively transgresses nation-states' boundaries. It looks for new political possibilities emerging out of the practices and experiences accumulated during encounters between local history and colonial history—that is, the new forms and energies produced by the mixing brought about by modernization. Internationalist localism respects tradition without essentializing it, and will not mobilize the resources of tradition simply for the sake of opposing the West. Its point of departure is not to reify the value system (which has happened in the Asian-values debate), but to reinvestigate it and its practices. Asia and the third world provide an imaginary horizon for comparison, or a method for what I call inter-referencing.

Rather than being constantly anxious about the question of the West, we can actively acknowledge it as a part of the formation of our subjectivity. In the form of fragmented pieces, the West has entered our history and become part of it, but not in a totalizing manner. The task for Asia as method is to multiply frames of reference in our subjectivity and worldview, so that our anxiety over the West can be diluted, and productive critical work can move forward.

It is with this assumption that we will engage with Partha Chatterjee in the next section. His theoretical intervention, particularly his identification of the "political society" in the third world—which he calls "most of the world"—are on the same wavelength as the alternative strategy proposed here.

Political Society and Mínjiān: A Dialogue with Partha Chatterjee

Within the context of the third-world nationalist movement in Asia, liberal social sciences and Marxist analysis, as constituents of the modernizing project, have joined hands to censor concepts crucial to our understanding of non-Western social formations. Under the influence of mainstream Euro-American social thought, these intellectual and academic practices have copied, applied, and appropriated analytical categories historically rooted in early capitalist societies to understand our own social spaces. The dialectic of the state versus civil society, which came out of eighteenth-century Europe, is one example. Once a model of this sort is in place and endowed with liberal democratic imagination, it renders everything else invisible or irrelevant. It is as if the entire social formation falls exclusively within those two domains. Under such conditions, the rediscovery of spaces, sectors, and planes that existed prior to the moment of colonial encounter and global conquest, and that are still actively working in contemporary daily life, becomes an urgent task. Without such a rediscovery, we do not simply erase history, we also produce inadequate analytical understandings of our own societies. A condition of making this rediscovery possible is multiplying and shifting our points of reference to include historical comparisons within the former colonized spaces of the world.

In June 2000, Partha Chatterjee was invited to Taiwan to deliver a series of lectures, which was titled "Locating Political Society: Modernity, State Violence and Postcolonial Democracy."[6] Reading and translating his essays and listening to his talks triggered flashes of recognition in me. The Indian instances he cited—the struggles of a squatter community (Chatterjee 1998), the controversy surrounding the death of a religious sect's leader (Chatterjee 2001), and the debate over a public memorial ceremony (Chatterjee 2000)—had much in common with recent events in Taiwan. The heated struggle over the squatter community in No. 14/15 Park in Taipei in 1997, the two-year fight of licensed prostitutes against the Taipei mayor in 1997–99, the many instances of state violence against gays and lesbians, the community reconstruction projects after the earthquake in September 1999, the brutal crackdown on the sex industry by the police, the emergence of new communities of foreign laborers, the social discrimination against religious sects, and other events all resonated with Chatterjee's message.

Are events like these unique to the third-world formation of modernity in Asia? I do not think that is necessarily the case, since similar events also happen outside the third world, but somehow the structural location, the modernizing processes, and the subsequent historical experiences common to third-world Asia make these phenomena more visible. As Tejaswini Niranjana argues, "Within the new globalization, the paths to the first world will be more clearly defined than ever, rendered easier to traverse. Other locations on the map will appear all the more blurred, all the more difficult to reach. Now more than ever a critical perspective on our contemporary political-cultural identities requires that we place those other journeys on our agenda" (Niranjana 2000, 106). To echo Niranjana's programmatic statement, there is an urgent need to do comparative studies, or inter-reference studies, of modernity as it is experienced in third-world spaces. The underlying assumption is that ignoring others who have experienced similar pressures and trajectories of modernization makes it impossible to understand oneself. By shifting our points of reference, we can generate more strategically useful knowledge.

Whenever controversial issues involving subaltern or marginal subjects—such as squatters, "betel nut beauties,"[7] or sex workers—emerge in the social space, the tendency to perfunctorily moralize and assign blame can quickly divide various communities who otherwise share common interests. Because social controversies have always been subjected to such normative claims, analytical attempts at explanation are constantly undermined, but controversial events should nevertheless be occasions for us to better understand the forces and principles at work in the larger social formation. It is time to change this habitual practice and replace it with a more careful and analytical comparative approach. One may ask: Why are such comparative analyses within the third world so rare—perhaps even nonexistent? What needs to be done to facilitate this change in points of reference? Even if the desire and means to shift viewpoints exist, on what grounds is comparison possible and productive?

Opportunities for Asians to get to know each other intellectually are often intercepted by the structural flow of desire toward North America and Europe. Though the situation is changing, direct academic interaction among the neighboring countries in Asia is still uncommon. Intellectual exchange in the region is lagging far behind the flow of capital and popular culture. In reality, we have already been doing comparative studies, but the comparison has been between Euro-American theory and our local experiences. This is by now a familiar complaint: the West is equipped with universalist theory; the rest of us have particularist empirical data; and eventually our writings become a footnote that either validates or invalidates Western theoretical propositions. We serve as the native informant to the theoretically minded researcher. The agony implied by this relation is caused by a serious problem of our own: the worship of theory. Indeed, theory has been narrowly understood as a set of superior knowledge, and it is associated with the names of specific authors. We forget that these theoretical propositions are not universally applicable but have been advanced in response to concrete local problems. Foucault's *The History of Sexuality* (1988) is thus wrongly perceived as an account not of European experiences but of the experiences of the entire human race, and hence is used to explain, for example, the history of sexuality in premodern China.

This type of comparison has been problematized before. Resistance to theory on nationalist grounds is common enough, but the real problem is that Euro-American theory is simply not all that helpful in our attempts to understand our own conditions and practices. There is something wrong with the frame of reference. It makes more sense and is more productive to compare the formation of the society of consumption in Taiwan with that in Korea, the condition of the peasantry in India with that in China, or the form of the city-state in Hong Kong with that in Singapore, because their experiences of being colonized societies, routes of modernization, geographical sizes, and structural locations in the current global capitalist system are more similar, making these comparisons more useful than any with the West.

Indeed, these types of comparisons have been made by scholars working in area studies in Euro-America, but the underlying positions and theoretical problematics set out in such analyses still reside within Europe or America, and the analyses often miss the real historical contradictions at work. Let me note here that I have always insisted that those who are living and working outside the location of analysis can often produce useful and important research, and that those who live and work "in the local" are often mired in complex networks of relations that erode critical distance. But this does not prevent us from recognizing that research is never conducted in isolation, operating instead within a specific tradition of knowledge production. This tradition prioritizes certain assumptions and concerns, which can deflect analytical attention away from real energies and contradictions on the ground.

Once we set the points of comparison and dialogue in a new direction—toward the third world or Asia—different sets of issues emerge. With the shift, the division between researcher and native informant suddenly vanishes. Discussing the issue of ethnic politics in Taiwan with Indonesian activist intellectuals, am I still a native informant? The hierarchical positioning is suddenly turned into a horizontal one; we stand side by side, equally ignorant about each other's society.[8]

This call for a shift and multiplication of reference points is easily misunderstood as an anti-West gesture. In actual practice, the sources of the West have offered us multiple entry points for knowing each other. We can communicate in English, as well as through critical languages such as Marxism, structuralism, and feminism, so that Western experiences—say, the formation of the English working class—serve as a common referent for us to use in beginning conversations with each other. These experiences are, in fact, a way to break the ice, and it is through the process of getting to know each other that issues and experiences beneath the surface—deeper than the layer of the West—will emerge. At that point, it becomes possible to shift the ground of received theoretical propositions. The following dialogue with Partha Chatterjee is one instance of breaking the ice.

In his three lectures in Taiwan, Partha Chatterjee set out to articulate a new critical concept that attempts to identify and describe emerging forms and spaces of democratic struggle in postcolonial India. The implication of Chatterjee's argument is that the existing analytical distinction between the state and civil society cannot explain how subaltern classes and groups, quantitatively dominant and socially visible, have been able to invent alternative spaces of political democracy to ensure their survival and livelihood. Often, these "populations" (Chatterjee's analytical term) are agents of neither the state nor civil society; their existence is often considered to be illegal at best, and at worst they are seen as dirt to be eliminated or otherwise used by the nationalist modernizing elites. They are excluded from the center of politics, but at the same time, they are often mobilized by the social elites for the latter's own political ends. However political power is redistributed among rival elites, the subalterns are still the classes to be dominated and governed. In order to survive, they have to negotiate with both the state and civil society, the so-called public sphere—a domain overwhelmingly occupied and controlled by the middle-class bourgeois subjects and other social elites. Aiming neither to capture state power nor win hegemonic leadership within civil society, subaltern groups in the course of their struggle somehow open up a transient space between the state and civil society. Chatterjee terms this mediating space "political society."

In his essay "Community in the East," Chatterjee follows Gramsci's formulation of civil society, but with a twist to allow for the Indian context. Chatterjee argues that "the politics of democratization must therefore be carried out not through the classical transactions between state and civil society but in the much less well-defined, legally ambiguous, contextually and strategically demarcated terrain of political society" (Chatterjee 1998, 280). It is precisely in this process of mediation and negotiation that the desire for democratization is played out. Chatterjee analyzes three examples. The first concerns a squatter community that has existed along a railway in Calcutta for fifty years. The community has been facing eviction since 1990, and it has formulated a discourse around the moral right for survival in order to mobilize groups in the civil society to negotiate with the state on the community's behalf. In his analysis of this case, Chatterjee on the one hand challenges the poverty of debate between liberalism and communitarianism in the West, and on the other hand brings out the reverse Orientalism found in the mindsets of the nationalist elites of the non-West. These elites are complicit in essentializing both the West (which is understood to represent materialism, individualism, and the neglect of tradition) and the East (which is understood to represent spiritualism, community solidarity, and the respect for tradition). In this way, the elites are reproducing the Western framing of the debate between liberalism and communitarianism. None of these discourses adequately explains how the so-called illegal residents were able to organize themselves and mobilize representatives from both the civil society (nongovernmental organizations) and the state (the social-welfare division) in their fight to keep their community intact.

The second example is related in the essay "Democracy and the Violence of the State: A Political Negotiation of Death" (Chatterjee 2001), which analyzes the events surrounding the 1993 death of a religious sect leader in Calcutta. Believing that their leader was in a trance and not really dead at all, members of the sect refused to relinquish control of his body. The media and civil-society elites, in their role as spokespersons for the modernization project, called the sect members irrational and superstitious, and pressured the local government to intervene in the name of hygiene and public security. Soon after, 5,000 police officers arrived to seize the body, triggering a massive riot. The sect responded to this state violence by arguing that the state's authoritarian and antidemocratic actions deprived them of their religious and civil rights. Chatterjee's detailed analysis focuses on the characteristics of political society and the dynamics among different agents: state, media, social elites, and members of the sect.

The third example is explored in the essay "On Civil and Political Society in Postcolonial Democracy" (Chatterjee 2000), which undertakes a rereading of a debate at the end of the nineteenth century between the young Rabindranath Tagore and Nabinchandra Sen over whether India should allow a Western-style memorial meeting to take place after the death of the modernist writer Bankimchandra Chattopadhyay. After describing how the issue was debated at that time, Chatterjee traces how the contradictions of colonial modernity have continued and been transformed in postcolonial contexts.

These examples, Chatterjee maintains, are not isolated events. In fact, in the postcolonial era, they are typical of the dominant forms of struggle of the subaltern classes. Elites in both the state and civil society, however, do not see subalterns as political actors but treat them as being prepolitical, and consequently their struggles are treated contemptuously. Chatterjee's project aims to bring to light the important possibilities opened up when this newly identified space is strategically elevated. What happens when political society is taken seriously? Through these analyses, Chatterjee puts forward three theoretical propositions arising from his study of modernity in the non-West:

1. The most significant transformations during the colonial period took place in civil society; the most significant transformations occurring in the postcolonial period take place in political society.
2. During the colonial period, the debate over social transformation was framed in terms of modernity; in the political society of the postcolonial period, the central question is that of democracy.
3. In the current phase of the globalization of capital, we may well be witnessing an emerging opposition between modernity and democracy, that is between civil society and political society. (ibid., 98)

These are provocative theses. Challenging and inspiring, they help us to locate the driving forces underlying democratic transformation in the third world. But as acutely as these propositions describe operating logics in the modern history of South Asia, they may not apply so neatly to East Asia. Under authoritarian rule until the 1990s, civil society in postcolonial Taiwan and South Korea has been the agent and site for social transformation, while political debate has been framed by discussions of both modernity and democracy. Only after the start of the so-called democratic transition in the mid-1980s has something which might be called political society emerged as a central site of struggle. The divergence does not mean we have nothing to learn from Chatterjee's formulation. These ideas have radically challenged existing understandings of contemporary politics, for both liberalism and Marxism, and have opened new ways of thinking about politics and democracy generally. They are especially useful in imagining how to widen the operating space for new social movements both inside and outside civil society. Chatterjee's contributions also allow us to conceptualize the dynamics of the field of struggle within which subject groups' strategic relations with other agencies can be located. His theoretical propositions explain a great deal, but they require certain modifications in the East Asian context. Let me try to tell a different story, based on experiences in Taiwan.

In the late 1980s and early 1990s, a debate that came to be labeled "civil society versus popular democracy" (*mínjiān shèhuì* versus *rénmín mínzhǔ*) took place among critical circles in Taiwan. The scale of the debate was not huge, but it was a dispute that will probably be revisited by future generations of scholars and activists. At that time, I belonged to the popular democracy camp, which also included a labor activist (Wuo

Young-Ie), an unemployed analytical philosopher (Ka Wei-po, a pseudo-nym), a feminist activist (Wang Ping), a sex liberationist (Josephine Ho), a feminist critic (Ding Naifei), a formerly imprisoned academic (Fred Chiu Yan-liang), and others. The debate grew out of discussions about the 1989 Tiananmen Square protests, known to Chinese speakers simply as the June Fourth Incident.[9] At that time, it became clear to us that all the responses in Taiwan to the events in Tiananmen Square—from the state, the opposition DPP, and left-leaning forces—were couched in stat-ist terms, and the anticommunist rhetoric that had been slowly disap-pearing had been brought back to the fore and was being used to mobilize self-serving public support in the form of mass rallies and other forms of political organization. It was at that point that we intervened.

We advanced several straightforward challenges to the civil-society position. First, this position proposed that in order to capture state power from the KMT regime, the DPP should be allowed to occupy the leading position within civil society, unify different interest groups, and thereby subsume all social movements under its leadership. In response, we de-veloped a set of arguments aimed at preserving a relatively autonomous space for allies involved in the labor, women's, environmental, aboriginal, and alternative-culture movements. We maintained that in an authori-tarian society that had been constituted by right-wing ideologies (statist, developmentalist, and anticommunist), and in which the forces of the Left had been wiped out soon after the Second World War, the critical density of progressive social forces was low; but this was a moment when left-leaning forces could begin to carve out a small space for themselves. We argued that social movements should increase their own autonomy, rather than allowing themselves to be quickly glued into the political space of party politics. Cautionary examples are the Labor Party (which disbanded in 1988) and the Worker's Party (which still exists but is not functional), neither of which were able to build wide bases of support. Negotiating with the DPP as it took control of the government, first at the local and later at the national level, has been a constant struggle. Some groups previously associated with the democracy movement have aban-doned their work altogether, while others have been completely assimi-lated into the DPP. To collaborate with the government, many of these groups have transformed themselves into nongovernment organizations in order to have the legal status needed to receive public funding, thereby becoming de facto front organizations of the DPP regime. Some movement leaders have entered the state directly and joined the ruling elite. But this infusion of progressive elements was not strong enough to move the DPP away from its nationalist and statist direction, and today democratic politics as led by the DPP is in crisis. One wonders how these civil-society theorists will reflect back on their earlier positions.

Our second challenge was to develop a strategy that would allow social and cultural movements to operate beyond the rigid space of nationalism, a space dominated by the debate between unification with China and Taiwan independence. Such statist politics and positions not only split up different movements, but they also blocked the possibility of rebuilding critical subjectivity on the ground. The eight years of DPP control has proved that those movement groups lacking sufficient critical reflexivity are easily divided by the mainstream politics of ethnic and national identity. Since the emergence of Lee Teng-hui on the national stage, the deep conflicts and splits that occur with each round of election-year political mobilization have blocked the possibility of forging effective alliances.

Our third challenge was to move beyond the reductionist state versus civil society model, which we felt could not adequately account for popular democratic struggles within a complex social formation. In our context, and judging from our actual political practices, it is obvious that the two domains are interwoven. Appropriating the work of Ernesto Laclau (1977) on the Latin American experience and Stuart Hall on Thatcherism (1980), we proposed to displace the state versus civil society paradigm with a more dynamic and more fluid analytical opposition: the power bloc (with its shifting alliances among the state, capital, the media, and supporting institutions) versus the people (represented by an alliance of various social movements). This theoretical and political position allowed us to identify emerging social tensions and contradictions. Departing from the unitary politics of the Left, which had been subsumed under a party-dominated leadership that privileged the working class as the leading agent of change, we argued for a line of radical popular democracy, operating on the principle of unity in difference without the political party as the leading unifying agent.[10]

In the early 1990s, the popular democracy position was indeed able to carve out a marginal political space for alternative imagination, and two decades later, the issues raised are still relevant. Over the years, we have been accused by those holding positions in civil society of splitting progressive political forces, but time has shown that numerous people affiliated with the civil-society camp have been co-opted by the DPP regime, and thereby have lost both energy and credibility. With no illusion of ever becoming part of state power, we have been able to enlarge the autonomy of social spaces through our movements and affiliations, and we have won a certain amount of popular support. These experiences raise a number of questions: After the change of regime in Taiwan, what is the relation between social movements and the state? Did the living conditions of subaltern groups improve under the DPP? What can be done to increase the autonomy of social spaces and prevent the state from simply gobbling them up?

Reflecting on these issues in light of Partha Chatterjee's formulation of political society, I think the propositions put forward by the popular democracy position have generated empowering effects, and I believe their effectiveness stems from the attempt to confront the real local and historical issues at stake. The articulation of a political society shares the spirit and concerns of the popular democratic position. Political society marks the operating site of popular democracy, giving a much more precise name to the latter space. The most valuable part of this encounter with Chatterjee's idea of political society is the reminder that we should not allow ourselves to be defined by our enemy. Civil society, alternatively understood, has real strategic value. Civil society can become part of the power bloc, and in certain circumstances, it can launch merciless attacks on subaltern subjects. Under other conditions, it can become a useful ally for subject groups in struggle. Turning civil society from a normative category into an analytical category enables us to better understand the locations and directions of the social forces at work. For instance, as intellectuals who in many cases occupy positions within civil-society institutions, we have to make more conscientious decisions about how to use our resources and networks in ways that empower subaltern groups. The analytical distinction thus helps us to not blindly invest in the civil-society sector, but to support subaltern struggles in the political society, which may involve ignoring the civil society, opposing it, or working with it.

Before attempting to translate Partha Chatterjee's notion of political society—a process through which I hope to open up possibilities for new understandings of Taiwanese society—it is important to note that his proposal for a political society, as a theoretical concept and political strategy, did not come out of the blue but from his previous work as well as other work in the field of subaltern studies. In his pathbreaking book, *Nationalist Thought and the Colonial World: A Derivative Discourse*, Chatterjee argues that "Gandhi's relation to nationalism can be shown to rest on a fundamental critique of the idea of civil society" (Chatterjee 1993 [1986], 85). As Chatterjee sees it, Gandhi is breaking from earlier lines of nationalist thought when he argues that the reason India was colonized and governed by the English was not because India is backward or lacks elements of the modern, but because the privileged Indian elites were seduced by and lost to the modern civilization of the West. Thus, even if the colonized elites expelled the English colonizer, the condition would remain the same: "English rule without the Englishman" (quoted in ibid., 86). The real force dominating India is, according to Gandhi, not the Englishman but his civilization.

Gandhi goes on to attack the concepts of modernity and progress, as well as "machine civilization," which is based on instrumental rationality and therefore allows for the exploitation of human beings (quoted in ibid.). For Gandhi, India does not possess the conditions required to develop civil society in the Western European sense, because only a limited part of the Indian population, mainly social elites, could enter such a space. To carry out an anticolonial struggle, Gandhi believes that social revolution has to operate in a social space much wider than civil society. He further argues against parliamentary democracy in India, because it too would be practiced only by the elite. If reform in India took place only within the civil society, there would be no possibility of successfully including the peasantry in the political process, and therefore no possibility that the decolonization of India could succeed. These critiques of civil society made Gandhi opt for popular movements as the basis for political mobilization.

Chatterjee's notion of political society is also grounded in a persistent concern of the Subaltern Studies collective. In "Democracy and the Violence of the State: A Political Negotiation of Death" (2001), Chatterjee asks why, after Gandhi successfully mobilized the peasantry to participate in social revolution, have subaltern classes not become part of the governing body of India? Why, in the postcolonial era, have they been pushed even further away from state power? In order to explain the historical forces at work, subaltern studies argues that subaltern classes and elite classes operate in different domains, with different sets of operating principles. Without the desire to take control of the state, India's subaltern classes were excluded from the processes of both the state and civil society. Operating according to a different logic, they could not be articulating agents in either space, which are the product of—and monopolized by—modernizing nationalist elites. Hence, the major problematic for subaltern studies is to rethink and explain the political space and practices of the subaltern classes. Chatterjee writes:

> Some of you may recall a framework used in the early phase of the Subaltern Studies project in which we talked about a split in the domain of politics between an organized elite domain and an unorganized subaltern domain. The idea of the split, of course, was intended to mark a fault line in the arena of nationalist politics in the three decades before independence during which the Indian masses, especially the peasantry, were drawn into organized political movements and yet remained distanced from the evolving forms of the postcolonial state. To say that there was a split in the domain of politics was to reject the notion, common in both liberal and Marxist historiographies, that the peasantry lived in some "pre-political" stage of collective action. It was to say that peasants in their collective actions were also being political, except that they were political in a way different from that of the elites. Since those early experiences of the imbrication of elite and subaltern politics in the context of the anti-colonial movements, the democratic process in India has come a long way in bringing under its influence the lives of the subaltern classes. It is to understand these relatively recent forms of the entanglement of elite and subaltern politics that I am proposing the notion of a political society. (Chatterjee 2001, 9)

Here Chatterjee teases out the strategic implication of a political society. To understand politics in the space between the elite and the masses, he departs from a conventional hierarchical relation between the two domains and opts for a horizontal relation. Within each domain, there is an internal operating logic; because the logic of the elite domain is much more familiar, there is a need for subaltern studies. It follows that the political domain of the elite is composed of at least two sites: state and civil society. It is not that the subaltern populations have nothing to do with either site—transactions indeed go on—but the articulating agents who monopolize the leading positions are the elite. Once the logic of state versus civil society is in place and the rules of the game are set, subaltern political logic will not be able to operate. The notion of the political society is then deployed to capture the dynamic logic of the subaltern subject groups' negotiations with both the state and civil society.

Chatterjee's critical understanding of civil society can be seen as an inheritance of the Gandhian tradition, as manifested in the collective work of the Subaltern Studies collective. It radically calls into question whether civil society can be a meaningful space for democratic practices of inclusion. The question becomes: if civil society is highly exclusionary, is there a possibility for subaltern classes to invent an alternative to elite political space? Seen from this perspective, Chatterjee's new political society is a response to a critical demand that has existed ever since the time of Gandhi.

Through the discussion above, we can see that civil society in Chatterjee's system of thought is not markedly different from the concept of bourgeois society as it was used by Hegel and Marx (Chatterjee 2000, 89). Political society, once it begins to operate, mediates civil society, the state, and subaltern groups in struggle. It is, then, a dynamic and fluid analytical concept. Political society does not exist a priori but through the processes of negotiation and struggle; it is therefore a space that exists beyond the politics of democratic representation. Chatterjee makes this important point: "if we have to give a name to the major form of mobilization by which political society (parties, movements, non-party political formations) tries to channelize and order popular demands on the developmental state, we should call it democracy" (ibid., 94). If we juxtapose this statement with the three theoretical propositions listed earlier, then it is clear that Chatterjee is not merely giving democracy a wider definition—one that does not exclude subalterns from the political process—but that he is also proposing that the driving energy of democracy is no longer located in the civil society's struggle for power with the state. This energy, rather, is located in the space of the political society, where the interactions and contradictions between civil society and the subject group unfold.

Having clarified the sources of Chatterjee's thought and the political meaning of political society, we are now ready to discuss the possibility of translating his ideas. In various places where Mandarin is spoken (including Singapore and Malaysia), and also in Korean and Japanese contexts, the word "society" has been consistently translated using the characters for *shèhuì*, but the word "civil" has been rendered very differently. Sometimes it is translated as *mínjiān*, a key term for which I cannot find an appropriate English equivalent. "Mínjiān" roughly describes a folk, people's, or commoners' society, but not exactly—because while *mín* means people or populace, *jiān* connotes space and in-betweenness. Civil society is sometimes translated as *shìmín* (urban resident or, literally, "city people") society, and in Hong Kong it is rendered in more classical terms as *shìjìn* (urban space). Interestingly, civil society is rarely translated literally as *gōngmín shèhuì* (literally, a society of citizens). In Taiwan, mínjiān shèhuì has been the most commonly used term, whereas shìmín shèhuì was adopted mainly in relation to urban social and community movements in the mid-1990s. In China, mínjiān has been used as a separate category to refer to people and practices that are separate from "the official,"[11] while shìmín shèhuì has been the predominant academic translation.[12] In South Korea, the civic movement began to call itself *shimin sahoe* in the early 1990s to distinguish itself from the earlier oppositional *minjung* (people's) movement.[13] In Japan, *shimin* society has been common usage.

In sum, the translation of "civil society" into gōngmín shèhuì ("citizen society" in the Hegelian sense) is not the dominant translation, and in fact, a dominant translation does not exist. What are the implications of such linguistic fluidity?

In my view, the ambiguity is an indication that translated notions such as civil society and citizenship were not smoothly absorbed into the political culture of many spaces in Asia as they underwent modernization. In our context, no matter how much effort liberal nationalist elites have made to modernize and to propagate the concept of individual rights, these efforts have largely failed. The concept of the citizen (*gōngmín*) was, from the early twentieth century onward, displaced by the concept of *guómín*,[14] which literarily means "people subjugated to the state." The nation therefore becomes the only agent of modernization, and the guómín are reduced to being those who are to be mobilized for that project.

To understand why gōngmín has been unable to supersede guómín, it is necessary to look at another pair of terms from China's imperial period: guān (official) and mín (people, or commoners). The two are not necessarily in opposition to each other, and their social relations are the foundation of what Chatterjee calls the pastoral functions of the state. The state has the power to govern, but it also has responsibility to take care of the people. In Chinese, this relation is understood as jiāhù zhǎngzhì, which is not exactly patriarchy but a paternalistic system in which the head of the family is responsible for his family members. The metaphor of family is often expanded to the level of the state, so that the emperor is the head of the national family, and the people his children. The system functions not on the basis of any legal contract but with the understanding that the head of the state will wisely use its social and material resources to deal with foreign powers and internal conflicts.

This is one reason why in contemporary Chinese societies, the protection of civil law is not a priority. It is not even seen as a basic right in the popular consciousness except, perhaps, in Hong Kong and Singapore, which have been more modernized — or, rather, which have become more legalistic — than Taiwan and mainland China, where real respect for the rule of law has not developed. In actual practice, the jiāhù zhǎngzhì system regulates social relations on different levels through recourse to three historically constituted principles or doxa: qíng (sentiment), lǐ (reason), and fǎ (legality). Of the three, fǎ is always the last resort. It is a highly fluid and contextually determined practice, and it is not always located in the domain of state power. It operates differently on the levels of the family, the community, and the imperial court. However, when legalistic measures are employed by the state, it is not interpreted as the normal functioning of civil society but as the workings of a paternalistic system of punishment.

This mind-set still operates in contemporary daily life, and for good reason: no one can fully trust a legal system that has long been an apparatus of control for an authoritarian regime. When social conduct is socially regarded as humane or compassionate (qíng) and reasonable (lǐ), it will not be challenged, even if it is illegal. A squatter community is illegal, but if it has existed for decades, it is humane for people to go on living there, and it is reasonable for the state to provide alternate housing if the community is relocated. Based on such living practices, mínjiān and guān have set the tone for imagining what in the Western analytic framework is understood as the relation between civil society and the state.

It is important to note that the legitimacy of the state is predicated on the fulfillment of its moral obligations. These obligations, which can be described as the paternalistic function of the state, are most visible in a crisis. After the 21 September 1999 earthquake in Taiwan, thousands of homes were destroyed. Legally, it was each homeowner's responsibility to purchase disaster insurance, but most low-income homeowners had not done so; some did not even know that such insurance existed. Many people, especially in rural areas where the damage was most severe, lost their jobs and could not pay their mortgages. The state called upon banks to absorb a portion of the unpaid mortgages, and the supposedly independent banking system complied. At no point did liberal economists — or anyone else — come forward to challenge this extralegal practice. Meanwhile, mínjiān groups moved in to help the victims much more quickly and effectively than the state. Food, water, clothing, and sleeping bags were sent in immediately; construction crews donated their time and equipment to the rescue effort; tents and temporary housing were efficiently built. Indeed, nonstate mutual-aid systems, such as clans and religious organizations, have existed in mínjiān spaces since at least the Ming Dynasty. Reflecting on these various responses to the earthquake, we see both the energy of mínjiān as well as the paternalistic function of the state.

To push this line of analysis a bit further, we have to recognize that mínjiān is an active social space that was not replaced during the process of modernization. Its power still has to be dealt with carefully, even by the authoritarian state. As an example of the place of mínjiān, think of the lunar calendar, which also has survived modernization. Throughout East Asia, though less so in Japan,[15] festivals, markets, and temples still use the lunar calendar to schedule their activities. Temples are highly organized mínjiān units. During political campaigns, candidates for public office have to visit temples to show respect to the gods and attempt to win the support of the believers. Another example is the economic activities of some mínjiān institutions, which have been categorized by scholars as belonging to the informal economy — a term for businesses that are illegal, are not taxed, or simply fall outside state regulation. In Taiwan, until the mid-1980s, the informal economy was the dominant form of economic activity.[16] In South Korea, the informal economy boomed after the 1997 financial crisis, with street vendors lining the sidewalks of Seoul's many shopping districts. In China, the state that arguably has the strongest hold over its citizens, there has been an enormous migration from rural to urban areas since the 1990s. A poor rural family can be supported on the income earned by a single urban worker. Often lacking official status, these migrant peasant workers have formed mutual-aid groups, and they survive mainly through working in the informal economy. The mínjiān tradition of networking and mutual support provides a basic mechanism for dealing with the harshness of life as a migrant worker in cities such as Beijing, Shanghai, and Guangzhou.

These examples indicate that mínjiān is the space where traditions are maintained as resources to help common people survive the violent rupture brought about by the modernizing of state and civil society. Note that this is an analytical statement. I am neither arguing that mínjiān is necessarily a progressive space that should be maintained, nor am I romanticizing it. The point is to recognize that mínjiān, in relation to the modern state and civil society, has always existed in Asia, and it did not disappear during the process of modernization. The modernizing state, often with support from elite groups in the civil society, has done everything it can to suppress and incorporate the common people. It uses moralizing words like "superstition," "feudalism," "antiquated," and "wasteful" to legitimize its attack on particular mínjiān groups and institutions, such as prostitutes, street vendors, and religious sects. But the historically accumulated density of the mínjiān space has proved strong enough to resist pressure from the civil society and violence from the state.

The annual festival for Mazu, the sea goddess, has become increasingly popular after years of unsuccessful suppression. Since the early 1990s, there has been an annual weeklong pilgrimage in which between 80,000 and 100,000 worshipers escort on foot a statue of the goddess as it travels to various towns and villages in central and southern Taiwan. The event has become politicized because it doesn't recognize national boundaries and has attempted to bring together believers and temples in central Taiwan with those in mainland China's southeast coastal provinces, where, according to legend, the goddess is originally from. This became a major controversy in June and July of 2000, when the Taiwanese pilgrims claimed that they should be allowed to travel directly to the mainland by boat, ignoring the official ban on direct travel between the countries. Not only was their motive religious rather than political, but the newly elected president had made a pledge during the election to support their wishes, and they felt this was the time for him to deliver on the promise he had yet to fulfill.

These kinds of activities express energies that are obviously not part of the civil society, which sees the Mazu festival as backward and superstitious. The reality is that mínjiān forces are organic and constantly adjusting to modern life, while maintaining their own relative autonomy.

If mínjiān is not a historical legacy but an evolving set of practices that operates more and more visibly in the present, what is its relation to civil society? In various instances in Taiwan, we have observed that it is the desire to modernize that motivates individuals and groups in the civil society to mobilize modern state institutions to oppose the practices of supposedly backward mínjiān groups. At these times, civil society allies itself with the state and pressures it to launch attacks on specific mínjiān sectors. For example, an alliance between self-proclaimed progressive feminists and the modernizing nationalist Taipei city government was formed in 1997 to eradicate licensed prostitutes. This is exactly what Partha Chatterjee calls the violence of modernity.

Here, the distinction between mínjiān and civil society is clear, but the boundary between civil society and the state is more fluid. With each change of government, a large number of people from the elite sector of the civil society (not members of mínjiān society) move into government jobs.[17] One needs only to have observed the Kim Dae-jung regime in South Korea or Chen Shui-bian's government in Taiwan to identify the essential relation between civil society and the state: civil society becomes the state. Rather than serving as a balancing force to defend the autonomy of social life, the desire for power among the elite of civil society always tips the scales in favor of the state. In contrast, mínjiān remains mínjiān: it remains in constant negotiation with civil society and the state, no matter who is in power.

In adopting Chatterjee's analytical framework to consider the living social conditions in Taiwan, the importance of political society becomes clear: it enables a strategic mapping of the forces flowing through and around civil society. At the same time, this map needs to be continually redrawn. Political society mediates not only state and civil society, but also other historically constituted social spaces, such as mínjiān and the society of consumption, a relatively recent formation in which the media play a central role.

The subject group that activates the momentary space of political society has to use the language of mínjiān society, build alliances with groups in civil society such as nongovernment organizations, negotiate with official state units, and win over the sympathy and support of the consuming classes, a task that requires skillful engagement with the media. The licensed prostitutes in Taiwan, for example, wore hats with a pink veil to cover their faces during all of their public protests. During the two years of their struggle, the hats became a familiar symbol to the public, and it is due to such negotiations with the public and the media that they finally won the right to survive for another two years. It is through these moments, regardless of winning or losing, that people write history.[18]

"Can the subaltern speak?" Gayatri Spivak asks (1988). The sex workers eloquently and forcefully voiced their protests on the streets and in front of television cameras. During the struggle, some of the women removed their pink veils, and some of those women have become well-known public figures. There was one particularly memorable moment during a 1998 press conference held by Chen Shui-bian, who was mayor of Taipei at that time. Chen was to present his achievements of the past year, and, to emphasize the supposedly popular-democratic nature of his government, the press conference was held in the first-floor lobby of Taipei City Hall, a large open space that had been carefully arranged for the occasion. When the mayor started to speak, the press conference was suddenly disrupted by shouts of protest. Thousands of white pamphlets were thrown from the upper floors by sex workers and activists, who had sneaked into the building earlier. The mayor was visibly upset, but because the cameras were rolling, he could only pretend nothing had happened. He continued his presentation, but no one bothered to listen. The cameras were directed at the pamphlets, which fluttered down like falling snow, or followed the sex workers and activists as they were driven out of the building by the police. Broadcast live, the scene engraved this heroic struggle in popular memory and reminds us of the important role that media consumption can play in political movements.

These concrete experiences have led me to attempt an expansion of

Chatterjee's analysis. In popular-democratic forms of struggle, political society does not just mediate the state and civil society; it also mediates mínjiān and the society of consumption. It is within the dynamic processes of political negotiation and transaction carried out among these agents that political society is able to insert itself into history. Because political society is unlikely to be institutionalized, these processes might be temporary or transitional, but they may have long-lasting impacts and important strategic lessons. Through dialogue with Chatterjee's work, the weaknesses in our previous position on popular democracy become visible. In other words, it is through translation and comparison that we not only begin to understand Indian society, but also to open up a different way of rethinking the characteristics of our own.

I hope by now it is clear what can be learned from the inter-referencing process in Asia. Useful ways of understanding our own societies have lain dormant, mainly because our points of reference have been the United States or Europe, where civil society as it is defined in those locations is well established, but also because we are constantly being pushed by our nationalist elites to follow and catch up with the West by reproducing those Euro-American forms of civil society. Thus, a potentially rich form of comparative work is ignored in favor of what is essentially a bad grading system. This is how Chatterjee puts it:

> This, I am suggesting, is one of the principal tasks of political theory today: to provide a conceptualization map of the emerging practices of the new political societies of the East. The normative models of Western political theory have, more often than not, only served to show the non-Western practices as backward or deviant. What we need is a different conceptualization of the subject of political practice — neither as abstract and unencumbered individual selves nor as manipulative of government policy, but rather as concrete selves necessarily acting within multiple networks of collective obligations and solidarities to work out strategies of coping with, resisting or using to their advantage the vast array of technologies of power deployed by the modern state. (Chatterjee 1998, 282)

This alternative mapping is impossible without shifting the frame of reference. If the points of reference remain within the old colonial framework, the process of translation will never be undertaken, and we will be blind to forces operating outside civil society and the state. However, once the dialogue is shifted and local and regional referents become the focus, unnoticed translation problems are necessarily brought to the fore and have to be confronted.

In dialogue with Partha Chatterjee, I have thus come to an understanding that, in our part of the world, translations on all levels (from analytical vocabulary to institutional forms to normative concepts such as democracy) have been driven by the century-long process of modernization. The object to be translated has to be subjected to existing social forces and must negotiate with dense local histories if it is to take root in foreign soil. What comes out of this long process of negotiation is not what was imagined at the initial moment of translation at all,[19] but a localized product of this blending process. It is something new. This is indeed a moment to maintain the critical distance necessary to rethink and reinvestigate the practices and effects of the supposedly modern process of translation. The type of high-intensity translation that we are discussing has been going on for more than a century. As they circulate, these ideas are organically embedded in the social space and become parts of our histories.

I take it that this is what modernity is all about. Modernity is not a normative drive to become modern, but an analytical concept that attempts to capture the effectiveness of modernizing forces as they negotiate and mix with local history and culture. In other words, modernity as an analytical term refers to the overall effects of modernization. Tradition is not opposed to modernity but is an integral and living part of it. The diversity and density of local histories guarantee the emergence of multiple modernities, a recently formulated concept that, in my view, is redundant. Translation thus gives us a way to conduct reinvestigations that allow the organic shape and characteristics of local society and modernity to surface. In this sense, translation is not simply a linguistic exercise but a social linguistics, or an intersection of history, sociology, and politics. In the end, translation allows us to more precisely identify what aspects of modernity have been articulated to the existing social formation. Civil society has indeed been able to translate and insert itself in Asian contexts, but in a limited and profoundly different way than in the West. At the same time, mínjiān has not been dissolved but continues to operate and evolve.

In the conceptual remapping Chatterjee refers to, we need not only to formulate a new category such as political society, but also to rearticulate existing categories such as mínjiān, which have survived the challenge of modernization and are still widely used by the state, the media, and the populace. To the modernist eye, mínjiān as a living concept and category may seem too particularistic and therefore cannot possibly possess theoretical value or analytical precision. But if mínjiān is able to offer us a tool to capture the specificity of a local social formation, we need to suspend the pretentious frame of universalism and particularism. We must be able to understand specificity as a fundamental working assumption of critical cultural studies. Universalism is not an epistemological given but a horizon we may be able to move toward in the remote future, provided that we first compare notes based upon locally grounded knowledge.[20] Universalist arrogance serves only to keep new possibilities from emerging, since it allows only one set of accepted analytic language to enter the dialogue and is itself a product of a specific set of historical experiences.

In the competition for universality, asking which civilizational values are more universal than others will only result in our falling back into cultural essentialism. The early mode of the Asian-values debate was just that. What is needed is a comparison not of enduring values but of practices on all levels, including studies of how values have been put into practice and how they are transformed. The resources needed to rediscover diverse forms of modernity, through comparisons and from alternative forms of knowledge production, are actually located in the concrete practices found within the open-ended local history of what Mizoguchi Yūzō (1996 [1989]) calls the ever-changing "base-entity" (jītǐ) upon which the forces and practices of modernization work.

Asia as Method: A Dialogue with Mizoguchi Yūzō

In the previous sections, we have dealt with the question of the West and have tried, in our dialogue with Partha Chatterjee, to indicate what can be gained from shifting our points of reference toward Asia. We are now prepared to address the theoretical problematic of Asia as method. In the process of thinking through the notion of Asia as method, what are the intellectual resources that we can inherit, revise, and further develop to reground ourselves in this new context? Because of Japan's particular history, Japanese critical intellectual circles have, since the mid-nineteenth century, taken quite seriously the question of Asianism and have accumulated a substantial body of intellectual assets (Sun Ge 2000), but Mizoguchi Yūzō's *China as Method* (1996 [1989]) is one of the few I have felt truly inspired by. Parts of that book were published as articles throughout the 1980s before appearing in book form. Although the context, issues, and directions of discussions have changed, twenty years later it still has much to teach us.[21]

In a lecture given in 1960, Takeuchi Yoshimi intuitively proposed the notion of Asia as method as a means of transforming the Japanese subject.[22] Reading the text of this lecture in the present context, one cannot but feel strongly that the issues posed by Takeuchi are as relevant as ever. A bit like Lu Xun's cultural criticism, Takeuchi's critical reflections during an earlier moment of history on the conditions of knowledge production are still challenging. In his lecture, as he discusses various differences between China and Japan, Takeuchi reflects on his own experiences of studying modern Chinese literature to consider the convergence of modernization and war. In Japan and China, he sees two very different models for late-developing countries undergoing modernization. Japan is the model student: it is the only Asian country to have fully embraced the West and learned from it. China represents the opposite pole: it has attempted to modernize while at the same time resisting the West. For Takeuchi, India is closer to the Chinese end of the spectrum. He suggests that it would be helpful to include the experiences of China and India within the Japanese horizon so that Japan's situation could be better understood. At the end of the lecture, he admits that he cannot yet say exactly what he means by Asia as method.[23]

Over a quarter-century later, Mizoguchi Yūzō published *China as Method* (1996 [1989]), which can be read as an attempt to rework Takeuchi's unfinished project. *China as Method* is a complex book. Because it was aimed at a Japanese audience, it is difficult for those not very familiar with critical intellectual discussions in Japan in the 1980s to fully unpack the many points of dialogue that are addressed. However, it is clear that Mizoguchi formulates his own theory through engagement with two intersecting discursive fields, and because of this, his intervention is conditioned by a dialogic structure. One wider field is Japanese intellectual production, and the second field, *Chūgokugaku* (Chinese studies), is located within the first.

Mizoguchi reenters the debate on the question of modernization, but he does so from a critical distance, in an attempt to move beyond the standard epistemological framework of progress versus backwardness that had been the dominant paradigm of Japanese intellectual history for the previous two centuries. In the beginning of the first chapter, titled "Examining the Horizon of 'Modern China,'" he points out how Chūgokugaku after the Second World War was conditioned by the prewar view of China, as represented in the writings of Tsuda Sōkichi. Tsuda's modernism considered Europe as the pinnacle of civilization against which China was evaluated and found lacking. He could therefore justify supporting the official position of the Japanese government, which partly justified the invasion of China by arguing that Japan, like Europe, was superior. Chūgokugaku in the postwar period began with the critique of Tsuda's modernism. Mizoguchi sees Takeuchi as a representative figure in this wave to restore the status of China.[24]

In Mizoguchi's account, Takeuchi's contribution was to reverse Tsuda's Eurocentric story: Takeuchi negated Japan's conformism and affirmed China's resistance. This is Takeuchi's famous theory of two opposing modalities: turning direction (*zhuǎnxiàng*) and returning to the core (*huíxīn*). Japan is the perfect example of turning direction, which is giving up the self, taking in Europe, and imagining becoming European. China represents the centripetal model of returning to the core, which resists Europe even as it constantly tries to overcome it. The result is that "Japan is nothing"—Takeuchi's catchphrase. In spite of Takeuchi's reversal of the narrative, Mizoguchi argues that Tsuda and Takeuchi were operating within the same epistemological structure.

How does one move beyond this pitfall? It is here that Mizoguchi puts forward his own method. He argues that total affirmation and total negation are equally ahistorical and hence equally problematic: "Such a-historical or non-historical points of view on modern China and Japan do not objectively and historically recognize that both have their own relative autonomy (just as Europe does). In other words, such a historical view cannot see how *both bear their own past, or inherit from the past (even if it is a negative inheritance), and how they now are conditioned by the past*" (Mizoguchi 1996 [1989], 5; emphases added). In this important passage, Mizoguchi's position is brought to the fore. I will return to this discussion in a moment, but at this point, suffice it to say that his method is to historicize Europe, Japan, and China in order to show how the history of each conditions the present, and results in their differences.

Mizoguchi continues: "In reality, China's modern(ity) is neither a European type, nor is it lagging behind Europe. From the very beginning, China has taken a special historical route different from both Europe and Japan" (ibid., 7). To illustrate what this distinctiveness is, he uses Sun Yat-sen's writings on *wángdào* (the kingly way, or benevolent government) as an example. After tracing the meanings of wángdào and corresponding social-structural transformations from the time of the *Book of Rites* over two thousand years ago all the way to the nineteenth century, Mizoguchi sums up his argument: "China's modern is a result of its own pre-modern '*mǔtǐ*' [mother's body, matrix, or originating basis]; therefore, it imminently inherits the historical specificities of the pre-modern . . . From the very beginning, China did not have the tendency of the European modern type. This is not a 'lack' or 'blankness,' but a necessary substance. Because of the inheritance of this substance, it will have to be conditioned by the *mǔtǐ*" (ibid., 9–10).

Here Mizoguchi moves beyond the limited mode of measurement and assessment of Takeuchi's generation. Instead, he calls for an inter-referencing of elements in different base-entities. Locating the relation between the operation of public (*gōng*) and private (*sī*) in Japanese and Chinese societies throughout history, he argues that "just as China's modern unavoidably has its own pre-modern as the *mǔtǐ*, and therefore unavoidably has its inscription, Japan's modern also has its own pre-modern *mǔtǐ*, and is correspondingly inscribed by it" (ibid., 13). He continues: "that is to say, history determines what is distinctive of each other's modern(ity), therefore, this proposition to consider the former's [China's] modern as 'Eastern,' and the latter's [Japan's] as 'nothing,' as a result of only following Western Europe, is historically speaking incorrect" (ibid., 14). At this point, Mizoguchi is obviously in dialogue with Takeuchi.

Mizoguchi's problematic exceeds the conventional boundaries of intellectual history. Pointing toward the base-entity of history immediately implies the existence of a social totality. If we approach his concern only from the point of view of the academic division of labor, we are missing the point, because the basis of his problematic does not begin or end with academic disciplines. Operating on the level of social ontology, he argues, "with regard to the question of connecting the main elements of the modern with the pre-modern, from today on, we can longer simply study intellectual history. We need to look at, as widely as possible, the everyday ethics, folk customs, and the very basis of social relations" (ibid., 39) — in other words, all forms of social practices. The positing of a social totality not only implies the methodology held by one who poses the question, but also presupposes a historically grounded theory of social ontology.

It is here that my formulation of a geocolonial historical materialism, described in chapter 2, meets Mizoguchi's theory of the base-entity.

> Perhaps, someone may ask: what then is your methodology? . . . If I were forced to answer this question, I could only say that I am [developing] a theory of *jǐtǐ* [base-entity]. Though it is a theory, it is simply trying to suggest that China has its own path of development, that is, starting from the mixing of the south and north, the conflicts and integration with other alien population groups (*yì mínzú*) such as Liao, Jing, Yuan, Qing, etc. On one hand, it has transformed, but on the other hand, its main branch has continuously inherited from the base-entity. When I say "China has its own path of development," I mean the inner drive developed out of the base-entity is the central motor for the dialectic of development.
>
> The reason why it is called a theory of the evolving base-entity, in sum, is because I do not want to see China's modern simply as a carrier passively responding to the impacts of the West, such as the understanding of a process of changing from "Chinese substance" (*zhōngtǐ*) to "western substance" (*xītǐ*), or a [disintegration] of the "old China." Instead, what I want to emphasize is to understand it as a process of casting off a skin of the "old China." Casting off a skin is to live again, which can also be understood as a new life, but a snake will not cease to be a snake simply because it casts off a skin. (ibid., 37)

It would be unproductive to criticize Mizoguchi's choice of words here. He is obviously in dialogue with Japanese intellectuals, among whom Europeanizing tendencies run strong, and for the sake of debate, he also gets sucked into the mainstream language of linear, evolutionary progression. That should not distract us from recognizing the original insight in Mizoguchi's theory of *mǔtǐ* and *jǐtǐ*. The insight is a historical ontology that conceives of a current multiplicity of local spaces in relation to world history.

In chapter 2, the formulation of a geocolonial historical materialism suggested that world history is composed of many regionally based local histories. Interactions among the world regions are the encounters and collisions of local histories. A local history is constantly changing, transforming, and evolving. It does not have an unchanging essence, although historical pasts are always internal to the formation of the local. To intersect with Mizoguchi's language, the base-entity inherits and continues its original body even as it casts off skin after skin.

If we frame the issue in terms of subjectivity, then the base-entity can be neither only individual nor only collective: it is both at the same time. Body, thought, and desire flow through and connect with the base-entity. From this standpoint, the way any local history operates ontologically is by definition different from the way any other history does. We must return to the transformations and trajectories of the base-entity, and to the operating logic driving its interaction with outside forces, to fully understand the characteristics of the constantly changing base-entity. Within the base-entity are internal forces driving change, such as contradictions in the social relations that comprise the social structure. In different historical moments, outside forces, such as colonial imperialist invasion, may constitute an even more pressing drive to change. But no matter what the origin or strength of these forces, they all have to work on the existing base-entity; that is the space where relations are linked and transformed.

As Mizoguchi argues, "as far as Japan and China are concerned, 'the challenge' from the West has neither destroyed the structure built since pre-modern times, nor made it collapse, but contributed to the peeling of the skin of the pre-modern, or at most changed its shape" (ibid., 38). Because different base-entities have their own specificities, they cannot be measured against each other hierarchically in ontological or normative terms, unless one imposes instrumental frames—such as mode of economic development, volume of gross national product, or degree of technological sophistication. The purpose of the inter-referencing mode of analysis is to avoid judging any country, region, or culture as superior or inferior to any other, and to tease out historical transformations within the base-entity, so that the differences can be properly explained.

Mizoguchi's theory of the base-entity has been attacked in Japan for promoting cultural essentialism. In my view, such a reading is in itself an essentialist account of Mizoguchi's work and is ultimately unproductive. If the theory of the base-entity points to a totality, it has to be materialist and cannot simply be culturalist; if it emphasizes the constant shifts and transformations, it cannot be essentialist.[25] What I call geocolonial historical materialism is precisely an attempt to revise historical materialism from this basis. It foregrounds the existence of multiple base-entities, so that Marx's basic theory can be understood anew. To repeat Marx's most quoted words again: human beings make history, but they always do so under conditions already given by and transmitted from the past. This idea can be understood in light of the theory of the base-entity. With this assumption, each geographical space—be it village, city, region, country, or continent—has its own base-entity and local history, with different depths, forms, and shapes. The methodological questions are: How can these base-entities be analyzed in terms of their internal characteristics? How can we best identify and analyze the interactions between and among different base-entities? It is in light of these questions that Asia as method can advance its inquiry.

The second field in which Mizoguchi makes an intervention is Chūgokugaku. As he points out, in contrast with the earlier belittling and despising of China by Japanese, the achievement of Chūgokugaku in the postwar period was to bring China back into the flow of Hegelian evolutionism and to situate postrevolutionary China side by side with European modernity. These moves reaffirmed that China was of equal value (ibid., 90). The problem is that the understandings of China have been "from things and sentiments [xīnqíng] internal to Japan" (ibid.). Mizoguchi calls this method of understanding, which has existed since the Edo period, "a tradition of reading China by setting aside China," or "a study of China without China." It is a functional instrumentalist mode based on the internal conditions, demands, and needs within Japan. He goes on to argue that this is why Chūgokugaku was in complicity with Japanese nationalism and could be a part of a "national-populist Greater East Asianism" (ibid., 92).

It is with such a critique that Mizoguchi opens a space for his proposal of China as method. He argues that "its purpose is neither for China itself, nor the heart of our inner self; that is to say, its end cannot be dissolved in

China or in us. On the contrary, its end should be the 'study of China' that transcends China" (ibid., 93). In my reading, what Mizoguchi means is that China as method is not only a way to understand China from the inside out, but a way of mutually relativizing both China and Japan through a mediating process of objectification so that both can be understood in different ways. In this way, the narcissistic being can be liberated and transformed into becoming.

The importance of this theoretical insight needs to be explored further. To reach a deeper understanding of the Other is a precondition of transcending one's self. To reach a different understanding of the self is a step toward the Other's understanding of itself. These ongoing dialectical processes enable mutual transcendence and make it possible to pose different historical questions, and eventually reach a different understanding of world history. China's postwar socialist transformation, for example, has to be understood in terms of its base-entity, but only by locating China in the East Asian context can we begin to see the inner logic of the transformations within the capitalist spaces of East Asia. Through this constant inter-referencing and the dialectic of comparison, we can transcend the understanding of China based simply on our own interpretation and, at the same time, transcend the understanding of ourselves based only on our own narcissistic perspective. In doing so, we can see beyond the received categories of socialism and capitalism as the only forces which can be used to describe modern world history and explore alternative possibilities. Mizoguchi puts it this way:

> To conceive of China as method (or means) is to conceive of the world as an end.
>
> In the past . . . the study of China that conceives of China as an end [in itself] is actually looking at China through the world as method . . . in other words, using the world as a standard to measure China, and therefore this world has become completely considered as the model "world." It is only that this world is a "world" of existing method . . . and this "world" is in fact Europe . . . The world that conceives of China as method must be a different world . . . The world that conceives of China as method is a multiplied world, in that China is an element of its composition. In other words, Europe is also an element. (ibid., 94–95)

Mizoguchi should not be misunderstood here as erecting a Sinocentrism to replace Eurocentrism. On the normative level, he is proposing an egalitarian, pluralistic, and multicultural worldview, avoiding the past analytical mistake of using Europe as the standard against which all other places are measured. He corrects the mistake of conflating the self-Orientalizing mind-set that maps European history onto all other base-entities. On the analytical level, Mizoguchi's version of Chūgokugaku points toward a different way of doing world history—that is, using China as a reference point to understand the local histories of other regions, and then, based on our understanding of the base-entities of these other world regions, establishing a clearer picture of world history. However, as is the case with any region, China in relation to East Asia is never the only reference point for seeing the world. By insisting on multiple reference points, Mizoguchi avoids the parochialism of certain versions of area studies, including the provincialism of the "study of China without China."

There are three profound implications. First, to study a place anywhere on earth, be it India, Ethiopia, Palestine, or Brazil, is simply one route toward an understanding of world history. To understand any place is a way to understand an aspect of the contemporary world. Second, the purpose of a renewed understanding of the world is to perceive ourselves differently in relation to our new vision of the world. Through this process, the self can be understood differently and hence transformed. In this sense, to do area studies is not simply to study the object of analysis but also to perform a self-analysis through a process of constant inter-referencing. Viewed from this perspective, if there is such a thing as Asian studies in Taiwan, it should be as much about Taiwan as it is about Asia. And in the context of Asian studies in the United States, Asian studies is and must be American studies. Third, relativizing the understanding of the self as well as the object of the study is a precondition for arriving at different understandings of the self, the Other, and world history.

I believe that this is the moment for us to inherit Mizoguchi's thinking. If I am allowed to shift the context of his dialogue from Japan to that of the critical circles in Asia, smuggling in Asia to replace China and sliding from China as method to Asia as method, I hold that the arguments still stand. I do not think this move contradicts Mizoguchi's thinking. In his writings and speeches, Asia and China often coexist, sometimes displacing each other. He writes: "No matter what is being suggested, the time to discuss or examine Asia based on a singularized 'world' is gone forever. I believe if a relative consensus can be reached, then we can evaluate Europe via *China and Asia*; of course this is a kind of reversal, and through this exchange we can move towards the picture of creating a new image of the world. . . . To conceive of China as method is to search for a theoretical creation, and at the same time a creation of a new world" (ibid., 96; emphasis added).

In moving toward the creation of a new world, Asia as method is then an open-ended imagination. In the specific contexts of certain practices, both discursive and nondiscursive, Asia can be a synonym for China, Malaysia, India, Sri Lanka, and Indonesia; or Seoul, Taipei, and Bangalore; or the third world. In this sense, the emerging field of Asian studies in Asia will have a very different historical mission than the Asian studies practiced in Europe and North America. Asian inter-referencing is a process of relativization. Its task is not only to understand different parts of Asia but also to enable a renewed understanding of the self. More importantly, the agenda of the transformed self is to transcend existing understandings of Asia and thereby change the world.

China as method was proposed around the end of the 1980s, when the cold war was in the initial stages of winding down. Around this time, interaction among critical circles in Asia was minimal. The situation since then has changed. Mizoguchi himself was involved in organizing the six-year Community of Knowledge project, a forum for intellectual dialogues between scholars in China and Japan.[26] I am not certain how Mizoguchi would renew his formulation given the current historical conditions, but the subject and object of dialogue with which Mizoguchi engaged matters as much as ever. Chūgokugaku in Japan, for instance, has become a more open field, with Japanese scholars now joined by scholars from Korea, China, and many other locations. The same is true of the wider intellectual field in Japan. Once the momentum for interaction within Asia builds, the subject of dialogue will also shift beyond the assumed national boundary of Japan.[27] "If you cannot find friends to talk to within the country, go somewhere else to find them" has become a new condition of knowledge.

By proposing and renewing the proposition of Asia as method in the present Inter-Asia context, we find ourselves the inheritors of Mizoguchi's vision of a new intellectual and political world. The differences between China as method and Asia as method lie in choices of emphasis. First, the main object of dialogue of Asia as method is local (Seoul, Tokyo, Shanghai, or Taipei, for example), but it is also transborder, regional, and even intercontinental. Second, it recognizes that elements of the West have become internal to base-entities in Asia, and hence there is no desire to stress our distinctiveness. Third, in making a shift toward Asia, it expands the Northeast Asia–centric imagination to include other parts of Asia, with the hope that our worldview will include heterogeneous horizons. Fourth, it self-consciously puts an emphasis on practices to suggest that in the unfolding of modernity, intellectual thought is only one of many historical practices, and the analysis of base-entities will have to operate on different levels of abstraction and in different domains. Fifth, its core theoretical and political agenda is to transform our subjectivities. Through imaginings of a new Asia and a new third world, diverse frames of reference cross our horizon, multiply our perspectives, and enrich our subjectivity. It is here that decolonization, deimperialization, and de–cold war—as one and the same movement—can begin to locate concrete methods for self-transformation. Asia as method is not a slogan but a practice. That practice begins with multiplying the sources of our readings to include those produced in other parts of Asia.

In dialogue with Partha Chatterjee, we have discovered not only the importance of political society as a driving force for social transformation in postcolonial spaces, we have also rediscovered mínjiān as a zone indispensable to our own social formation. To bring these discoveries into dialogue with Mizoguchi's theory of the base-entity, we must return both political society and mínjiān to their historical base-entities in Asia. Chatterjee's theoretical discovery of the political society as the site for democratic struggle has not yet provided sufficient historical explanation, just as our rediscovery of mínjiān awaits a fuller historical description of how it has operated as a carrier of modernity. I would like to think these ongoing tasks challenge us to see politics and democracy in a radically different light.

THE IMPERIAL ORDER OF THINGS,
OR NOTES ON HAN CHINESE RACISM

Deimperialization is an ongoing intellectual project, and therefore a conventional conclusion would be inappropriate here. I end the book with a type of self-critique so as to invite concerned readers undertaking other forms of reflexive practice to bring to light issues that are close to home yet often forbidden to address. As a Han Chinese, I find the task of critically engaging the oppressive aspects of the Chinese empire to be central to the deimperialization movement. I suggest that the problem of racism in the Han-centric worldview is located within the structure of the imperial order.

A tragic event motivates my self-critique.

I first met Martin Jacques in 1996. He was the editor of the London-based journal *Marxism Today* in the 1980s and is a respected journalist, television producer, and political analyst. Commissioned to produce a documentary called *The Decline of the West and the Rise of East Asia* for BBC Two, Martin asked his close friend Stuart Hall to approach me for help in making the necessary contacts in East Asia. Martin and I soon became good friends, often sharing thoughts on the dynamics of the region. Two years later, he moved to Hong Kong with his family and started a book project on the transformation of the East Asian economy and culture in the global context. The move was also occasioned by the career of his beloved wife, Harinder Veriah (Hari to her friends), a lawyer whose London-based firm assigned her to its Hong Kong office — partly, I would guess, because she was Asian. As an Indian Malay growing up in a Chinese neighborhood, Hari had learned Cantonese, which she thought would be a great advantage for working in Hong Kong.

When Martin came to Taipei to do research and interviews for his book in 1998, I helped arrange his visit, and it was then that I first met Hari and Ravi, their newborn son. In my role as the local host, I took Hari, Martin, and Ravi out to dinner. I found Hari very thoughtful and warm, the kind of person who would always think first of friends rather than herself. After we got to know each other better, she started to talk about her experiences of discrimination in Hong Kong. Hari had thought her ability to speak Cantonese would have made her life easier, but no: few people in Hong Kong could see past her dark skin and South Asian features. She did not feel respected anywhere she went—in the office, at the market, or on the subway. Whenever we met after that, the three of us analyzed Chinese racism. Alas, our informal discussions proved inadequate to prevent the tragedy.

In late December 1999, I was invited by Martin and Hari to stop in Hong Kong on my way home to Taipei from Beijing, to meet their old friends, the Hobsbawm family. I happily went to stay with them and had a wonderful evening. Several days after I returned home, Andy Hobsbawm called to inform me that Hari had died on 2 January in a local hospital. The reason was unknown, and the Hong Kong police were investigating the case.

Hari's death triggered strong responses in foreign communities in Hong Kong. There were charges that she did not receive prompt and proper treatment at the hospital because of her race. A lawsuit was filed, and the case sparked a broad antidiscrimination campaign.[1] The loss of such a wonderful human being can never be lessened through analysis. But it is the responsibility of the living to move forward and honestly confront and change the unacceptable conditions of life.

In the course of the legal proceedings, it has been difficult to establish a definitive causal relation between racism and Hari's death. At the same time, no one can confidently deny the strong possibility of that connection. My purpose here is not to argue that Hari's death was the result of racism, but to expand on the discussion of Han racism that this tragic event prompted in Hong Kong, and to attempt to provide some explanations. In Hong Kong, Taiwan, Singapore, and Malaysia, diverse forms of labor migration are increasingly visible, and previously latent conflicts are beginning to emerge. The prevailing triumphalist sentiment underlying the so-called peaceful rise of mainland China has also evoked anxieties and could easily trigger racial confrontations. Reports on the insensitive ways in which mainland Chinese businesses operate in Africa suggest that Han Chinese racism may become a global problem. As Chinese intellectuals, these circumstances compel us to take up this issue and seriously consider our responses.

How was the racism of the Chinese empire different from that of other colonial and imperial powers? What is the specificity of Han racism today?

The conceps of Han and racism must be analyzed. Han has never referred to a homogeneous population but to a historically fluctuating, imagined community. In mainland China, the Han are by far the largest official ethnic group. The nation's official language is *Hànyǔ* (Mandarin, also known simply as the national language, or *guóyǔ*), which uses *Hànzì* (Chinese characters). In the global context, the word "Han" is increasingly being displaced by "Chinese" (for people, Huárén or *Zhōngguórén*). My insistence on the use of Han (rather than simply Chinese) is to indicate analytically that even as the meanings of "Han" continue to evolve, the Han people's long history continues to condition our practices in the arenas of daily life, intellectual thought, and cultural production. Politically, the Han are one of the dominant populations in the world, and distinguishing the Han from the many minority groups subsumed under the category Chinese (Huárén) is a necessary step toward critically confronting the history and current expressions of Han racism. To problematize racism is to call attention to the fluidity of terms such as race (*zhǒngzú*), ethnicity (*zúqún*), and nationality (*mínzú*), which now overlap in both Chinese and English. For instance, we would say that in Malaysia the three major "ethnic" groups are Malay, Chinese, and Indian, and that there is a "racial" problem among these populations; in mainland China, Han is a category of "nationality," and its relation to minorities is not a matter of "racial" but of "national" (*mínzú*) difference. The ambiguity of these concepts cannot be analytically resolved but will have to be constantly problematized.

The predominant approaches to racism in the social-science literature are to analyze economic and class differences or to resort to culturalist interpretations, such as Huntington's (1993) "clash of civilizations," but these modes of explanation do not sufficiently capture the immanent logic and specificity of racism in Han Chinese societies. Such a blunt assertion is not a claim for Han Chinese particularism. Han racism existed long before China's encounter with the West and is found today in mainland China's interactions with its Asian neighbors and within the Han population itself. Unpacking the specificity of racist logic in our own societies may open up new perspectives on racist practices in other locations.

Methodologically, the analysis could begin by tracing Han relations with the group's Others through different moments of history, and could then track the developments and divergences of those relations in different Chinese societies.[2] Here I can operate only on the level of theoretical reflection, with the hope that concerned intellectuals in different Chinese communities will address the specificities in their own locations.

Two important feminist works on the Qing Dynasty inspire the following analysis. Maram Epstein's essay "Confucian Imperialism and Masculine Chinese Identity in the Novel *Yesou Puyan*" contrasts descriptions of the sexual encounters of the Han protagonist in the 1880s edition of the novel with those in the abridged version published in the 1930s. As the narrative unfolds, the protagonist interacts with characters from far-off lands such as Italy, Portugal, Spain, and India, as well as those living in places on the periphery of the Chinese empire, including Taiwan, Japan, Burma, Siam, Ceylon, and the Miao and Yao Kingdoms. What emerges from reading Epstein's account is a set of three discursive and psychic strategies for dealing with the Other. The first is to demonize (*guǐhuà*) the unfamiliar subjects. These Others are imaginatively portrayed as having "green faces with exposed long teeth," or sometimes with tails, feathered bodies, and the like. This is a genre of fascination with—and fear of—what Chinese have traditionally called the foreign devil. Within this category there are various subsets, such as Western foreign devils, who are physically imposing, and Eastern foreign devils—the Japanese—who are shorter. To demonize the Other is part of a familiar Han imaginary in which the self is human while the Other is not.

The second strategy is to animalize the Other. When the protagonist travels to Taiwan, he discovers the island to be a wild land inhabited by "human bears" (*rénxióng*); in southern China, where the Miao reside, he encounters six pairs of white pythons who subjugate the Miao people and encourage them to rebel against the Chinese empire. The pythons resemble humans, but they have long bodies covered in scales, white hair, and cold, numb sexual organs. Arriving in India, he describes it as a Buddhist country: "those who are Buddhists exert no effort, they are as stupid as cows, ugly as dogs, and all they do is recite sutras, and fast" (Epstein 1998, 17). What is interesting is that even these animalized Others stimulate the protagonist's sexual desire. This desire for sex with animals is amusingly justified because in such encounters "chaos transforms itself into civilization" (ibid., 12). This is once again the story of the Han civilizing mission. Animalized Others can ostensibly become human through being educated by us, though at the gut level, we know they can never really become like us.

The third strategy, often applied to neighboring minority peoples, is to differentiate outsiders through even finer distinctions, thereby producing additional sets of hierarchies. These peoples were divided into two broad groups: the "cooked" and the "raw," with the cooked being those who were "culturally different but could be easily 'digested' (*xiāohuà*) into the sphere of influence of Chinese culture." Unlike the decadent Eastern devils (the Japanese), who were considered hopelessly raw, the Miao were "dancing their way into the Chinese consciousness" (ibid., 14). They were being Hanified, yet with the knowledge that since they are not fully human, not quite the same as us, the assimilation process would never be successfully completed. This strategy of pushing the Other through a humanization project while forever maintaining a superior position in the social hierarchy is intrinsic to the functioning of colonialism.

Epstein's feminist analysis relies on a gendered understanding of yin-yang logic—in which yang is always superior to yin—to interpret the hierarchical relation between the Han (yang) and the Other (yin). My own reading is that what unifies these three strategies is a hierarchical distinction between human and nonhuman—or, more specifically, an assertion of the power to judge the degree of humanness of others. This hierarchy is articulated by a speaking position above the constituted categories, and this position is occupied by a male subject who has cultivated himself through long and rigorous training and has attained the highest levels of cultural capital and power. The hierarchy presupposes that there are beings who can physically pass as human but who cannot be qualified as having fully achieved humanity. Reading and reciting the classics (*sìshū wǔjīng*) and cultivating one's body and virtue (*xiūshēn yǎngxìng*) are the routes by which one moves toward humanness. Confucianist ethics and moral thought as practiced philosophy can be understood in this light, and in this sense the human is above the categories and speaking positions of yin and yang, man and woman.

This is the key to understanding the logic of Han racism. But where does this logic come from? Let me first clarify that we are not addressing the idealist issue of Asian values. Instead, we are addressing materialist practices, which are shaped by a particular worldview. Within the system of Han racist practices, this logic has long been an instinctual response when encountering the Other. This means that the encounter always presupposes the subject's knowledge of an accumulated set of practices, which in turn condition and mobilize the subject's practices when confronting the unfamiliar Other.

One source of these practices can be found in the theory and historical practices that developed around the notion of *nèishèng wàiwáng*—internally like a sage, externally a ruler. The sage-king cultivates the inner virtue of a saint while governing through winning the hearts and consent of his subjects (*bǎixìng*). Here I rely on Liu Jen-peng's work. In "The Disposition of Hierarchy and the Late Qing Discourse of Gender Equality,"[3] the first chapter of *Feminist Discourse in Early Modern China: Nation, Translation and Gender Politics* (2000), Liu borrows from Louis Dumont's analysis of the Indian caste system in his classic *Homo Hierarchicus: The Caste System and Its Implications*, published in 1980, to understand the Chinese construction of hierarchy. She sees Dumont's theory of hierarchy as an articulation of a relation between "the encompassing" and "the encompassed": within the totality of a system of relations, the higher position is able to encompass the lower one, but not the reverse. For instance, male positions can encompass female, but the female cannot encompass the male. On some levels, the male and female are mutually supportive, but structurally they are not equal.

In another chapter of the same book, "'Penumbrae Questions the Shadow'—Sexual Subject Outside 'Gender Equality,'" Liu cites an allegory used by Chuang Tsu to rethink the development of hierarchical relations among different speaking positions and their subsequent unequal representations in the public arena.[4] The allegory includes three positions: the subject (*xíng*, which literally means form or substance), the shadow of the subject (*yǐn*), and the penumbra (*zhòngwángliǎng*), which is the slight shade outlining the shadow. If the subject is the form or body, the shadow relies on the subject to exist, and the penumbra, as the outer shadow of the shadow, relies on the shadow to exist. Because the penumbra is not clearly defined, and hence cannot be identified in terms of an individual subject, it is seen as a cluster of lumps crowding around the shadow. In the space of the social, this encompassing epistemological framework is based on the principle that subject and shadow cannot be separated (*xíngyǐn bùlí*). Because the penumbra cannot present itself—or, if seen as a cluster, themselves—directly, its presence is represented by the shadow in the public arena.

Liu's distinctions can be more easily understood if they are viewed in terms of identity politics: if the structure is a heterosexual patriarchy, where the subject is a male, and the shadow is a feminist, then the penumbra is a lesbian group, which cannot be properly presented except—at least in the contexts of Taiwan and mainland China—by masquerading as a cluster of feminists. If the structure is capitalism, the capitalist is the subject, the working class is the shadow, and the penumbra is the migrant worker who cannot be presented in civil society except through mediating "shadow" organizations such as churches or activist labor groups. If the structure is the world system, the subject is the dominant race, the shadow is the minority, and the penumbra is the demon, the animal, the raw, the nonhuman. In these three instances, the subject occupies a position from which a structural universe is formed and thereby encompasses the other speaking positions. The subject is above other categories and controls the dynamics of the structure.

This formulation of differentiated subjects has wider implications. It radically questions the normative assumption of public-sphere theory, which assumes that all subjects have direct and more or less equal access to public spaces. In my view, this allegory should be applied only with caution. Its importance lies in its descriptive and analytical acuity, which accurately captures the objective existence of the hierarchical dispositions of human subjects. This level of analysis needs to be kept separate from normative and strategic considerations. Whether the allegory can be used to develop strategies that empower subaltern subject groups cannot be theoretically predetermined; rather, it has to be weighed by subjects in action. One thing is certain: any useful strategy would have to involve political analysis of the specific objective conditions within which the action takes place.

According to Liu, in the Chinese scholarly tradition, the relation between the subject and object is not conceptualized as a binary opposition. Rather, it is a relation of yin and yang, a relation of complementarity, negotiation, and division of labor. But Liu points out that this tradition ignores a crucial structural relation. She argues that the Taoist concept of *taiji*, as a structural totality in place prior to the existence of yin and yang, has to be analyzed on two levels. On the higher level, the unity of yin and yang is complementary and indeed encompasses a totality. But on the lower level, yang is higher than yin, and the former governs and encompasses the latter.

To bring the discussion to the level of social analysis, we see that the enunciative position—from which the ontological and epistemological foundation is produced, and which thus provides the basis for the disposition of all social hierarchies—is in fact the same transcendent human implied by the Othering processes identified by Epstein. In other contexts, this position may be described as the man of moral integrity (*jūnzǐ*), the saint (*shèngrén*), or the sage-king (*shèngwáng*). Put bluntly, in the late Qing discourse on gender equality, the saint is the source of equality. In the words of the scholar and political reformer Liang Qichao, whose life spanned the late Qing Dynasty and the early republican era, "in the teaching of the Saint, man and woman are equal" (*shèngrén zhījiào nánnǚ píngděng*) (quoted in Liu 2000, 52). In other words, only the saint can teach the true meaning of gender equality; the speaking position of the saint encompasses and operates above the categories of both man and woman. The existence of the saint presupposes that humanity's diversity is hierarchically constituted: the saint is on top, the untouchables below, and demons and animals—the nonhumans—are even further down in the hierarchy.

At this point, we are ready to return the discussion to the logic of Han racism. For the Han, the position of human at the top of the hierarchy applies not only to gender relations but also to race and class relations. "We are equal, yet you are not quite human enough to take over my speaking position as a saint" is the psychic mechanism constantly mobilized in encounters with the Other, a basic formula of self-defense through the maintenance of psychic superiority.

This logic, I submit, is the epistemological foundation of the Chinese empire; this imperial order of things is embedded deeply in the psyche and practices of Han Chinese.⁵ As part of the modernization project that accompanied the Western imperialist invasion, reform-minded Han literati were forced to adopt notions such as tolerance and equality, especially in their interactions with imperialist Others. But the mind-set, the psychic structure, and the ideological practice of the formula "we are equal, yet you are not quite human enough" was and is entrenched in the political unconscious. The human-nonhuman distinction still persists. The formula is contextually mobilized to deal with Others who might be classified into a spectrum of the superior (white), weaker (minority), and unfamiliar and inferior (dark-skinned South Asians). This universal chauvinism has provided a psychic mechanism for the Han to confront imperialist intervention and to make life more bearable: these (white) foreign devils can beat us by material force, but they can never conquer our spirit. This is precisely the logic of Lu Xun's famous character Ah Q. But the identical racist logic is used to discriminate against those living on the periphery of China and most likely contributed to the death of Hari Veriah. A sharp-edged shield can be used for self-defense, but it can be a lethal weapon when deployed carelessly.

Though the works of Epstein and Liu are mainly concerned with issues of gender and sexuality, they have opened up a discursive space at the core of the Chinese empire that has wide-ranging implications. Throughout the history of the Han, multilayered discrimination has been an expression of practices growing out of a particular conception of the human, a conception that is constituted within an inherently discriminatory hierarchy. On the surface, human is a universal horizon; once that plane is reached, differences in gender, sexuality, class, nation, and race are transcended. In other words, hierarchical differences within the categories of gender, sexuality, class, nation, and race are the natural expressions of human as an operating regime. This regime is shaped like a pyramid, where human is on top, and the half-human and nonhuman (the shadow and the penumbra) look up in admiration as they continue their slow, futile climb. Meanwhile, the human looks downward. He is the authority who determines how far the Other is from reaching the top and becoming a real human being like him. This transcendent human has no traits: he is above gender, sexuality, class, and race. He manifests discrimination at precisely the moment when he patiently and conscientiously tells you, "Work harder and you can make it!" If you wish to move away from the logic of the pyramid by telling him that the rules of the game are invented by the Han, the male, and the literati, he will kindly tell you: your intelligence and wisdom (*huìgēn*) are not yet fully cultivated; you have not yet crossed the horizon into true humanity; you are much too Westernized; and you have been poisoned by feminism, Marxism, or postcolonialism.[6]

I think the supposedly heated debate on Chineseness is not nearly hot enough. It has not reached the heart of the matter: universal chauvinism. If one accepts the understanding of the Han perception of human presented here, can one not support the call for deimperialization? As Chinese living in Taiwan, Hong Kong, Singapore, Malaysia, and mainland China, we need to work together to think through the issue of racism in comparative terms. In Taiwan, racism is expressed in the dominant population's treatment of aboriginal peoples, foreign laborers, migrant domestic workers, foreign and mainland Chinese brides, and foreign English-language teachers. The so-called democratization of Taiwan has not yet resulted in more democratic ways of relating to others. Unless a reflexive deimperialization movement can be actively staged, we are still a long way from achieving Sun Yat-sen's dream of world equality (*tiānxià dàtóng*).

On 30 September 2005, Denmark's *Jyllands-Posten* published a dozen cartoons caricaturing the prophet Muhammad, several of which portrayed him as a terrorist. According to Islamic teachings, any visual representation of the Prophet is blasphemous, and the publication of the cartoons triggered strong protests from the Islamic world, as well as heated debates within Europe. In February 2006, the London-based *Guardian* published an essay by Martin Jacques (2006) titled "Europe's Contempt for Other Cultures Can't Be Sustained," a piece critically reflecting on the problem of racism across Europe. The deck copy clearly brings out his main argument: "A continent that inflicted colonial brutality all over the globe for 200 years has little claim to the superiority of its values." Martin sees the wide-ranging reactions to the Danish cartoons within Europe as a revealing combination of "defensiveness, fear, provincialism and arrogance." The controversy clearly demonstrated that Europe is ill prepared to cope with the changing world. This is not the first time that Martin has written on the need for Europe to seriously consider the imperialist damage it inflicted around the globe. In his frequent contributions to the public debate, with his persistent concern with the rise and transformation of Asia—China and India in particular—he seeks to shake up European parochialism.

Even though Hari most likely lost her life to the racism of Hong Kong Chinese, Martin has never emotionally turned against the Chinese. On the contrary, he hopes that his beloved son, Ravi, will learn Mandarin, and in addition to having him study Indian music, Martin is also encouraging him to play the *erhu*, a two-stringed Chinese musical instrument. Instead of fostering resentment, Hari's tragic death has been the driving force behind Martin's persistent exploration of contemporary racism and its intimate connection with the history of European imperialism.

Two days after his piece on the Danish cartoons was published in *The Guardian*, Martin told me that he had received more than two hundred strongly worded e-mails, most of them unfriendly. He was very pessimistic that Europeans would critically reexamine their imperialist histories, which he believes is the most important issue for Europeans to address in the coming decades. After reading Martin's essay, I asked him what the reaction would have been if the piece had been published not in his name but mine. He said readers in Europe would have ignored it or thought that I was just another Chinese who did not understand Europe. Indeed, I imagine some would have responded by saying that China was also an empire, that it too was rife with racial discrimination, and that I therefore had no right to question them. I also imagine that if this epilogue addressing the issue of Han Chinese racism were written by a European or an American, it would be quickly cast aside by Chinese readers.

If these speculations are true, then we really do need to take this issue seriously. Identity politics has not faded away, and it will not in the foreseeable future. Critical intellectuals have to make more proactive use of our own inescapable identities to speak from within, so that the subject groups we belong to will respond to the problems in question. In the words of an old expression, to criticize others, one has to first examine oneself. It all starts with reflexive self-criticism.

This book now comes to a close. Though I do not naively think that the problems currently facing the world can all be reduced to the problematic of deimperialization, conflicts and clashes within national borders and those between nations and regions are all too often inescapably connected to the history of colonialism and imperialism. To explain such contradictions in flat, abstract, and simple conceptual terms has always been the collaborationist mode of knowledge production, one that deflects responsibility away from imperialism. One often hears that racism occurs everywhere, that there is no need to track the specificities of its practices, that history is always the result of imperialist rivalries and conquests, and that there is no need to change those truths — indeed, no possibility of changing them. This book challenges those assumptions and the arrogant conditions of knowledge production that sustain them. These conditions attempt to regulate academic production into a singularity, coated with professionalism but stripped of critical concerns and political positions. The imperialist apparatus and the collaborationist desire of the colonized to catch up have ensured that the mechanisms which have evolved to shape intellectuals into professional academics are now firmly in place throughout the globe. But the rules of the game were set by the empire. Carrying with us the historical experiences of the colonized third world, we cannot allow ourselves to be swept up in the rush toward neoliberal globalization. We have to insist on advancing the critical work of deimperialization, decolonization, and de–cold war, and facilitating regional integration on the level of knowledge production through the practices of Asia as method.

NOTES

Introduction: Globalization and Deimperialization

1. "Chinese empire" is, of course, a modern phrase in English. It is used here to denote Chinese regimes which underwent regular dynastic shifts, and their relations with other political entities in the region. According to Wang Hui's recent study, "Chinese empire" is a phrase heavily charged with evolutionist imagination. The narrative of the modernizing nation-state requires the construction of an imaginary backwards empire against which the nation-state measures its development. For a detailed discussion, see Wang (2004).
2. See the important chapter by Hamashita (2003) in Arrighi, Hamashita, and Selden (2003). This book is highly recommended for its sophistication and explanatory power, though it is somewhat uncritically committed to a positive, romantic narrative of the rise of East Asia, especially China, as a counterbalance to the Euro-American hegemony of the past two centuries. Needless to say, the dialogue is once again directly shaped by a Eurocentric view of world history.
3. Okinawa remained a vassal state until the 1870s.
4. Perhaps because of this unclear mix, it is still difficult for East Asians to fully understand the notion of the nation-state, or at least to agree on what it is. The translations of "nation-state" in Japanese, Korean, and Chinese indicate completely different understandings of the term.
5. The statement is arguable because of the complex history of Hong Kong. The Kowloon Peninsula was ceded to the English in 1842 after the First Opium War. In 1898, the New Territories, which make up 92 percent of Hong Kong, were leased to England for ninety-nine years. Whether Hong Kong was a colony or a concession depends upon which historical moment we refer to.
6. For earlier research on this period, see the important volume edited by Myers and Peattie (1984).
7. For recent scholarship on the subject, see Duara (2003).
8. For an important, historically grounded account of the differences between assimilation and imperialization in the context of Japanese colonialism, see Ching (2001).

9. For a detailed account of this period, see Dower (1999). Okinawa did not revert to Japan until 1972, and in the interlude, Okinawans lived a hard life under an authoritarian and militaristic U.S. regime, which is perhaps the most shameful and neglected chapter in the history of U.S. imperialism. For an important recent work on Okinawa after the Second World War, see Toriyama (2003). We have yet to hear any word of apology from the U.S. government for its 27-year (1945–72) authoritarian rule in Okinawa.

10. See Bruce Cumings's (1981 and 1990) pathbreaking work on the Korean War.

11. Cumings (1999) is an important work on U.S. hegemony in East Asia.

12. Perhaps because these movements are ongoing, there is very little empirical research detailing their processes. In both Taiwan and South Korea, the movements have moved beyond the level of cultural production and consumption to encompass the spaces and practices of daily life. For instance, having cold rice tea after a summer meal in Seoul, or having cold bean-curd soup in Taipei, is now seen as part of the local tradition.

13. See the Chinese-language edition of the *Modern History of Three East Asian Countries* (2005). These words are printed underneath the title on the title page: "Learning from history, facing the future. Let us together build a peaceful and friendly new relationship in East Asia."

14. See chapter 4 for a detailed discussion. My own dialogue with one critical circle in Japan was published as "The Question of Asia's Independence" in the June 2005 Anti-Japan special issue of the Tokyo-based journal *Contemporary Thought* (*Gendai Shiso*).

15. Sovereign, that is, from the Chinese point of view. The exceptions are Hong Kong, which was reintegrated into China in 1997; Macao, which was returned to China in 1999; and Taiwan, whose status is unresolved.

16. See Qian Liqun's (2005) powerful account of that era and its long-lasting impact on Chinese intellectual culture.

17. Based on my own interactions in the region, I have to say this is a complex issue which cannot be handled in a simple, politically correct way. The sizes of the countries matter a great deal. For example, an intellectual circle in Singapore cannot be expected to take on the same amount of responsibility as its counterpart in China. This issue is taken up again in the final chapter.

18. In 1924, when he visited Japan, Sun Yat-sen gave a famous speech on Great Asianism, calling for Asian peoples' solidarity against any form of imperialism.

19. I have in mind the recent situation in Taiwan. The Taiwan independence movement bloc (the Democratic Progressive Party, or DPP) was in power

from 2000 to 2008, but in the later years of its rule, the regime relied on the United States even more heavily than the KMT did. The anticommunism–pro-Americanism structure was strengthened, not weakened.

20. I am referring to the "counter-empire" proposed by Michael Hardt and Antonio Negri (2000). In my view, their formulation of the "multitudes" as an agent of change lacks the critical angle of deimperialization. A powerful challenge to neoliberal globalization, their political proposal nonetheless cannot be advanced without reopening the deimperialization question in the imperial centers and former colonies.

Chapter 1: The Imperialist Eye

I wish to thank Yiman Wang for undertaking the huge task of translating an earlier version of this chapter from Chinese into English. As noted in the preface, that version was published in *Positions* in 2000.

1. For these opposing views, see Xu (1994) and Huang (1994). It is worth noting that within the discourse of transnational capital, Taiwan's investment environment in the 1970s and 1980s was described in the same terms used for Southeast Asia in the 1990s.

2. For classical theorizations of imperialism, see Lenin (1939 [1917]), Magdoff (1978), Hobson (1965 [1902]), and Luxemburg (1976 [1909]). For a recent reformulation, see Hardt and Negri (2000).

3. Actually, there is no "sixth" Export Processing Zone in the Philippines, but this was the exact language used by Juang Bingkun, the Taiwanese minister of the economy. The government built several export processing zones in Taiwan itself during the 1970s, so when the minister stated that the facility in the Philippines was "Taiwan's sixth export processing zone," he was viewing it as an extension of Taiwan's physical territory (L. Zhang 1994).

4. See Wuo's (1994) criticism of the Back Alley (Li-xiang) Studio's documentary *Taiwanese Friends*.

5. For the collaboration of national capital and the state apparatus, see Wang Cheng-hwann (1993).

6. For a recent account of the Bandung Conference and third worldism, see the special issue of *Inter-Asia Cultural Studies: Movements*, edited by Hee-yeon Cho and Kuan-Hsing Chen (2005).

7. I have benefited immensely from discussions on this point with Ashish Rajadhyaksha.

8. For a more detailed criticism, see my preface to the Chinese edition of Tomlinson's book (Chen 1994b).

9. For the first four points, see Magdoff (1978, 140, 242–44).

10. For a leftist analysis of Asia from an Asian perspective, see David and Kadir-gamar (1989).

11. See Hechter (1975) for a classic discussion of internal colonization. Strictly speaking, "internal" refers to the inside of a nation-state in the geographical sense.

12. For the most part, I follow Antonio Gramsci, Louis Althusser, and Stuart Hall in seeing ideology as a system of representation through which the social subject understands the world and lives in it.

13. Lee Yuan-tseh (1994). The written document, prepared by Lee's office, states that within ten years Academia Sinica hopes to be a center of Southeast Asian Studies (310). Lee insists, in his responses to legislators, that this plan has nothing to do with politics (326, 339, 357, 268).

14. There is no question that the Southeast Asia research project was a failure. It was officially abandoned in 2003, having been renamed the East Asia research project. A significant amount of research funds, accumulated over ten years, was wasted. But given Lee Yuan-tseh's powerful positions in both the academic hierarchy and the political arena, no one has been able to hold him responsible for this failure. From 2004 to 2006, I was a visiting research fellow at the National University of Singapore, a real center of Southeast Asian research, and I saw no trace of the Academia Sinica's huge investment in the project. When experts in the field mention the Southeast Asia project at all, it is spoken of as a joke. But there is absolutely no critical reflection on the project in Taiwan. The new East Asia project may well continue to be supported by the current and future governments, though whether it is academically influential or not is no longer the main issue: once academic work is subjugated to the will of the political regime, one can no longer evaluate it in academic terms.

15. The phrase "surrounding areas" is unclear in its reference, but the illustrations and captions in the special issue indicate that the phrase includes China and Japan. The next day's front page contained a picture captioned, "The close connections between China, Japan, and Southeast Asia." The phrase's ambiguity raises several questions: Does the unnamable region arouse subconscious anxiety or hostility? What are the Oedipal implications? This imaginary Other is the basis of ideological operations that I discuss in detail later in the book.

16. For a detailed account in English of Japan's southward advance in the 1930s, see Peattie (1996).

17. Independently of Charles Darwin, Wallace developed an evolutionary theory that was largely in agreement with Darwin's views; Wallace's presentation of

his views to Darwin convinced the latter to publish *On the Origin of Species.*
The Wallace line, which runs between several Indonesian islands, is a boundary separating Asian and Australian animal species. See Jones (1980, 10–34).
For the relationship between evolution and imperialism, see Hofstadter
(1965), especially the chapter on racism and imperialism. I thank Fu Dawei
for drawing my attention to this information.

18. This passage was cited in Wang Cheng-hwann's (1993) short essay on the
negative impact of the southward-advance policy on the working class.
Wang's essay is perhaps the only critical analysis of the southward-advance
policy published in the 1990s.

19. Pǎo dānbāng describes the activities of a person who makes frequent trips
overseas to buy goods to sell at home at a much higher price. This type of so-
called unproductive trade has historically been looked down on. Táishāng is
the common term for Taiwanese who conduct business abroad. That term
generally has neutral connotations.

20. For the local hostility to images of the Chinese, see Suryadinata (1975), and
Constantino (1992).

21. See Ang (1992) for a discussion of the negative consequences of identifying
with (or being identified with) Chinese culture for overseas Chinese.

22. "Mainlander" is the common English translation of *wàishěng rén*, literally
"people who come from outside the province" of Taiwan. It refers to the two
million people who came to Taiwan as part of the KMT exodus at the end
of the Chinese civil war, as well as their descendants. *Běnshěng rén*, literally
"people who come from the province," or so-called native Taiwanese, is the
common term for the Han Chinese (and their descendants) who had been
living in Taiwan before that time. It does not include aboriginal Taiwanese.
For a more detailed discussion of the meaning of these terms, see chapter 3.

23. In Taiwan's political system, the president appoints the prime minister. Lee
Teng-hui was the first Taiwanese president, taking over in 1988 after the
death of Chiang Ching-kuo. One story from that time was that after Lee
became president, he felt obliged to appoint Hau Pei-tsun as prime minister,
an old-line four-star general and former commander in chief of the army, in
order to forestall the possibility that the overwhelmingly mainlander military
might stage a coup. By 1993, Lee's government was secure enough that when
Hau retired, he could be replaced with Lien Chan, who is considered a native
Taiwanese. In effect, this was the moment of final victory for the Taiwanese
faction of the KMT. Yang's narrative, with its tensions of mainlander versus
Taiwanese, parallels the disintegration of the Lee-Hau regime and the rise
of the Lee-Lien regime.

24. For arguments on different classes and ideologies, see Wu and Cai (1971), Shi Ming (1980), Shi Xinyi (1988), and Yang Bichuan (1988).
25. The 1947 February 28 Incident—or 228 Incident, as it is usually referred to—was a pivotal event. Widespread civil unrest, sparked by an instance of police brutality, was met with state violence. In the weeks after the event, KMT troops, some newly arrived from mainland China, killed thousands of Taiwanese.
26. For a detailed sociological critique of Zhang Maogui, see Chao (1994).
27. For a more detailed discussion, see K.-H. Chen (1988).
28. For a Taiwan feminist criticism of nationalism, see Ping Fei (1994).
29. For Queer Nation, see Cruikshank (1992, 176–77). *Freedom Newspaper*, published by a Taiwanese lesbian group, made Queer Nation the topic of its second issue in 1994.
30. The statement was made in a public forum in 1994, by a woman who chose to be anonymous.
31. The claim that the KMT's project was "internal" is disputed. In the 1990s, President Lee Teng-hui described the KMT as an "external polity," by which he meant a nonnative colonial power.
32. Many of these political issues were first debated in the cultural sphere. The 1970s saw the rise of nativist literature (*xiāngtǔ wénxué*), which drew attention to and sharpened the divides between Chinese and Taiwanese identity. See Shi Minhui (1988).
33. The official name of the KMT is still the "Chinese KMT" (*Zhōngguó Guómíndǎng*), although some elements within the KMT advocate formally changing the name to the "Taiwan KMT."
34. A pleasure boat on Qiandao Lake in Zhejiang Province carrying twenty-four Taiwanese tourists and eight mainland Chinese was hijacked and burned, with the attackers killing everyone on board. Chinese officials were considered to have bungled the criminal investigation and were accused of treating the families of the victims with exceptional indifference.

Chapter 2: Decolonization

1. For a recent account, see the special issue of *Cultural Studies* on "Globalization and the De-Colonial Option," edited by Walter Mignolo (2007).
2. See Césaire (1972 [1953], 39–43). For instance, Césaire writes: "If you criticize the colonialism that drives the most peaceable populations to despair, Mannoni will explain to you that after all, the ones responsible *are not the colonialist whites* but the colonized Madagascans. Damn it all, they took the whites for gods and expected of them everything one expects of the divinity" (ibid., 41; emphasis in original).

3. *Black Skin, White Masks* was written in response to Mannoni. Fanon's fourth chapter, "The So-Called Dependency Complex of Colonized Peoples," begins with a quotation from Césaire and then attacks Mannoni.

4. For a discussion of Fanon from the field of queer studies, see Fuss (1994).

5. It is then understandable that since the postwar era, ethnic nationalism, which is the reproduction of the colonialism of an earlier moment, has dominated third-world political scenes. Fanon's analysis refers to experiences on the African continent, especially in the Ivory Coast, Senegal, Algeria, and the rest of North Africa. But the two forms of nationalism he identifies in *The Wretched of the Earth*—ethnic nationalism and regionalism—are common throughout the third world. Each of these forms has its own historical basis; often the differences predate the colonial period. In the case of Taiwan, ethnic nationalism is widespread, but regionalism is only an undercurrent. Regional difference was first mobilized in the mid-1990s, and only then as an electoral strategy. Although the logic of regionalism has recently shown signs of breaking down, it has been the dominant political logic of South Korea since the Second World War. There, the regional background of the presidential candidates is the most crucial factor in the election: if a candidate comes from a province with a small population, it is unlikely that she or he will be elected.

6. Nandy himself puts it like this: "The broad psychological contours of colonialism are now known. Thanks to sensitive writers like Octave Mannoni, Frantz Fanon and Albert Memmi, we even know something about the interpersonal patterns which constituted the colonial situation, particularly in Africa. Less well known are the cultural and psychological pathologies produced by colonization in the colonizing societies" (Nandy 1983, 30). He goes on to analyze the situation in India.

7. See for instance, Wang Ji-shih (1995), an edited volume in response to Huntington's article. Also, in September 1997, Huntington was invited to Singapore and Malaysia to debate with Asian scholars.

8. The essay was originally published in *Antipode* in 1977; it was reprinted in the 1985 special issue, "The Best of Antipode, 1969–1985." The essay was then rewritten as chapters 1 and 2 of Soja's *Postmodern Geographies* (1989). I have consulted the 1985 version.

9. The relative autonomy of the local histories of world regions is echoed in Mizoguchi Yūzō's (1996 [1989]) theory of "base-entity." See chapter 5 for a detailed discussion.

Chapter 3: De–Cold War

1. Our position, popular democracy, was called integrationist by the separatists, and separatist by the integrationists; we simply thought we were on the Left but could not say so. Before the lifting of martial law in Taiwan in 1987, the entire political sphere was dominated by the right wing and people lived under the shadow of the White Terror; it would have been counterproductive at that point to claim to be on the Left. Only in the mid-1990s did we realize how completely the Left and the CCP were conflated in the popular imagination shaped as it was by the Right.

2. An independent left-leaning journal, *Taiwan: A Radical Quarterly in Social Studies*, started publication in 1988 right after the lifting of martial law. Although it has no institutional support, the journal has been able to survive for the twenty years. It is now seen as one of the most important intellectual journals in the Chinese-speaking world.

3. Five years later, in 2002, when I was a visiting professor at Beijing's Tsinghua University, one could no longer distinguish locals from foreigners by dress alone.

4. The only group which has been actively addressing the issue is the Cold-War and State Violence in East Asia project, which held its first conference in 1997, in Taipei. Subsequent conferences were held in 1998 in Cheju, South Korea, and in 2000 in Okinawa. The group's main organizers are Suh Sung, Chen Ying-zhen, and Sugihara Tōru, who are activist intellectuals working across borders.

5. For example, in Taiwan, 98 percent of students studying abroad in 1950 were in the United States; so were 82 percent in 1960, 88 percent in 1970, 93 percent in 1980, and 90 percent in 1990. See the Taiwan Ministry of Education report at http://www.edu.tw/bicer/content.aspx?site_content_sn=7590.

6. According to a 2003 report by the Chinese consulate in Chicago, "China began to send students to the United States in 1979, and saw the fastest growth and biggest number of students from 1989 to 1994. From 1995 its first place was taken over by Japan. India rose suddenly as a new force in the past two years, and stayed for the second year at the top of the list." See http://www.china consulatechicago.org/eng/jy/t40302.htm (accessed 21 May 2009).

7. For research on a total war from the Japanese perspective, see Yamanouchi, Koschmann, and Narita (1998).

8. Kōjin Karatani (1998) argues that empires by definition have a unified language, so in this sense, Japan does not qualify as an empire. Karatani is not trying to deflect responsibility from his country, but to deepen critical thinking on imperialism.

9. For the rhetoric of the discourse on the Greater East Asia Co-Prosperity Sphere, see Jansen (1984) and Peattie (1984).

10. For a discussion of the inability to see the problem of the interiority of the United States in Asia, see chapter 4.

11. For lack of better English terms to render the Chinese notions of *qínxù* and *gănqín*, I am flirting with Raymond Williams's "structure of feeling" here. A more accurate expression is Ding Naifei's (2000) "structure of sentiment," but I have to caution the reader that this translation is still somewhat imprecise. "Emotion" is not precisely equivalent to *qínxù*, which often has a strongly negative connotation, and *gănqín* has connotations beyond just "feeling."

12. "Great reconciliation" (*dàhéjiě*) is a local term, coined by Taiwanese politicians in the mid-1990s. It was used as part of an attempt to resolve the differences between the unification and independence movements, an attempt that proposed some middle ground of reconciliation between the two political positions.

13. During the high point of the nativist movement in the late 1980s, Hakkanese people openly challenged the Minnanese who equated "Taiwanese" and "Minnanese," thereby neglecting Taiwan's Hakka population.

14. In the 1960s and 1970s, when Chiang Kai-shek and, later, his son Chiang Ching-kuo addressed the nation, many people in Taiwan could not understand their heavy Zhejiang accent and had to rely on transcripts to get the complete message.

15. As a system to classify and control the population of Taiwan, "provincial register" refers to one's provincial origin printed on one's identification card. Through this official mechanism, one's provincial identity is registered and constructed as shěngjí (literally, "origin register"). A provincial register (shěngjí)contradiction (máodùn) is the local way of expressing a conflict between people from Taiwan and others.

16. For an analysis of related historical events, see K.-H.Chen (1992).

17. Lu Hau-tung designed the original Kuomintang flag. The design of the party flag was later incorporated into the national flag of the ROC.

18. Wang Jingwei has been portrayed in KMT nationalist history as a traitor for working closely with the Japanese and against Chiang Kai-shek. Now that most Taiwanese have had a nationalist education, Wang's name is widely used in Taiwan to mean "traitor," as Americans use the name Benedict Arnold or Europeans refer to Quisling.

19. In the 1960s and 1970s, pornography had to be smuggled into Taiwan (it came mostly from American soldiers stationed in the country), and teenage students would pass this rare commodity around to each other.

20. I had always thought that this sentiment existed only among the older generation of běnshěng rén, but I was wrong. On 28 February 2001, a public forum was organized by *Taiwan: A Radical Quarterly in Social Studies* to discuss the controversy generated by a Japanese comic book, *Thesis on Taiwan*. In the forum, a young man who spoke with a Minnanese accent confessed that he was very disappointed by the new DPP government and said that it might be better to be ruled by the Japanese.

21. Close to half a million soldiers came to Taiwan with the KMT regime. By the 1980s, they were aging and came to be collectively labeled "old soldiers." In the late 1980s, they were one of the first groups to visit their old homes on the mainland.

22. See Wuo (1993) for an account of "returning home" movies produced in late 1980s and early 1990s.

23. From the late 1980s to the mid-1990s, Hong Kong was where these family reunions took place. Many hotels offered accommodation packages specifically for that purpose.

24. I use the word "representation" reluctantly, for two reasons. First, the central concern of this chapter is emotional structures, which cannot easily be represented. And second, representation presupposes something that exists before it is reflected, whereas these films themselves are part of the social-real sphere.

25. Since at least the 1930s, "anti-Japanese" has been the dominant mind-set of the KMT regime, and the image of Japan has been the imaginary Other through which the KMT version of Chinese identity was constructed. Until the 1980s, for instance, the Taiwanese government tightly restricted the importation of Japanese films and in propaganda films always represented Japan as the enemy.

26. The Mukden Incident was the bombing on 18 September 1931 of a section of railroad in Manchuria owned by a Japanese company. Japan blamed Chinese dissidents for the attack and used it as a pretext to invade Manchuria, which Japan quickly made into the protectorate of Manchukuo. The Marco Polo Bridge Incident, a battle on 8 July 1937 between Chinese and Japanese troops near Beijing, marked the official beginning of the Second Sino-Japanese War, although the Mukden Incident is now regarded as an early event in that war.

27. In "Two Discursive Formations on Chineseness in Taiwan New Cinema," the second chapter of her Ph.D. dissertation, Shi Wei (2005) criticizes this view and argues that the most important difference between běnshěng rén and wàishěng rén is really the divergence of their attitudes toward mainland

China. Her criticism is well taken. As I see it, her account fills many of the gaps in the present chapter.

28. See Butalia (1998) for an important account, based on oral histories.

29. Mizoguchi's essay was first published in Japan and was intended for Japanese readers. A Chinese translation was published in the Chinese (Beijing) monthly magazine *Du-shu* in May 2001.

30. In May 1980 a popular uprising broke out in Gwangju City that was crushed by the Korean army under the Chun Doo-hwan dictatorship.

Chapter 4: Deimperialization

1. Taiwan's first presidential election involving universal suffrage and a direct vote took place in March 1996. The new policies were considered by mainland China as signs of a move toward Taiwan independence. Relations between the two countries were tense in the weeks leading up to the election, and the crisis escalated when the presidential candidates used separatist rhetoric during the campaign. It was in that context that mainland China held military exercises, including missile launches, in the Taiwan Strait.

2. All the quotes below are from the letter, dated 6 March 1996. The translations are my own.

3. This controversy was initiated by President Lee Teng-hui. It was a move to expand the autonomy of the Taiwan state in relation to the People's Republic of China.

4. According to this report, the main findings of the survey were: (1) considering Taiwan's security, 60 percent of Taiwanese oppose Taiwan's becoming a state of the United States, and 26 percent support it; (2) in a choice between joining the United States or being governed by mainland China, 37 percent prefer the former, and 20 percent prefer the latter; (3) if Taiwan could preserve its language and culture while joining the United States, 46 percent would support the move while 46 percent would oppose it; (4) among those who oppose Taiwan's joining the United States, 55 percent indicate it is because they are "Chinese," and 40 percent say it is because they are "Taiwanese;" and (5) to maintain the status quo, 70 percent think Taiwan will rely on U.S. protection, and 25 percent think it will not.

5. For details, see Chang (1996).

6. When I gave a presentation on Club 51 at an open forum in January 2002 in Seoul, a Korean friend reacted strongly saying that if similar activities took place in Korea, people might beat the organizers to death. At the same time, what might be called the America complex is very strong in Korea. Another friend, Cho Haejoang, pointed out in our conversation, after the Second

World War, the United States has generally displaced China in terms of cultural influence in Korea. Undoubtedly, this has also been the case in Taiwan. The classic Japanese notion of "leaving Asia for Europe" is not at all a phenomenon unique to Japan. In fact, "leaving Asia for America" is a postwar trend throughout East Asia. See the first section of chapter 5 for a detailed discussion.

7. According to Chang (1996), there are groups similar to Club 51 in Canada, Australia, and several island nations in the Pacific.

8. In Chou Wei-ling's book (1998), a small map of Taiwan appears alongside small maps of Alaska, Hawaii, and Puerto Rico, all of which are placed next to a larger map of the continental United States.

9. Chou Wei-ling's book (1998) is "dedicated to the People of Taiwan, who have no sense of security and certainty."

10. The term "radical plural opportunism" (jījìn duōyuán tóujī zhǔyì) was coined by Huang Zhi-xiang, a prominent writer of television dramas. His *Big Eunuch and Little Carpenter* was a popular show broadcast in 1994.

11. At one demonstration in Okinawa in 2000, over 27,000 people holding hands encircled Kadena Air Base to protest the presence of American forces. Protests like these indicate that the U.S. refusal to leave is not just unreasonable but downright shameless. The United States imposes its own democratic values onto the rest of the world, but when these values come into conflict with its perceived self-interest, it simply refuses to follow basic democratic procedures.

12. To be sure, Kaplan is not trying to deny the imperial status of the United States; rather, she is struggling to rewrite the dominant historiography. Writing in the context of American studies, Kaplan's strategy is to reconnect "United States nation-building and empire-building as historically coterminous and mutually defining" (Kaplan 1993, 17). Her argument seems to have struck a chord. In 1998, empire and imperialism was the theme of the annual meeting of the Association of American Studies.

13. Qian Liqun provides a succinct analysis of the worldviews held by mainland Chinese intellectuals during the 1950s (Qian 2005). What is important for our purposes is his description of the positions of the KMT (for the United States and against communism and the Soviet Union) and the CCP (against the United States and for communism and the Soviet Union), which is useful in understanding the conditioning effect the United States had on China during the cold war.

14. For the historical trajectories of anti-Americanism in Latin America, the Middle East, Europe, East Asia, and within the United States, see the timely *Anti-Americanism*, edited by Andrew Ross and Kristin Ross (2004).

15. According to a poll conducted by the *United Daily News* in March 2003, 55 percent of Taiwanese opposed U.S. military intervention in Iraq and 21 percent supported it. In a poll taken by TVBS the same month, over 60 percent were opposed and 20 percent in favor.

16. On 24 March and 18 April 2003, two public forums were organized by *Taiwan: A Radical Quarterly in Social Studies* to address the Taiwan-U.S. question.

17. For instance, Zheng Chun-chi, a labor leader and representative figure of the progressive forces in Taiwan, mentioned Club 51's positions on several call-in television shows in Taiwan.

18. "Why Does Taiwan Want to Send Troops to Iraq?," http://www.yam.com (accessed 30 April 2004).

19. For a detailed discussion, see Shin (2002).

20. In 1978, *Formosa Magazine* was closed down by the KMT, which sparked a violent popular revolt.

21. A gunshot was heard on the day before election day while Chen was campaigning in southern Taiwan, and Chen was found slightly injured. The supposed attack on him won the sympathy of some voters, which was deemed to give him the margin he needed to be reelected. After the election, controversy broke out, with many people believing that the attack had been faked by Chen's camp. Even today, what really happened remains a mystery.

22. According to a report in the *China Times* on 5 June 2004, Chiu had to go to Washington to read Chen's inauguration speech, line by line, to U.S. government officials (Liu 2004).

23. Mainland China's antisuccession law was enacted in 2005 to counter the Taiwan independence movement.

24. Public statement made by the Taiwan State Building Movement Organization, http://www.yam.com (accessed 16 March 2003).

25. For a recent account of the changing dynamic in Korean thinking, see Shin (2005).

26. The official name of the AMPO Treaty is the Treaty of Mutual Cooperation and Security between the United States and Japan. It was first signed in 1950 and revised in 1960. The treaty has been the legal basis for the U.S. military presence in Japanese territory.

27. Taiwan Defense Alliance website, http://www.taiwanda.org.tw/.

28. Here Ching cites Tomiyama Ichiro's analysis of the "Japanization" process in Okinawa. Tomiyama maintains that "battlefield" and "everyday life" are not separate spaces, and that subjectivity is dialectically formed.

29. All references in this chapter refer to the 2005 Chinese edition, published by Social Sciences Studies Publishing in Beijing.

30. The Yasukuni Shrine in Japan is dedicated to those who died for their country. For many East Asians the shrine is seen as a memorial to Japanese imperialism.

Chapter 5: Asia as Method

The title of this chapter is inspired by Mizoguchi Yūzō's *China as Method* (1996 [1989]). Takeuchi Yoshimi published an essay called "Asia as Method" (2005a [1960]). Although the contexts and specific issues and problems discussed here are quite different, there is nevertheless a connection. See the fourth section of this chapter for a detailed discussion of this point. For my purposes here, Asia refers to an open-ended imaginary space, a horizon through which links can be made and new possibilities can be articulated. As an attempt to move beyond existing limits, and as a gesture toward something more productive, my notion of method does not imply an instrumentalist approach, but is imagined as a mediating process.

1. For an account of the project, see Chen and Chua (2007).
2. We have to acknowledge the immensely important work done by Mutō Ichiyō, Suh Seng, Chen Ying-zhen, Matsui Yayori, and Hamashita Takeshi. Without the contributions made by these respected individuals over the past forty years, it would have been more difficult for the following generations to move forward.
3. This point was made by Professor Choi Wan Ju, the editor of the influential journal *Creation and Criticism*, in his round-up session at the East Asia Cultural Forum, organized at SungKongHoe University, Seoul, in 2002.
4. To be fair, Chakrabarty later turned to other parts of Asia. See Chakrabarty (2000b).
5. For a detailed discussion, see Nandy (1983, 1–63).
6. The three lectures were based on four papers (Chatterjee 1998, 1999, 2000, 2001). Translations of these lectures and selected essays were later published in Chinese in K.-H. Chen (2000). See also Chen (2001b). Some of the ideas presented in Taiwan were later published in Chatterjee (2004).
7. "Betel nut beauties" are young women who sell betel nuts and wear sexy clothing to attract customers. For visual images of the betel-nut culture, see Chin-pao Chen (2000).
8. Such a project has begun. See the special issue of *Inter-Asia Cultural Studies: Movements* edited by Chun and Shamsul (2001), in particular Shamsul (2001), Deshpande (2001), and Sun (2001b).
9. After the June Fourth Incident, a series of essays was published in an effort to open the discussion on popular democracy. See Nan (1989), Ping-fei Wu (1989), and Shi Si-hung (1989). The most thorough analysis was later pub-

lished as a book by the pseudonymous Ka Wei-po, using the pen name Robocop (1991).

10. A part of the story of the popular democracy position is available in English. See Chen (1994c).

11. For a sophisticated analysis in the context of modern Chinese literary history, see Shi-he Chen (1997).

12. Deng Zheng-lai (2002) is one of the key proponents of introducing the notion of civil society into China.

13. For a detailed account of the transition, see Cho Hee-yeon (2000b) and Cho Hee-yeon and Park (2002).

14. For a detailed historical account of the guómín discourse in relation to the Chinese nationalist discourse, see Shen and Chien (1999). The Mandarin notion of guómín is confusingly taken from the Japanese notion of kokumin, which uses the same two characters. Partly due to the Japanese colonial legacy, all public elementary and junior high schools in Taiwan are called guómín schools and have the ostensible purpose of training children to become subjects of the state. The term is also used in Korean and Japanese political discussions. For details, see Cho Han Haejoang (2000).

15. The lunar calendar has not been widely used in Japan since the Meiji era, but that does not mean that mínjiān spaces no longer exist. Traditional festivals are still celebrated, but they are now scheduled according to the Gregorian calendar. The Buddhist calendar still used in Thailand and the Islamic calendar widely used by Muslims are both lunar.

16. For instance, according to Wuo Young-Ie's study on the construction trade in Taiwan, in 1984, out of 16,000 companies, only 2,687 had acquired legal licenses, while the rest operated without a license. See Wuo (1988, 221).

17. When Chen Shui-bian took power, numerous members of the civil society joined the government, including one feminist who became a member of his cabinet.

18. Two related papers in English on the politics of sex work are Ho (2000) and Ding Naifei (2000).

19. I have benefited from work on translation by Niranjana (1992), L. Liu (1994), and Sakai (1997).

20. On the question of universalism, I have benefited from discussions with Ashish Rajadhyaksha, Kim Soyoung, Wang Hui, Ding Naifei, Paul Willemen, and Stuart Hall.

21. I should note that my conversations with Professor Mizoguchi have always been inspiring and enjoyable. He is one of a group of intellectuals who, though now in their 70s, are still always on the move. The word retirement does not exist in their dictionary.

22. Takeuchi Yoshimi (1910–77) was an important modern thinker in Japan. Though he taught for a while, his intellectual interventions were never conducted in an academic style. The issues he was concerned with and the cultural and political activities he participated in spanned the full range of major problematics facing intellectuals in modern Japan. In 1944, he published *Lu Xun*, one of his most important works. Lu Xun became a system of reference, an interlocutor, throughout Takeuchi's life. Through his study of the inner world of Lu Xun, Takeuchi proposed the highly intuitive proposition of Asia as method, which challenged the Eurocentrism of the Japanese intellectual world. Because his intellectual style was unique, and because he often had no sense of political correctness, it is very difficult to label him. For a long time after his death, his work was simply forgotten. Recently, in Japan his original contributions to Japanese intellectual history have been rediscovered.

23. I read translations of the lecture in both English and Chinese. I am grateful for Richard Calichman's English translation in *What Is Modernity? Writings of Takeuchi Yoshimi* (2005a), and for Hu Dong-zhu's Chinese version, published in 2007 in *Taiwan: A Radical Quarterly in Social Studies*, no. 65.

24. Takeuchi's *Lu Xun* and his important essay "China's Modern and Japan's Modern" (1948) are the representative texts analyzed by Mizoguchi.

25. I must thank Professor Sakamoto Hiroko for bringing this issue to my attention, and for further clarifying the point in the context of the Sixth Community of Knowledge Conference, which took place at the Japan Foundation in Tokyo in August 2002.

26. For details of the project, see Sun (2001b). The six-year project, organized by Mizoguchi Yūzō and Sun Ge, officially ended in 2002. It was a series of forums in Beijing and Tokyo with the purpose of bringing critical intellectuals from China and Japan together to address important historical and political issues, which was not possible through existing modes of academic exchange. The memory of the Sino-Japanese War was one of the many important topics discussed.

27. I have observed a trend of increasing interactions within Asia, especially in Northeast Asia. The Cultural Typhoon project, initiated in Japan, has become an annual conference open to participants from outside Japan, mainly from Taiwan, Hong Kong, and South Korea. The annual conference of Taiwan's Cultural Studies Association has also become an international gathering, with participants from Singapore, Malaysia, Japan, Korea, and Hong Kong. If there were an annual Chūgokugaku gathering in Japan, scholars from neighboring places would probably also be present. That would change the logic and language of dialogues, and a relatively closed national space would be opened up.

Epilogue: The Imperial Order of Things

The earliest version of this epilogue was written in English and titled "'Foreign Devil' and 'Han Chinese Racism.'" It was written in response to a talk given by Immanuel Wallerstein at the Hong Kong University of Science and Technology on 21 September 2000. A Chinese version was presented in January 2005 as part of a panel on Han Chinese racism in the context of migration at the annual conference of the Cultural Studies Association of Taiwan, where Qua Sy Ren of Singapore, Josh Hong of Malaysia, Yan Hairong of China, Hsiao Hsiao-chuan of Taiwan, Ben Ku of Hong Kong, and I began to address this issue together. In June 2007, we gathered again at the 2007 Inter-Asia Cultural Studies Conference at Shanghai University, to further our discussions.

1. For details, see the Harinder Veriah Trust website at http://www.harinderveriah.com (accessed 28 May 2009), as well as Jacques (2002). The Hong Kong government finally passed an antidiscrimination law on 10 July 2008.

2. For a systematic study of the Chinese discourse of race, see Dikotter (1992). M. Dujon Johnson's (2007) *Race and Racism in the Chinas: Chinese Racial Attitudes towards Africans and African-Americans* is a major contribution on Chinese racism in mainland China and Taiwan. His research finds no "qualifying difference" in these two places.

3. A shorter version of the chapter in English can be found in Liu Jen-peng (2001).

4. The full fable in English is quoted in Liu Jen-peng and Ding (2005, 49–50), which addresses the problem of queer politics in Chinese contexts. This line of thinking is also developed in Liu Jen-peng, Perry, and Ding (2007).

5. I believe that China's tributary system can also be understood through this framework.

6. Perhaps because the notion of the transcendent human based on a moralistic universalism is so difficult to overthrow from within, Liu's (2002) later work turns toward science fiction, from which she formulates a concept of posthuman.

228 Incident: On 28 February 1947, the newly arrived KMT army clashed with local Taiwanese residents triggering a series of protests, strikes, and riots. Estimates of the number of people killed and injured range from ten to thirty thousand. The event has had long lived consequences. Symbolically it is seen as the beginning of the KMT's authoritarian rule, as well as a marker of ethnic conflict.

ASEAN: The Association for Southeast Asian Nations was established in 1967. Its purpose has been to facilitate economic cooperation and to promote regional peace. ASEAN Plus Three was institutionalized in 1999 to coordinate cooperation between ASEAN and China, Japan, and South Korea.

Asian-values debate: This scholarly debate emerged in the second half of the 1990s in the context of efforts to explain the extraordinary growth of East Asian economies. Some academics attributed this economic success to traditional Asian values such as collectivism, family cohesion, and Confucianism. Others argued that there was no single unity of values across the region. Yet others thought that the stress on the dichotomy of Asian versus Western values would abet the authoritarianism of many East Asian governments.

Bandung Conference: In April 1955, leaders of African and Asian states met in Bandung, Indonesia, to promote direct economic and cultural cooperation between their countries and to oppose colonialism. The meeting was seen as central to the formation of a third world — outside of the spheres of influence of cold-war rivals, the United States and Soviet Union — and as leading to the development of the non-alignment movement.

Běnshěng rén 本省人 (literally, "inside-province people"): People who come from the Taiwan province. This is the common term for Han Chinese who were living in Taiwan before the KMT exodus from mainland China from 1945 to 1959, as opposed to aboriginal Taiwanese. See also wàishěng rén.

CCP, the abbreviation for Chinese Communist Party (共產黨, Gòngchǎndǎng): The CCP has ruled mainland China since 1949 after defeating the KMT (see below) in the Chinese civil war.

Cheju Uprising: Also known as the 4.3 Event, the uprising started on 3 April 1948 on Cheju Island, South Korea. The rebellion was suppressed by the Korean army with an estimated fourteen to thirty thousand civilians killed or injured. The incident marked the beginning of the South Korean state's authoritarian rule, seen as part of the struggle against communism.

Chen Shui-bian 陳水扁: Representing the DPP (see below), dominated by běnshěng rén (see above), Chen was elected president of Taiwan in 2000. His victory ended the KMT's fifty year tenure in government. He was reelected in 2004, but is now in jail, convicted of abuse of power and corruption.

Comfort women: Women who were forced to work as prostitutes in the Japanese military brothels located throughout Asia during the Second World War. Since the 1990s an international movement has emerged seeking compensation and to reclaim the dignity of these women.

DPP, the abbreviation for the Democratic Progressive Party (民進黨, [mínjìndǎng]). Founded in 1986, the DPP was the main opposition party in Taiwan during KMT (see below) rule. The DPP took power in 2000 with the election of Chen Shui-bian (see above) as president.

Greater East Asia Co-Prosperity Sphere (大東亞共榮圈 Dàdōngyàgòngróngquān): An idea formulated by the Japanese military government in the 1930s and 1940s. The idea was to create an autonomous bloc of Asian countries to liberate it from the domination of Western imperialist powers.

Gwangju Uprising: In May 1980, a popular uprising broke out in the Gwanju city that was crushed by the Korean army under the Chun Doo-hwan dictatorship. More than one hundred thousand students and citizens participated. The uprising marks a moment of democratic action against authoritarianism, militarism, and U.S. imperialism.

KMT, the abbreviation for Kuomintang (國民黨, Gúomíndǎng, literally "national people's party"): Founded by Sun Yat-sen in 1894, the KMT was defeated by the CCP (see above) in the Chinese civil war in 1949. Its leaders and many of its members moved to Taiwan to set up a government that claimed to control the mainland as well as the island. It was defeated by the DPP (see above) in 2000 and returned to power in 2008.

Lee Teng-hui 李登輝: Lee became the first ethnically Taiwanese President of the Republic of China and KMT Chair in 1988 after Chiang Ching-kuo, the son of Chiang Kai-shek, passed away. In 1996 he became the first popularly elected president, and in 2000 passed his power to Chen Shui-bian (see above). Lee is known for his anti-China, pro-America, pro-Japan, and pro-Taiwan independence positions. Now in his late 80s, Lee continues to be active in national politics.

Wàishěng rén 外省人 (literally, "outside-province people"): People who came from outside the Taiwan province. Commonly translated as "mainlander," this is a common term for the two million people who came to Taiwan as part of the KMT (see above) exodus at the end of the Chinese civil war, as well as their descendants. See also *Běnshěng rén*.

Wang Jing-wei 汪精衛: Originally a member of the KMT (see above), Wang disagreed with Chiang Kai-shek and other KMT leaders about how best to fight the communists and formed a government in Nanjing that collaborated with the Japanese. KMT history treats Wang as a traitor, and his name is widely used in Taiwan as a synonym for traitor.

White Terror (白色恐怖, Báisèkǒngbù): A totalitarian campaign under the KMT in Taiwan in the 1950s and 1960s to control dissidents, especially leftists. Its name contrasts its users, the "white" nationalists, with the "red" communists on the Chinese mainland.

BIBLIOGRAPHY

Ahmad, Aijaz. 1992. *In Theory: Classes, Nations, Literatures.* London: Verso.

Anderson, Benedict. 1991. *Imagined Communities: Reflections on the Origin and Spread of Nationalism.* 2nd edition. London: Verso.

Ang, Ien. 1992. "On not Speaking Chinese — Diasporic Identity and Postmodern Ethnicity" ("不會說中國話—論散居族裔之身份與後現代之種族性"). Translated by Shih Yiming 施以明. *Chung-Wai Literary Monthly* (中外文學) 21, no. 7: 48–69.

Arrighi, Giovanni, Takeshi Hamashita, and Mark Selden, eds. 2003. *The Resurgence of East Asia: 500, 150, 50 year Perspectives.* London: Routledge.

Baik, Young-seo. 2002. "China's Asia: A Korean Perspective." *Inter-Asia Cultural Studies: Movements* 3, no. 2: 277–86.

Barlow, Tani. 1993. "Colonialism's Career in Postwar China Studies." *Positions: East Asia Cultures Critique* 1: 224–67.

Blaut, James M. 1987. *The National Question: Decolonising the Theory of Nationalism.* London: Zed Books.

————. 1993. *The Colonizer's Model of the World: Geographical Diffusionism and Eurocentric History.* New York: Guilford.

Butalia, Urvashi. 1998. *The Other Side of Silence: Voices from the Partition of India.* New Delhi: Viking.

Césaire, Aimé. 1972 [1953]. *Discourse on Colonialism.* Translated by Joan Pinkham. New York: Monthly Review Press.

Chakrabarty, Dipesh. 1992. "Provincializing Europe: Postcoloniality and the Critique of History." *Cultural Studies* 6, no. 3: 337–57.

————. 2000a. *Provincializing Europe: Postcolonial Thought and Historical Difference.* Princeton, N.J.: Princeton University Press.

————. 2000b. "'Asia' and the Twentieth Century: What Is 'Asian' Modernity?" *'We Asians': Between Past and Future — A Millennium Regional Conference*, 15–32. Singapore: Singapore Heritage Society.

Chang, Pingyi 張平宜. 1996. "The Slogan of Club 51: For Neither Unification Nor Independence, Let Us Be American, Let Taiwan Be a State of the U.S."

("51俱樂部—口號: 既不統也不獨, 讓我們成為美國人: 讓台灣變成美國一州"). *China Times* (中國時報), 29 May.

Chao, Kang 趙剛. 1994. *Watch Out for the "Nation": Critical Social Movements and Critique of Social Movements* (小心國家族: 批判的社運及社運的批判). Taipei: Tangshan.

Chatterjee, Partha. 1993 [1986]. *Nationalist Thought and the Colonial World: A Derivative Discourse*. Minneapolis: University of Minnesota Press.

———. 1998. "Community in the East." *Economic and Political Weekly* 33, no. 6: 277–82.

———. 1999. Introduction to *Wages of Freedom: Fifty Years of the Indian Nation-State*, edited by Partha Chatterjee, 1–22. New Delhi: Oxford University Press.

———. 2000. "On Civil and Political Society in Postcolonial Democracy." In seminar booklet, "Locating Political Society: Modernity, State Violence and Postcolonial Democracy," 80–98, 4 June. Taipei.

———. 2001. "Democracy and the Violence of the State: A Political Negotiation of Death." *Inter-Asia Cultural Studies: Movements* 2, no. 1: 7–22.

———. 2004. *The Politics of the Governed: Reflections on Popular Politics in Most of the World*. New Delhi: Permanent Black.

Chen, Chin-pao. 2000. "Bezel-Nut Beauties." *Inter-Asia Cultural Studies: Movements* 1, no. 2: 301–4.

Chen, Fangming 陳芳明. 1990. *An Observation on Taiwan's Inner Democracy* (台灣內部民主的觀察). Taipei: Independent Evening News.

Chen, Kuan-Hsing 陳光興. 1988. "'The Toad in the Garden': Stuart Hall on Thatcherism" ("花園裡的癩蝦蟆"). *Contemporary* (當代), April, 66–77.

———. 1992. *Media/Cultural Criticism's Popular Democratic Line of Flight* (媒體／文化批判的人民民主逃逸路線). Taipei: Tangshan.

———. 1994a. "The Imperialist Eye: The Cultural Imaginary of a Sub-empire and a Nation-state" (帝國之眼). *Taiwan: A Radical Quarterly in Social Studies* (台灣社會研究季刊) 17:149–222.

———. 1994b. "'Jie-du' *Cultural Imperialism*" ("解讀《文化帝國主義》"). Preface to the Chinese edition of *Cultural Imperialism* (文化帝國主義), by John Tomlinson, translated by Feng Jiansan. Taipei: Times Publishing House.

———. 1994c. "Positioning Positions: A New Internationalist Localism." *Positions: East Asia Cultures Critique* 3, no. 3: 680–710.

———. 1996. "Not Yet the Postcolonial Era: The (Super) Nation-State and Transnationalism of Cultural Studies." *Cultural Studies* 10, no. 1: 37–70.

———, ed. 2000. *Partha Chatterjee Seminar: Locating Political Society: Modernity, State Violence and Postcolonial Democracy* (發現政治社會). Taipei: Chu-liu.

———. 2001a "America in East Asia: The Club 51 Syndrome." *New Left Review*, 12 (November-December): 73–87.

———. 2001b. "Intellectual/Political Commitments: An Interview with Partha Chatterjee." *Inter-Asia Cultural Studies: Movements* 2, no. 1: 23–34.

Chen, Kuan-Hsing, and Chua Beng Huat. 2007. "Introduction: The *Inter-Asia Cultural Studies: Movements* Project." *Inter-Asia Cultural Studies Reader*, edited by Kuan-Hsing Chen and Chua Beng Huat, 1–6. London: Routledge.

Chen, Shi-he 陳思和. 1997. *Self-selected Works* (自選集). Guilin: Guangxi Normal University Press.

Chen, Tsun-shing 陳傳興 1994. "Race Discourse and Class Writing" ("種族論述與階級書寫"). Conference on Chinese Novels in Taiwan, Hong Kong and Mainland China, 40–90 (兩岸三邊華文小說研討論會), Taipei.

Chen, Ying-zhen 陳映真. 1998. "The Making of Taiwan's Americanization" ("台灣的美國化改造"). Preface to *The Trip of Return* (回歸的旅途) by Dan Yang 丹陽, 1–14. Taipei: Renjian.

Ch'ien, Edward T. 1986. *Chiao Hung and the Restructuring of Neo-Confucianism in the Late Ming*. New York: Columbia University Press.

Ching, Leo T. S. 2001. *Becoming "Japanese": Colonial Taiwan and the Politics of Identity Formation*. Berkeley: University of California Press.

Cho, Haejoang 趙惠淨. 1999. "Constructing and Deconstructing 'Koreanness' in the 1990s South Korea" ("建構與解構九０年代的韓國性"). Translated by Chia-hsuan Lin. *Taiwan: A Radical Quarterly in Social Studies* (台灣社會研究季刊) 33:65–102.

Cho Han, Haejoang. 2000. "'You Are Entrapped in an Imaginary Well': The Formation of Subjectivity within Compressed Development—A Feminist Critique of Modernity and Korean Culture." *Inter-Asia Cultural Studies: Movements* 1, no. 1: 49–70.

Cho, Hee-yeon. 2000a. "The Structure of the South Korean Developmental Regime and Its Transformation: Statist Mobilization and Authoritarian Integration in the Anticommunist Regimentation." *Inter-Asia Cultural Studies: Movements* 1, no. 3: 408–26.

———. 2000b. "Democratic Transition and Social Movement Change in South Korea." *The Journal of Sungkonghoe University* 15: 9–48.

Cho, Hee-yeon and Kuan-Hsing Chen. 2005. "Bandung/Third Worldism." Special issue, *Inter-Asia Cultural Studies: Movements* 6, no. 4.

Cho, Hee-yeon and Won-soon Park. 2002. "Democratic Reform and Civic Movements in South Korea." *Joint U.S.-Korea Academic Studies* 12, no. 2: 81–102.

Chon, Shi-yong. 2000. "Tearful Greetings End Years of Separation: Korean Families Meet in Seoul, Pyongyang." *The Korean Herald*, 16 August.

Chou, Wan-yao. 1996. "The *Kominka* Movement in Taiwan and Korea: Comparisons and Interpretations." *The Japanese Wartime Empire, 1931–1945*, edited by Peter Duus, Ramon H. Myers, and Mark R. Peattie, 40–70. Princeton, N.J.: Princeton University Press.

Chou, Wei-ling. 1998. *A Date with the U.S. — The Ultimate Resolution of Taiwan's Future: Taiwan Becomes a State of the U.S. in 2013; Say Yes to America* (與美國有約). Taipei: International Village.

Chua, Beng Huat. 1998. "Culture, Multiracialism, and National Identity in Singapore." *Trajectories: Inter-Asia Cultural Studies*, edited by Kuan-Hsing Chen, 186–205. London: Routledge.

Chun, Allen, and A. B. Shamsul. 2001. "Other 'Routes': The Critical Challenges for Asian Academia." Introduction to special issue "Critical Challenges for Asian Academia." *Inter-Asia Cultural Studies: Movements* 2, no. 2: 167–76.

Constantino, Renato. 1990. *The Philippines: The Continuing Past*. Quezon City, the Philippines: Foundation for Nationalist Studies.

———. 1991. *The Making of a Filipino: A Story of Philippine Colonial Politics*. Quezon City, the Philippines: Malaya Books.

———. 1992. *The Philippines: A Past Revisited (Pre-Spanish–1941)*. Quezon City, the Philippines: Foundation for Nationalist Studies.

Cruikshank, Margritte. 1992. *The Gay and Lesbian Liberation Movement*. New York: Routledge.

Cumings, Bruce. 1981 and 1990. *The Origins of the Korean War*. 2 vols. Princeton, N.J.: Princeton University Press.

———. 1984. "The Legacy of Japanese Colonialism in Korea." *The Japanese Colonial Empire, 1895–1945*, edited by Ramon H. Myers and Mark R. Peattie, 478–96. Princeton, N.J.: Princeton University Press.

———. 1999. *Parallax Visions: Making Sense of American–East Asian Relations at the End of the Century*. Durham, N.C.: Duke University Press.

David, Kumar, and Santasilan Kadirgamar, eds. 1989. *Ethnicity: Identity, Conflict, Crisis*. Hong Kong: ARENA Press.

Deng, Zheng-lai 鄧正來. 2002. "Introduction: State and Civil Society" ("導論：國家與市民社會"). *State and Civil Society: A Social Theory Approach* (國家與市民社會：一種社會理論的研究路徑), edited by Deng Zheng-lai and J. C. Alexander, 1–21. Beijing: Central Compilation and Translation Press.

Deshpande, Satish. 2001. "Disciplinary Predicaments: Sociology and Anthropology in Post-colonial India." *Inter-Asia Cultural Studies: Movements* 2, no. 2: 247–60.

Dikotter, Frank. 1992. *The Discourse of Race in Modern China*. Palo Alto, Calif.: Stanford University Press.

Ding, Naifei. 2000. "Prostitutes, Parasites and the House of State Feminism." *Inter-Asia Cultural Studies: Movements* 1, no. 2: 97–108.

Dirlik, Arif. 1997. "Eurocentrism, the Fatal Distraction? Globalism, Postcolonialism and the Disavowal of History." Paper presented at the Colonialism and Its Discontents Conference, Academia Sinica, Taipei.

"Disclosing the 'Anti-war, Anti-US, Anti-Taiwan' Syllogism of the Pro-China Force Conspiracy" ("揭穿親中勢力反戰、反美、反台的三段論陰謀"). 2003. *Taiwan Daily* (台灣日報), 26 March.

Dower, John W. 1999. *Embracing Defeat: Japan in the Wake of World War II.* New York: W. W. Norton.

Duara, Prasenjit. 2003. *Sovereignty and Authenticity: Manchukuo and the East Asia Modern.* Lanham, Md.: Rowman and Littlefield.

Duras, Marguerite. 1986. *The Lover.* Translated by Barbara Bray. New York: Harper and Row.

Epstein, Maram. 1998. "Confucian Imperialism and Masculine Chinese Identity in the Novel *Yesou Puyan.*" Paper presented at the 1998 Inter-Asia Cultural Studies Conference on Problematising "Asia," Taipei.

Fanon, Frantz. 1967 [1952]. *Black Skin, White Masks.* Translated by Charles Lam Markmann. New York: Grove.

―――. 1968 [1961]. *The Wretched of the Earth.* Translated by Constance Farrington. New York: Grove.

Foucault, Michel. 1988. *The History of Sexuality: An Introduction.* Translated by Robert Hurley. New York: Vintage.

Fu, Jianchung 傅建中. 2005. "Political Advertisement Published in Washington D.C.—'Taiwan Defense Alliance' Calls for the U.S. to Take over Taiwan" ("政治廣告登上華府 保台大聯盟籲美接管台灣"). *China Times* (中國時報), 21 September.

Fuss, Diana. 1994. "Interior Colonies: Frantz Fanon and the Politics of Identification." *Diacritics* 24, nos. 2–3: 20–42.

Garcia, Neil. 1996. *Philippine Gay Culture: The Last 30 Years—Binabae to Bakla, Silahis to MSM.* Quezon City, the Philippines: University of the Philippines Press.

Gauhar, Altaf. 1987. "Asia: The Experience of the Sub-continent." *Decolonization and After: The Future of the Third World,* edited by Bruno Kreisky and Humayun Gauhar, 51–61. London: Southern Publications.

Gu, Xiuxian 顧秀賢. 1993. "Preface: Yang Zhao, Cultural Critique and His Enemy" ("楊照，文化批判和他的敵人，序"). *Yang Zhao: Thinking at the Threshold* (臨界點上的思索), 1–5. Taipei: Zili Wanbao.

Hage, Ghassan. 1993. "Republicanism, Multiculturalism, Zoology." *Communal/ Plural* 2: 113–38.

Hall, Catherine. 2002. *Civilising Subjects: Metropole and Colony in the English Imagination 1830–1867.* Cambridge: Polity.

Hall, Stuart. 1980. "Popular Democracy vs. Authoritarian Populism: Two Ways of Taking Democracy Seriously." *Marxism and Democracy,* edited by A. Hunt, 157–85. London: Lawrence and Wishart.

———. 1992a. "The Question of Cultural Identity." *Modernity and Its Futures,* edited by Stuart Hall, David Held, and Tony McGrew, 274–316. Cambridge: Polity.

———. 1992b. "The West and the Rest: Discourse and Power." *Formations of Modernity,* edited by Stuart Hall and Bram Gieben, 275–332. Cambridge: Polity.

———. 1995. "Negotiating Caribbean Identities." *New Left Review* no. 209: 3–14.

Hamashita, Takeshi. 2003. "Tribute and Treaties: Maritime Asia and Treaty Port Networks in the Era of Negotiation, 1800–1900." *The Resurgence of East Asia: 500, 150 and 50 Year Perspectives,* edited by Giovanni Arrighi, Takeshi Hamashita, and Mark Selden, 17–50. London: Routledge.

Hanasaki, Kōhei. 2000. "Decolonialization and Assumption of War Responsibility." *Inter-Asia Cultural Studies: Movements* 1, no. 1: 71–84.

Hardt, Michael, and Antonio Negri. 2000. *Empire.* Cambridge: Harvard University Press.

Hechter, Michael. 1975. *Internal Colonialism: The Celtic Fringe in British National Development, 1536–1966.* Berkeley: University of California Press.

Heng, Geraldine, and Janadas Devan. 1992. "State Fatherhood: The Politics of Nationalism, Sexuality and Race in Singapore." *Nationalisms and Sexualities,* edited by Andrew Parker, Mary Russo, Doris Summer, and Patricia Yaeger, 343–64. London: Routledge.

Ho, Josephine. 2000. "Professionalization and Self-empowerment: Conversations with Taiwanese Sex Workers." *Inter-Asia Cultural Studies: Movements* 1, no. 2: 97–108.

Hobson, J. A. 1965 [1902]. *Imperialism: A Study.* Introduction by Philip Siegelman. Ann Arbor: University of Michigan Press.

Hofstadter, Richard. 1965. *Social Darwinism in American Thought.* New York: Braziller.

Huang, Yulin 黃毓麟. 1994. "Facing the South: What for?" ("南向，究竟為那椿"). *China Times* (中國時報), 31 March.

Huntington, Samuel P. 1993. "The Clash of Civilizations?" *Foreign Affairs* 73, no. 3: 22–49.

Ichiang, Baluer, and Lawagau Laigelaer. 1992. "A History of Aboriginal Nations in Taiwan" ("台灣原住民族的發展史"). *Hunter's Culture* (獵人文化) 16: 30–41.

Ishihara, Shintaro 石原慎太郎, and Akio Morita 聖田昭夫. 1990. *The Japan that Can Say No* (一個可以說NO的日本). Translated by Lui Xiuqin. Taipei: Central Daily.

Jacques, Martin. 2002. "A Season in Paradise." *The Guardian*, 30 November.

———. 2006. "Europe's Contempt for Other Cultures Can't Be Sustained." *The Guardian*, 17 February.

Jansen, Marius B. 1984. "Japanese Imperialism: Late Meiji Perspectives." *The Japanese Colonial Empire, 1895–1945*, edited by Ramon H. Myers and Mark R. Peattie, 61–79. Princeton, N.J.: Princeton University Press.

Johnson, Chalmers. 2000. *Blowback: The Costs and Consequences of American Empire*. New York: Henry Holt.

Johnson, M. Dujon. 2007. *Race and Racism in the Chinas: Chinese Racial Attitudes towards Africans and African-Americans*. Bloomington, Ind.: Author House.

Joint Press Corps. 2000. "After 50 Years Two Korean Brothers Meet Again." *The Korean Herald*, 16 August.

Jones, Greta. 1980. *Social Darwinism and English Thought: The Interaction between Biological and Social Theory*. Brighton: Harvester.

Kaplan, Amy. 1993. " 'Left Alone with America': The Absence of Empire in the Study of American Culture." *Cultures of United States Imperialism*, edited by Amy Kaplan and Donald E. Pease, 3–21. Durham, N.C.: Duke University Press.

Karatani, Kōjin 柄谷行人. 1998. "Language and Nationalism: A Postscript" ("語言與民族主義：后記"). Paper presented at the Second Community of Knowledge International Conference (第二回知識共同體國際會議), Beijing Foreign Studies University.

Ker, Rey-ming 柯瑞明. 1996. *Taiwan Can Say No* (台灣可以說不). Taipei: Yeh-Chiang.

Kim, Seongnae. 1996. "Mourning Korean Modernity: Violence and the Memory of the Cheju Uprising." Work in progress.

———. 2000. "Mourning Korean Modernity in the Cheju April Third Incident." *Inter-Asia Cultural Studies: Movements* 1, no. 3: 461–76.

King, Heng-wei 金恒煒. 2003. "The Logic of 'Anti-War and Anti-America'" ("反戰反美的邏輯"). *Taiwan Daily* (台灣日報), 26 March.

Kreisky, Bruno, and Humayun Gauhar. 1987. Introduction to *Decolonization and After: The Future of the Third World*, edited by Bruno Kreisky and Humayun Gauhar, 1–7. London: Southern Publications.

Laclau, Ernesto. 1977. *Politics and Ideology in Marxist Theory*. London: Verso.

Lamming, George. 1992 [1960]. *The Pleasures of Exile*. Foreword by Sandra Pou-chet Paquet. Ann Arbor: University of Michigan Press.

Lee, Geok Boi. 1992. *Syonan: Singapore under the Japanese (1942–45)*. Singapore: Singapore Heritage Society.

Lee, Yuan-tseh. 1994. "The Fifth Meeting of the Education Committee." *Lifa-yuan (Legislative Yuan) Bulletin* 83, no. 21: 285–372.

Lefebvre, Henri. 1976 [1973]. *The Survival of Capitalism: Reproduction of the Rela-tions of Production*. Translated by Frank Bryant. New York: St. Martin.

———. 1991 [1974]. *The Production of Space*. Translated by Donald Nicholson-Smith. Malden, Mass.: Blackwell.

Lenin, V. I. 1939 [1917]. *Imperialism in the Highest Stage of Capitalism*. New York: International.

Li, Guangzhen 李光真. 1994. "The Vanguard of Critical Discourse—An Inter-view with Yang Zhao" ("批判論述的尖兵—楊照專訪"). *Guanghua* (光華) 2:91–92.

Li, Hongxi. 1994. Editor's introduction to "Taiwan under the Flag of the Sun." Special issue, *Japan Digest*, no. 100.

Lin, Huazhou 林華洲. 1992. "Aboriginals in History" ("歷史上的原住民"). *Hunter's Culture* (獵人文化) 16:42–49.

Liu, Jen-peng 劉人鵬. 2000. *Feminist Discourse in Early Modern China: Nation, Translation and Sexual Politics* (近代中國女權論述：國族、翻譯與性別政治). Taipei: Student Bookstore.

———. 2001. "The Disposition of Hierarchy and Late Qing Discourse of 'Gen-der Equality.'" *Inter-Asia Cultural Studies: Movements* 2, no. 1: 69–80.

———. 2002. "On the Margin of 'Classics' and 'Human'" ("在「經典」與「人類」的旁邊"). *Tsing Hua Journal of China Studies* (清華學報) 32, no. 1: 167–202.

Liu, Jen-peng and Ding Naifei. 2005. "Reticent Poetic, Queer Politics." *Inter-Asia Cultural Studies: Movements* 6, no. 1: 30–55.

Liu, Jen-peng, Amie Perry, and Ding Naifei. 2007. *Penumbrae Query Shadow: Queer Reading Tactics*. Taoyuan, Taiwan: Center for the Study of Sexualities, National Central University.

Liu, Kexiang 劉克襄. 1994. "A Disappeared Line" ("一條消失的線"). *China Times* (中國時報), 2 March.

Liu, Lydia H. 1994. *Translingual Practices*. Palo Alto, Calif.: Stanford University Press.

Liu, Ping. 2004. "Chen's Inauguration Speech Read and Approved by the U.S." *China Times*, 5 June.

Luo, Zhi-tian 羅志田. 1998. "Nationalist Concerns in Hu Shih's Thought on Cosmopolitanism" ("胡適世界主義思想中民族主義的關切"). *Nationalism and Modern Thought in China* (民族主義與中國現代思想), 193–221. Taipei: Dung-da.

Luxemburg, Rosa. 1976 [1909]. *The National Question: Selected Writings of Rosa Luxemburg,* edited by Horace B. Davis. New York: Monthly Review.

Magdoff, Harry. 1978. *Imperialism: From the Colonial Age to the Present.* New York: Monthly Review.

Malialiaves, Monanen 莫那能. 1989. "Burning" (燃燒). *The Beautiful Rice Straw* (美麗的稻穗). Taichung, Taiwan: Chen Xing.

Mannoni, Octave. 1990 [1950]. *Prospero and Caliban: The Psychology of Colonization.* Translated by Pamela Powesland. Ann Arbor: University of Michigan Press.

Maruyama, Masao. 1963. *Thought and Behaviour in Modern Japanese Politics.* Edited by Ivan Morris. London: Oxford University Press.

Marx, Karl. 1898 [1852]. *The Eighteenth Brumaire of Louis Bonaparte.* Translated by Daniel De Leon. New York: International Publishing.

Memmi, Albert. 1991 [1957]. *The Colonizer and the Colonized.* Translated by Howard Greenfeld, introduction by Jean-Paul Sartre. Boston, Mass.: Beacon Press.

Mignolo, Walter D., ed. 2007. "Globalization and the De-Colonial Option." Special issue, *Cultural Studies* 21, nos. 2–3.

Miyoshi, Masao. 1993. "A Borderless World? From Colonialism to Transnationalism and the Decline of the Nation-state." *Critical Inquiry* 19: 726–51.

Mizoguchi, Yūzō 溝口雄三. 1996 [1989]. *China as Method* (日本人視野中的中國學). Translated by Li Suping 李甦平, Gong Ying 龔穎, and Xu Tao 徐滔. Beijing: Chinese People's University Press.

———. 2001. "Creating Space for a Sino-Japan Community of Knowledge" ("創造日中間知識共同空間"). *Du-Shu* (讀書), May Issue, 3–11.

Modern History of Three East Asian Countries: Learning from History, Facing the Future, Building a New Peaceful and Friendly Framework Together (東亞三國的近現代史). 2005. Beijing: Social Sciences Academic Press.

Mutō, Ichiyō. 1998. "Alliance of Hope and Challenges of Global Democracy." *Trajectories: Inter-Asia Cultural Studies,* edited by Kuan-Hsing Chen, 346–59. London: Routledge.

Myers, Ramon H., and Mark R. Peattie, eds. 1984. *The Japanese Colonial Empire, 1895–1945.* Princeton, N.J.: Princeton University Press.

Nan, Tian-men 南天門. 1989. "Anti-communism Is Not Equivalent to Democracy" ("反共不等於民主"). *Independent Daily* (自立早報), 8 June.

Nandy, Ashis. 1983. *The Intimate Enemy: Loss and Recovery of Self under Colonialism.* Bombay: Oxford University Press.

————. 1994. *The Illegitimacy of Nationalism: Rabindranath Tagore and the Politics of Self.* New Delhi: Oxford University Press.

Ngugi wa Thiong'o. 1986. *Decolonising the Mind: The Politics of Language in African Literature.* Nairobi: Heinemann Kenya.

Niranjana, Tejaswini. 1992. *Siting Translation: History, Post-structuralism and the Colonial Context.* Berkeley: University of California Press.

————. 2000. "Alternative Frames? Questions for Comparative Research in the Third World." *Inter-Asia Cultural Studies: Movements* 1, no. 1: 97–108.

Peattie, Mark R. 1984. "Japanese Attitudes towards Colonialism." *The Japanese Colonial Empire, 1895–1945,* edited by Ramon H. Myers and Mark R. Peattie, 80–127. Princeton, N.J.: Princeton University Press.

————. 1996. "Nanshin: The 'Southward Advance,' 1931–1941, as a Prelude to the Japanese Occupation of Southeast Asia." *The Japanese Wartime Empire, 1931–1945,* edited by Peter Duus, Ramon H. Myers, and Mark R. Peattie, 189–242. Princeton, N.J.: Princeton University Press.

Ping, Fei 平非, ed. 1994. "Women's Country, Home (Fake) Identity" (女人國、家（假）認同). Special issue of *Isle Margins* (島嶼邊緣), no. 9.

Pletsch, Carl E. 1981. "The Three Worlds, or the Division of Social Scientific Labor, circa 1950–1975." *Comparative Studies in Society and History* 23:565–96.

Qian, Liqun. 2005. "The World View of My Generation." *Inter-Asia Cultural Studies: Movements* 6, no. 4: 565–34.

Qiu, Guifen 邱貴芬. 1992. "Discovering Taiwan: Constructing Postcolonial Discourse in Taiwan" ("發現台灣：建構台灣後殖民論述"). Paper presented at the 16th Comparative Literature Conference (比較文學會議), Chungli, Taiwan.

Robocop 機器戰警. 1991. *Taiwan's New Oppositional Movement: Road to New Democracy* (台灣的新反對運動——到新民主之路). Taipei: Tang-san.

Ross, Andrew, and Kristin Ross, eds. 2004. *Anti-Americanism.* New York: New York University Press.

Said, Edward. 1979. *Orientalism.* New York: Vintage Books.

————. 1993. *Culture and Imperialism.* New York: Knopf.

Sakai, Naoki. 1988. "Modernity and Its Critique: The Problem of Universalism and Particularism." *The South Atlantic Quarterly* 87, no. 3: 475–504.

————. 1997. *Translation and Subjectivity: On "Japan" and Cultural Nationalism.* Minneapolis: University of Minnesota Press.

Schiller, Herbert. 1991. "Not Yet the Post-imperialist Era." *Critical Studies in Mass Communication* 8:13–28.

Sedgwick, Eve Kosofsky. 1985. *Between Men: English Literature and Male Homosocial Desire.* New York: Columbia University Press.

Shamsul, A. B. 2001. "Social Science in Southeast Asia Observed: A Malaysian Viewpoint." *Inter-Asia Cultural Studies: Movements* 2, no. 2: 177–98.

Shen, Sung-chiao 沈松僑, and Chien Yung-xiang 錢永祥. 1999. "Delimiting China: Discourse of 'Guomin' (國民) and the Construction of Chinese Nationality in Late Qing." Paper presented at the Conference on Nationalism: East Asia Experience, Academia Sinica, Taipei.

Shi, Ming 史明. 1980. *The Four-Hundred-Year History of the Taiwanese* (台灣人四百年史). Taipei: Pengdao Culture.

Shi, Minhui 施敏輝, ed. 1988. *The Selected Collection of Taiwan Consciousness Debate* (台灣意識論戰選集：台灣結與中國結的總決算).Taipei: Chien-wei.

Shi, Si-hung 史思虹. 1989. "Populism" (人民主義). *China Tribune* (中國論壇), no. 336: 34–42.

Shi, Wei. 2005. "Undoing Chineseness in Contemporary Chinese Cinemas." Ph.D. dissertation, University of London.

Shi, Xinyi 史新義. 1988. "We Are All Sons and Daughters of the Taiwanese Nation: The Taiwanese Nation and Taiwanese Nationalism, Part I" ("我們都是台灣民族兒女：台灣民族與台灣民族主義（上）"). *Taiwan New Culture* (台灣新文化) 16:69–91.

Shin, Gi Wook. 2002. "Marxism, Anti-Americanism, and Democracy in South Korea: An Examination of Nationalist Intellectual Discourse." *New Asian Marxisms*, edited by Tani E. Barlow, 359–84. Durham, N.C.: Duke University Press.

———. 2005. "Asianism in Korea's Politics of Identity." *Inter-Asia Cultural Studies: Movements* 6, no. 4: 616–30.

Soja, Edward. 1989. *Postmodern Geographies: The Reassertion of Space in Critical Social Theory*. London: Verso.

Soja, Edward and Costis Hadjimichalis. 1985 [1977]. "Between Geographical Materialism and Spatial Fetishism: Some Observations on the Development of Marxist Spatial Analysis." Reprinted in "The Best of Antipode, 1969–1985." Special issue, *Antipode* 17, no. 2–3: 59–67, edited by Richard Peet.

Spivak, Gayatri. 1988. "Can the Subaltern Speak?" *Marxism and the Interpretation of Culture*, edited by Cary Nelson and Lawrence Grossberg, 271–313. Urbana: University of Illinois Press.

Sun, Ge 孫歌. 2000. "How does Asia mean?" *Inter-Asia Cultural Studies: Movements* 1, no. 1: 13–48; no. 2: 319–342.

———. 2001a. "Confronting the Entanglement of History" ("直面相互纏繞的歷史"). *Du-Shu* (讀書), May: 19–26.

———. 2001b. "Globalization and Cultural Difference: Thoughts on the Situation of Trans-cultural Knowledge." Translated by Allen Chun. *Inter-Asia Cultural Studies: Movements* 2, no. 2: 261–76.

Sundaram, Jomo Kwame. 1989. "A Nationalist Alternative for Malaysia?" *Partisan Scholarship*, edited by Peter Limqueco, 213–32. Manila: Journal of Contemporary Asia Publishers.

Sung, Chiang 宋強. 1996. *China Can Say No* (中國可以說不). Taipei: Renjiang.

Suryadinata, Leo. 1975. *Primubi Indonesians, the Chinese Minority and China*. Kuala Lumpur: Heinemann.

Takeuchi, Yoshimi 竹內好. 2005a [1960]. "Asia as Method." *What Is Modernity? Writings of Takeuchi Yoshimi*, edited and translated by Richard F. Calichman, 149–65. New York: Columbia University Press.

———. 2005b [1952]. "Independence and Ideal of the Nation" ("國家的獨立與理想"). *Overcoming the Modern* (近代的超克), edited by Sun Ge 孫歌, and translated by Li Dongmu 李東木, Zhao Jinghua 趙京華, and Sun Ge, 272–84. Beijing: Sanlian.

Tambiah, S. J. 1986. *Sri Lanka: Ethnic Fratricide and the Dismantling of Democracy*. Chicago: University of Chicago Press.

Tan, Gerald. 1993. "The Next NICs of Asia." *Third World Quarterly* 14, no. 1: 57–73.

Tan, Shi 譚石. 1994. "A Literary Critic Who Ought Not to Be Absent" ("不該缺席的文評家"). *China Times* (中國時報), 31 March.

Tomlinson, John. 1991. *Cultural Imperialism: A Critical Introduction*. Baltimore, Md.: The Johns Hopkins University Press.

Toriyama, Atsushi. 2003. "Okinawa's 'Postwar': Some Observations on the Formation of American Military Bases in the Aftermath of Terrestrial Warfare." *Inter-Asia Cultural Studies: Movements* 4, no. 3: 400–418.

Vergès, Françoise. 1995. "Monsters and Revolutionaries: Colonial Family Romance and Métissage." PhD dissertation, University of California, Berkeley.

Wang, Cheng-hwann 王振寰. 1993. "The Formation of an Alliance between State and Corporate Sectors in Taiwan" ("台灣新政商關係的形成與政治轉型"). *Taiwan: A Radical Quarterly in Social Studies* (台灣社會研究), no. 14: 123–63.

———. 1994. "Lee Teng-hui Goes to Nayang" (李登輝下南洋). *Taiwan's Labor Movement* (台灣工運), no. 5: 70–72.

Wang, Fuchang 王甫昌. 1992. "The Nature of Integrating Provinciality: An Examination of Experience and Theory" ("省籍融合的本質:一個經驗與理論的探討"). *Ethnic Relation and National Identity* (族群關係與國家認同), edited by Zhang Maogui 張茂桂, 53–100. Taipei: Institute for National Policy Research.

Wang, Hui 汪暉. 2002. "Imagining Asia: A Genealogical Analysis" ("亞洲想像的系譜學"). *Horizons* (視界) 8:144–208.

————. 2004. *The Rise of Modern Chinese Thought* (現代中國思想的興起). Vol. 1. Beijing: Sanlian.

Wang, Ji-shih 王緝思, ed. 1995. *Civilization and International Politics: Chinese Scholars on Huntington's Theory of the "Clash of Civilization."* (文明與國際政治—中國學者評亨廷頓的文明衝突). Shanghai: People's Publisher.

Wittfogel, Karl A. 1985 [1929]. "Geopolitics, Geographical Materialism and Marxism." Translated by G. L. Ulmen. *Antipode* 17, no. 1: 21–72.

Wu, Micha 吳密察. 1991. *Research on Taiwan Modern History* (台灣近代史研究). Taipei: Daosiang.

————. 1994. "Reconsidering Taiwan's location" (重新認識台灣的位置). *China Times* (中國時報), 3 March.

Wu, Ping-fei 吳平非. 1989. "What Is Popular Democracy?" ("什麼是人民民主？") *Independent Daily* (自立早報), 20 June.

Wu, Sanlian 吳三連, and Cai Peihuo 蔡培火. 1971. *A History of the Taiwan Nationalist Movement* (台灣民族運動史). Taipei: Independent Evening News.

Wuo, Young-Ie 吳永毅. 1988. "State, Capital and Labor in Taiwan's Construction Industry: A Case Study of an Informal Contractor" ("論營造業中的家—資本—勞動的關係——由非正式部門的個案研究所作的推論"). *Taiwan: A Radical Quarterly in Social Studies* (台灣社會研究季刊) 1, nos. 2–3: 211–30.

————. 1993. "Banana, Pig-King, Nation: Mainlanders' National Identity in 'Returning Home' Cinema" ("香蕉、豬公、國家：返鄉電影中外省人的國家認同"). *Chung-Wai Literary Monthly* (中外文學) 22, no. 1: 32–44.

————. 1994. "The Difference between Localism and the Local Left—The Hospitality and Hostility in the Premiere Forum of 'Taiwanese in Mainland'" ("一字之差的本土派和本土左派—《台胞》首映座談會的善意與敵意"). *Isle Margins* (島嶼邊緣) 9: 100–106.

Xu, Zongmao 徐宗懋. 1994. "Critical Reflections on the Ecology of Dialogues on the 'Southward policy'" ("用「南向熱」孵化玫瑰園？反省國內「南向政策」的對話生態"). *China Times Evening News* (中時晚報), 26 February.

Yamanouchi, Yasushi, J. Victor Koschmann, and Rykuichi Narita, eds. 1998. *Total War and "Modernization."* Ithaca, N.Y.: East Asia Program, Cornell University.

Yang, Bichuan 楊碧川. 1988. *A History of the Taiwanese Resistance during the Japanese Occupation* (日據時代台灣人反抗史). Taipei: Daosiang.

Yang, Bo 楊波. 1994. "Mysterious Chinese" ("神祕的華人"). *China Times* (中國時報), 3 March.

Yang, Changzhen 楊長鎮. 1994. "Gazing at Low Lattitude: Taiwan and the 'Southeast Asia Movement'" ("凝視低緯度：台灣與東南亞運動"). *China Times* (中國時報), 2 March.

Yang, Zhao 楊照. 1993a. "Memorandum of the Past" ("往事追憶錄"). *United Literature* (聯合文學) 101:54–102.

———. 1993b. *Thinking at the Threshold* (臨界點上的思索). Taipei: Zili Wanbao.

———. 1994. "From the Periphery of China to the Center of *Nanyang*: A Neglected Episode of History" (從中國的邊陲到南洋的中心：一段被忽略的歷史). *China Times* (中國時報), 2–4 March.

Yoo, Sun-young. 2001. "Embodiment of American Modernity in Colonial Korea." Translated by Francis Lee Dae Hoon. *Inter-Asia Cultural Studies: Movements* 2, no. 3: 423–42.

Yoshimi, Shunya. 2000. "Consuming America: From Symbol to System." *Patterns of Consumption of Asia's New Rich*, edited by Chua Beng Huat, 202–24. London: Routledge.

———. 2003. "'America' as Desire and Violence: Americanicanization in Postwar Japan and Asia During the Cold War." *Inter-Asia Cultural Studies: Movements* 4, no. 3: 433–50.

Zhang, Lingzhu. 1994. "First Action to Support President Lee's 'Southward Policy.'" *China Times*, 20 February.

Zhang, Maogui 張茂桂. 1992. "Provinciality and Nationalism: Questions and Reflection" ("省籍問題與民族主義：問題與反省"). *Ethnic Relation and National Identity* (省籍—族群與國家認同), edited by Zhang Maogui, 233–78. Taipei: Institute for National Policy Research.

Zhang, Yanxian 張炎憲. 1994. "Fifty Years of Blood and Tears in Politics" ("五十年政治血淚"). *Japan Digest* (日本文摘), no. 100: 16–40.

Zheng, Hong-sheng. 2002. "How Could a Great Reconciliation Become Possible?" Translated by Oiwan Lam. *Inter-Asia Cultural Studies: Movements* 3, no. 1: 107–13.

Academia Sinica, 27, 272 nn. 13–14

Algeria, 23, 81

American-centrism, 107, 174, 219

Americanism: as internal to East Asian subjectivity, 8, 10, 115, 120, 123, 127, 132, 161, 163–67, 170–72, 175, 176–81, 186–87, 190, 191, 198, 279 n. 6

AMPO Treaty, 194, 281 n. 26

anti-American sentiment, 178–84, 186, 187, 280 n. 14

anti-Chinese sentiment: in Southeast Asia, 32; in Taiwan, 57, 132–33

anticommunism: as alibi for authoritarianism, 123, 135; in South Korea, 123, 175–76, 187, 191, 288; in Taiwan, 56–57, 115, 118, 123, 135–37, 153, 157, 166–67, 190, 231

anticommunism–pro-Americanism structure, 7–10, 115, 153, 175, 199, 208, 271 n. 19; in Taiwan and South Korea, 121, 123, 186–91

anti-imperialism, 23, 47, 115, 151–52, 187, 188

anti-Japanese sentiment: in East Asia, 122, 191; in Southeast Asia, 31; in Taiwan, 129, 149–50, 278 n. 25

area studies, 3, 28, 226, 253; Asian studies, xv, 1–3, 225–27, 253–54; Chūgokugaku, 246–54, 284 n. 27

ASEAN (Association of South East Asian Nations), 5, 15, 23, 31, 32, 183, 214, 234, 287

Asia: as center of global capitalism, 67–68, 181–82; meanings of, x, 212–16, 254, 282; nationalism in, ix, 22–23, 123; regionalization of, 12–13, 15, 120, 121, 122, 197–98, 203, 213–15, 246, 251, 268, 270 n. 18; rise of, 3, 214, 267, 269 n. 2

Asia as method, xv, 15, 284 n. 22; meanings of, 211–16, 246; practices of, xii, 223, 251, 254–55, 268, 282. See also inter-referencing

Asianism, 13, 121, 246, 251, 270 n. 18. See also Greater East Asia Co-Prosperity Sphere; regionalization: of Asia

Asian studies, 28; in Asia, xv, 1–3, 225–27, 253–54. See also Chūgokugaku; inter-referencing; Southeast Asia project

Asian-values debate, 123, 223, 245, 262, 287. See also Neo-Confucianism

assimilation: colonization and, 86, 261; hybridity and, 98; imperialization vs., 6–7, 200–201, 269 n. 8; multiculturalism vs., 97

Australia, 94, 97, 184, 215, 280 n. 7

Banana Paradise (Wang), 124, 135–49, 155

Bandung Conference, 12, 20, 192, 271
n. 6, 287

base-entity (jǐtǐ), 245, 248–53, 255, 275
n. 3

běnshěng rén (Taiwanese), 55, 124–25,
273 n. 22, 287; Japanese/colonial
subjectivity of, 133–34, 149–56;
solidarity with wàishěng rén, 139,
141. *See also* wàishěng rén

běnshěng–wàishěng conflict, 41–44,
138–39, 146–54, 278 n. 27; politicization of, xiv, 9, 53–59, 135, 190, 232;
as provincial register contradiction, 124–25, 142, 155–57, 277 n. 15;
Taiwan consciousness vs. Chinese
nationalism and, 55–59, 135

Black Skin, White Masks (Fanon), 14,
40, 74, 77–78, 275 n. 3

black tide (black tide cultural sphere),
27–31

Blaut, James, 54, 108–9

Bush, George H. W., 182

Bush, George W., 15–16, 183–85

capitalism: colonialism and the development of, 22, 108–9; cultural
studies and, 21, 24, 66; East Asian
zone of, 7, 12, 15, 18, 121, 181, 199,
202; global centers of, 67, 108;
globalization and, 4, 9, 165, 208,
230; hierarchy of nations under
global, 18, 20, 62; identity and,
38–40, 96, 263; local history's
encounter with global, 66, 214,
215; Marxist analysis of, 69, 70–71,
104–6, 224; nation-state and, 23, 82,
108; neocolonial imperialism and,
22–23, 165, 174; radical plural opportunism and, 173; regionalization

of global, 178, 214; socialism vs., 8,
11–12, 118, 252

Césaire, Aimé, 77, 78, 82, 274 n. 2, 275
n. 3

Chakrabarty, Dipesh, 218–19

Chatterjee, Partha, x, 211, 216, 223–30,
233–37, 241, 243–45, 255

Cheju Uprising, 123–24, 175–76, 288

Chen Shui-bian, 153, 242, 288; assassination attempt on, 189, 281 n. 21;
civil society and, 241, 283 n. 17;
U.S.–Taiwan relations under, 184,
188–89, 191. *See also* DPP

Chen Ying-zhen, x, 68, 115, 161, 276
n. 4

Chiang Ching-kuo, 56–58, 170, 273
n. 23, 277 n. 14

Chiang Kai-shek, 58, 118, 170, 198, 277
n. 14, 277 n. 18, 289

Ch'ien, Edward T., 98–99

China: Asia's relation to, 5, 12–13, 213–
15, 260; civilizationalism in, 93–94;
cultural, 37, 39–41, 171; běnshěng
rén disdain for, 133–34, 152; decolonization and deimperialization in,
12, 68, 197, 201–2; imperialism in,
5–6, 118, 121–22, 150–52, 157, 197,
247; Japan's relationship with, 11,
191, 196, 246–47; mínjiān society
in, 237–40; modernity of, 12, 151,
246–50; modernization of, 11, 157,
237, 246–48, 265; nationalism in,
12, 22, 151–52; opening of, 7–8, 12,
56, 61, 107, 144, 181; responses to
colonialism and imperialism of,
11–12, 150–52; rise of, 12–13, 191,
196–99, 214, 258, 267, 269 n. 2;
socialist revolution in, 11–12, 31,
32, 201, 252; as Taiwanese cultural

referent, 127–28, 132–33; Taiwanese investment in, 17–19, 62; Taiwanese reconciliation with, 124, 156–57, 171, 190–2; Taiwanese visits to, 9, 117–18, 142–44; as Taiwan's Other, 10, 56–57, 170; triumphalism in, 13, 258; U.S. as internal to subjectivity of, 120, 181, 198, 276 n. 6; U.S. relations with, 13, 181–84, 188–89, 197; the West vs., 12, 13, 41, 93, 181, 217. *See also* Greater China

China as Method, 246–55, 282

Chinese Civil War, 55, 146, 213, 273 n. 22, 288, 289; end of, 157, 191–92; as struggle over China's modernity, 11, 151–52

Chinese Communist Party (CCP), 150, 170, 280 n. 13, 288; authoritarianism of, 57, 197; defeat of the KMT, 11, 55, 151–52, 157; economic control over Greater China of, 47; as the KMT and DPP's Other, 10, 56, 61; KMT rapprochement with, 190–92. *See also* Chinese Civil War

Chinese empire, 5, 11, 31, 171, 197, 208, 260, 269 n. 1; identification with, xv, 198; oppressive legacy of, 6, 12–13, 197, 257; racism in, 259, 264–66, 267

Ching, Leo, 200–201

Chou Wei-ling (David C. Chou), 161–63, 280 nn. 8–9

Chua Beng Huat, 178

Chuang Tsu, 262–63

Chūgokugaku (Chinese studies), 246–54, 284 n. 27

Chun Doo-hwan, 187, 279 n. 30, 288

civilizationalism: decolonization and, xiii, 67, 81; as defense mechanism, 151; forms of, 93–94; imperial desire and, 178; little subjectivity and, 92–93; Nandy on, 69, 89–94, 219–21; nationalism and, 92, 94–95, 220–21; nativism as form of, 89, 94–95, 178; universalism and, 245

civil society: Gandhi's critique of, 234; mínjiān society vs., 238–41; political society and, 241–43; popular democracy's challenges to, 230–33; state and, 184, 224, 227–33, 241, 283 n. 17; strategic value of, 233; subaltern studies' critique of, 235–36; translations of in East Asia, 237, 244

Clash of Civilizations, The (Huntington), 94, 182, 259

Clinton, Bill, 182–83

Club 51: American dream of, 170–71; cold-war sensibility of, 167; deimperialization and, 164–65, 208; desire for security of, 166–67, 172–73; globalization and, 167, 173; history of, 162; imperial desire of, xv, 171, 173, 186, 200, 208; mainstream Taiwan politics and, 162, 185; media presence of, 161–62, 185; nationalism and, 167, 172; other 51st-state movements and, 163, 280 n. 7; Taiwan independence movement and, 163, 164, 167, 168, 190; U.S. policy support of, 161–62, 179, 185–86, 188; U.S. statehood and, xiv, 161–63, 190, 199, 279 n. 4

cold war: as colonial–postcolonial mediator, xiv, 8, 111, 149, 157, 175–76; decolonization and, 4, 67, 123, 124, 205; deimperialization and, 11, 193, 206; end of, 47, 67, 118–20, 157,

cold war (*continued*)
181–82, 184, 193–94; globalization
and, 9, 14, 67, 119, 182; legacy of, 10,
71, 118–19, 124, 167, 184; nationalism and, x, 123, 125, 159; structure,
7, 121–22, 135, 175, 180–81, 191, 205,
208. *See also* de–cold war
colonialism, 2, 80, 91, 220; civilizing
mission of, 73–74, 84–85, 87, 134,
261; cold war and, xiv, 8, 120–24,
149, 157, 175; continuing effects of,
14, 24, 68, 110–12, 121, 135; culture
and, 24–25, 84–85, 110–11; historical
responsibility for, 21–22, 153, 204–7,
266–67; history of, 5–7, 108–10;
imperialism vs., 6, 8, 200; as indigenous process, 220; internal, 22, 23,
41, 55, 84, 272 n. 11; modernization
and, 66, 84, 133–34; psychology of,
44–45, 50–51, 72–80, 94–97, 200,
275 n. 6; racism and, 77–78, 80, 83,
95, 97, 121; transition to capitalism
and, 22, 108–9. *See also* decolonization
Colonizer and the Colonized, The,
(Memmi), 74, 85–89
comfort women, 10, 11, 203, 288
comparative analysis. *See* inter-
referencing
Constantino, Renato, 31, 33
critical syncretism, xiii, 72, 99–102, 112
cultural imaginary, 108, 110–13; Asia
as, x, xv, 212, 223, 282; China as, 127,
151, 215, 260; civilizations as, 92, 151;
imperialist, 45, 60, 63, 65–66; Japan
as, 127, 133; Marxism as, 69; Taiwan
as part of Southeast Asia as, 25–26,
33, 37, 48–50, 52, 61; U.S., 127, 165,
173, 177, 178; the West as, 216, 222

cultural imperialism, 89, 176–77
Cultural Imperialism (Tomlinson), 21
cultural studies, 1, 111; Birmingham
tradition of, 101–2; as decolonization movement, 69, 72, 102, 112–13;
deimperialization and, 165–66;
methodologies and practices of,
xi, xvi, 21, 66–67, 102, 110–13; third
world and, xiii, 21, 24, 63–64, 69,
72, 102; universalism vs. particularism in, 245
Culture and Imperialism (Said), 24–25,
99–101, 111
Cumings, Bruce, 180–81

de–cold war, 208, 255, 268; Asia as
method and, 212; decolonization
and, 120–21, 123, 124, 201; defined,
x, 4, 120
decolonization, 13, 15–16, 255, 268;
civilizationalism as form of, 67, 81,
90, 94; of the colonizer, 75; critical discourses of, 68–69; critical
syncretism and, xiii, 72, 99–101,
112; of the cultural imaginary,
65–66, 111–12; cultural studies as
movement for, 69, 72, 102, 112–13;
de–cold war and, 120–21, 123, 124,
201; deimperialization vs., 3–4, 6,
23, 173, 200, 201; forms/effects of,
11–12, 66–67, 81; Gandhi on, 234;
geocolonial historical materialism
and, 65, 102, 111; incompleteness
of, vii, xiii, 14–15, 53, 61, 63, 65, 112,
204–8; interrupted by cold war, 4,
8–10, 121, 205; Marxism and, 69–72,
106; nationalism as form of, 23,
81–84, 94, 112, 125, 164; nativism
as form of, 9, 65, 67, 81, 84–89, 94;

psychology of, 72–80, 96–97, 111; subjectivity as site of, x, xiii, 166. *See also* neocolonialism

deimperialization, vii; Asia as method and, 2, 212; in China, 12, 197–98, 257, 266; cultural studies and, 165–66; de-cold war and, 201; decolonization and, 3–4, 6, 23, 173, 200, 201; globalization and, 2, 3, 14, 164–65; in imperial centers, 7–8, 14–15, 193, 200, 202–7; imperial desire and, xiv, 198, 205–8, 257; incompleteness of, 4, 7–8, 14, 193, 200, 201, 208, 211; knowledge production and, 211, 268; necessity of, 13–16, 201, 209, 266–68; of theory, 3, 246

democracy: global, vii, 208–9, 280 n. 11; in Japan, 193; limits of, ix, 183–84, 191, 194, 208–9; movement in South Korea, ix, 9, 10, 187, 193, 288; movement in Taiwan, 9, 56, 185–88, 190, 193, 266, 279 n. 1; movements in India, 227–30, 234–36, 255; suppression of, 8, 123, 187–88, 190, 193, 199; U.S. imperialist, 183, 186, 187, 199, 208–9, 280 n. 11; U.S. as symbol of, 170, 186, 199. *See also* political society; popular democracy

developmentalism, 8, 12, 62, 122, 123, 126, 158, 193

diaspora, 95, 154

Dou-sang: A Borrowed Life (Wu), 124–35, 138–39, 149, 154

DPP (Democratic Progressive Party), 288; CCP and, 184; ethnicity, politicized by, xiv, 9, 53–59, 135, 190, 232; KMT and, 47, 153, 155, 191; social

movements co-opted by, 231–33; southward advance support of, 17, 62; U.S. dependence of, 188–89; U.S. policy support of, 185, 186, 270–71 n. 19

Duras, Marguerite, 38–41, 44, 61

East Asia: China's relation to, 5, 12–13, 214–15, 260; cold-war structure in, 9, 118–21, 181–82, 191; history of, vii, xii, 4–7, 33, 110, 158, 180–83; independence of, 195. *See also* regionalization: of Asia

England. *See* United Kingdom

Epstein, Maram, 260–61, 264, 265

ethnicity, 259; multiculturalism and, 97–98; nationalism and, xiv, 53–54, 83, 87, 94, 275 n. 5; politicization of, 9, 23, 83–84. *See also* běnshěng-wàishěng conflict

ethnocentrism, 40, 45, 52, 60, 65, 93, 95

Eurocentrism, 215, 217–19, 224–27, 243, 247–48, 253, 284 n. 22; American-centrism vs., 174, 219; of Mannoni, 75–77; of Marxist theory, 70, 102–4, 106–8

Europe, 15, 89, 133; as cultural referent, 133, 247–48; global capitalism and, 67, 108–9; racism in, 266–67. *See also* West, the

European studies, 3, 226, 254

European Union, 5, 15, 23, 183

Fanon, Frantz: on colonial identification, 40, 50–51, 68–69, 72–74, 85; criticisms of, 80, 275 n. 4; critique of Mannoni by, 77, 275 n. 3; critique of nationalism by, 23, 67, 80–

Fanon, Frantz (*continued*)
84, 275 n. 5; on decolonization, x, 14, 23, 79–80, 95, 111, 200; neocolonialism and, 110; on psychology of the colonized, 74, 77–80, 85, 178
February 28 Incident. *See* 228 Incident
femininity, 91, 155. *See also* yin-yang logic
feminism, 71, 96, 206, 227, 263, 266; antinationalism and, 54–55; as common language, 227
Feminist Discourse in Early Modern China (Liu), 262–64
First Sino-Japanese War, 5, 202
Formosa Magazine Incident, 188, 281 n. 20
Four Little Tigers, 20, 196
France, 40, 164, 133, 204

Gandhi, 90–92, 200, 220, 234
Garcia, Neil, 221–22
gay cultures, 155, 221–22; decolonization and, 53, 71; identity politics and, 55, 96, 99, 263; the state and, 224
geocolonial historical materialism, xiii, 1, 65; base-entity and, 249–51; cultural imaginary and, 110–12; in third-world spaces, 23, 66. *See also* history: local history and the encounter with colonization
geographical-historical materialism, 105–8, 110
geographical materialism, 103–6
geography, 30–31, 66, 104–8
globalization: cold war precondition for, 4, 8–9, 119, 182; as continuation of colonialism and imperialism, 2, 108, 112, 173; contradictory effects of, 100; cosmopolitanism as form of, 101, 165; decolonization enabled

by, 3, 9; defined, 4; deimperialization and, 2–4, 14; democratization and, 9, 209, 230; as depoliticizing force, 21, 158; of identity politics, 71; imperialism and, 4, 21, 100; insecurity and, xiv, 165, 173, 178; the local vs., xvi, 23; Marxism and, 71; national identification and, 100, 164; nativism as reaction to, 89; neoliberal, 4, 9, 12, 16, 67, 165, 182, 209, 268, 271 n. 20; regionalization as result of, 5, 9, 67, 107–8, 159, 183, 209, 214; studies, xv, 1, 2
Gramsci, Antonio, 34–35, 105, 228, 272 n. 12
Greater China, 183; Taiwan negation of, 46–47, 52
Greater East Asia Co-Prosperity Sphere, 10, 31–32, 35, 37, 121–22, 288
great reconciliation. *See* reconciliation
Gwangju Uprising, 158, 187, 279 n. 30, 288

Habermas, Jürgen, 3, 217
Hadjimichalis, Costis, 104–5
Hage, Ghassan, 97–98
Hall, Stewart, x, 54, 65, 100, 101–2, 216–17, 232, 272 n. 12
Hanasaki Kōhei, 205–7
Han Chinese, 257; as colonizers of Taiwan, 20, 30–31; meanings of, 259
Han Chinese racism, 258–59, 266–67; hierarchical construction of humanness in, 261–65; othering strategies of, 260–61; transcendent human and, 261–64, 285 n. 6
historical materialism: colonialism and, 108; culture and, 110; decolonization of, 72, 102–4; geographical materialism and, 103–4; as method

of cultural studies, 21, 66, 72, 102; singularizing tendency of, 70, 107; spatialization of, 66, 102–4, 106–7, 251. *See also* geocolonial historical materialism; geographical-historical materialism

history: colonial, 10, 18, 50–51, 66, 68, 77–79, 95, 102, 111–13, 122, 218; de-cold war and, 120; decolonization and, 3, 4, 8, 9, 14, 16, 93, 107–8, 121, 158–59, 190, 193, 201–2; deimperialization and, vii, 4, 7, 12–13, 16, 158–59, 193, 198, 200, 204, 267; as field of study, 35, 218–19; geography and, 103–7; globalization's disregard for, 2, 21; inter-referencing of history in Asia, 107, 224, 250–51; local history and the encounter with colonization, 5, 23, 66, 70, 102, 106–11, 118, 163–64, 177, 214, 215, 218, 221–23, 244, 245, 250–53; nativism and, 9, 178; reconciliation and, 156–59, 198, 201; southward advance discourse and, xiii, 27, 28, 29, 31, 35–37, 46, 50–53, 60–61; world, 102, 109, 215, 250–53; writing of, 9, 10, 32, 35, 50, 52–53, 55, 62–63, 102, 158, 202–4, 206, 218–19. *See also* base-entity (jītǐ); historical materialism; Southeast Asia project

Hong Kong, 226, 238; Chinese take-over of, 166; colonization of, 5, 269 n. 5; as cultural exporter, 63, 177; decolonization in, 8, 63, 201; racism in, 258, 267, 285 n. 1. *See also* Four Little Tigers

Human Space (Rénjiān) special issue, 25–41, 45–52, 60

Huntington, Samuel, 94, 182, 259

hybridity, 75, 98, 100

identification: civilizationist, 92, 93; colonial, 39–40, 44–45, 68–69, 77–80, 85, 90–99, 177–78; critical syncretism as strategy of, xiii, 72, 99–102, 112; disidentification and, 99, 177–78; imperial, xv, 45, 171, 176, 197; multiplying objects of, xv, 2, 99, 100–101, 112, 227, 255; nativist, 85, 97; questioning objects of, 69, 96–97, 176–78, 193, 198; racial, 37–41, 45, 52–54, 61, 98, 259. *See also* identity; United States: as internal to East Asian subjectivity

identity: cultural, 62, 72; diaspora and, 95; of the empire, 7; false, 138, 148; hybrid, 100; national, 11, 43–44, 54–61, 98, 100–101, 170–76, 223; structural production of, 95–96, 124; transitional national, 206–7

identity politics, 2, 69, 263, 267; colonial identification and, 96–97, 99; deimperialization and, 201; Fanon on, 80; globalization and, 71, 100

ideology: Althusser's concept of, 111, 272 n. 12; anti-communist, 56–57; Chinese nationalist, 56; cultural imaginary and, 111; Gramsci's theory of, 34–35, 272 n. 12; history as support for, 62–63; imperialist, 24–25; of modernization, 134; neo-liberal, 9; state apparatuses of, 58; Taiwanese nationalist, 52

imperial desire (imperial consciousness), 198; in Asia, 178; in China, 13, 41, 197; critical syncretism and, 101, 112; deimperialization and, xiv, 4, 63, 200; in Taiwan, 17–20, 24, 37, 45, 51, 60, 61, 171, 173, 200; in the U.S., 5, 16 imperialism: colonialism vs., 6; cold war and, 8; cultural, 89, 176–77; cultural imaginary and, 24–25, 111, 177–78; cultural studies and, 21, 24, 66, 101–2, 112; democracy and, 186–87, 199, 209; disregarding of, 21–22, 166, 173–75, 178, 204; globalization and, 2, 4, 21–22, 69, 108–9, 165; historical responsibility for, 200, 203–4, 206, 268; knowledge production and, 33–34, 74, 211, 268; modernity and, 157–58, 177; modernization and, 165, 265; nationalism and, x, 31–32, 82, 154; racism and, 267; responses to, 23, 68, 122, 150–52, 165, 197–98, 216–23; subimperialism and, 18, 20, 24, 25, 51, 59, 62, 63. *See also* deimperialization; neocolonialism; *specific countries*

imperialist eye, 3, 59–60

imperialization, xv, 4, 208; assimilation vs., 6–7, 200–201, 269 n. 8; of colonial centers, 7; of the subject, 6–7, 72, 201, 203. *See also* deimperialization

imperial order, the, 257, 264

India, 174, 200, 213, 215, 217, 267; civilizationalism in, 89–93, 219–21; democracy in, 227–30, 234–36; Japan and, 196, 246; nationalism in, 91–92, 234; Taiwan and, 224–25, 243

Indonesia, 213; Taiwanese investment in, 18–19

Inter-Asia project, 212–13, 254. *See also* inter-referencing

internationalist localism, 223

inter-referencing, xii, 106–7, 212, 223, 225–27, 243–45, 248, 250–55. *See also* identification: multiplying objects of

Intimate Enemy, The (Nandy), 75, 89, 220

Iraq wars, 15–16, 161, 174, 182–87, 189, 202

Jacques, Martin, 257–58, 266–67

Japan: anticommunism–pro-Americanism structure in, 121, 123, 175, 191, 193, 205; Asianism in, 178, 245–46, 270 n. 18; China's relationship with, 191, 196, 246–47, 250–52; colonial legacy in Taiwan, 51–52, 122, 133–34, 149–52, 155–56, 172, 277 n. 20; colonization of Asia by, 5–6, 31–37, 48–52, 121–22; decolonization in, 8, 11, 192; deimperialization in, 7–11, 159, 193, 195, 203–8; developmentalism in, 193; historical responsibility for imperialism of, 157–58, 192–93, 203–8; imperialization of the subject (kominka) by, 6–7, 72, 201, 203, 206; independence of, 193–96, 198; modernization of, 246–48; nationalism in, 159, 206, 251; as symbol of modernity, 132–34; as Taiwanese cultural referent, 127–35, 149–50, 152; transition from colonizer to colonized, 7, 10, 193; U.S. as internal to subjectivity of, 8, 176–80; U.S. military mandate in, 119, 181, 192–95. *See also* Chūgokugaku; Greater East Asia Co-Prosperity Sphere

Johnson, Chalmers, 119

June Fourth Incident, 57, 231

Kaplan, Amy, 174, 280 n. 12

Kim Dae-jung, 119, 183, 184, 241

Kim Jung Il, 119, 183
Kim Seongnae, 117, 123, 175–76
KMT (Kuomintang), 153–55, 288; anti-Japanese policies of, 149–50, 278 n. 25; authoritarianism of, 146, 153, 188, 287; běnshěng rén and, 133–34, 147, 152; CCP othering of, 10, 56, 153, 167; CCP rapprochement with, 144, 191–92; Chinese nationalism promoted by, 47–48, 52, 56, 58, 126–29, 133–34, 149–52; colonization of Taiwan by, 20, 49, 55, 154, 274 n. 31; DPP and, 47, 153, 155, 191; dream of recovering the mainland, 56, 151–52, 188; exodus from mainland China of, 55, 151, 153, 278 n. 21; mainlander and Taiwanese nationalist factions of, 44, 47, 56–59, 61–62, 273 n. 23, 274 n. 33; Taiwan as temporary base for, 143, 151; U.S. support of, 56, 188. See also běnshěng rén; běnshěng–wàishěng conflict; Chinese civil war; Lee Teng-hui; wàishěng rén; Taiwan: White Terror in; 228 Incident
knowledge production, vii, x, 29; Asia as method and, 2–3, 23–24, 120, 212–13, 268; imperialism and, xii, 33–34, 211; traditions of, 227; universalism and, 71, 245, 268; the West and, 216. See also area studies; Asia as method; geocolonial historical materialism; inter-referencing
Kobayashi Yoshinori, 150
Koizumi Junichiro, 184, 191, 192
Korea: Japanese colonization of, 5, 121–22; U.S. as internal to subjectivity of, 180
Korean War, 7, 154, 181, 213

Korean wave, 186
Kyoto Protocol, 183

language: English as colonial, 117, 213; English as common, 227; as foundation of nativism, 85, 87; language politics in Taiwan, 126–29, 134, 139, 149, 152–53
Lee Hsiao-fung, 170
Lee Teng-hui, 26, 60, 161, 289; KMT chairmanship of, 47, 56, 58, 59, 273 n. 23, 274 n. 31; Southeast Asia tour by, 27, 35–37, 46; Taiwan nationalism and, 57–58, 59, 153, 232, 279 n. 3. See also KMT
Lee Yuan-tseh, 27–29, 47, 272 nn. 13–14
Leung, Ka-Fai Tony, 38–40
Levfebre, Henri, 105
Lien Chan, 163, 191–92, 273 n. 23
Liu Jen-peng, 262–65
Liu Kexiang, 26, 33–34, 52
Los Angeles, 107, 162, 167–69
Lover, The (Duras), 38–41
Lu, Annette, 189
Lu Hau-tung, 128–30, 132, 277 n. 17
Lu Xun, x, xi, 68, 246, 265, 284 n. 22

Macao, 6, 8, 201, 270 n. 15
Magdoff, Harry, 109–10
mainland China. See China
mainlander. See wàishěng rén
Malaysia, 19, 31, 32, 33, 213, 258, 259
Manchukuo, 6, 7, 278 n. 26
Manchuria, 121–22
Mannoni, Octave, 68, 74–77, 80, 85, 274 n. 2, 275 n. 3
Marxism: as common language, 227; decolonization and, 69–72; Eurocentrism of, 70, 224; geocolonial

Marxism (*continued*)
    historical materialism and, 103–11,
    251; political society and, 230, 236
masculinity, 39–40, 91, 126, 155. *See also*
    patriarchy
Ma Ying-jeou, 190
Memmi, Albert, 14, 74, 94–95; cri-
    tique of nativism by, 67, 84–89
Memorandum of the Past (Yang), 41–44
mínjiān society, 216, 237, 283 n. 15;
    civil society and, 238–39, 241; mod-
    ernization and, 239–41, 244–45,
    255; mutual assistance in, 239–40;
    political society and, 241–43
Minnanese, 124, 277 n. 13. *See also* lan-
    guage: language politics in Taiwan
Mitani Taichirō, 205–6
Miyoshi, Massao, 22, 110
Mizoguchi Yūzō, x, 157–58, 216, 245–
    54, 282, 283 n. 21
*Modern History of the Three Countries
    in East Asia*, 10, 202–4, 270 n. 13
modernity: capitalist vs. socialist
    roads to, 11–12, 151, 157; colonial
    and postcolonial aspiration for,
    133–34, 165, 241; colonizer as em-
    bodiment of, 85, 90, 149; compara-
    tive studies of, 225–26; democracy
    vs., 230; Gandhi's critique of, 234;
    hierarchy of cultural referents
    under, 127–28, 132–33, 152; imperi-
    alism and, 157–58; as mixture of
    colonial and local elements, 66,
    220–23, 237, 244; nativist critique
    of, 81, 87; violence as inherent to,
    158, 176, 241
modernization: Chinese vs. Japanese
    model of, 246–48; colonial, 84, 122,
    133–34, 152, 165; imperialism and,
    265; knowledge production and,

224; mínjiān society and, 239–41,
    245, 255; nationalist, 123, 134, 151;
    state as agent of, 237, 269 n. 1;
    translation in local contexts, 244
moralizing, 122, 164, 225, 240, 285 n. 6
multiculturalism, 94, 97–98, 253
Mutō Ichiyō, 11, 207

Nandy, Ashis, 9, 45, 75, 275 n. 6; on
    civilizationalism, 67, 69, 89–94,
    219–21; on colonial identification,
    85; on internal colonialism, 84
Nanyang. *See* Southeast Asia
national bourgeois elites: collabo-
    ration with colonizers, 23, 61–62,
    81–84, 166, 174–75, 180, 268; nego-
    tiation with mínjiān society, 237,
    239–41; power struggles among, 59,
    83, 135, 190; subalterns relation to,
    228–29, 234–36; use of nationalism
    by, 54; the West/U.S. as model for,
    161, 177, 237, 243
nationalism: articulating agents of,
    54–55; civilizationalism and, 91–92,
    94, 220–21; cold war and, x, 123;
    colonialism and, ix, 32, 82–83,
    91–92, 125, 154, 159, 275 n. 5; co-
    option by nationalist elites, 54, 59,
    61, 83, 123, 135; critical syncretism
    and, 100–101; cultural studies over-
    investment in, 24, 63–64, 165; de-
    cold war and, 125; decolonization
    and, 23, 81–84, 94, 112, 125, 164, 166;
    deimperialization and, 166; ethnic,
    xiv, 57, 87, 94, 135, 275 n. 5; Fanon's
    critique of, 67, 68–69, 81–84; glob-
    alization and, 100; imperialism
    and, x, 82, 123, 154, 176, 216, 217, 219;
    nativism and, 84, 87, 94; negation
    of, ix, x, 164, 167; racism and, 83.

See also individual countries; KMT:
Chinese nationalism promoted by;
Taiwan consciousness
nationality: Chinese construction of,
259; as national identity, 52, 167,
170
nation building, 3, 23, 65, 82; Club 51's
strategy for, 164, 167, 168; Taiwan
nationalist, 58, 59, 61–62; United
States and, 280
nation-state: as agent of modernization, 237; civilizationalism and, 91–
92; in East Asia, 5, 269 n. 4; empire
and, 173, 269 n. 1, 280 n. 12; global
capital and, 22–23, 66, 107–8, 177;
neocolonialism and, 82, 92; provi-
sional identification with, 206–7;
regionalism and, 21, 89, 214; as unit
of analysis, 23, 63–64, 112, 125, 159,
214, 215, 223
nativism: civilizationalism as form of,
94, 178, 220–21; cultural studies
and, 165; as form of decolonization,
9, 65, 67, 81, 84–89, 94; globalization and, 89; identification and, 85,
97, 99, 100–101; nationalism and,
84, 87, 94; as self-negation and
rediscovery, 3, 9, 84–89, 95, 178, 221.
See also Taiwan consciousness
naturalism, 30–31, 33–35, 52
nature, 103–5, 107
neocolonialism (neocolonial imperialism, neoimperialism), 18, 110; area
studies and, 28; critical syncretism
and, 101; cultural studies and, 21;
decolonization and, 23, 63, 66, 67,
79, 81–82, 97, 112; effects of, 22;
multiculturalism and, 97–98
Neo-Confucianism, 39, 40, 94, 98, 178.
See also Asian-values debate

newly industrialized countries
(NICs), 20, 122
Niranjana, Tejaswini, 225
North Korea, 71; cold war and, 175–
76; rapprochement with South
Korea, 9, 115–17, 118, 119, 182–83,
214; U.S. relations with, 182–84

Okinawa: colonization of by Japan,
5; decolonization in, 8, 12, 157;
deimperialization in, 11, 12; desire
to join the U.S., xiv, 163; U.S. occupation of, 7, 8, 11, 119, 181, 194, 270
n. 9, 280 n. 11
Orientalism, 103–4, 228, 253
overseas Chinese, 31, 32, 37–38, 40–41,
259

particularism: universalism vs., 217–18,
226, 245
patriarchy, 58, 96, 99, 126, 146, 155, 258.
See also masculinity
peace movements, 11, 184, 185
Philippines: anti-Chinese sentiment
in, 32; communism and socialism
in, 32–33; desire to join the U.S.,
xiv, 163; Japanese colonialism in,
31; nativism in, 221–22; Taiwanese
investment in, 18, 19, 271 n. 3; U.S.
imperialism in, 33, 166
political economy, 104, 106, 110
political society, 223, 228; civil society
and, 230, 233, 234, 236, 241–43;
democracy in, 230, 236; mínjiān
society and, 216, 242, 243, 255;
political implications of, 230, 235–
36; popular democracy and, 233;
society of consumption and, 242,
243; Subaltern Studies collective
and, 234–36

politics of resentment, xiii, 2, 67, 72, 81, 94–96

popular democracy movement, 117, 243, 276 n. 1; challenges to civil society of, 230–33; political society and, 233

postcolonial studies, xv, 1–2, 66–69, 80–81, 95, 165, 174, 204–5, 217

provincial register contradiction. *See* běnshěng-wàishěng conflict

psychoanalysis: of the colonized's identification with the colonizer, 40, 43–44, 50–51, 77–78, 82, 90, 94–95, 177–78; of the colonized's identification with the self, 85–89, 92, 96, 178; of the dependency complex of the colonized, 76–77; of the inferiority complex of the colonizer, 44, 76, 77; as weapon of anticolonial struggle, 74, 79. *See also* assimilation; critical syncretism; identification: colonial; politics of resentment

psychology: collective, 47–48, 73, 77; of the colonizer, 74–76, 86; of the people, 74; relation to politics and social structure, 45, 48, 73, 77, 79–80, 96, 111, 146, 178

Qiandao Lake Incident, 57, 274 n. 34

queer nation, 55

queer theory, 45

race: articulating agents of, 54, 79, 98; Chinese construction of, 259; ethnic nationalist disregarding of, 53, 61; identification and, 37–41, 45, 52–54, 61, 98, 259

racism, 268; colonialism and, 39, 45, 75, 77–80, 83, 87, 95, 97–98, 121, 266; nationalism and, 83; nativism and, 87, 95, 165; as product of nationalist power struggles, 135, 165. *See also* Han Chinese racism

radical plural opportunism, 172–73, 186, 280 n. 10

Reagan, Ronald, 182, 187

Reconciliation: between běnshěng rén and wàishěng rén, xiv, 124, 128, 153, 156, 157, 277 n. 12; between colonizer and colonized, vii; between countries in East Asia, 9, 10, 111, 198, 203; between Japan and its colonies, 157–59, 201; between Taiwan and China, 156–57, 190, 191–92

reference points. *See* inter-referencing

regionalization: of Asia, 12–13, 15, 120, 121, 122, 197–98, 203, 213–15, 246, 251, 268, 270 n. 18; balance of power sustained by, 15–16, 182, 209, 214; as expression of nativism, 89; globalization and, 4, 5, 67, 108–9, 178, 209; knowledge production and, 2–3, 284 n. 27; obstacles to, 5–6, 9, 10, 109, 123–24, 192; superstate organizations as expression of, 5, 23, 31, 183. *See also* Greater East Asia Co-Prosperity Sphere

Roh Moo-hyun, 187, 191

Said, Edward, 24–25, 99–101, 110, 111, 222

Sakai, Naoki, 217–18

Second Sino-Japanese War, 6, 118, 149–50, 153, 155, 278 n. 26

Sedgwick, Eve Kosofsky, 45

self-determination, 55, 82, 180, 182

September 11, xv, 4, 14, 22, 171, 186, 199, 209; global responses to, 5, 11, 15, 161, 179, 183, 184, 186, 187; U.S.

response to, 174, 182. *See also* Iraq wars

Shi Ming, 53–54

Singapore, 204, 213, 238, 258; Asian identification of, 178; colonization of, 31–32; nationalism in, vii–ix, 32; suppression in, 54. *See also* Four Little Tigers; Greater China

Singapore Ga Ga (Tan), vii–ix

Sinocentrism, 5, 13, 36, 52–53, 253, 257; promoted by KMT, 47–48, 52, 56, 58, 126–29, 133–34, 149–52

Sino-Japanese War: First, 5, 202; Second, 6, 118, 149–50, 153, 155, 278 n. 26

socialism: capitalist triumph over, 8, 22, 69–70, 118–19, 181; as form of modernity, 12, 151; legacy of, 71; rise of, 31; in Taiwan, 55; U.S. suppression of socialism in Southeast Asia, 33

society of consumption, 226, 242, 243

Soja, Edward, 104–7

Southeast Asia (Nanyang): ASEAN, 5, 15, 23, 31, 32, 183, 214, 234, 287; China's marginalization of, 215; decolonization in, 14, 204–5; Japan's colonization of, 5–6, 31–37, 48–52, 121–22; Lee Teng-hui's tour of, 26–27, 35–36, 37, 46; nationalism in, 31–33; Taiwanese investment in, xii, 17–19; as Taiwan's alternative to China, 17, 25, 30–31, 33–35, 36, 46–49, 51–52, 271 n. 1. *See also* southward advance discourse

Southeast Asia project, 27–29, 272 nn. 13–14

South Korea: anti-American sentiment in, 187; anticommunism–pro-Americanism structure in, 7, 119, 121, 123, 175–76, 191; anti-Japanese sentiment in, 191; authoritarianism in, 123, 175–76, 187, 288; Cheju Uprising, 123–24, 175–76, 288; civil society in, ix, 237, 241; colonization of by Japan, 5–6, 122, 157, 180; decolonization in, 8, 10, 63, 157, 193, 201; democratic movement in, ix, 9, 10, 187, 193; developmentalism in, 123, 193; Gwangju Uprising, 158, 187, 279 n. 30, 288; mínjiān society in, 240; nationalism in, ix, 191; nativism in, 9, 178, 270 n. 12; North Korea and, 9, 115–17, 118, 119, 182–83, 214; political characteristics of, 123; subimperial desire in, 63; Taiwan and, 123, 155, 186–88, 226; U.S. dependency of, 181, 191, 201; U.S. as internal to subjectivity of, xiv, 8, 120, 163, 178, 187–88, 279 n. 6; U.S. military bases in, 119, 188, 191; U.S. relations with, 7, 10, 182–84, 187

southward advance discourse, xii–xiii, 17–18, 20–21, 25–39, 45–52, 59–63, 65, 122

southward advance policy, 17–19, 29, 46–48, 51, 52, 60–63, 208, 273 n. 18. *See also* Japan: colonization of Asia by; Southeast Asia: as Taiwan's alternative to China

space, 66, 104–8

statism, 61, 94, 123, 154–55, 231, 232

structure of sentiment, 277 n. 11; as site of analysis in cultural studies, xiv; globalization as, 118, 165; little subjectivity as, 93; as mediator of colonizer and colonized, 111; rise of Asia as, 214; in Taiwan, xiv, xvi, 58, 124, 125, 133–35, 148, 149–50, 155–56, 159 subalterns, 159, 242, 263; identification and, 95–96, 99; national bourgeois elites vs., 23, 59, 72–73, 134, 227–29, 233–36; political society as space of, 228, 233–36

subaltern studies, 68, 218, 234–36

sub-imperialism, third world, 24, 25, 63. *See also* Taiwan: sub-imperial desire and practices of

subjectivity, x; of cold war subjects, 118, 119, 120, 130, 201; of the colonized, 5, 43–45, 53, 72–73, 94–95, 149, 151, 152, 165, 201; critical, 195, 232; cultural and social, 59, 70, 98, 107, 127, 208, 250; decolonized (critical syncretic), 98–101, 112, 223; deimperializing, 4, 198; desire for dignified and balanced, 3, 81; hybrid, 98, 100; imperialist, 24–25; indigenous, 221; as internally generated, 165, 190–91, 220; little, 92–93; mutual constitution of, 24–25, 38, 74, 78, 94, 149; nationalist, ix, 221; nativist, 85–88; rebuilding of, xv, 8, 166, 212; regional, 8, 83, 215; state-produced, 155; sub-imperialist, 35, 38, 39, 45, 62, 171; transformation of the self and, xv, 212, 253, 255

Sun Ge, 158

Sun Yat-sen, 13, 121, 196–98, 248, 266. *See also* Asianism

syncretism, 98–99. *See also* critical syncretism

Tagore, Rabindranath, 91–92, 229

Taiwan, xi–xii; aboriginal peoples of, 30–31, 52–53, 55, 124, 266; anti-communism in, 56–57, 115, 118, 123, 135–37, 153, 157, 166–67, 190, 231;

Chinese military threat to, 162, 166–67, 172, 173, 192; colonialism in, xii, 5–6, 20, 31, 35–37, 48–52, 57, 121–22, 149–50; decolonization in, xiii, 8, 10, 12, 20, 63, 65, 121, 157, 173, 188, 201; democratic opposition movement in, 9, 56, 185–88, 190, 193, 266; deimperialization in, 8, 164, 201, 208; ethnic conflict in, xiv, 9, 53–59, 135, 190, 232; hierarchy of cultural referents in, 127, 132–33; history and, 10, 35, 52–53, 55, 62–63; identity in, 39–44, 124–25, 142–44, 156; imaginary location in Southeast Asia, 25–27, 29–31, 33–37, 46–52, 60–62; independence vs. unification debate in, 48, 117, 164, 167, 171, 190, 192, 232, 277 n. 12; international investments of, xii, 18–20, 46–48, 62; international marginalization of, 48, 51, 56, 93; as KMT's temporary home, 142, 143, 151, 188; the Left in, 56, 57, 173, 230–33, 276 n. 1; little subjectivity and, 92–93; mínjiān society in, 239–42; nationalism in, xiii, 46, 48–49, 52–59, 61–62, 149–52, 172, 232, 275 n. 5; native leftists in, 26, 46, 49, 62; new Taiwanese, 169, 171; "Orphan of Asia" narrative in, 152; political characteristics of, 58, 123; reaffirmation of and nostalgia for Japanese colonial modernity in, 51–52, 122, 133–34, 149–50, 172, 277 n. 20; reconciliation with China, 156–57, 190, 191–92; Southeast Asia and, 17, 25, 30–31, 33–35, 36, 46–49, 51–52, 271 n. 1; South Korea and, 115, 117, 123, 186–88; structure of sentiment in, xiv, xvi, 58, 124, 125, 133–35, 148,

149–50, 155–56, 159; subimerperial-
ist desire in, xii–xiii, 17–20, 35, 37,
45, 46, 51, 59–61, 62, 63, 122, 171, 173,
186, 200, 208; third-world location
of, 20–21, 22–23, 33, 63; travel to
China allowed by, 9, 117–18, 142–
44; undetermined status of, 48, 161,
163, 167, 168, 173, 199; U.S. dependency of, 152, 162, 163, 167–68, 170,
172, 181, 188–91, 199, 270 n. 19; U.S.
education of intellectuals from, 26,
28, 115, 120, 161, 276 n. 5; U.S. as internal to subjectivity of, 10, 115, 120,
127, 161, 170–71, 178–79, 181, 186–87,
190, 198, 208; U.S. neocolonialism
in, 8, 18, 20, 52, 56–57, 62, 174–75,
177–78, 179, 181; White Terror in,
56, 58, 62, 123, 137, 153, 188, 276
n. 1, 289. *See also* běnshěng rén;
běnshěng–wàishěng conflict; Club
51; DPP; KMT; popular democracy
movement; southward advance
policy; wàishěng rén
*Taiwan: A Radical Quarterly in Social
Studies*, 117, 276 n. 2
Taiwan-centrism, 35, 36–37, 47, 48–50,
51
Taiwan consciousness, 9, 10, 52–54,
55–59, 62, 144
Taiwan Defense Alliance, 198–99
Taiwan independence movement, 53,
55, 57–58, 184, 199, 270 n. 19, 277
n. 12, 279 n. 1, 281 n. 23; pro-American and pro-Japanese politics of,
153; support for the southward
advance policy of, 62; Taiwan's
dependence on the U.S. and, 163,
168, 189–90; Taiwan State Building
Movement, 166, 185; wàishěng rén
and, 144. *See also* Club 51

Taiwan Strait missile crisis, 157, 161–
62, 166, 167, 279 n. 1
Takeuchi Yoshimi, 194–96, 211, 246–
48, 282, 284 n. 22
Tambiah, S. J., 93
Tan Pin Pin, vii–ix
third world: Asia as method and,
212, 223, 225, 227, 255; as categori-
cal alternative to nation-state, 21,
63–64; China's solidarity with, 12,
13; cultural studies and, xiii, 21, 24,
64, 66; decolonization in, 18, 23, 65,
68–69, 74–75, 120–21, 200; globalization and, 21–22, 268; Marxism
in, 21, 23, 66, 69–70, 224; nationalism in, ix, 22, 25, 82–83, 91, 123, 164,
217, 219, 224, 275 n. 5; subimperialism in, 24, 25; three-worlds theory
and, 20, 22
Tomlinson, John, 21
Tiananmen Square Massacre, 57, 231
traditionalism, 67, 89–91, 92, 216. *See
also* civilizationalism
translation, 237, 243–44, 269 n. 4
Tsuda Sōkichi, 247
228 Incident, 53, 55, 62, 123, 141, 153,
158, 274 n. 25, 287

United Kingdom: Asian imperialism
of, 5, 31–33, 91, 93, 204, 220, 269
n. 5; cultural studies in, 21, 101–2;
deimperialization in, 14; Gandhi's
desire to liberate, 91, 200; Glorious Revolution in, 108; perceived
inferiority compared with Europe,
133; support for Iraq war of, 184
United Nations, 182, 209; Japan's bid
for seat on security council of, 191,
192; Taiwan's attempts to rejoin, 58,
167, 199

United States: area studies and, 2–3, 28, 243, 253; authoritarian regimes in East Asia supported by, 8, 9, 175, 187–88, 190, 193; betrayal of the ideals of, 82, 173–75, 183, 187; China as competitor to, 13, 183, 197; containment strategy of, 175, 181; declining influence of, 179, 182; education of East Asian elites in, 26, 28, 115, 120, 161, 162, 177, 212, 276 nn. 5–6; imperialism in East Asia, 21, 123, 163, 166, 168, 173–75, 189–90, 204–5; as internal to East Asian subjectivity, 8, 10, 115, 120, 123, 127, 132, 161, 163–67, 170–72, 175, 176–81, 186–87, 190, 191, 198, 279 n. 6; lack of deimperialization in, 8, 14, 15, 202; military presence in East Asia, 7, 8, 11, 119, 174, 181, 187–88, 191–95, 202, 270 n. 9, 280 n. 11, 281 n. 26; neocolonialism/neoimperialism in East Asia, 8, 18, 20, 28, 52, 56–57, 62, 82, 110–11, 115, 165–68, 170, 174–81, 188–95; superpower status of, 15, 179, 181–83, 197, 209; as symbol of democracy and modernity, 10, 127, 132, 167–68, 170–71, 174–75, 177–78, 180, 181, 186, 199. See also American-centrism; cold war; Iraq wars; September 11

universalism: civilizationist claims to, 90–92, 220–21; history and, 109; nativism vs., 221; particularism vs., 217–18, 226, 245; race and, 79; theory's claim to, 3, 64, 70, 71, 226; transcendent human as embodiment of, 264–65, 285 n. 6; the West and, 89, 217–19, 226. See also civilizationalism; Eurocentrism

University of California, Berkeley, 28

Vergès, Françoise, 74

Veriah, Harinder, 257–58, 265, 267, 285 n. 1

Vietnam, 18, 19, 32, 39, 91, 175, 204

Vietnam War, 8, 182

wàishěng rén (mainlanders), 55, 124–25, 138–39, 154, 273 n. 22, 289; China vs. Taiwan as "home" for, 142–44; Chinese-nationalist/cold-war subjectivity of, 149–56; forced immigration of, 153, 155; gender roles of, 146–47; as "old soldiers," 135, 143, 278 n. 21; solidarity with běnshěng rén, 139, 141. See also běnshěng–wàishěng conflict

Wallace, Alfred Russel, 33, 272 n. 17

Wallace Line, the, 33–35, 61, 272 n. 17

Wang Hui, 214, 269 n. 1

Wang Jingwei, 128–30, 277 n. 18, 289

Wang Shiao-di, 135

Wang Tung, 135

West, the: "and the rest," 216–17, 222; civilizationalism as response to, 81, 90–92, 93, 94, 219–21; as common referent, 227; deconstruction as response to, 217–18; East Asian triumphalism as response to, 67; as fragments internal to local subjectivity, 223, 255; nationalism as response to, 216, 217; nativism as response to, 89, 221–22; negation of, 90, 220, 247; as object of desire and resentment, 40, 217, 222, 243, 247, 265; obsessive postcolonial critiques of, 1–2, 24; as Other, 11, 13, 40–41, 121, 122–23, 151, 181, 214–16, 222, 223, 246, 249; as postcolonial imaginary, 89, 94, 234; provincialization as response to, 218–19;

universalism and, 3, 90, 92, 217–19, 226

Wittfogel, Karl A., 103–4, 106

World Trade Organization, 173, 182

Wretched of the Earth, The (Fanon), 14, 23, 50–51, 81, 83, 275 n. 5

Wu Micha, 26, 35–37, 45, 46, 47, 48–49, 52

Wu Nian-chen (Nien-Jen Wu), 125, 134

Yang Bo, 26, 37–41, 44, 45, 52

Yang Changzhen, 26, 30–34, 47, 52

Yang Kui, 68

Yang Zhao, 26, 41–52

yin-yang logic, 27, 91, 261–62, 264

Yoshimi, Shunya, 165–66

Kuan-Hsing Chen 陳光興 is a professor in the Graduate Institute
for Social Research and Cultural Studies, Chiao Tung University,
Taiwan. He is the author of *Media/Cultural Criticism: A Popular-
Democratic Line of Flight* (1992, in Chinese), *The Imperialist Eye*
(2003, in Korean), and *De-Imperialization—Asia as Method* (2006,
in Chinese). His edited volumes include *Stuart Hall: Critical Dia-
logues in Cultural Studies* (1996), *Trajectories: Inter-Asia Cultural
Studies* (2000), and *Inter-Asia Cultural Studies Reader* (2006).
He is a co-executive editor of the journal *Inter-Asia Cultural
Studies: Movements*.

Library of Congress Cataloging-in-Publication Data
Chen, Kuan-Hsing.
Asia as method : toward deimperialization / Kuan-Hsing Chen.
p. cm.
Includes bibliographical references and index.
ISBN 978-0-8223-4664-7 (cloth : alk. paper)
ISBN 978-0-8223-4676-0 (pbk. : alk. paper)
1. East Asia—Study and teaching. 2. Culture—Study
and teaching—East Asia. 3. Postcolonialism—East Asia.
4. Globalization—East Asia. I. Title.
DS510.7.C44 2010
950.072—dc22 2009047585